THE MAN WHO
WOULD BE
SHERLOCK

THE MAN WHO WOULD BE SHERLOCK

THE REAL-LIFE ADVENTURES OF
ARTHUR CONAN DOYLE

CHRISTOPHER SANDFORD

Thomas Dunne Books
St. Martin's Press
New York

To Maynard Atik

THOMAS DUNNE BOOKS.
An imprint of St. Martin's Press.

THE MAN WHO WOULD BE SHERLOCK. Copyright © 2017 by Christopher Sandford. All rights reserved. Printed in the United States of America. For information, address St. Martin's Press, 175 Fifth Avenue, New York, N.Y. 10010.

www.thomasdunnebooks.com
www.stmartins.com

Library of Congress Cataloging-in-Publication Data

Names: Sandford, Christopher, 1956– author.
Title: The man who would be Sherlock / Christopher Sandford.
Description: First U.S. edition. | New York : Thomas Dunne Books, December 2018. |
    Includes bibliographical references and index.
Identifiers: LCCN 2018027165 | ISBN 9781250079565 (hardcover) |
    ISBN 9781466892217 (ebook)
Subjects: LCSH: Doyle, Arthur Conan, 1859–1930. | Doyle, Arthur Conan,
    1859–1930—Characters—Sherlock Holmes. | Holmes, Sherlock. | Chantrelle,
    Eugene—Trials, litigation, etc. | Authors, Scottish—19th century—Biography. |
    Authors, Scottish—20th century—Biography.
Classification: LCC PR4623 .S26 2018 | DDC 823/.8 [B]—dc23
LC record available at https://lccn.loc.gov/2018027165

Our books may be purchased in bulk for promotional, educational, or business use. Please contact your local bookseller or the Macmillan Corporate and Premium Sales Department at 1-800-221-7945, extension 5442, or by email at MacmillanSpecialMarkets@macmillan.com.

First published in Great Britain by The History Press

First U.S. Edition: December 2018

10 9 8 7 6 5 4 3 2 1

Some judge of authors' names, not works, and then
Nor praise nor blame the writings, but the men.

Alexander Pope
Essay on Criticism

❖

Art in the blood is liable to take the strangest forms.

Arthur Conan Doyle
The Greek Interpreter

❖

You know my methods, Watson.

Arthur Conan Doyle
The Crooked Man

CONTENTS

ACKNOWLEDGEMENTS

This is not a biography of Arthur Conan Doyle, nor of Sherlock Holmes. Anyone interested in reading more about either one of them will find some suggestions in the bibliography at the back of the book. Nor would I ever be rash enough to enter the briar-patch of a debate on, say, the prevalence of certain sorts of human tattoo in one part of Victorian Britain as opposed to another one, or on the precise location of Dr Watson's war wounds, or the order of his marriages, or on any number of other matters best left to that devoted cult of followers going under the banner of 'Sherlockians'. Nor, in particular, could I comment with any presumption of authority on Doyle's famously mixed feelings about Holmes, who clearly belonged to that 'different and humbler plane of literature' that the author himself sometimes pursued and sometimes mocked, although my old English master and friend Alan Kennington, who at one time actually knew Doyle, always liked to quote *Macbeth* on these occasions, 'We but teach bloody instructions, which, being taught, return to plague the inventor'.

Instead, I've tried to show the ways in which Doyle himself consistently applied both the intellect and innate sense of justice (if not always the mercurial powers of observation) of his immortal creation. In at least two cases, that of the young Anglo-Indian solicitor George Edalji, imprisoned for a bizarre series of cattle mutilations near his home in the English Midlands, and of Oscar

Slater, a German-born Jew who served eighteen years (and narrowly avoided execution) for having bludgeoned to death an elderly spinster in her Glasgow flat one night in December 1908, Doyle found himself at the centre of events every bit as outlandish as any he devised for Holmes. Although these would be the two great set-piece mysteries of Doyle's detective career, he brought a similar blend of basic investigative ability and campaigning zeal to several other cases drawn to his attention, on both sides of the Atlantic, over the course of forty years. As we'll see, they continued even after the author himself modified his materialist beliefs and began to commune with the spirits of the dead following the heavy toll of his family losses in the First World War.

Although Doyle was always at pains to separate 'the doll' and his 'maker', as he called Holmes and himself, both characters shared an intriguing mixture of the coldly scientific and rational on one hand, and the morally keen and chivalrous on the other. It's this seeming contradiction, along with a generous helping of those peculiarly foul crimes that seemed to predominate as Victorian Britain splashed around in a sea of immorality, that help to give Holmes his enduring appeal, and hopefully also apply here in the real-life adventures of his author.

For archive material, input or advice I should thank, professionally: AbeBooks; Alibris; the *American Conservative*; *Atlantic Monthly*; the late Saul Bellow; Birmingham City Council; the Bodleian Library, Oxford; Bonham's; Book Depository; Sophie Bradshaw; the British Library; the British Newspaper Library; *Chronicles*; Stephen Cooper; the Cricket Society; the *Daily Mail*; the Dogs of War Theatre; the FBI – Freedom of Information Division; Dominic Farr; the General Register Office; Glasgow City Archives; *Hansard*; the History Press; Michael Hurley; Jane Jamieson; Roger Johnson; Barbara Levy; the Library of Congress; Sue Lynch; Barbara McLean; the Magic Circle; Magicus; Marcia Markland; Michigan State Department of Health; the Mitchell Library, Glasgow; the National Archives; the National Records of Scotland; the 1976 Coalition; Mary Pilan; Premier Tutors; Renton Library; Rebecca Romney; St Martin's Press; Seaside Library, Oregon; the *Seattle Times*; the Sherlock Holmes Society; Staffordshire Record Office; Zoe Stansell; Liz Street; Andrew Stuart; Thomas Toughill; Cynthia Tyrrell; University of Montana; University of Puget Sound; Vital Records; the William Salt Library; Windlesham's Manor; and Qona Wright. I would also like to thank Robin B. James for indexing.

And personally: Lisa Armstead; Reverend Maynard Atik; Pete Barnes; Jane Blunkell; the late Ryan Boone; Rocco Bowen; the late David Bowie; Robert and Hilary Bruce; Jon Burke; Don Carson; the late Pat Champion; Changelink; Hunter Chatriand; James Clever; Common Ground; Christina Coulter; Tim Cox; the Davenport; Monty Dennison; Micky Dolenz; the Dowdall family; John and Barbara Dungee; Reverend Joanne Enquist; Explorer West; Tom Fleming; Malcolm Galfe; the Gay Hussar; Gethsemane Lutheran Church; James Graham; the late Tom Graveney; Jeff and Rita Griffin; Charley Grimston; Grumbles; Steve and Jo Hackett; Hermino; the late Frank Hinsley; Alex Holmes; the Hotel Vancouver; Hyde Park Executive Apartments; Jo Jacobius; the Jamieson family; Lincoln Kamell; Terry Lambert; Belinda Lawson; Eugene Lemcio; the Lorimer family; Robert Dean Lurie; Les McBride; Heather and Mason McEachran; Charles McIntosh; the Macri family; Lee Mattson; Jim and Rana Meyersahm; Missoula Doubletree; the Morgans; John and Colleen Murray; Kaiyo Nedd; Greg Nowak; Phil Oppenheim; Gary O'Toole; Robin Parish; Owen Paterson; Peter Perchard; Chris Pickrell; the late John Prins; Robert Prins; the Prins family; Scott P. Richert; Ailsa Rushbrooke; St Matthew's, Renton; Sandy Cove Inn; Susan Sandford; Peter Scaramanga; Fred and Cindy Smith; Reverend and Mrs Harry Smith; the late Thaddeus Stuart; Jack Surendranath; the late Ben Tyvand; Mary Tyvand; Robert Valade; Diana Villar; the late Peter Way; Karin Wieland; Soleil Wieland; West London Chemists; Debbie Wild; the Willis Fleming family; Aaron Wolf; the Woons; and Zoo Town Surfers.

My deepest thanks, as always, to Karen and Nicholas Sandford.

C.S.
2017

1

THE DOLL AND ITS MAKER

Who was Sherlock Holmes?

One of the paradoxes of Arthur Conan Doyle's indestructible sleuth is that he seems both to embody the past and belong to the present. Although there's a generous amount of period detail to the Holmes stories, with their soupy miles of cobblestone streets, he's also a thoroughly modern, even futuristic human calculating machine, who takes full advantage of such emerging disciplines as psychiatry, forensics, toxicology, ballistics, analytical chemistry and anthropometrics – the use of precise body measurements to 'profile' criminals – to complement his legendary powers of observation. Although Conan Doyle, like most authors, deplored the habit of identifying 'real-life' models for his characters, he also took the opportunity to pay Dr Joseph Bell (1837–1911) the compliment of calling him the 'true Holmes'.

The frock-coated Bell was 39 years old when Doyle, an impoverished medical student, first attended one of his lectures at Edinburgh University. Described as a 'thin, white-haired Scot with the look of a prematurely hatched bird, whose Adam's apple danced up and down his narrow neck', the doctor spoke in a piping voice and is said to have walked with a jerky, scuttling gait 'suggestive of his considerable reserves of nervous energy'. Bell was a keen observer of his patients' mental and physical characteristics – 'The Method', as he called it – which he used as an aid to diagnosis. A lecture in the university's gaslit amphitheatre might, for example, open with Bell informing his audience that the subject standing beside him in the well of the auditorium had obviously served, at some time, as a non-commissioned officer in a Highland regiment in the West Indies – an inference based on the man's failure to remove his hat (a Scots military custom) and telltale signs of tropical illness, among other minutiae. Added to his impressive powers of deduction, Bell also liked to bring an element of drama to his lectures, for instance by once swallowing a phial of malodorous liquid in front of his students, the better to determine whether or not it was a deadly poison. (He survived the test.) For much of the last century, Bell has been the individual most popularly associated with the 'real Holmes'.

That notwithstanding, there would be several other ingredients in what Conan Doyle called 'the rather complex chain' leading to his detective's creation. Pinning down Doyle's real-life models should be a straightforward matter of checking the known facts of his life in the years prior to March 1886, when he put pen to paper on the first Holmes tale, *A Study in Scarlet*. We know that he read voraciously, and that he drew heavily on the analytical-detective fiction of Edgar Allan Poe and Emile Gaboriau. It's also known that Doyle was concerned with finding a narrative way to show the potential of forensic science for solving crime. And it can be safely said that he brought a moral dimension to the stories, at the end of which, however outlandish their plots, affairs were successfully restored to their rightful, late Victorian order. Many of these strands came together in the person of Joe Bell, who in 1878 picked Doyle out to serve as his outpatient clerk, the beginning of a relationship between the brilliant man of reason and his somewhat stolid accomplice that would foreshadow that between Holmes and Dr Watson. As we'll see, there are also various other candidates whose individual talents and eccentricities mirrored those of the fictional inhabitants of 221b Baker Street.

At this point, one begins to see why so many readers are convinced that the author of the Sherlock Holmes stories was really one Dr John Watson, and that Conan Doyle was merely a kind of glorified literary agent behind the scenes. (There are many more strange theories about the series than that.) But writing, to Doyle, was very much an imaginative or moral exercise, and not just a parlour game where the intellectual elite would try to identify the models for his best-known characters. Sherlock Holmes, it seems fair to say, was a composite of several historical, living or invented figures. We'll touch on some of these in later pages. But, critically, Holmes also reflected the personality of his creator, a man who combined a lifelong passion for scientific inquiry with a finely honed sense of honour and justice and, just as important, an absolute willingness to offend the political or religious orthodoxy of the day.

This, then, is a tale of two detectives. The first one is the mythological figure of Sherlock Homes, a combination of several pioneering Victorian professionals, and of his author's imagination. The result is a character who has endured for some 130 years, and whom we still associate today with wearing an Inverness cape, smoking a calabash pipe and uttering the immortal line, 'Elementary, my dear Watson', none of which appear in any of his sixty originally published appearances. Along the way, Holmes has survived everything from his creator's periodic attempts to kill him, to being hijacked for countless literary sequels and knockoffs – including one, with the title *A Samba for Sherlock*, in which a nearly blind detective gropes his way around the barrios of Rio de Janeiro, and another, *The Beekeeper's Apprentice*, which outs him as a feminist.

Part of Holmes's appeal, surely, lies in Conan Doyle's skilful creation not just of a memorable leading man, but also a *dramatis personae* that helps sustain our interest in the series as a whole. The characters 'ring well', as the author Saul Bellow (something of a closeted gothic-crime fan) once told me. 'They may not be realistic, but they feel real and they feel right … If it isn't what the Victorian underworld was like, it's what we like to *think* it was like.'

As well as the pairing of Holmes and Watson that would become the prototype of a whole raft of comically mismatched yet interdependent double acts, from Jeeves and Wooster to Morse and Lewis, we're perhaps equally drawn, with a shudder midway between joy and revulsion, to that 'Napoleon of crime', Professor Moriarty. Like Holmes's deerstalker hat and signature cape, the notion of Moriarty far exceeds his physical presence in the published stories, where he appears just twice, but even so he's insinuated himself into our consciousness as the archetypal evil genius. It's all part of the process of bringing the series closer to real life than Doyle himself might admit.

Today there are thriving clubs and societies and, thanks to the internet, enjoyably spirited long-distance discussions that try and establish such matters as which train, exactly, Holmes might have taken to Baskerville Hall, or the correct location of the wound Watson suffered in the Afghan War. It's in no way intended as a slight to note again that there may be no other characters in English literature, not excluding those of P. G. Wodehouse, who continue to excite such fanatical and, at times, slightly dotty devotion.

Sherlock Holmes is an austere masterpiece; a universally recognisable character made up of several true-life or imagined ingredients. But he's also the literary embodiment of his author. Conan Doyle was eminently well qualified to write about the horrors of Victorian urban life, having worked as a young medical assistant in 1870s Sheffield and Birmingham, among other character-forming experiences. Fifty years later, Doyle could still shock audiences with a variety of macabre tales of his youth, such as the time he was led into an ill-lit back parlour where a 'grotesquely misshapen form, with pitted complexion, hooded eyes and a face gnawed by pox' lay pathetically awaiting his care. Nor was his subsequent six-month spell as the ship's surgeon on an Arctic whaler without its colourful incident, as seen by his 1904 story, 'Black Peter'.

While this whole period was grist for Conan Doyle's later career, it also touched off or accelerated his lifelong dread of drunkenness – the 'great frailty' that afflicted his own father Charles, who spent several years as an inmate of the Montrose Lunatic Asylum before his premature death in another institution. In short, the man who invented Sherlock Holmes was on terms of more than passing familiarity with the forces of social and criminal darkness.

Joseph Bell may have been the basic template for the character, but Holmes also reflected Doyle's own mixture of scientific reason and almost monomaniacal pursuit of justice in the face of the blundering and often corrupt Establishment. It's true that in December 1912 Doyle rebuked a critic with a poem ending in the lines, 'So please grip this fact with your cerebral tentacle/The doll and its maker are never identical'. It's also true that Joseph Bell himself – not a man to unduly shun any available credit – once wrote a letter to Doyle stating, 'You are yourself Sherlock Homes and well you know it'.

The machine-like impersonality of Holmes's methods mirrors the impenetrability of Holmes the man. Even to scholars and those countless ordinary fans around the world who devote themselves to a close textual study of the series – the so-called Holmesians or Sherlockians – there are still tantalising gaps and unresolved discrepancies. To this day, apparently well-adjusted and intelligent minds eagerly debate the character's family background (solidly British, although related to the Vernet dynasty of French painters), or matters such as where he went to university, and whether he was truly a confirmed bachelor or, rather, one of those tragic literary figures who have had their hearts broken earlier in life and turn their backs on romantic love as a result.

Might Holmes have been schizophrenic? Was he a practical joker? Or totally humourless? Did he vote? Enjoy a night out? Could he have suffered the childhood trauma of seeing one or both of his parents killed by street robbers, an event that, as in the case of Batman, served as the motivation for his whole subsequent crime-fighting career? In all likelihood, we'll never know. Nowhere in the roughly three-quarters of a million words Conan Doyle wrote about Holmes do we ever learn the character's exact age, his birthplace, or his birthday. In 2015, eighty-eight years after his last official appearance, Holmes seemingly made a comeback in a story that had allegedly lain undisturbed for decades in a Scottish loft. Entitled 'Sherlock Holmes: Discovering the Border Burghs and, by Deduction, the Brig Bazaar', the tale in turn became a mystery – a true addition to the canon, or merely a pastiche by a hand that may or may not have been Doyle's? To review the books, monographs, films, and other, more ad-hoc projects inspired by Holmes today is not to note a revival of interest, but simply to let down a bucket into a bottomless well.

But perhaps the greatest enigma of all is how a morally austere Scotsman who had barely set foot in London before his thirtieth birthday, and who was convinced his true literary calling lay in Napoleonic-historical romance, could have created a thoroughly contemporary dramatic hero, who also happened to be a bipolar drug addict given to shooting up cocaine three times a day to overcome his lassitude, and whom we associate with an intimate working knowledge of the English capital's underworld and back streets. It's a tribute to Doyle's powers of improvisation that London, which he knew largely from the contemporary Post Office Directory, the nearest thing to Google Maps of the day, is often described as another character in the stories.

It's also well known that Doyle, unlike the detective's millions of diehard fans, soon grew weary of Holmes, once admitting, 'I feel towards him as I do to pâté de foie gras, of which I once ate too much, so that the name of it gives me a sickly feeling to this day'. Having brought the character to life in 1886, he was trying to kill him again as soon as 1890. Holmes's apparent watery end in 'The Final Problem', published in the December 1893 edition of *The Strand* magazine, scarcely two years after his debut there in 'A Scandal in Bohemia', triggered the perhaps apocryphal story that bereaved readers had walked around the streets of England wearing black armbands. Doyle himself was more stoical, jotting only the words 'Killed Holmes' in his notebook.

He took a similarly laconic approach when the American *Collier's Weekly* offered him the fabulous sum of $25,000, or roughly £6,000, to revive Holmes in a series of six stories. 'Very well, ACD', he scribbled back on a postcard. Even so, Doyle was always shrewd enough to see a long-term future for Holmes. Rather like an iconic 1960s rock band contemplating a reunion, there would be periodic hints of a one-off comeback, if not a full-scale return to public life. Although Holmes the detective remained dead, there was 'no limit to the number of papers he left behind or the reminiscences in the brain of his biographer,' Doyle wrote in *The Strand*'s sister paper *Tit-Bits* in December 1900. The inevitable followed with the first published instalment of *The Hound of the Baskervilles* just eight months later. When the American actor William Gillette brought the character of Holmes to the stage at around the same time, Doyle allowed, 'It's good to see the old chap again'. The old chap would continue to appear in periodic new adventures until as late as 1927, taking Holmes up to an era when fictional detectives were dealing with pushy leading ladies and fascist spies. By then he had outlived many of the late Victorian conventions and physical trappings (gloaming and gaslight, swirling river fogs) of his heyday, and Doyle himself survived the character he had long felt so conflicted about by just three years.

✳ ✳ ✳

Holmes's own 'Rules of Evidence' tell us that, around 1885, Conan Doyle, a modestly successful provincial doctor with literary ambitions, was growing tired of the standard detective yarn which relied more on plot devices such as divine intervention, coincidence or intuition than on systematic thought or scientific analysis to achieve its result. Doyle had the idea to do away with the haphazard and instead to present the whole story as an intellectual challenge to the reader, giving him or her an equal opportunity with the detective to solve the mystery. All that then remained was a leading man who was not only logical but troubled as well, thus allowing us to identify with at least some of his humanising contradictions.

As we've seen, Doyle's old mentor Joseph Bell was the basic prototype, but there were others who clearly influenced the final product. One of the true pioneers of forensic medicine, Dr Henry Littlejohn (1826–1914) was an unmistakable figure around Victorian Edinburgh, where among other duties he advised the police in a number of high-profile criminal cases. In January 1878, for example, he was able to determine that the 'vomited data' of a woman found dying in her bed were more in keeping with narcotic poisoning than gas exposure, as the rather cursory official examination had concluded, with the result that the victim's husband was charged with her murder. (Some years later, Littlejohn's son Harvey, also a forensic scientist, crossed swords with Conan Doyle in their contrasting interpretations of a sensational Scottish murder case: see Chapters 7 and 8.)

There are those who claim also to see glimpses of Holmes in Jerome Caminada (1844–1914), a legendary figure in the history of the Manchester Police who was known both for his logical faculties and unorthodox methods. Over the years, the burly, luxuriantly bearded Caminada employed a variety of imaginative disguises, including that of a visiting Tanzanian warlord, a drunken, one-legged sailor and various working-class roles, in order to infiltrate the local criminal classes. He even once successfully impersonated a female opera singer. Like Holmes before him, Caminada went on to investigate a seemingly well-educated, aristocratic woman who was actually a consummate forger and crook, before becoming infatuated by her, and in time he found an arch-nemesis with a number of similarities to the academic turned criminal fiend, Professor Moriarty.

There are vocal schools in support of several other names as being the 'real Holmes'. Some see a touch of the pathologist Sir Bernard Spilsbury (1877–1947) in the character, although he could only have influenced the later stories, while others confer the mantle on one Francis 'Tanky' Smith (1814–88), who bestrode the Leicester CID at the time Conan Doyle was growing up. Also partial to disguises, Smith's most famous assignment came when as a private detective he solved the disappearance of his county's high sheriff, whose lifeless body he eventually found floating in the River Moselle in Germany. As well as the above, there are literally dozens of other candidates said to have inspired Doyle from among the ranks of the official or semi-official forces in Italy, Belgium, Spain, Luxemburg, Austria, Brazil, Colombia, Barbados and the United States; the list is far from exhaustive.

Unlike most of these characters, Conan Doyle himself presents a figure of comparatively conventional temper and settled habits, spending long hours each day at his desk, as disciplined in his writing routine as he had been as a doctor, an instinctive Tory, a teetotaller, devoted to his widowed mother, and with little that could be called truly nonconformist or even eccentric about his private life, at least until he started regularly communing with ghosts at around the age of 58.

Doyle's appearance seemed thoroughly correct. He was tall, squarely built, heavily moustached, with plastered-down brown hair. He carried his umbrella at the furl; his bearing was military; and for long stretches of his life he lived in a series of suburban villas stuffed with mahogany tables, marble busts and hunting prints. He loved cricket, and once succeeded in dismissing W.G. Grace, the titan of the Victorian game, an achievement he ranked 'above any prize the literary world could confer'.

When Doyle sat down to work he often prepared sheets of paper with multiple versions of individual scenes, or specific lines of dialogue, intended for whatever story was under construction. One version might show a certain amount of archaic if energetically sustained idiom like 'quothas' and 'windage', another one favoured a perfectly serviceable, 'flat' style devoid of any noticeable technique, and the third draft typically betrayed some modestly experimental touches such as the omission of inverted commas in direct speech. Doyle chose the middle course in almost every case, before going on to neatly write out the manuscript, with minimal further revisions, in a text 'always as clear as print', as his editor at *The Strand* remarked appreciatively.

Doyle's patient, bricklaying method when it came to his writing reflected his essentially practical, temperate approach to life as a whole. 'There was nothing lynx-eyed, nothing "detective" about him,' wrote the American journalist Harry How, who interviewed Doyle in his first flush of fame from the Holmes stories. 'He [was] just a happy, genial, homely man; tall, broad-shouldered, with a hand that grips you heartily, and, in its sincerity of welcome, hurts.'

That the 'automatic writing' view of Conan Doyle and his immortal detective appears something of a simplification the following pages will, perhaps, show. Conversely, there are those who depict Doyle as a classic case of a journeyman author who merely stumbled onto a winning formula and practised it, with little variation, practically throughout his life, repeating the ritual phrases and stock plot devices, while rigorously maintaining his own outward appearance of stuffy moral and social conformity until the last. This, too, is an inadequate picture of the man.

Conan Doyle may not have 'been' Sherlock Holmes. But there's abundant evidence that the detective conformed to a fundamental logic and precision of thought in his maker's mind. The presentation of the Holmes stories was sometimes clumsy, and the writing wooden. They could be justly criticised for their frequent technical lapses and faulty grip of their subject matter, just as much as they could be praised for their pervasive sense of atmosphere and their many unforgettable individual scenes or bursts of dialogue. The adventure of 'Silver Blaze', published in 1892, demonstrates both these extremes. Although Doyle's all-important grasp of the world of horse-racing is shown as only fair (as he later admitted, if the events had taken place in real life as he described them, half the characters would have been arrested, and the other half 'warned off' for life), we continue to quote the deathless exchange between Holmes and the befuddled local police inspector:

> 'Is there any point to which you would wish to draw my attention?'
> 'To the curious incident of the dog in the night-time.'
> 'The dog did nothing in the night-time.'
> 'That was the curious incident,' remarked Sherlock Holmes.

The satisfying thing is not only the neat twist of the line, but the obvious contrast it creates between the subtle, insightful mind of the maverick consulting detective and that of the plodding official investigator. Clichés now, Doyle's treatment of such matters showed his originality in the 1890s. Any writer who dares to think up and carry off such a persuasively anti-authority theme as embodied by Holmes in his dealings with Scotland Yard would not, in all probability, be a slave to the judicial or governmental orthodoxy when it came to matters of real-life miscarriages of justice.

'A few of the problems which have come my way have been very similar to some which I had invented for the exhibition of the reasoning of Mr Holmes,' Conan Doyle wrote in his 1924 *Memories and Adventures*. 'I might perhaps quote one in which that gentleman's method of thought was copied with complete success,' he added, for once throwing modesty to the winds. Almost all the contemporary accounts show how confident Doyle was in his own powers of calculation and deduction, even if in public he generally chose to play the role of a sort of anonymous medium who had just happened to summon Sherlock Holmes into being.

The case began at London's Langham Hotel – that great Victorian pile that still 'sits atop Regent Street like a grand yet faded dowager', to quote the *Smithsonian*, and one of those places where Sherlock Holmes and his creator frequently overlap. In August 1889, Doyle went to dinner there with the managing editor of *Lippincott's* magazine, and left again with a commission for the second Holmes novella, *The Sign of the Four*, which itself name-checks the hotel.

One of the perennials of the Holmes canon is the individual who mysteriously vanishes, and the case here had most of the essentials. 'A gentleman had disappeared,' Doyle wrote:

He had drawn a bank balance of £40 which was known to be on him. It was feared that he had been murdered for the sake of the money. He had last been heard of stopping at [the Langham], having come from the country that day. In the evening, he went out to a music-hall performance, came out of it about ten o'clock, returned to his hotel, changed his evening clothes, which were found in his room [the] next day, and disappeared utterly. No one saw him leave the hotel, but a man occupying a neighbouring room declared that he had heard him moving during the night. A week had elapsed at the time that I was consulted, but the police had discovered nothing. Where was the man?

Doyle's subsequent investigation showed both deductive reasoning of a high order and a degree of something closer to common sense than to true forensic science. The man had evidently meant to disappear, he rapidly concluded. Why else would he draw all his money? More than likely, he had come back to the hotel late that evening, changed his clothes, and then slipped out again unnoticed in the crowd of other returning theatregoers. The police inspector who called Doyle in on the case assured him that he and his men had undertaken the 'most diligent researches' into where the man might have gone in London at eleven or twelve o'clock at night.

Their enquiries did not, however, extend to checking the railway timetables for the day in question. Doyle did this, and quickly deduced that the man had departed on the midnight express bound for Edinburgh. The abandonment of his evening suit suggested that he had then intended to adopt a life free of the conventional social niceties. By a similar process of deduction, or perhaps more of a working knowledge of human nature, Doyle further determined that there was a woman involved other than the missing party's wife. At this point the police belatedly turned their attention to Edinburgh's less fashionable suburbs, and soon found the man in the circumstances described. The fellow guest who believed he had heard his neighbour moving around his room at night had simply been confused by the normal sounds of a large hotel. Once explained, as in any good Sherlock Holmes story, it was all so simple – if you knew how.

In a broadly similar case, Doyle again demonstrated that what he called the 'general lines of reasoning advocated by Holmes' had a practical application to real life. A young woman had become engaged to a French businessman, living in England and known to be reticent about his past life, who had then abandoned her at the altar. On their wedding day, several witnesses had seen the groom set off for the church to meet his bride, but he had never arrived. The police investigated, apparently believing that foul play was involved, possibly touching in some way on the Frenchman's extensive business interests.

Doyle looked into the matter, and quickly reached a sadly different conclusion. The man had never seriously intended to marry his English fiancée, for the simple reason that he already had a wife waiting for him at home in France. He had 'disappeared' by simply stepping in at one door of a hansom cab and out at the other – oddly enough, a plot device identical to one in the 1891 Holmes tale 'A Case of Identity'. 'I was able to show the girl very clearly both whither [her fiancé] had gone and how unworthy he was of her affections,' Doyle wrote, combining his coldly analytical and profoundly moral sides in one neat summary.

Time and again, whether in fiction or real life, Conan Doyle brought this old-fashioned sense of chivalry to bear in his detective exploits, never quite coming to terms with what he deemed the 'sophisticated decadence' of the modern age. For the Scotsman born in 1859 and raised in a religious household, the protection of the vulnerable members of society was a matter of 'honour', a word that resounded deep within his Victorian soul. To Doyle, the fairer sex conjured up images of the defenceless young girl, the cruelly abused wife, the jilted lover, and the 'fate worse than death itself'. When investigating such cases, he made up for any shortcomings he may have had as a forensic detective by a fiercely moral sense of the particular iniquities that often befell young women, and how these same victims were failed by the criminal justice system.

Doyle's reaction to the affair of the Fox sisters of Hydesville, New York, demonstrated this lifelong propensity to take up the sword on behalf of the young, female or otherwise supposedly weak members of society. In 1848, Margaret Fox, aged 14, and Kate, 12, had apparently begun to hear nocturnal 'bumps and raps' in the bedroom of their small farmhouse. The girls' mother became convinced that an unseen spirit she named 'Mr Splitfoot' was communicating with them, and that 'distinct manifestations of an undead soul' continued even when she and the children moved home.

Within a year, the sisters and their mother had become a popular music-hall attraction up and down the American east coast, and won over a number of influential backers, including Horace Greeley, editor of the *New York Tribune*, who took up their cause in a series of sensational front-page articles. As a result, the young Fox girls effectively launched the modern spiritualist movement. They kept the act going even as grown women, although the abstemious Greeley was left to regret that by then Margaret and Kate had regularly 'taken a sip', the beginning of a serious drinking problem in their later days.

In time, Conan Doyle would come to cautiously endorse the Foxes' 'apparent mediumship' and their 'strong sense within their own minds of communion with worlds unseen'. While on a lecture tour of the USA in 1923, Doyle announced his intention to erect a monument to the sisters, both of whom had died in poverty in the 1890s. The public response to this was only 'sparing', he was forced to admit. 'The reaction to my appeal for some central memorial of our Cause has been so scanty that I cannot bring myself to present it,' he wrote in the psychic journal *Light*. 'I am, therefore, returning the money to the various subscribers, whom I hereby thank.'

Although Conan Doyle evidently had doubts about whether the young Fox sisters had been truly channelling some diabolical agency, or merely engaging in a juvenile prank, he leapt to their defence when the magician Harry Houdini publicly insisted that the girls had done no more than 'lie abed and crack their own toe-joints … thus producing the unworldly "rapping" … an effect any fool can reproduce by clicking two coins together over the head of a blindfolded person.' Doyle was incensed at what he called 'this viciously partisan assault upon virtual infants', reasoning that 'at such tender age they could hardly have been such practiced hoaxers'. According to his friend and fellow spiritualist Oliver Lodge, when Doyle subsequently discussed the Foxes with Houdini they fell into a 'noisy debate', at which time 'the iron had entered Sir Arthur's soul; he swore that he would never stand by while an innocent's name was besmirched … He would hit at the villifiers and sceptics, and hit hard.'

Some of these same ingredients were at work in Conan Doyle's spirited defence of 16-year-old Elsie Wright and her 10-year-old cousin Frances Griffiths, who disappeared with a camera one hot afternoon in July 1917 into the glen behind the Wrights' home in the village of Cottingley, West Yorkshire, and returned with an image that seemed to show Frances leaning on the side of a small hill on which four fairies were dancing. 'It is a revelation,' Doyle wrote to Houdini.

On 24 July 1928, Doyle appeared as a defence witness in the criminal trial of a Miss Mercy Phillimore and Mrs Claire Cantlon, respectively the secretary of the London Spiritualist Alliance and a medium who practised there, whom the police had charged under the 1604 Witchcraft Act. Doyle was so infuriated at the 'medieval' proceedings against these 'honest, cruelly abused English ladies' that he went on to make an appointment with the Home Secretary in an unsuccessful bid to change the law as it applied in their case.

There seemed to be almost no limit to how far he would go, whether by a gift of money, his time, or some other form of public campaign, when he saw one of these 'honest gentlewomen' subjected to the same sort of 'ill-considered and vindictive attack by our ruling class'. 'Sir Arthur was mesmerising,' a sceptical *Daily Express* journalist admitted, after hearing him speak on the subject to a packed house at the Royal Albert Hall. 'I felt that if he wanted to sell us a house with the roof missing, he would achieve his purpose by an eloquent and sustained eulogy of the features that remained.'

A few weeks later, while on a speaking tour of South Africa, Conan Doyle was again able to take up the cause of a wronged woman, though 'wronged' hardly conveys the fate of 18-year-old Irene Kanthack, who had been raped and stabbed to death while out walking her dog in a park near her family home in a respectable neighbourhood of Johannesburg. The investigating police chief, a Colonel Trigger, seemed to speak in the authentic voice of Doyle's Inspector Lestrade when he announced that he had swiftly solved the crime by the expedient of arresting a 'black native' with a history of petty theft. Some of the circumstantial evidence would seem to have fit the suspect, but rather more of it to completely exonerate him. The man was soon released without charge.

Other white women then came forward to claim that they, too, had been assaulted over the course of the previous weeks or months, close to the spot where Irene Kanthack's body had been found. Was a serial homicidal rapist on the loose? Could it have been, as Colonel Trigger theorised, 'some black man in the grip of his unquenchable urges'? On the day Conan Doyle arrived in town, it was apparently learnt that a voodoo cult was in operation only a mile away from the murder scene, and that this was in the habit of holding 'messianic services' including a communion ritual involving the use of freshly shed human blood.

That was at least one account; but the accounts are as various and lurid as the scenes they claim to describe, and the only certainty is that at the time Doyle arrived in Johannesburg on his lecture tour there had been a thirty-fold increase in the already impressive daily number of local firearm sales, from approximately seventy to 2,100, and 'no white women, whether singly or together, were to be seen anywhere on the city streets' after dark.

By all accounts, Doyle's investigative antennae were soon alert to the double injustice he saw in Johannesburg. Not only had a helpless young woman been viciously assaulted; the police had clearly concluded that a black man had done it. 'What confronted one was this rank determination to equate skin colour with criminality,' he wrote. Doyle and a local journalist named Stephen Black set out to investigate, and soon turned up at least one lead that 'should have rung loudly, even in the seemingly deaf ears of Col. Trigger', Doyle remarked. This followed their interview of a janitor at an apartment block near the scene of Irene Kanthack's murder who had witnessed a white man with a distinctive facial scar wringing out a bloodstained shirt in a washroom there on the evening of the attack. Doyle and his colleague went to the building and persuaded the janitor to show them the room where the mysterious scarred man had lived. It was empty, but not entirely free of evidence. According to Black, 'Sir Arthur was shocked … The walls were covered by indecent drawings, more or less life size … women in the most clinical and obstetric attitudes.' Doyle recovered his poise sufficiently to then arrange to pay the rent on the room for a month, apparently hoping that Colonel Trigger might be interested in visiting it.

We'll return to the outcome of the case; but for now it again illustrates the lengths to which Doyle would go on behalf of a wronged party, particularly if some form of officially tolerated prejudice or bigotry was involved. As the local *Weekend Argus* wrote of a speech he gave at the time:

> Sir Arthur's talk was familiar, often dry, but his more inspired passages throbbed with the heady moral rhetoric of a great avenger, and grew shrill and staccato in their impassioned climaxes, crashing down together in a peal of continuous thunder and lightning.

Conan Doyle was sometimes content to let the natural crusader in him do the work of the coldly reasoning detective. In some ways, too, he was more of a Dr Watson than a Sherlock Holmes. 'I am the man in the street,' Doyle insisted, which surely sums up Watson himself, whatever one makes of his later interpretations by everyone from Nigel Bruce to Jude Law. Attributing all the Holmesian virtues to his author would be to stretch what was only a fair working knowledge on Conan Doyle's part of matters such as toxicology, ballistics and handwriting analysis.

Doyle's 6,000-word investigation in 1907 of a series of anonymous letters that accompanied the George Edalji cattle-maiming case (see Chapters 4 and 5) perhaps owed more to his sense of indignation at the wrongful imprisonment of the young Parsee convicted of the crime than it did to a close textual study of the letters. His subsequent presentation of his findings to a committee at the Home Office was not only unwisely long, but so oblivious to some of the established facts of the case that at least one of the officials present used the opportunity to discreetly take a nap. Doyle's legendary self-confidence was not, however, impaired: he recorded in his case notes, 'I trust that I have convinced every impartial man that the balance of evidence is enormously against Edalji having had anything to do with the letters'. Perhaps, at heart, he enjoyed sparring with the Establishment as much as he did fighting for victims of injustice.

Those who love such sport know that the best place to look for a fight in the late Victorian or early Edwardian literary worlds is on the occasions when Conan Doyle felt that honour – sometimes his own, more often someone else's – was at stake. Returning by sea from the Boer War in July 1900, he fell into a quarrel with Roger Raoul-Duval, a French novelist temporarily serving as an army observer, over the latter's claim that the British troops had been in the habit of using the particularly destructive 'dumdum' bullets of the kind that tore apart the internal organs on striking a body. According to his first biographer, 'Sir Arthur turned beetroot-red and called him a liar. The [Frenchman] tendered a written apology.'

Several other such cases followed over the years. George Bernard Shaw's public questioning of the bravery of the captain and crew of the *Titanic* after it went down in 1912 had Doyle figuratively spitting his teeth into his hand and saying that he was distressed to see that such an intelligent man as Shaw lacked 'that quality – call it good taste, humanity, or what you will – which prevents one from needlessly hurting the feelings of others'. When H. G. Wells later went into print describing a certain medium and her 'spirit guide' as 'wrought of self-deception, [as] pathetic as a rag doll which some lonely child has made for its own comfort', Doyle again leapt to the defence. The individual circumstances varied, but as a rule the feuds show how Doyle saw himself: a responsible intellectual of rigid moral probity, who if necessary could quietly demolish an adversary.

If Conan Doyle had the right moral stuff to invest in what he once called his 'monster' of Sherlock Holmes, he was also lucky enough to have a vast and receptive market waiting for him. The 1890s saw the birth or rapid growth of a number of British retail businesses like John Lewis, Marks and Spencer, Sainsbury's and Boots that remain familiar today. Appealing to broadly the same, increasingly urbanised middle class, it was also a golden era of mass circulation family periodicals like the new *Strand* magazine, at sixpence, half the price of most monthlies of the day, where Holmes found an immediately appreciative audience.

'A Scandal in Bohemia' appeared in *The Strand*'s July 1891 issue, which enjoyed a total subscription of 485,000 copies, meaning perhaps 2 million readers out of a literate English population of some 17 million men, women and children: a story today would have to be read by roughly 7 million people, which is more than the combined circulation of *The Times*, *The Daily Telegraph*, *The Guardian*, the *Daily Express*, the *Daily Star*, the *Daily Mirror* and the *Daily Mail*, to claim a similar hold on the public. Doyle may have been frustrated that it was his detective fiction, not his 'lasting work', that the public craved, but the increasingly lucrative commissions and healthy royalty cheques proved a palliative silver lining.

Doyle was also fortunate in his timing on another level. The turn of the twentieth century was uniquely ripe for the arrival of a moral avenger like Holmes, and it's no surprise that so many readers came to think of him as a living person. The truly grisly murder mystery was then a staple of British life. Compared to the farrago of horrors that Doyle and his generation read about or personally experienced on a daily basis, much of today's high-profile crime seems as innocuous and bloodless as a case of a purloined cow-creamer out of the pages of P.G. Wodehouse.

Doyle's London was a soiled, sad place whose inhabitants habitually murdered, stole, lied and cheated as they slithered around in a sea of immorality. It seemed the various outrages were all absurdly and graphically bloody and gory, the motivations behind them often ghoulish, and the cast of characters uniformly macabre and grotesque. This was the world that Conan Doyle knew was ready for the introduction of a contemporary moral equaliser like Holmes. It was also the one that provided Doyle himself with a wealth of bizarre and often outlandishly gothic adventures to rival anything in his fiction.

The list that follows is far from exhaustive, but in just the decade from 1904 leading to the outbreak of the First World War there was the case of 'George Chapman' (actually a Pole named Klosowski) who joined the long list of London's notable lady-killers when he was convicted of poisoning three successive wives. A year later a chemist's assistant named Arthur Devereux murdered his young bride and their twin sons, placed the bodies in a trunk, calmly deposited this at a nearby warehouse and was going about his life as usual until his suspicious mother-in-law investigated; Devereux was tried and hung for his crimes in August 1905. Meanwhile, having been released from custody after murdering his father by bludgeoning him with a chamber pot, a journalist named William Benn would see his wife Florence commit suicide by hanging herself from a tree in their garden. The Benns' young daughter would go on to become the actress Margaret Rutherford.

Shortly afterwards there was the doubly poignant case of 13-year-old Thomas Polmear, described as a 'village idiot', who drowned and decapitated an infant in the belief that this was a normal thing to do, and then spent the remaining twenty-eight years of his life in a lunatic asylum. In 1909 George Joseph Smith, a Londoner, began his practice of marrying and deserting an unspecified number of women before deciding to drown three of them in quick succession; the 'Brides in the Bath' murderer was in turn executed in 1915.

Meanwhile, a relatively rare case where the woman was the perpetrator, not the victim, came when 23-year-old Kittie Byron stabbed her lover Reginald Baker to death in the doorway of a London post office; although sentenced to hang, she was reprieved and eventually spent nine years in jail. Framing these various events was the brief but sensational reign of Jack the Ripper in 1888, and the infamous case of Dr Hawley Crippen, who after murdering his wife at their London home in January 1910 fled with a female companion disguised as his son and boarded an Atlantic liner in order to start a new life together in Canada. Crippen became the first criminal to be captured with the aid of wireless telegraphy, and was hanged at Pentonville.

The cases of George Edalji and Oscar Slater, which follow, were among the most notorious of an era when each successive 'crime of the century' appeared to be followed by a greater and even more hideous one with each passing year. It sometimes seems almost surprising that anyone got out of early Edwardian London in one piece, given the prevalence of violent offences, quite apart from the era's other set-piece tragedies, such as the loss of the *Titanic* and the discovery seven months later of the frozen bodies of Captain Robert Scott and his companions in the Antarctic ice.

As a whole, Britons were expected to be phlegmatic about death, and they often were. At the same time, people were clearly ready for someone who could make sense of the spectacular series of stabbings, shootings, poisonings, strangulations, assaults and petty betrayals that seemed to take place on such a regular basis, and so many of which involved a female or (so it was then thought) equally helpless member of society. It was Conan Doyle's unique genius to provide this service on two levels: as the creator of Sherlock Holmes, and as a detective of formidable skills in his own right.

'A writer is a maker, not a man of action', W.H. Auden once claimed, but even he went on to admit that all fiction is, in a sense, autobiographical. In the case of Conan Doyle, this is more than usually true. It's difficult to study any individual major crime in Great Britain between around 1890 and 1925 without encountering Doyle in one form or another. His name was either being bandied about as a surrogate for the detective most needed to help redress a grievance, or failing that, Doyle was personally on the miscreant's trail. He even found time to join a small group of senior policemen, lawyers, pathologists, academics, writers and other invited parties to discuss particularly controversial cases, past or present, where the justice system seemed to have failed.

Called, simply, the Crimes Club, it met roughly six times annually from its inception in July 1904. It was a prestigious line-up: Doyle himself; Sir Arthur Pearson, founder of the *Daily Express*; Samuel Ingleby Oddie, soon to be one of the prosecutors in the Crippen case and later the Coroner of Westminster; Fletcher Robinson, the *Express* journalist who first came up with the basic plot of *The Hound of the Baskervilles*; and George Sims, a writer who had campaigned successfully for the release of Adolf Beck, a Norwegian engineer twice wrongfully convicted in British courts because of mistaken identity.

As a rule, the club met in a private dining room of one of the great London hotels like the Langham, but there were occasional field trips: Doyle and his fellow members took at least one tour of Jack the Ripper sites in Whitechapel, where he was said to have inspected the various crime scenes through his magnifying glass – if true, a pleasingly Holmesian touch. Several years earlier, Doyle had visited Scotland Yard and been shown a letter supposedly written by the Ripper, remarking that Holmes would surely have made a facsimile of the signature and published it far and wide in the press in the hope someone would recognise it, an initiative that had escaped the official police force.

As Sir Basil Thomson, the long-time Assistant Chief Commissioner at the Yard and a widely quoted authority on crime and criminology (until an arrest for public indecency with young girls put an end to his career) noted, 'Conan

Doyle would have made an outstanding detective had he devoted himself to crime detection rather than authorship. There was much of Sherlock Holmes in him.' It was perhaps the singular tragedy of Doyle's life that he saw himself as a 'serious' author, that with certain notable exceptions the reading public looked on the results with disdain, and that there was also a part of him drawn irresistibly, like Holmes himself, to the ghoulish or macabre. When you add a powerful moral compulsion to see justice served and a later unshakable belief that the living could communicate with the dead, the stage is set for high drama.

2

'THE DARKNESS OF DOYLE'S MIND'

To answer the main question first: about seven. That was how old Conan Doyle was when he first personally encountered a murderer. In September 1866, Doyle was dispatched to Newington Academy, an Edinburgh fee-paying school just three streets away from his latest family home. The building itself, bleak, gabled and weather-stained, was in gothic style, decorated with snarling heraldic animals and a hellfire biblical injunction etched over the front door. It does not make for a sympathetic account in Doyle's memoirs. 'A tawse-brandishing schoolmaster [Dr Patrick Wilson] of the old type made our young lives miserable,' he wrote in a punitive account more than fifty years after the event. 'From the age of seven to nine I suffered under this pockmarked, one-eyed rascal who might have stepped from the pages of Dickens … Home and books were my sole consolation.' It was the start of a mutual antipathy, Doyle disliking Wilson for his stupidity and cruelty, Wilson despising Doyle for his literacy and general independence.

He was a bright enough pupil, although he already showed signs of being both self-willed and resistant to some of the excesses of a traditional Roman Catholic education. Doyle served his requisite two years at the Academy without being expelled, but that was about the best that could be said of his time there. 'My comrades were rough boys and I became a rough boy, too,' he wrote.

Although superficially the most respectable of Victorian educational establishments, the Academy had a viper in its midst. Shortly before Doyle arrived there, the school had appointed an eminently well-qualified Frenchman named Eugene Chantrelle to teach languages. Chantrelle had been born in Nantes in 1834, showed some early aptitude for chemistry, and later toyed with the idea of a career in medicine. In the charged political atmosphere of mid-nineteenth-century France he had also developed certain strong republican sympathies.

While still at school, Chantrelle was both wounded and arrested in the course of an anti-government march in Paris. Shortly after his release from custody, he chose to move abroad, first to the United States, then England, and finally to Edinburgh, where he arrived in 1865. Aged 31, Chantrelle boasted among his achievements (and boast he did) fluency in English, French, German, Latin and Greek. He had written at least one textbook, though it remains unclear if this was commercially published or more privately available, and was known to furnish medical and political opinions freely around the Edinburgh pubs.

To the local young women, Chantrelle must have cut a dashing figure, with his elegant Parisian frock coat, close-clipped, brilliantined black hair, luxuriant side-whiskers and mournful dark eyes. At the Academy, which was co-educational, he was known to stride into class, the gorgeous, if unearned, gown of l'Ordre des Médecins billowing behind him, and address his female students with a suave 'Bonjour, mademoiselles'.

By the time Doyle came to know him in the autumn of 1866, Chantrelle was already carrying on an affair with an attractive Academy fifth-former named Elizabeth Cullen Dyer. She was 15 years old. The relationship seems to have gone undetected until the late winter of 1867, when Dyer fell pregnant. This situation was too much for Dr Wilson, who dismissed both parties from his school. Thirty-four-year-old Chantrelle and then 17-year-old Dyer married in Edinburgh on 11 August 1868, and the first of their four sons was born ten weeks later.

Doyle himself left the Academy at about the same time, and spent the next seven years at successive boarding schools in Lancashire. Although he omits it from his memoirs, he would have known very well about the scandalous affair he left behind in Edinburgh. He could hardly have avoided it, since an exotic foreigner like Chantrelle had inevitably excited gossip at the Academy even before he had seduced one of his students there. Among other things, it was rumoured that he had wives in several North American cities, as well as one at home in France, and that his sexual relations tended to the sadistic.

The Chantrelles' subsequent marriage was wretchedly unhappy, and could have served as one of those pitiful accounts of domestic woe that form the prologue to several Sherlock Holmes cases. In the words of the editor of the transcript of Chantrelle's eventual trial:

> That he ever had any affection for his wife is doubtful. A more melancholy story of married life has seldom been told in a Court of Justice … Through the years, he frequently abused her without reason, made her the butt of his blasphemy, laid violent hands on her, terrified her by his threats, and to her knowledge was systematically unfaithful to her.

In December 1876, Elizabeth complained to the police that Chantrelle had thrashed her 'unmercifully' on her bare buttocks with a horsewhip, which even in the Scotland of those days, where severe beatings of wives were not uncommon, being considered good for the soul, was enough to merit an official caution. The following October, he took out a policy for £1,000 (roughly £90,000 today) with the Scottish Star Assurance Company in the event that his young wife should predecease him. At Chantrelle's trial it was noted that he had gone to some trouble to understand the definition of 'accidental death' in the contract, and specifically whether 'cramps' and mishaps with 'noxious vapours or fumes' would be included.

On the morning of 2 January 1878, a servant girl found Elizabeth Chantrelle lying unconscious in her bed. There was a strong smell of gas in the room, apparently caused by a broken valve in a nearby fireplace. After being examined by a local doctor who diagnosed a then not unusual case of coal poisoning, the victim was taken to the Royal Infirmary, where she died later that afternoon without regaining consciousness. Elizabeth Chantrelle was 26 years old.

This was the case that brought the attention of Dr Henry Littlejohn, Edinburgh's first Medical Officer of Health and one of the pioneers of the use of toxicology in criminal investigations. Littlejohn set himself to closely studying the vomited matter found on Elizabeth Chantrelle's bedclothes. This showed the presence of opium, which had evidently combined with the effects of gradual gas inhalation to induce death. Eugene Chantrelle was put on trial for his wife's murder, found guilty, and executed on 31 May 1878. He protested his innocence, but at least managed a note of resignation at the end. 'If it is to be, it must be,' Chantrelle remarked as he was led to the gallows.

Although Conan Doyle plays only a walk-on part in the Chantrelle affair, it sets the scene for several of his later criminal investigations. There was the central fact of a cruelly abused young woman, the starting point for several of Sherlock Holmes's cases, and always of particular concern to Doyle himself. The London *Globe*, which Doyle took, published a long account filled with circumstantial detail about the frequent arguments between Elizabeth Chantrelle and her husband, and about how the latter had behaved more 'smoothly' towards her in the last weeks of her life, apparently to lull her into a sense of false security. It also alleged that the victim's 'intimate organs' had been horribly bruised, and that there were other signs of 'vile use'.

Then there was the question of the actual poisoning, which enjoyed something of a vogue among late Victorian homicides. A few years before the Chantrelle tragedy, a young Glasgow woman named Madeleine Smith had gone on trial charged with serving her lover cocoa laced with arsenic (Doyle's father Charles had drawn sketches of the courtroom scene for the press), just one of several such criminal adulterations in the Scotland of that time. Thanks to men like Henry Littlejohn and Joseph Bell (who also consulted on the Chantrelles), recent advances in forensic medicine made it increasingly likely that cases of deliberate poisoning would result in a successful conviction.

Finally, there was Doyle's personal connection to the Chantrelles; he had known both the husband and wife, he was studying under Joseph Bell at the time of Chantrelle's trial, and the murder scene at 81 George Street in central Edinburgh was only a short walk away from his childhood home. It's surely not coincidental that toxins and venoms play such a prominent role in the Sherlock Holmes adventures, or that Holmes was given what Dr Watson calls 'profound knowledge of chemistry … well up in belladonna, opium, and poisons generally', among several other skills of the modern-day medical examiner. Along with the 'low Toby' (today's mugger), the 'cracksman' (or house-breaker), the 'snoozer' (who specialised in hotel jobs), the 'inheritance hurrier', or poisoner, were all criminals typical of the period when Doyle came to create the definitive consulting detective.

'It was the sort of age,' Doyle later remarked, 'when you copy out bits of Poe and carry them around as if you'd written them.' He was referring to his early twenties, when he enjoyed a dual career as a seemingly respectable qualifying family doctor and an author of 'spookist' tales like 1883's 'J. Habakuk

Jephson's Statement', a chiller inspired by the real-life case of the *Mary Celeste*, the brig found drifting unmanned off Gibraltar ten years earlier. 'It will make a sensation,' Doyle confidently predicted, suggesting that under the veneer of gentlemanly diffidence he already had a clear vision both of himself and his ability. Although he pocketed a handsome 29 guinea fee for his efforts, a significant step down the road of convincing the 24-year-old author to take up the pen full-time, overnight fame eluded him. The magazine published the story without a byline, leading many readers to speculate that it had been written by Robert Louis Stevenson.

Ironically, Conan Doyle was far from pleased at the enormous publicity he duly attracted only a few years later. As early as 1892, when he was 33, he was fretting about having squandered his 'entire mental life' on his 'small creation' of Sherlock Holmes, returning to the character in later years chiefly to pay his bills. Perhaps just as painful to Doyle as the nagging sense of his slumming it with Holmes was the unwelcome attention of the detective's curious or obsessed fans. The author complained with some justification that his daily postbag soon brought him dozens of 'highly charged' and 'lunatic' requests for his services as a criminal investigator. Many other applicants arrived in person at Doyle's home, whose doorstep soon teemed with men and women bearing everything from a pack of slavering bloodhounds on a leash to a deceased loved one's apparent coded communications from beyond the grave. A number of callers doggedly refused to leave the premises without a personal consultation with Sherlock Holmes.

In August 1892, when a journalist outed Joseph Bell as the inspiration for Holmes, Doyle immediately wrote to his old professor to warn that he, too, could now expect to receive letters from 'raving idiots'. He wearily quoted some of his own correspondence, which then included a series of appeals from a merchant in Liverpool anxious to know Holmes's views on Jack the Ripper; some equally profuse notes from a young man in Glasgow, who would record the exact time of composition – down to the second – of the beginning and end of his messages; and others 'who believe their neighbours are starving maiden aunts to death in hermetically sealed attics'.

Conan Doyle's ambivalence about Holmes was only part of an elaborate tapestry of conflicting beliefs and ambitions that afflicted the author throughout his life. One part of him was content to turn out a stream of thrilling, if relatively undemanding yarns of a gaunt, drug-taking hero saving his clients, and sometimes England herself, from dastardly plots. Another side wanted to be remembered as a great creative artist and historian. There was a Doyle who was eminently sane, solid, clubbable and conservative, a 'birthright Catholic', as he put it, whose acceptance of the infallibility and literal correctness of the Bible eventually gave way to a broadly Unitarian faith which held that there was a 'wonderful poise' to the universe and 'tremendous power of conception' behind it. And there was the formally-trained man of science who struck out in a new direction early in his medical career. Beneath his surface orthodoxy, Doyle was soon attending his first séances and following the reincarnation and time travel theories of Madame Helena Blavatsky, a Russian-born spiritualist who had emigrated to New York and founded the Theosophical Society there, apparently in the belief that the power of the modern state 'constantly encroaches on our Aryan supremacy'.

In 1883, Doyle fell in with one of those faintly eccentric polymathic figures so prevalent in Victorian public life. Alfred Drayson, a fellow member of the Portsmouth Literary and Scientific Society, was a distinguished former soldier and a prolific author on everything from the game of billiards to the rotation of the earth, on which he wrote a sophisticated, if controversial, monograph.

One night in January 1887, Doyle, Drayson and some other like-minded researchers met in the darkened dining room of a house in the north end of Portsmouth. The initial results of their séance were disappointing, although after half an hour of silence the dining table itself began to tap up and down in a kind of Morse code they interpreted as 'You are going too slowly! How long are you going to take?'

A few weeks later, Doyle met with a local professional medium named Horstead, 'a small bald grey man with a pleasant expression', who was apparently able to make household items such as a box of eggs materialise in front of them, as well as to summon the departed. At a sitting in Portsmouth on 16 June 1887, Horstead dropped his head to his chest and began to speak in a low, tremulous voice in which he announced that the spirits were among them. For some time, the group sat staring down at the heavy oak table in front of them. Then, slowly at first, it began to rise up, apparently of its own accord. Horstead waited for a moment, during which the room grew appreciably colder, and then passed Doyle a scrap of paper. The writing on it read, 'This gentleman is a healer. Tell him not to read Leigh Hunt's book.' As Doyle had then been thinking of buying that critic's *The Comic Dramatists of the Restoration*, it appeared to be a notable feat of psychic prediction. After a few more seconds, the table banged down to the floor again.

When the lights came back up, Doyle sat silent for several moments. The inquisitive but still devoutly Catholic 28-year-old doctor had just undergone a conversion into a disciple of the occult, who would one day become the de facto head of a new worldwide religion. Doyle would later note that this event 'marked in my spiritual career the change of "I believe" into "I know"'.

✳ ✳ ✳

Conan Doyle's eight years in residence at No. 1, Bush Villas, Elm Grove, in the Portsmouth suburb of Southsea, not only marked his spiritual reawakening. They proved to be the turning point of his whole life. Arriving there as a 'feckless' bachelor GP with less than £10 to his name, he left again as a well-received author and man of affairs, with a wife and young daughter in tow. It was here that Doyle brought Holmes to life when he began *A Study in Scarlet* in March 1886, finishing the full 45,000-word manuscript in just seven weeks, although it took a further nineteen months before it finally saw the light of day in the popular *Beeton's Christmas Annual*.

Situated between a church and a pub, Doyle's home was a sooty, three-storey brick house with little pretension to elegance. Although the downstairs consulting room was adequately furnished, the actual living quarters were spartan, asphalt-floored and minimally heated in wintertime. When Doyle first took possession, he had been caught short by the sight in the dimly lit scullery of several rows of human skulls grotesquely smiling up at him. Recovering from his shock, he discovered that they were plaster of Paris models, apparently abandoned by the building's previous tenant, a dentist.

Having failed to persuade his mother to allow his 14-year-old sister Connie to live with him in Portsmouth, Doyle successfully asked her to send his 9-year-old brother Innes instead. With the eventual addition of a housekeeper and the regular arrival of messengers knocking at the door, Bush Villas would come to assume at least some of the characteristics of the fictional ménage at Baker Street. By the late 1880s, the household also included a resident cook, a shuffling valet-doorman, and a part-time maid who was paid a shilling a week. A visitor recalled that the upstairs rooms were increasingly cluttered with a 'medley of the refined and the Bohemian. There were military prints displayed alongside whimsical paintings of fairies, shelves of various chemical apparatus, clouds of pipe smoke', and a 'muscular atmosphere' symbolised by a harpoon, a bear's skull and a seal's paw, among other souvenirs of Conan Doyle's service as ship's doctor on the whaler SS *Hope*, all making for another real-life link to the murky pantomime set of Baker Street. When Doyle finally left Southsea in December 1890, he was given a farewell dinner presided over by his friend and colleague Dr James Watson.

Doyle, like Holmes, valued his privacy, and in addition had the author's natural capacity for introspection. But as a struggling young doctor, he was always aware of the need to advertise his services. A week after his arrival, the *Portsmouth Evening News* carried the paid announcement, 'Dr Doyle begs to notify that he has removed to 1 Bush Villas, Elm Grove, next to the Bush Hotel'.

One wet evening later that summer, a young cotton salesman apparently named 'Hynes' or 'Hines' rode by the house on his way up Kings Road towards the docks. A clap of thunder caused his horse to rear up, and Hynes was thrown to the ground. He fell heavily on the cobblestones and lay there, either unconscious or badly winded, for some half an hour. During this time several patrons sauntered in or out of the door of the nearby pub, but, evidently believing the man to be drunk, they left him undisturbed in the gutter. He was still there as night began to fall, wearing only the light clothes in which he had been making his way across town to the harbour. Eventually, the door of Bush Villas opened and Conan Doyle emerged to perform his nightly ritual of vigorously polishing the brass nameplate on his front wall.

When Doyle saw the injured man, he went to action. Within a minute he had picked him up and carried him back inside the house, where he swiftly bandaged his head and then sent for a carriage to take him to hospital. Hynes later remembered that his rescuer – 'a big, square-chested man with a deep Scots burr' – had passed the time while they waited by speaking, a little incongruously, of his interest in matters such as mesmerism, telepathy and reincarnation. 'Death cannot end all,' he assured his patient. After a few minutes, two uniformed attendants arrived at the door to bear Hynes off to the Royal Portsmouth Infirmary.

The second they were safely on their way, Doyle himself jammed on his coat and hat and ran the 2 miles to the offices of the *Evening News* in order to breathlessly recount the adventure of 'the bloodstained body in the street', as the paper put it in their account of the story. Doyle's own name was prominently displayed throughout. In time the injured salesman made a full recovery and returned to work in his native Liverpool. He received a bill from Doyle for 2 guineas. Some nine years later the first batch of Sherlock Holmes stories began to appear in *The Strand* magazine, marking the moment at which Doyle's literary vocation decisively overtook his medical career. It was then that Hynes realised that the man who had spoken quietly to him about the paranormal that evening in Portsmouth was also the inventor of a character 'who dealt in phenomena altogether more solid and earthbound than did his creator'.

※ ※ ※

As a career, the writing of world-renowned mystery adventures would seem to be remarkably flexible in accommodating varying personal circumstances. There have been authors like Edgar Allan Poe, the godfather of the modern detective genre, whose profoundly melancholy life and enigmatic early death somehow seem to be of a piece with his published fiction; and others, like Agatha Christie, who with certain rare exceptions (see Chapter 10) have appeared to lead the life of a churchgoing provincial English schoolteacher of the most sound traditional habits. Conan Doyle makes such an interesting case because he seems to embody both these extremes: on the one hand, a solidly Establishment type, patriotic and middlebrow, who as time went on seemed to cut a reassuringly old-fashioned if not mildly fogeyish figure, liking nothing more than to potter around his garden or to get up in plus fours for a round of golf; on the other, a closet radical, a latent occultist and table-tapper, and a champion of those persecuted for their political or spiritual beliefs.

Was he really a Holmes, or a Watson? Or a bit of both? Doyle's son Adrian – who went off the rails in later life, moving around Switzerland and various hotels on the French Riviera and often leaving no forwarding address, negotiating the sale of his father's papers as he went, and thus who may not be an entirely credible witness – later wrote of a childhood with a distinct flavour of Baker Street to it:

My memories are mottled with sudden, silent periods when following upon some agitated stranger or missive, my father would disappear into his study for two or three days on end … The hushed footfalls of the whole household, the tray of untasted food standing on the threshold, the subconscious feeling of tension that would settle on family and staff alike, were not less than the reflected essence of the brain, the lamp and the letter that wrought their unpublicised drama on the inner side of the curtained door.

In short, Doyle was that comparative rarity, a contented author, sharply focused when circumstances demanded, and at all other times a genial companion to his family and friends. One American reporter thought him:

> A prime slab of Merry England … He laughed easily, and loudly, with great gusto, usually slapping his knee in exclamation at the same time … The emotions were always healthily near the surface. He was blessed with a marvelous expressive face that turned beet-red when he was angry, which was seldom, and lit up when he was pleased.

And yet Conan Doyle's equilibrium was often tested by the most irregular circumstances and the most curious events. 'Those who knew him best will testify, I think, to the darkness of Doyle's mind in its contemplation of human nature,' said Bernard Ernst, an author and lawyer who became a friend. 'He was a smoothly polished vessel filled with the most toxic content.'

In March 1885, Conan Doyle's near neighbour and colleague Dr William Pike, a fellow Scot, sought his opinion on a patient who appeared to be suffering from recurrent headaches and nausea, which Pike thought might be symptoms of something more serious. The victim was a 25-year-old man named Jack Hawkins. He had been living for the previous six months in a Southsea boarding house with his widowed mother and elder sister, but as Jack's condition worsened they had moved into a private home at 2 Queen's Gate, Osborne Road, a few minutes' walk to the south of Elm Grove.

Doyle's examination confirmed what Dr Pike had feared: Hawkins was suffering from 'dropsy', or cerebral meningitis, an inflammation of the brain lining for which there was then no known cure. Under the circumstances, the doctors could do little more than prescribe a course of bedrest, fluids and analgesics. It's possible that Dr Pike may have subsequently tried to 'ventilate' his patient by pumping air into his lungs with a household bellows. In any event, the treatment was unsuccessful. Jack Hawkins continued to deteriorate rapidly, and neither his mother nor sister could provide the constant care he required. In time, Doyle, who had a spare room, made a suggestion that was undoubtedly humanitarian as well as narrowly commercial. Hawkins could come to live with him as a paying guest at Elm Grove, where he would at least be kept as comfortable as the circumstances allowed.

Although there are obvious dangers in taking the Holmes stories too literally, the detective's 1893 adventure of 'The Resident Patient' gives a workable account of what followed. In the fictional treatment, the 'Hawkins' character is a renegade member of a criminal gang who chooses a doctor's house in which to hide out from his vengeful former associates. There are one or two other significant embellishments, such as the arrival at the surgery of a mysterious Russian nobleman prone to cataleptic fits, unique to the published tale. But the essence of the plot, the taking of sanctuary by a distressed individual in a medical practice, is common to both versions. It was an example of how Doyle would often confront and dramatise the events of his own life in order to make a suitably intricate case for Holmes.

Within only a day or two of Jack Hawkins being brought to Elm Grove, his condition worsened significantly. The headaches gave way to seizures, and by his third night in residence Doyle was administering his patient the powerful sedative chloral, which if taken in excess can itself produce convulsions, heart irregularities and even death. On the evening of the fourth day, Doyle called in Dr Pike for another consultation. They agreed that there was nothing further to be done. Early the following morning, 25 March, Doyle was awakened by the sound of his housekeeper screaming from the next room. She had gone in to take Hawkins his daily medication, and found him dead in his bed.

Conan Doyle's immediate reaction to the tragedy seemed to dwell less on the narrowly medical and instead to favour a more spiritual interpretation of events. 'There is great promise, I think, in the faces of the dead,' he wrote, impressed by the way in which Hawkins now appeared to be so 'thoroughly serene'. 'They say it is but the post-mortem relaxation of the muscles, but it is one of the points on which I would like to see science wrong.'

Two days later, on the morning of Friday, 27 March, Doyle helped to carry Hawkins's coffin out of the front door of his house (uncongenial to a doctor still trying to win the confidence of his local community) and rode at the head of the small funeral cortège to the nearby cemetery. By this stage, he had come to take notice of the dead man's sister Louisa, or 'Touie', a handsome and soft-spoken 27-year-old spinster who, like Doyle himself, had a family secret: her older brother Jeremiah had spent the last fifteen years confined in a mental ward, where he tirelessly filled sketchbooks with drawings that ranged from the classically religious to the obsessively anatomical, 'displaying the human form at its most stark', in one contemporary account. With her round face and brown-red hair, which she often wore in a bun, it's perhaps also worth adding that Louisa bore a passing resemblance to a younger version of Doyle's mother, Mary.

Later on the night of the funeral, Conan Doyle returned home to find a police inspector waiting for him on his doorstep. There had been an allegation of murder against him, the caller announced. Recalling the incident many years later, Doyle justifiably remarked that the visit had come 'like a thunderbolt out of the blue sky'. Once inside, the inspector explained that he had received an anonymous letter questioning the speed with which Jack Hawkins had succumbed to his final illness while in Doyle's care. He was there now, he added, as an 'objective explorer' trying to illuminate the facts in the case. What medications had Dr Doyle prescribed for his patient? Who had signed the death certificate? Why had it been thought fit to bury Jack Hawkins with such haste? For the imaginative and sensitive Doyle, the inquisitive official sitting before him writing in his notebook must have seemed a sinister, threatening figure, if not one quite on the order of Professor Moriarty. Under the circumstances, it was perhaps fortunate that Dr Pike was able to confirm that he had seen the patient the night before he died, and that his colleague Doyle had done everything possible for the poor man.

Although the police soon concluded their enquiries into Jack Hawkins's death, the anonymous correspondent might conceivably have felt justified in renewing his efforts in the light of what followed. In the course of the next few weeks, an affection formed between Hawkins's doctor and bereaved sister, who now enjoyed a sole legacy of £100 a year from her late father's estate, circumstances broadly similar to those contained in the 1890 Holmes tale *The Sign of the Four*. The sweet-natured Louisa was duly presented to Doyle's mother, who approved. In all, it was to be a year of wildly fluctuating fortunes for the young literary doctor. A strange mixture of emotional fragility and moral poise, he reported feeling 'rapturous again' soon after he began courting Louisa, whom he married on 5 August 1885.

Even so, Doyle retained 'potent memories' of the Hawkins affair, and the uneasy sensation of how even an innocent man might feel while under official suspicion, for the remaining forty-five years of his life. Speaking of his broader sense of the precariousness of the human condition, he later coined the phrase 'The abyss under every soul'. It's perhaps not coincidental that Doyle first began to write *A Study in Scarlet* sitting in that same downstairs interview room, on the first anniversary of the inspector's visit. He would often return to the theme of a man unjustly accused in the course of the fifty-nine Holmes tales that followed.

A Study in Scarlet did not prove easy to place, and even its eventual appearance in the Christmas *Beeton's* anthology was little cause for celebration. It brought its author neither fame nor fortune. The publishers paid Doyle the unpromising sum of £25 for the copyright, and 'I never at any time received another penny for it,' he recorded in his memoirs. The story resurfaced in a modest book edition the following year, but even then it avoided any significant sales. At that stage Doyle had few plans to revive the eccentric inhabitants of 221b Baker Street, and, in common with the reading public, clearly had no idea that they were bound for immortality.

Reviewing his prospects in 1889, shortly before the pivotal commission for *The Sign of the Four*, the struggling young author could note only that his life at the time consisted of his medical practice, his paranormal interests and his writing, in that order, 'with a little cricket as a corrective'. As he approached his thirtieth birthday, Conan Doyle was still obliged to take whatever literary hack work he could, of which his translation of a technical German submission to the *Gas and Water Gazette* was but one milestone down a long road of 'serial indignities [and] burdens'. In 1888, one publisher declined Doyle's historical novel *Micah Clarke*, set at the time of the Monmouth Rebellion of 1685, with the scathing verdict that it lacked 'the one great necessary point for fiction, i.e. interest'.

For Doyle, however, returning to crime writing almost seemed to be a case of predestination. It was as if the material was searching him out. Sometimes this took the form of a curious, true-life encounter with the criminal fraternity, while at others the inspiration was of a more occult nature. Both sets of circumstances clearly appealed to Doyle's adventurous imagination and met his requirement for a suitably dramatic denouement. As he understood it, he was being led by unseen but insistent hands 'down an indefeasible path, towards a career sometimes expressly, often dimly, stated'.

In early 1887, Conan Doyle had such an experience while sitting in a séance room in Portsmouth that would affect him for the rest of his life. Alfred Drayson was present, along with a mutual friend, a young architect named Henry Ball, as well as four or five others. The sitters prayed together around a small table, with the proceedings led by Ball, who also practised as a clairvoyant. All of those gathered had previously affirmed their belief in the distinct prospect of communion with the dead. During the prayers, Ball, small and bespectacled, and seemingly the most conventional of figures, was seized by what he took to be a visitation of the Holy Spirit. The tone and message of his prayer changed, and he prophesied that Doyle – still unknown in literary circles – would become a world-famous author. Another participant in the session who was clasping Doyle's hand felt 'a bolt of current' run through it. Ball's own hand was shaking uncontrollably at the time. When the lights came up again a few moments later they revealed only the spectacle of half a dozen formally dressed Victorian men sitting around a suburban Portsmouth dining table, but Ball regarded it as an authentic paranormal message. Doyle also accepted the prophecy as valid.

In time, there were to be more material sources of inspiration for Doyle's subsequent series of detective fiction. A letter written by a member of the Portsmouth Literary and Scientific Society touches on the curious case of the swarthy young man who presented himself one morning at Doyle's surgery in Elm Grove. The caller's hand was heavily bandaged, supposedly as a result of a late-night industrial accident. Doyle deduced from the precise serrations of the man's wound, and the telltale evidence of ink blotches, that his patient had in fact been involved in a counterfeiting operation gone wrong. This particular diagnosis effectively combined the routinely medical with some of Holmes's own powers of logical observation. It was 'quite a turn-up,' the correspondent would go on to note.

The hurried departure of the injured man out of the back door of the surgery, and the swift subsequent arrival of the police to interview Doyle – their second appearance on his doorstep in successive years – provide another real-life Victorian puzzle plot, one which countless readers have gone on to enjoy as the classic 1892 Holmes tale (one of only two such cases Dr Watson ever brought to his friend's attention) 'The Adventure of the Engineer's Thumb'.

In particular, the criminal ambience of late Victorian Portsmouth, with its bustling docks where women in tight skirts loitered in doorways or 'disported themselves with drunken sailors until daybreak', must have commended itself to the aspiring detective writer, always vicariously thrilled by the court pages in the *Evening News* and ready to appropriate them for his fiction. The contemporary press reveals an underworld of thieves and imposters, and a published account of Christmas week, 1886, records the various judicial proceedings taken against 'bawdy-house keepers, night crawlers, pick-pockets, robbers, coshers … and fraudulent merchants who take advantage of the annual merriment', even in that season of supposed peace and goodwill.

Conan Doyle was clearly in his element as an ambitious young author whose most famous character relied for his existence on a continually replenished supply of varied and dramatic criminal activity. It was as if the more roguish members of the community actively sought Doyle out. There was the lady patient, for example, who called on him one morning in 1887 with a request for a 'highly specialised and unusual reconstructive procedure' (a disguise not intended for her face), a commission he declined; and others whom he remembered for their 'boisterous, individualistic and sometimes violent' natures. As a young medical student, Doyle had made the acquaintance of Sir Robert Christison, a distinguished former president of Edinburgh's Royal College of Physicians, and a man of 'obscure [and] faintly shady' personal habits, widely thought to have combined with the German-born criminal Adam Worth to serve as models for the notorious Professor Moriarty, although others have conferred the honour on Christison's successor Thomas Fraser, a classically austere Scot chiefly remembered today as a tireless advocate of vivisection, briefly one of Doyle's own enthusiasms.

At some stage early in 1891, in the first flush of his success with Holmes, Doyle went to London's Portman Square, immediately off Baker Street, to be photographed by the society portraitist Herbert Barraud. It was another case of art mirroring life, as Barraud, a blackmailer, served at least in part as inspiration for the character of Charles Augustus Milverton, perhaps the greatest single ogre to be found anywhere among the 100-odd criminals in the Holmes canon. A dictionary of 1897 (the year after Barraud's death) lists him as 'a base and impudent man [about whom] there was an atmosphere of sulfur and reeking fish'.

Doyle was also familiar with the details of the suggestively named Charles Augustus Howell (1840–90), an art dealer and alleged swindler who notoriously organised the exhumation of Dante Gabriel Rossetti's wife Elizabeth Siddal and the retrieval of the poems Rossetti had left buried in her coffin seven years earlier. Shortly after his fiftieth birthday, Howell was found lying in the street outside a Chelsea pub with his throat slit, and a coin jammed in his mouth, possibly an allusion to a life given over to extortion and slander. The poet Algernon Swinburne wrote of Howell that he hoped he was 'in that particular circle of Malebolge where the coating of external excrement makes it impossible to see whether the damned dog's head is or is not tonsured'. It's both a sign of the times and a curious fact of his own life that even as a provincial family doctor Conan Doyle should have consistently encountered such a rich and varied cast of ruffians.

All of these were of course dwarfed by the activities of Jack the Ripper between August and November 1888, a period when Conan Doyle was still at work in Portsmouth and frequently travelling to London to arrange the publication of his book *Micah Clarke*. The 'theory' that Doyle himself was the Ripper belongs in fairyland, although, as briefed by his old tutor Joseph Bell, he certainly knew of both the more graphic details of the Whitechapel killings and the widespread panic they caused.

One way or another, the eminently respectable general practitioner seemed to be personally acquainted with many of the more memorable murders in Britain. According to Adrian Conan Doyle, his father 'thought it likely that [the Ripper] had a rough knowledge of surgery. He also thought it probable he clothed himself as a woman to approach his victims without arousing suspicion on their part.'

As his own beliefs changed, Doyle came to feel that the police should make more use of clairvoyance in gaining what he called 'divine insight' into cases like the Ripper's. Joseph Bell later remarked that he and 'a medical man who liked puzzles' had separately investigated the series of five murders. Bell recalled:

> There were two of us in the hunt and when two men set out to find a golf ball in the rough, they expect to find it where the straight lines marked in their mind's eye to it, from their original positions, crossed. In the same way, when two men set out to study a crime mystery, it is where their researches intersect that we have a result.

In November 1888, Bell and Doyle each wrote down the name of his prime suspect in the Ripper case and placed it in a sealed envelope. When they opened the envelopes they found that they had written down the same name: James Kenneth Stephen, an Old Etonian poet and author, known equally for his brooding good looks and prodigious physical strength, who until recently had been employed as tutor to Prince Albert Victor, the eldest son of the Prince of Wales. Stephen had suffered a serious head injury in the winter of 1887, and this had seemingly exacerbated his natural tendency to bouts of psychosis and violence, which he believed 'could only be explained by the most pronounced insanity'. He spent much of the next four years alternating between a post at Kings College, Cambridge, and a mental asylum in Northampton. In January 1892, Stephen heard that his erstwhile pupil and friend, 28-year-old Prince Albert, had died of pneumonia. From that moment onwards, he refused to eat, and died just twenty days later. He was 32. The official cause of death was given as 'mania'.

3

DUET WITH AN OCCASIONAL CHORUS

It's not clear exactly when Conan Doyle became aware that his first brief flirtation with Sherlock Holmes might evolve into a lifelong marriage. Even as crowds lined up in the street to buy each successive issue of *The Strand* featuring the detective's latest adventure, his author doggedly forged ahead with his novel *The Refugees: A Tale of Two Continents*, dealing with the oppression of the seventeenth-century Huguenots and their exodus to America. If anything, Doyle continued to look on literature as the lesser part of his dual career, and on Holmes himself as a definite if increasingly lucrative distraction.

In late 1891, when he was 32, the self-described 'ink-stained physic' was still keeping his options open. The character 'seems to have caught on,' Doyle would remark calmly as the global Sherlock Holmes publishing phenomenon got under way, before adding, 'It augurs well for the new book'.

Whether a doctor with a paying sideline in fiction, or a writer who also happened to keep a medical practice, Conan Doyle consistently came to the defence of the persecuted or oppressed. If the aggrieved party happened to be a lady, so much the better. Doyle may not have been a 'feminist' in the later sense of the word, but he was, in his way, a comparatively modern man. In 1897 he published a story called 'The Confession', in which a Catholic woman speaks of her feelings of guilt over a youthful love affair.

Doyle's novel *A Duet with an Occasional Chorus* followed two years later, just as he grappled with challenges in his own marriage. It, too, touches on sexual infidelity. Most modern readers would take both these works in their stride, but at the time they rattled the bars that defined the limits of respectable literature. When a friend named Jeannie Bettany was suddenly widowed in 1892, Doyle wrote her a letter with the suggestive hope that she would not squander 'upon household and maternal duties what is meant for the world'. In broadly similar vein, there's the description of *A Duet*'s Frank Crosse that seems to speak just as much of his author:

> There was sometimes just a touch of the savage in Crosse ... He left upon women the impression, not altogether unwelcome, that there were unexplored recesses of his nature to which the most intimate of them had never penetrated. In those dark corners of the spirit either a saint or a sinner might be lurking, and there was a pleasurable excitement in peering into them, and wondering which it was. No woman ever found him dull.

A man of the world, then, but also one who worked tirelessly on behalf of divorce law reform and other initiatives intended to liberate 'the fairer – and higher – sex from mindless convention'. Doyle 'undoubtedly thought that women were superior,' his daughter Jean would later remark, reflecting on his belief that 'a wife would, in a happy home, influence her husband'. To Doyle, women were sometimes shallow and vain, more often able and resolute, and, whatever their character, invariably the target of his finely honed sense of chivalry and compassion if wronged.

On 30 September 1896, a wealthy San Francisco tea importer named Walter Castle, his wife Ella and their 9-year-old son Frederick checked in to the Cecil Hotel on the Thames Embankment in London. The venue, which sported a Moorish façade, carved marble columns, velvet pile and an Indian smoking room, was then the last word in opulence, and not normally associated with episodes of petty crime. The Castles were on the final leg of a grand European tour, and planned to return across the Atlantic a week later. Both adult members of the family were confirmed Anglophiles, and had often spoken of their plans to bring various souvenirs of the old country back home to America. 'My own special interest in silverware developed during this period,' Ella later explained, 'and I knew how a beautiful tablepiece from Garrard or Asprey would captivate our friends when next we sat down to dine together in California.'

But if Mrs Castle thought that her visit to London would be merely an enjoyable extended shopping trip, she was to be cruelly disappointed. On 5 October, the police arrived in the family's hotel suite and began a thorough search of the premises. They had been alerted by a suspicious nearby shopkeeper, who reported – in the words of the official complaint – 'that the pieces left on display [there] had been reduced in number by at least one Great Exhibition cream jug, fancy tea-cup, [and] Imperial Russian Pillbox Clock (blue)', following Mrs Castle's visit. There were other allegations, too, that someone had recently removed items of cutlery from the hotel's dining room. 'We know nothing about it,' Walter Castle told the police. 'We are just here for some peace and quiet.' There had been absolutely nothing untoward about their stay in London to date, he added, except that a dog had bitten his wife on the ankle, and she had become 'incensed' as a result.

Once in the suite, the police quickly took possession of several diamond brooches, some rings and 'a fancy necklace of Egyptian design' found in the bottom of a steamer trunk. Mr Castle still remained calm, inviting his guests to sit down and politely asking the lead investigator, a Detective Arrow, 'What's this all about, friend?' A moment later, one of the officers opened a large oak wardrobe and discovered not only the missing shop chinaware, but also:

Seventeen ornate fans, a score of tortoiseshell combs, sixteen brooches, diverse mufflers, scarves [and] gloves, three sables, four engraved toast racks, two hallmarked egg-cups, assorted utensils and a tall cream-pot.

While Mr Castle remained silent, his wife began to rapidly pace up and down the room, sobbing quietly. The couple were arrested on charges of theft, and spent the next several nights in prison.

Eventually, a court decided that Walter Castle, if seeming 'oddly removed' from events, had no case to answer. His wife, who appeared in the dock half-swooning, and supported by two uniformed nurses, pleaded guilty to a reduced charge of shoplifting. Her QC, Sir Edward Clarke, introduced evidence to suggest that his client was a mentally unstable, physically ill woman, who from the onset of puberty had exhibited 'various troubles incidental to female life'.

In a future, less reticent age these same ailments would be referred to as premenstrual syndrome, later joined by post-natal depression.

Testimonials from Mrs Castle's American friends revealed that her disordered state of mind had been a 'pathetic secret ... for many years'. The judge agreed with the defence counsel that, while technically guilty – indeed, 'an incorrigible kleptomaniac' – the accused should be spared the full penalty of the law, which allowed for up to four years of hard labour. Instead, she was sentenced to three months' confinement at Holloway Jail. The prisoner left the court in Clerkenwell amidst a barrage of reporters and photographers, providing an early glimpse of a celebrity media frenzy that Conan Doyle, for one, thought unedifying. 'It was prurience,' he later noted, 'masquerading as journalism.'

Much of the press, in fact, seemed to be gripped by an advanced form of schizophrenia when it came to reporting the Castle case. On the one hand, there were constant articles and editorials (fourteen in the *San Francisco Chronicle* alone) deploring that accounts of a woman's 'most delicate physiology' had been publicly aired in a 'grotesque breach', to quote the *Chronicle*, of her 'rights and privacy'. On the other hand, those same guardians of Mrs Castle's dignity felt able to engage in an almost psychotic discussion, by the standards of the day, of the more clinical details of the case, including, but not limited to, the exact state of the accused's menstrual cycle and the possible condition of her uterus. These were not terms readily bandied about during the latter days of the reign of Queen Victoria, and Doyle's prompt letter on the subject in the press combined a becoming delicacy with a rigorous degree of logic that approached Holmes's own methods:

Dear Sir,

Might I implore your powerful intercession on behalf of the unfortunate American lady, Mrs Castle, who was condemned yesterday to three months' imprisonment upon a charge of theft? Apart from the evidence of the medical experts, it is inconceivable that any woman in her position in her sane senses would steal duplicates and triplicates – four toast racks, if I remember right. Small articles of silver with the hotel mark upon them, so they could not be sold or used, were among the objects which she had packed away in her trunk. It can surely not be denied that there is at least a doubt as to her moral responsibility, and if there is a doubt, then the benefit of it should be given to one whose sex and position as a visitor amongst us give her a double claim upon our consideration. It is to a consulting room and not a cell that she should be sent.

The following day, the Home Secretary announced that Mrs Castle was indeed 'mentally [and] morally irresponsible for her actions', and would be released from custody forthwith 'on her husband's promise to take charge of her'. The family immediately sailed home to America. At Christmas the following year, Ella Castle sent Conan Doyle a book of Walt Whitman poems. In it was a note, 'To Sir Arthur, who serves as the world's conscience.'

✳ ✳ ✳

In the summer of 1891, Conan Doyle, his wife Louisa and their 2-year-old daughter Mary (a son, Kingsley, would follow in 1892) moved into a large, red-bricked house at 12 Tennison Road, South Norwood, a London suburb roughly an hour's hansom cab ride south of Baker Street. The fourteen-room villa reflected the family's growing prosperity. Thanks largely to Sherlock Holmes, Doyle earned £1,616 that year, the bulk of it from his pen, which was roughly five times his annual income as a young practitioner in Southsea. In regular notes to his mother, or 'the Mam', as he called her, he extolled the pleasures of being 'in my own lovely little home, with the sweetest and prettiest of all little wives' – and talked about how he was never happier than when taking Louisa on a 30-mile spin on their tandem bicycle.

The following year, Conan Doyle packed the family off for an extended stay in Davos, Switzerland, where, a stout, ruddy-faced 34-year-old Briton dressed in tweed knickerbockers, he became a somewhat unlikely pioneer of alpine skiing. Affairs in general were 'most satisfactory', Doyle assured his mother – 'I have saved enough now to make Touie's position & that of the children quite secure in case I should die.'

Although a collaboration with James Barrie on a comic opera called *Jane Annie* proved a flop ('the most unblushing outburst of tomfoolery that two responsible citizens could conceivably indulge in publicly,' George Bernard Shaw wrote, in one of its better reviews), Doyle followed this with his one-act play *A Story of Waterloo*, which opened successfully in the West End to warm notices, and went on to become a staple of late Victorian theatre. In 1892, he earned the significant sum of £2,279, or roughly £200,000 ($300,000) in today's terms.

'It appear[ed] almost too good to last,' Doyle later wrote, and in fact it was. The pleasant routine of life was soon interrupted by a series of frustrations and private sorrows that eclipsed any possible professional disappointment. Following Doyle's sister Annette's loss to pneumonia at just 33, and his father's lonely death in a Scottish asylum, came the news that Louisa herself was dangerously ill. It proved to be a case of tuberculosis. In those pre-antibiotic days there was little hope of recovery from the disease, which generally proved fatal within only a few months, or at best a year or two. It was a chain of events that even the constitutionally optimistic Arthur admitted was 'a little overwhelming'. Seeking a more rarefied climate than the London suburbs, Conan Doyle and his family settled in a house in the elevated village of Hindhead, Surrey, which he perhaps charitably called the 'English Switzerland'. After a winter of monsoon-like rain he was soon forced to revise his estimate of its benefits to Louisa's health. Despite this, Doyle was to make Hindhead his home for the next eleven years, and finally disposed of his property there, Undershaw, only in 1921.

On 15 March 1897, meanwhile, in circumstances he chose to omit in his autobiography, Doyle met a 23-year-old Anglo-Scots woman named Jean Leckie. He would celebrate the anniversary for the rest of his life by presenting her with a spring flower, suggesting that he associated her with an act of renewal, or rebirth. Ironically, Doyle had also met Louisa on or around the same date − the Ides of March − twelve years earlier. The lively and attractive Jean, said to have possessed a 'chatty' manner and 'dazzling' green eyes, was both an expert horsewoman and a trained opera singer. She was also descended from an ancient Highland clan that had shown various signs of artistic and literary ability over the years.

The exact nature of Doyle's relationship with Jean while he struggled with his responsibilities to Louisa and the children can only ever be a matter of guesswork and hearsay. It may well be that he was flagrantly unfashionable in terms of today's morality, and remained faithful to his wife during her long physical decline. Strikingly, however, just weeks after meeting Jean, Doyle began work on his short story 'The Confession', before turning to his novel *A Duet*, among various other tales dealing broadly with domestic or married life. All these works are tastefully done, and can be innocently enjoyed on any number of levels. If one were to summarise their common theme, it would be a surprisingly bold exploration of social taboos, and, more specifically, of sexual infidelity.

In January 1889, just as, in Southsea, Conan Doyle prepared to deliver his first child, the police came to arrest 17-year-old Elizabeth Foster, who worked as a servant girl at the Church of England vicarage in Great Wyrley, near Walsall. She was accused of sending threatening letters to her employer, the Reverend Sharpurji Edalji, who, as an Anglican vicar of Indian origins, was something of a novelty in the English Midlands of that time. Foster appeared at Cannock Police Court, where she pleaded guilty to a lesser charge and was bound over to keep the peace. Few of those who read the short local news report of the trial, including Doyle himself, can have guessed that it was to be the starting point of one of the most sensational and protracted criminal cases of early twentieth-century Britain.

Some years later, there was a second outbreak of anonymous letters to Reverend Edalji's home. They came in a variety of handwriting styles and under a number of pseudonyms. If the correspondence could be said to have a mutual theme, it was that Edalji and his family were Satan-worshipping infidels of highly unusual personal habits who would roast eternally in hell. 'Do you think, you Pharisee, that because you are a parson God will absolve you from your iniquities?' enquired one note. Another characterised Edalji as a 'confirmed lunatic' – surely a case of projection – and promised the Edaljis' three children and their Scots-born mother Charlotte an afterlife distinguished by perpetual fire and brimstone. Much of the language employed was intemperate, quite often embellished by crude graffiti, and some of it positively demented in its tenor and allusion. The blameless Mrs Edalji, for example, was 'a kunt, liar, divil, confounded hypocrite, silly blasted bloody fool', in the words of a complainant who could apparently not spell the words 'cunt' and 'devil', but who had no difficulty with 'confounded hypocrite.'

The local police were no closer than they had been at the time of the first threatening letters to identifying the culprit or culprits, although there seems to have been a growing belief that the teenaged George Edalji, the eldest child, was in some way implicated in harassing his own family. This began the truly bizarre chain of events that led to George's eventual arrest and imprisonment on a charge of cattle mutilation. Conan Doyle investigated the case, and quickly concluded that at the heart of it there lay not so much a diabolical ripper as the technical shortcomings of the turn-of-the-century rural English police, added to George Edalji's provocative combination of brown skin and precocious intelligence as one of the first Anglo-Asians to successfully embark on a career as a lawyer.

We'll return in the next chapter to the Edalji affair, which took several further dark turns before reaching its climax in 1907. In time, Doyle imposed at least partial order on the mounting chaos of the case, insisting that the persecution of George Edalji owed more to racial prejudice and to rank blundering on the part of the authorities than to a rational investigation of the facts. 'The sad truth is that officialdom in England stands solid together,' he wrote:

> … and that when you are forced to attack it, you need not expect justice, but rather that you are up against an avowed Trade Union, the members of which are not going to act the blackleg to each other, and which subordinates the public interest to a false idea of loyalty.

More than a century later, it's still striking how this apparently conventional, Imperialist figure would lay his hard-won reputation on the line to defend a half-caste young Birmingham solicitor against the full force of the Edwardian Establishment.

As his campaign attracted more and more attention, however, Doyle began to be criticised for some of his underlying methodology – was he really all that 'Holmesian' in his core investigative technique, or more of a social crusader who saw elaborate criminal conspiracies everywhere, instead of mere incompetence or bigotry? Doyle felt these criticisms keenly. He had a depressive side anyway, and as we've seen was something of an eccentric, a believer both in fairies and in the supernatural powers of ectoplasm, as secreted from under a medium's skirts.

Through it all, he never once wavered in his support of George Edalji, and as a result can be said to have become a founding father of England's Court of Criminal Appeal, for which he should be a national hero. Edalji himself lived until 1953, and once told a reporter, 'Sir Arthur may be chiefly remembered for Sherlock Holmes, but he was also the bravest man in Britain. I owe him everything.'

✳ ✳ ✳

In June 1894, as the torrent of offensive letters continued to rain down at Great Wyrley, Conan Doyle packed a weekend bag and accompanied two fellow members of the Society for Psychical Research (SPR) on a field trip to the remote coastal village of Charmouth, in Dorset. They were there to investigate an allegedly haunted house occupied by an Irish family and their mute, elderly maid – 'a gothic ménage,' Doyle noted.

On their first night in residence, the three men sat up with a specially modified camera and other equipment with which to capture any spirits that might appear. None did. On the second night, Conan Doyle reported that he had been startled to hear a series of loud bangs coming from the kitchen, but that nothing looked out of place when he and his colleagues ran downstairs to investigate. He seems to have suspected at the time that they were the victims of a hoax, possibly perpetrated by the family's 19-year-old son in league with the maid. As Doyle's own beliefs changed, so did his interpretation of what he came to call the 'Charmouth possession'. When he wrote about the incident some thirty-five years later in his book *The Edge of the Unknown*, Doyle added that the house in question had burned down a short time later, and that the skeleton of a young boy was discovered buried in the garden. The inference was that the child's spirit had somehow been responsible for all the commotion.

Conan Doyle the materialist and sceptic also recognised a strain of mysticism in himself which often imbued his prose. What gave the early Holmes stories the ring of truth was their combination of human warmth and scientific spirit. Doyle's own occult experiences at this time were still restricted to a few sittings with seaside mediums, a continuing belief in the practicalities of mesmerism, telepathy and levitation, and an 'unbreakable' faith in the materialising power – or apport – of solid objects at a séance.

A more traditional psychic incident came one night at home, where Doyle suddenly awoke 'with the clear consciousness that there was someone in the room, and that the presence was not of this world'. After lying seemingly paralysed for some moments, he had heard steps slowly approach his bed, and then a voice murmur, 'Doyle, I came to tell you that I am sorry' – a case, he believed, of a formerly sceptical friend who had, in the afterlife, recanted his views on spiritualism.

Pursuing his more conventional career, Doyle let off several furious broadsides at members of his own trade whom he deemed guilty of excessive ambition. A prime target was Hall Caine, bestselling author of the prototype feminist novel *The Christian*, whose talent for self-advertisement Doyle addressed in a letter to the *Daily Chronicle*:

I think it unworthy of the dignity of our common profession that one should pick up paper after paper and read Mr Caine's own comments on the gigantic task and the colossal work which he has just brought to a conclusion … It is for others to say these things.

As we've seen, there were subsequent feuds with George Bernard Shaw and H.G. Wells, among others. Doyle told his editor friend W.T. Stead that he made a distinction between the writing of 'real work' and that of a mere yarn in a newspaper or magazine. The latter 'must be uneven, disjointed and superficial,' he insisted, in another implied reproach of the Holmes stories by their author.

Fortunately, Conan Doyle had bills to pay, resulting in a steady flow of work which still gives pleasure today. In December 1894 he published the first batch of his well-received Brigadier Gerard tales, which happily married his love of early nineteenth-century historical romance with some of the narrative fizz of Holmes. Another, less successful Napoleonic saga, *Uncle Bernac*, followed in 1897. Never one to rest on his laurels, Doyle then began work on a Regency prizefighting novel he called *Rodney Stone*, followed in turn by *The Tragedy of the Korosko* – 'a book of sensation,' he admitted, if still visionary in dealing with the theme of Islamic terrorism. Were that not enough, the 'cheerfully gamut-running' author produced both a series of paranormal tales that became known as the *Round the Fire Stories* and a volume of poems, *Songs of Action*, in the same two-year period.

When the journalist Harry How went to interview Conan Doyle, he was struck by the author's voluminous postbag. The 'lunatic letters' were a problem, Doyle admitted, although others were more suggestive. 'On the morning of my visit the particulars of a poisoning mystery had been sent to him from the Antipodes,' How recorded. This was the sensational case of the Yorkshire-born Thomas Hall, who had emigrated to New Zealand as a teenager and in 1885 went on to marry the former Kate Espie in Timaru, a whaling port roughly 100 miles south-west of Christchurch. Two months after the wedding, Hall presented his wife with her will, and requested that she sign it. It left him all her property. The following month, he took out two life insurance policies in her name; between them, these would benefit him by £6,000 (some £480,000 today) in the event of Kate's death within seven years.

In an echo of the Chantrelle case, Kate fell ill shortly after the birth of her only child, Nigel, in June 1886. For weeks, this 'gentle, affectionate girl', as a judge later called her, lay bedridden with crippling stomach pains. She 'vomited until [she] was exhausted, and then vomited again, unable to think or sleep'. In time her hair and teeth fell out. She was 'pitiful thin, spent and ghastly', a 'desperate old crone' while still in her early twenties. Kate's doctor, Patrick McIntyre, who was said to be good on minor ailments but weak on serious diseases, eventually arranged for a sample of her stomach contents to be sent to Dunedin for analysis. When the police came for Thomas Hall a few weeks later and said that his wife's system contained enough antimony sulfide (produced by filing off the heads of safety matches) to poison ten women, he looked amazed and distressed. 'How could such a thing happen?' he asked.

Hall was arrested for attempted murder. Joining him in the dock was the family's live-in companion, Margaret Houston, with whom he was said to have had an affair. It did not help Hall's case that he had bought a book called *Taylor on Poisons* while on his honeymoon, and highlighted the section on antimony in red pen. At the trial in Christchurch, Houston was acquitted; Hall was sentenced to life imprisonment. The presiding judge called him 'the vilest criminal ever seen in New Zealand'. In a dramatic postscript, the body of Hall's wealthy father-in-law was then exhumed, and it too was found to be riddled with poison. This seemed to confirm what many of the local papers had already told their readers – that the case was about a sociopathic man 'employing one of the cruellest of all forms of assault for monetary gain'. Hall was duly tried a second time and condemned to hang, although his sentence was commuted on appeal. After serving twenty-one years in prison, he returned to England to die.

When Hall wrote to Conan Doyle from his jail cell in January 1892 appealing for his help, Doyle seems to have declined to actively investigate the case. Hall recorded in his diary, 'No interest beyond mercy'. Doyle was, however, to refer to the precedent of the New Zealand Appeal Court when he came to campaign for a similar institution to provide relief for George Edalji and other victims of miscarriage of justice at home in England.

It's perhaps not accidental that in a story called 'The Naval Treaty', published in 1893, Sherlock Holmes takes a keen interest in poisons. As we first see him, Holmes is at his table in Baker Street, clad in a dressing gown, and in the midst of an intense chemical investigation. In a moment he introduces a slip of litmus paper to a test tube containing a solution. 'You come at a crisis, Watson,' the detective announces. 'If this paper remains blue, all is well. If it turns red, it means a man's life.' Doyle, as Watson, remarks, 'He then dipped it into the test-tube, and it flushed at once into a dull, dirty crimson. "Hum! I thought as much!" he cried … "A very commonplace little murder," said he.'

In time, Doyle intervened more directly in the case of Moat Farm, near Clavering in Essex. A middle-aged woman named Camille Holland had disappeared, and suspicion fell on her common-law husband Samuel Dougal, a short, shaven-headed retired army officer of unusual domestic habits. Dougal's case wasn't helped when it was learnt that he had quickly installed another woman in the house as his mistress, and that in the summer months he was in the practice of going bicycling in the nude accompanied by his similarly free-spirited teenaged servant girl.

Again, it seemed raw greed was the primary factor involved. Dougal was found to be systematically moving funds from the missing Camille's accounts into his own, sufficient for the police to take possession of the farm in the hunt for clues to her whereabouts. As the *Essex County Chronicle* reported, the phrase 'take possession' was literally true, as 'the police actually move[d] into the home ... The officers engaged in the search now occupy the farmhouse, preparing their meals and making their beds for themselves. Detective-Sergeant Scott acts as chef.' It was also one of the first criminal investigations in Britain to attract the decadent voyeurism of later major cases. 'Throughout the week, people have flocked to the Moat Farm in crowds, the majority being ladies,' the *Chronicle* reported. 'Oranges and nuts were sold as at a village fair, and the raucous voices of the vendors were heard on every side. Souvenir postcards commanded an enormous sale.'

Despite this intense scrutiny, the police drew a blank until Conan Doyle, sitting at his desk 100 miles away in Hindhead, was asked by an inquisitive reporter if there was any point in the affair to which he might wish to draw the investigators' attention. 'To the curious fact of the property's name,' he remarked, in so many words.

'The property is called Moat Farm.'

'That is the curious fact,' Doyle replied.

The following day, police pulled the body of Camille Holland from a trench that had been dug into the moat surrounding the estate. She had evidently been shot through the head at close range and then buried in the muddy soil. In July 1903, Samuel Dougal went to the gallows at Chelmsford Jail, aged 57. In the split-second before the trapdoor opened beneath him, he uttered the word 'guilty'.

✳ ✳ ✳

In November 1899, at the age of 40, Conan Doyle felt duty-bound to volunteer to serve with the British forces fighting the Boers in South Africa. Doyle's mother – the Mam – was not pleased, rather tactlessly noting that her son's 'very breadth' would make him an easy target for the enemy. Although the army declined his services, Doyle was eventually to spend four months working as a surgeon in a field hospital in Bloemfontein, a town only recently taken by British troops, where he arrived in March 1900.

Initially, this seems not to have been too arduous. The hospital was set up in the grounds of the Ramblers Cricket Club, and Doyle continued to enjoy ample meals served to him in the pavilion dining room by his butler Cleeve, who he paid to accompany him on the journey. But conditions worsened appreciably when, in mid April, the Boers managed to sever the town's supplies.

Conan Doyle's first intimation that life would rapidly deteriorate from there came when he tried to run his pre-dinner bath one evening and found that there was no hot water, 'nor water of any kind, but a trickle of viscous slime dripping from the tap'. In short order, Doyle and his fellow doctors were confronted by the 'hellish vista' of a full-scale typhoid epidemic. The artist Mortimer Menpes, covering the war for the *Illustrated London News*, later wrote of Doyle:

> Throw[ing] open the door of one of the wards … The only thing I can liken it
> to is a slaughter-house. The place was saturated with enteric fever, and patients
> were swarming in at such a rate that it was impossible to attend them all.

Even in the midst of this horror, Conan Doyle remained characteristically cheerful, organising a series of football matches where players 'slithered around on a field of blood and waste'.

He returned safely to England in July 1900. The chief result of his time at the front was his publishing of a book-length sixpenny pamphlet *The War in South Africa: Its Causes and Conduct*, which combined his usual stout defence of the British fighting man with trenchant criticism of the backwardness of some of the military establishment – 'essentially unchanged in tactics since Waterloo', and which 'urgently needed to be dragged into the new century'. Doyle's paper quickly went through eighteen editions, and was thought to have weighed heavily in the new king's decision to give him a knighthood.

The other upshot of Doyle's South African adventure was a revival of Sherlock Holmes from his apparent watery grave: first in the discrete, satanic canine melodrama *The Hound of the Baskervilles*, and then in a burst of Holmesredux stories beginning with 'The Empty House'. At their best these were dazzling, vividly recreating the fading, gaslit era of the 1890s, while providing some modest twentieth-century allusions both to new scientific methods and sexual mores, if, at the same time, betraying Doyle's only fragile command of technical detail involving plot devices such as thumbprints or bicycle tyres.

From all indications, Doyle had been highly indignant to learn that the enemy troops in South Africa, while for the most part not lacking physical courage, adopted guerrilla tactics in the field. A particular Boer ruse was to hoist a dummy convincingly dressed as a soldier somewhere on the horizon. Only when the British fired on it did they come to appreciate ('with some bitterness,' Doyle noted) that it was a trap intended to give away their position. As often as not, there were heavy casualties in the subsequent counter-assault by well-entrenched Boer snipers. Doyle himself later insisted that the plot twist of Holmes's return in 'The Empty House', in which the detective foils a would-be assassin by tricking the man into firing at a wax effigy of him, was chiefly the brainchild of his friend Jean Leckie. It's tempting to wonder if he was also thinking of his experience of the front lines in South Africa less than three years earlier.

Although Holmes remained anchored solidly in the material world, Doyle himself now saw spiritualism as an increasingly valuable aid to traditional detective skills. There was the case, for instance, of James Robert Hay, who was born in Australia to Scottish migrant parents, worked for a time as a primary schoolteacher, and then joined the Mormon Church and moved to Salt Lake City, Utah. There, in 1896, Hay married Aggie Sharp, the daughter of a prominent businessman and community leader. Their wedding was a 'swagger' affair, the *Salt Lake Herald* reported, complete with printed guest list and embossed invitations, servants dressed up in powdered wigs, a full orchestra, and 'no late-night outbreak of the hoochy-koochy, or other such abdominal embellishments that now pass for dancing'.

All went well for the next few years, during which the couple had three children. Then, in December 1901, James Hay disappeared one snowy night after visiting his friend and neighbour, 36-year-old Peter Mortensen. Mortensen insisted that they had parted amicably, and the local sheriff initially seemed inclined to believe him. Thinking otherwise, Hay's father-in-law, James Sharp, a practising spiritualist, took his suspicions to the *Herald*. The paper was not slow to discover that Mortensen had been a customer of Hay's timber company, to which he 'owed big', a story it ran under a banner headline on the morning of 18 December. That night, James Sharp had a vision in which he saw his son-in-law's frozen corpse buried in a familiar location; not a hunch or a premonition, he was later at pains to point out, 'but an actual picture inside my head' of Hay's hastily dug grave.

The following morning, the police found Hay's body, a bullet through his head, in the very spot James Sharp had described for them. Sharp then corresponded with Conan Doyle, sharing some of the particulars of the crime and in time asking him if he felt he could help the prosecution case by 'now reading the mind of the suspect'. Doyle thought it 'a rude and elementary affair' as a murder mystery, but 'highly instructive on the psychic level'. His reply to Sharp was measured. 'Brain waves' might be hard to interpret at that distance, he allowed, but:

> A friend here has passed on a vision to me. I know by many means the power of this person's mediumship. In the vision, a message came through which spelled out the letters 'PLC' in some financial connexion. There is also a more hazy impression of a line of guns being fired. 'I am not able to get more detail than that,' the medium has assured me, 'but there is a definite atmosphere of deceit and fraud to be investigated.' I give this for what it is worth.

Nowhere in the correspondence does Doyle specify the name or even the sex of his mysterious clairvoyant, although it's possible to speculate that it may have been his companion Jean Leckie, who went on to show a talent for 'ghost writing', among other psychic abilities, a few years later. By the time of this particular exchange, the *Salt Lake Herald* had already revealed that Peter Mortensen had owed some $4,000 to Hay's business, and that this traded as the Pacific Lumber Company, although it's by no means certain, given the communications technology of the era, that Doyle himself would have known of this. There are various non-psychic techniques, collectively called 'chaining', that enable a skilled performer to make a series of ambiguous but broadly accurate observations about an individual or object, but it seems unlikely that such a person could have stumbled on the initials 'PLC' purely by chance. In due course, Peter Mortensen was found guilty of first-degree murder, and was put to death in the early hours of 20 November 1903. At his own request, he was executed by a firing squad.

At about the same time as James Hay's disappearance in Utah, 60-year-old Adolf Beck emerged from Portland Jail off the coast of Dorset in southern England, where he had served five years' hard labour for fraud. Portland was among the most notorious outposts of the nineteenth-century British penal system; among other afflictions, the place featured both the 'stairs of death', a vertiginous rock quarry up whose ninety-eight steps prisoners struggled carrying hefty concrete slabs, and a system of physical punishments, including flogging, that might not have disappointed Captain Bligh at his most pitiless on the deck of the *Bounty*. Beck, an educated, if somewhat shiftless Norwegian-born mining engineer with a seafaring background, emerged from confinement 'wasted and careworn', the *Daily Mail* reported, 'with an unsteady gait and the mark of his ordeal impressed upon his stooped shoulders and downcast eyes'.

On his first morning back in London, Beck received a heartfelt letter from a supporter that described the 'misery which your friends have suffered from your long imprisonment', and added that 'to none has this been more acute than me'. The letter rejoiced in Beck's liberty:

> Your release has gladdened those who have waited, as you endured all the privations of a convict. The authorities have gone from excess to excess in this matter … That the rest of your days may be triumphantly happy can be the only wish of those who deplore the injustice of your treatment.

The writer went on to conclude that the 'whole squalid affair' stood as an example of Britain's judicial and political Establishment having closed ranks following the 'shameful delinquency' of those who had persecuted Beck in the first place. The letter was signed by Arthur Conan Doyle.

Doyle, in fact, had taken a supporting role in the case to that of his fellow Crimes Club member, George Sims. Sims, who knew Beck socially, had published a series of articles in the *Daily Mail* that pointed to serious flaws in the original trial. It's still difficult to know with complete clarity if this was primarily a matter of corruption or of mere ineptitude, but in either event the proceedings mark a low point in the annals of late Victorian British criminal justice.

Beck had first been arrested in December 1895, after a woman confronted him in a London street and accused him of having recently swindled her out of some jewellery by the expedient of representing himself to her as 'Lord Willoughby', a fabulously wealthy man with 'a great estate in Lincolnshire and a private yacht'. Suitably impressed, the woman had given him a watch and several rings, which he promised to replace with more valuable pieces. That was the last she had seen of Lord Willoughby until her chance encounter with Beck some three weeks later.

Following his arrest, no fewer than twenty-two other women came forward to claim that they, too, had been defrauded by the mysterious Willoughby. Beck was not only summarily found guilty; he was sentenced as a repeat offender. Eighteen years earlier, a man named John Smith had been convicted of swindling unattached women by using the alias 'Willoughby', and went to prison for five years. He had disappeared after his release, and it was assumed that Beck and Smith were one and the same. In time, Doyle and Sims were able to convincingly discredit the Crown case by the Holmesian technique of stripping away any accompanying emotion and conjecture and instead presenting two objective, material facts which established it as about as clear a case of mistaken identity as can ever have been brought before a British court: first, Beck had been travelling in Argentina, not living in London, at the time of the original crime of 1877; second, the man then incarcerated as John Smith was Jewish and thus had been circumcised, while Beck was not. As Holmes remarks in *A Study in Scarlet*, 'before turning to those mortal and mental aspects of the matter which present the greatest difficulties, let the enquirer begin by mastering more elementary problems'.

Incredibly, in 1904 Beck was arrested a second time for swindling another young woman out of her jewellery. He was again sent for trial and swiftly found guilty, although on this occasion the judge himself expressed doubts about the verdict, and decided to defer sentencing. During the interval, yet more women came forward to complain that they in turn were victims of a confidence trickster posing as 'Lord Willoughby' who in a fresh predatory campaign had just relieved them of their watches and rings. It sometimes seems surprising to learn that any female could have walked the streets of London at this time and emerge with her valuables intact.

Since Beck himself was already in custody, awaiting sentencing, the police were forced to conclude that he might thus be innocent of these latest offences. Instead, they arrested a man giving his name as William Thomas, who proved to be the elusive 'John Smith' of the original 1877 trial. Charged under his real name of Wilhelm Meyer, he was sent to prison for both the 1895 and 1904 crimes. He bore a passing physical resemblance to Adolf Beck. Beck himself received a royal pardon and £2,000 in compensation, but a public outcry – again orchestrated by Doyle and Sims – raised this to a total of £5,000, or roughly £375,000 ($550,000) today. He died just five years later, aged 68.

It's worth dwelling on the tragedy of Adolf Beck a moment longer, if only because it serves as a direct forerunner to two separate criminal cases that came to occupy, and often to obsess, Doyle for the rest of his life. In all three instances, he distilled the specifics of the case down to one central issue: could the British Establishment (which largely meant the Home Office) be trusted to act vigorously and impartially when made aware of an apparently grave breach of justice?

More particularly, Doyle would take up matters such as the correct technical procedure for a police line-up; the fallibility of much, if not most, eyewitness testimony; and the vagaries of specialist scientific analysis. These were early days for criminal forensics as a whole, meaning that some of the same small group of professionals would recur in all three cases. Just because a particular handwriting expert had erred in the Beck trial, for example, was no reason to prevent him from testifying a few years later against George Edalji. To Doyle, as to Holmes, it was the rare case that failed to reward a new investigative approach or a fresh mindset. Everything was incremental, and each small discovery was an opportunity to learn something more. If one expert was wrong, conceivably another one was also wrong.

> Perhaps I am too demanding and exacting; perhaps I lack what is essential: the careless attitude of officialdom, which teaches you to tie a thick ribbon around a file you consider to be closed, and then to forget it; I cannot.

Although Doyle spoke these words, they could just as easily have been Holmes ruminating on his continual struggle to assert 'the mind' of intelligence and reason over 'the heart' of emotion and prejudice.

* * *

In December 1900, Conan Doyle went into print to admit that, while Sherlock Holmes might still be regarded as dead, there was 'no limit to the number of papers he left behind or the reminiscences in the brain of his biographer'. The following August, The Strand began serialising The Hound of the Baskervilles, after which it appeared in book form and immediately sold out its first print run of 30,000 copies. It would be hard to overstate the reaction of the reading public at large to Holmes's return, an event greeted as something akin to the discovery of an eleventh commandment, or a later full-scale comeback tour by the Beatles.

As we've seen, Doyle had been stoical when first disposing of his 'poor hero of the anemic printed page', jotting only the words 'Killed Holmes' in his notebook. He took a similarly relaxed approach to the subsequent offer from *Collier's* to revive the detective for a fee of $25,000, or roughly $1.7 million in modern money. Just for purposes of comparison, in 1911 (before which they were unpaid) a senior British Cabinet minister received an annual salary of £400 (the equivalent today of £28,000, or $40,000) for his services to the nation.

As well as its phenomenal sales success, *The Hound of the Baskervilles* also has the distinction of involving Doyle as a leading character, rather than mere author, in a compelling murder mystery. The tale of the infernal dog haunting the Devon moors had initially been brought to him by his friend and occasional golf partner Fletcher Robinson, the *Daily Express* correspondent who was on the same boat returning from the war in South Africa. Doyle soon negotiated an unheard of advance of £100 per 1,000 words for first-publication rights of his long story in *The Strand*. Since the magazine sold 33,000 more copies than usual that August, its proprietors can't have been too unhappy with the arrangement. Doyle appears to have paid roughly a third of his initial fee to Fletcher Robinson, though there's some doubt about their future relationship; like Dr Watson's first name, it's one of those insoluble Holmes riddles to have excited a lively exchange of views over the years.

More than a century later, a team led by the author Rodger Garrick-Steele applied unsuccessfully to exhume Robinson, who died in 1907 at the age of 36. Their initiative followed years of speculation that Doyle had somehow 'arranged to have his unacknowledged collaborator poisoned in order to avoid exposure as a fraud', a charge that seems fanciful even by the most acute Sherlockian standards. Robinson (who was credited in full under the first column of text of the story's appearance in *The Strand*) almost certainly succumbed to typhoid fever, like an estimated 56,000 other Britons that year. While it conjures up a vivid image of Conan Doyle furtively introducing arsenic to his colleague's drinks back in the clubhouse after a round of golf, set against this are Doyle's continuing, if sporadic, payments to Robinson throughout the period 1901–1907, as well as his frequent cheerful admission of his moral debt in the matter. Writing to 'the Mam' in April 1901, for instance, Doyle proudly announced that *The Hound* was 'a real Creeper' and, further casting modesty to the wind, added, 'Holmes is at his very best, and it is a highly dramatic idea – which I owe to Robinson'.

In July 1907, Conan Doyle found himself involved in a Holmesian case about stolen jewels, miscarriages of justice and murderous revenge, although it's possible the morally austere detective might have shied from some of the crime's more dissolute subplot. The basic story was that one hot summer's night someone made off with a collection of 394 gems, worth some £12 million today, from a safe inside Dublin Castle. Known popularly as the 'Irish Crown Jewels', they had been under the care of Conan Doyle's maternal cousin, the Ulster King-at-Arms, 44-year-old Sir Arthur Vicars.

His custodial regimen seems to have been a relaxed one, and it was reported that the dipsomaniac Vicars had sometimes awoken from a stupor on the floor of his office wearing one of the most valuable pieces round his neck, among other lapses of protocol, although in his defence he explained that these had merely been instances of his 'personally checking security arrangements' for the collection. One can imagine Holmes's pursed lips as he listened to accounts of the 'unsavoury types, some of them members of Vicars's own staff, indulging in depraved late-night entertainments in the Castle's state rooms', where the parties tended to be of the all-male variety.

Among the principal cast of characters was a Captain Richard Gorges, lately a Boer War hero, of 'sexually equivocal' reputation; the 9th Duke of Argyll, King Edward VII's brother-in-law and a former Governor-General of Canada, who had a known fondness for guardsmen; Lord George Haddo, the king's official representative in Dublin, who travelled with his own satin-clad pageboy; and Vicars's nephew and secretary, Pierce Gun Mahony, who, in addition to sounding like a 1930s Chicago gangster, was reputed to have 'eyes that could make a girl do anything'. Looming above them all as a suspect in the theft that came briefly to be known as the 'crime of the century' was 30-year-old Francis Shackleton, the disreputable younger brother of the polar explorer, who shortly afterwards left Ireland, possibly with official encouragement, and never returned.

Immediately he read of the matter, Doyle wrote to his cousin Vicars offering to consult on the case. Vicars replied that he would be very glad of the help, adding that whatever the eventual outcome he was already 'quite ruined', his job and pension in jeopardy, thanks to the 'well-connected debauchers and sodomites' who lay at the heart of the scandal. Doyle was quickly able to establish that there had been no fewer than seven keys to the door of the room where the valuables were kept, and access to the vault itself 'casual, [to] the point of criminally negligent'. No one had bothered to check the contents of the safe at any time between 11 June, when Vicars had briefly inspected the jewels, and the morning of 6 July, when he discovered their theft.

A further cause for concern was that the king and queen were expected in Dublin on an official visit just four days later, and His Majesty was reportedly not amused by this 'brazen relocation' of pieces that had originally been a gift of his grandfather, William IV. The crime also came during one of those cyclical crises in Anglo-Irish affairs, when the barricades 'will surely soon be manned against the thunder of hooves and mutinous terror on the streets of England,' as the London *Globe* chillingly put it. Could the robbery, Vicars mused, have somehow been part of a larger plot intended to 'incite our Union to the brink of civil war?'

Conan Doyle took the pragmatic approach to the case. First, he acquired an architect's blueprint of Vicars's office in Dublin Castle, as well as a detailed sketch map showing the adjacent doors and staircases. Having satisfied himself on the basic layout of the crime scene, he turned to the 'immemorial questions of motive and opportunity – who might have desired the jewels' removal, and had the means to carry them off?' Doyle's suspicions quickly fell on 'that feckless man' Frank Shackleton as the culprit, if for no other reason than that he was known to be chronically short of funds, 'and not discriminating in how he obtained them'. Vicars seems to have supported this theory, and in January 1908 publicly accused Shackleton of the crime.

Playing Lestrade to Doyle's Holmes, meanwhile, was the stolid figure of Detective Chief Inspector John Kane of Scotland Yard, who eventually submitted a lengthy report, never publicly released, blaming 'two persons, neither of them previously familiar with Dublin Castle', and adding that these individuals had 'almost certainly since broken up the pieces for individual sale'. Kane explicitly denied to a Viceregal Commission that Shackleton was involved in the theft. That same body reached the less controversial verdict that Vicars had 'not exercise[d] due vigilance or proper care in his role as custodian of the regalia', and relieved both him and his staff of their duties.

Doyle continued to see his cousin as a scapegoat. Modestly remarking that he would prefer not to be quoted on the subject, lest the British public come to see him as an 'infernal busybody', he wrote to Vicars in May 1920 to say that the original case had been relatively simple to solve, and that the only complication had been 'the obtuseness [and] misreporting' of the official inquiry. In November 1912, the *Daily Mail* had alleged that Vicars had allowed a woman reported to be his mistress to obtain a copy of his key to the safe, and that she had since fled to Paris with the gems in her possession. A year later, the paper was forced to issue an apology and to admit that the story was a complete fabrication – 'there was never any such female,' the *Mail* admitted. Vicars went on to accuse Shackleton by name in his will, which also referred to certain 'wicked and blackguardly acts of the Irish government', who were 'backed to the hilt by the late King Edward VII whom I had loyally and faithfully served'.

Many of the principal characters in the case fared poorly, if not considerably worse than that, in the years ahead. Captain Gorges went on to be convicted of manslaughter, and emerged from prison to die in poverty. At the time of his original investigation, Doyle had been able to establish what the official force had somehow overlooked: Gorges and Shackleton had served together in the same army unit in South Africa, where their money troubles had been the stuff of regimental legend, and thus might conceivably have gone on to become accomplices in the Irish affair. Shackleton himself was imprisoned in 1914 for passing a cheque stolen from a widow. On his release he took the alias 'Mellors' and lived under that name until his early death in 1940. Vicars's nephew Pierce Gun Mahony was later found floating dead in a lake in County Wicklow. It was said that he had tripped while out walking, accidentally shot himself twice through the heart, and then stumbled backwards into the water. In April 1921, masked men broke into Arthur Vicars's home in County Kerry and set it on fire. They then marched Vicars out to the lawn, tied him to a tree, and shot him through the head. A sign found attached to his body read, 'Spy Informers beware – IRA never forgets'.

The Irish jewels were never recovered, but they returned in spirit, at least, eighteen months later, when *The Strand* published Conan Doyle's story of 'The Bruce-Partington Plans'. Although there are several differences between the Holmes adventure and its real-life precursor, the central idea of stolen goods in high places, and the subsequent disgrace of their custodian, is common to both versions. It seems safe to assume that Colonel Frank Shackleton might be the model for Colonel Valentine Walter, the reprobate brother of an eminent Englishman 'whose decorations and sub-titles fill two lines of a book of reference' in the fictional tale. There is also a shared connection to royal patronage. While Edward VII had privately offered a reward for the return of the Dublin jewels, in the Bruce-Partington case, set in the year 1895, we learn that Holmes goes on to 'spend a day at Windsor, whence he returned with a remarkably fine emerald tie-pin', the gift of 'a certain gracious lady in whose interests he had carried out a small commission'.★

Shortly after he published 'The Bruce-Partington Plans', Doyle heard from a young woman named Joan Paynter, who worked as a nurse at the North Western Hospital in Hampstead, London. 'I am appealing to you as I can think of no one else who could help me,' she wrote, in terms that might have come direct from the prologue to another Holmes mystery, which Dr Watson would surely have given the title 'The Disappearing Dane':

> About five weeks ago, I met a man, originally a native of Copenhagen. We became engaged and although I did not wish to say anything about it for a little while he insisted on going down to Torquay to meet my people.

Following this introduction, the Dane had simply vanished from the scene. There had been no attempted fraud or extortion on his part, and his fiancée was understandably distressed at his abrupt departure. 'Please don't think it awful cheek on my part, I feel so awfully miserable and it was only this morning that I thought of you, please do all you can for me, and I shall be eternally grateful,' she wrote. To Doyle it must have seemed an irresistible opportunity to put chivalry in the service of detection.

In fact, he had only to make enquiries through the Danish press to quickly learn the truth. In July 1909, a number of Copenhagen newspapers carried notices which roughly translated as, 'Reward offered for information on missing London man'. A second line in bold print added, 'Idlers need not apply'. One of the non-idlers who replied was the missing party's cousin, who filled in some of the less salubrious detail for Doyle. This again mirrored at least some of the basic plot of the 1891 Holmes story 'A Case of Identity' (itself inspired

---

★ The plot of 'The Bruce-Partington Plans' also mirrors some of the sad details of the 'Merstham Tunnel Mystery' of September 1905, when the body of a young woman, Mary Money, was found lying across a set of railway lines to the south of London. She had been the victim of an assault. In the Holmes story, published three years later, a junior government clerk, Arthur Cadogan West, is found dead next to the Underground tracks outside Aldgate Station. In both cases, it appeared that the victim had been killed elsewhere, and their body then thrown from a train.

by the saga of the Australian butcher, Thomas Castro, who in 1866 emerged from the Wagga Wagga bush purporting to be the missing heir to the Tichborne baronetcy, a claim that ultimately led an English court sentencing him to jail for perjury), if without the fictional tale's more complex web of family deceit.

Put bluntly, it seemed the man had simply used Miss Paynter for his own ends, and seeing no prospect of enrichment on the Torquay premises, had moved on. It was another case in which Doyle was able both to solve the mystery and to show his innocent young client how fortunate an escape she had had. 'Brain fever' might have been the rather broad term that Doyle, like many others, applied to a wide range of 'female hysterical disorders', as they were then called, but there were few British men of the era who listened with more sympathy while women talked about themselves, their hopes and their fears than he did.

✳ ✳ ✳

There was a strand to the Sherlock Holmes stories apparent as early as the detective's appearance in *The Sign of the Four*. Holmes, bored and despising the world around him, chiefly the loyal Watson, exercising self-destructive skills of a high order. The deeper Holmes sinks into melancholy, the deeper his retreat into the 'seven per-cent solution' of cocaine. 'Count the cost,' Watson remonstrates with his friend:

> Your brain may, as you say, be roused and excited, but it is a pathological and morbid process which involves increased tissue-change and may at least leave a permanent weakness. You know, too, what a black reaction comes upon you. Surely the game is hardly worth the candle.

In this particular case, Holmes finds relief in an enjoyably melodramatic adventure involving oriental treasure, revenge, romance and a blowgun-firing pygmy, a sufficiently potent mix to hold his depression at bay until the crime is solved and Watson in turn announces his engagement – eliciting only a 'dismal groan' from his companion. Affairs having been successfully returned to their correct state, Holmes similarly finds himself back at the starting point, his sense of tedium and futility almost morbid in its intensity and unreason. 'For me,' he remarks, in the story's closing line, 'there still remains the cocaine bottle,' before stretching his bony white hand up for it.

DUET WITH AN OCCASIONAL CHORUS

71

There was a broadly similar pattern to Conan Doyle's life in 1906–1907 following the death of his wife Louisa. By then it was nearly twenty-one years since the couple had married, and thirteen from the time she had been diagnosed with a 'hopeless' case of tuberculosis. The family had continued to move restlessly about in search of the best possible climates to curb the disease, including a return trip to Southsea, where they found that the old surgery where they first lived together had become a corsetry shop named Doyle House. By the spring of 1906, Louisa was permanently bedridden, pitifully frail, and could speak only in a whisper. Towards the end, she is said to have summoned her 17-year-old daughter Mary and told her 'not to be shocked or surprised if my father married again, but to know that it was with her understanding and blessing'. Louisa died peacefully at home on Wednesday, 4 July. She was 49. 'My father sat by the bedside,' Mary remembered later, 'the tears coursing down his rugged face, and her small white hand enfolded in his huge grasp.'

Unsurprisingly, Conan Doyle fell into a period of deep dejection as he struggled not only with his immediate loss, but also the prospect of single-handedly raising two teenaged children. It was an excruciating time. Among other things, Doyle was tortured by insomnia, a condition possibly exacerbated by his pangs of guilt that, to one degree or another, he had begun to enjoy the company of a mistress – Jean Leckie – while his wife lay terminally ill.

We know that Doyle attended séances in London during August and September 1906, and that he later recalled a period of 'long solitude' spent wandering through the Scottish moors once the children had returned to school in the autumn. On 19 October, he wrote to his mother of having been 'all alone for three days … One collects oneself and finds one's soul.' Doyle told another correspondent that day that he felt 'paralysed' when it came to doing any productive work, and urgently in need of some 'driving force' to carry him through his depression. The following morning the papers reported that the young lawyer George Edalji had been released from Pentonville Prison after serving three years of a seven-year sentence for the crime of cattle mutilation.

4

THE CREEPING MAN

When George Edalji walked out of the prison gates on the morning of Friday, 19 October 1906 he carried a brown paper parcel of civilian clothes, a gratuity of £2 9s 10d (representing about 7 pence, or 10 cents, for each month of his confinement) and a printed form requiring him to report to the police at regular intervals during the unexpired four years of his custodial term.

As the authorities were at pains to point out, Edalji's conviction had not been overturned and he was not being pardoned. This was purely 'a degree of goodwill [and] mercy,' *The Times* reported blandly, possibly the result of the 'many letters, petitions and appeals' addressed to the Home Office over the previous three years protesting the young man's innocence. In particular, the satirical magazine, *Truth* – a sort of precursor to *Private Eye* – had run a series of articles between January and March 1905, which had remarked that 'the crime against the poor victims was a relatively slight affair compared with the ordeal of a completely blameless soul hurl[ed] into the hell of slavery in a jail-cell'. According to this reading, the prosecuting authorities in the Edalji case – and more especially the Chief Constable of Staffordshire, Captain George Anson – had drawn their conclusions largely as a result of crass incompetence and blind racism, rather than the proven Holmesian formula of meticulous observation and reasoning.

Later in 1905, a correspondent to *The Times* had asked whether the Edalji affair might not 'arouse the brain [of] that great presiding genius of No. 221b Baker Street', containing as it did a somewhat enigmatic Anglo-Indian family, a series of apparently motiveless and brutally violent crimes perpetrated at night, and an official investigation not distinguished by its forensic brilliance. No wonder, perhaps, that Doyle was soon able to report that he had overcome his depression and turned his energies towards 'an entirely unexpected channel'.

There is some doubt about the exact sequence of events that led Doyle to first involve himself in the Edalji affair. In his 1924 memoirs, he claimed that during 'the days of darkness' following Louisa's death, and apparently thinking it to be a cricket title, 'I chanced to pick up an obscure paper called *The Umpire*, and my eye caught an article which was a statement of [the] case'. But writing in 1907, Doyle recalled that Edalji, a jailhouse enthusiast of Sherlock Holmes, had contacted him direct, enclosing details of his trial and conviction. In either event, the recently bereaved author could hardly have avoided some of the widespread press coverage that followed Edalji's conditional release in late October 1906. We know that Doyle was visited at home that Christmas by his fellow Crimes Club member, John Churton Collins, and that Collins wrote that he 'had a delightful time with ACD, who is on fire with the Edalji case'.★ Similarly, Doyle's 33-year-old brother Innes recorded in his diary on 12 January 1907, 'Much talk of Edalji'.

As we've seen, the case had its origins in a hate mail campaign of unusual stamina and variety directed at the Bombay-born vicar of St Mark's Anglican church of Great Wyrley, Staffordshire, and his family. The Reverend Shapurji Edalji had first been appointed to the parish in January 1876, when he was 35, and would serve there continuously until his death forty-two years later.

Despite, or because of, his outsider status, he seems to have readily understood and appreciated the cultural role faith played in Victorian Britain. The 'more practical and less dogmatic' men became about religion, the reverend often preached, the better lives they would lead; in turn 'the life of the nation [would] become more virtuous'. There was 'much good sense emanat[ing] from the

***

★ Collins was one of a number of Crimes Club members to come to an untimely end. In September 1908, he was found drowned in a ditch near Lowestoft, Suffolk, possibly a suicide. He was 60.

pulpit at Wyrley,' the daily *Birmingham Gazette* once editorialised. It would be wrong to assume that Reverend Edalji's views, which tended to the politically Liberal, were universally popular, however, and his vicarage was the target of unappreciative graffiti, usually of the racial kind, even before the anonymous correspondence began.

Taken as a whole, the Edaljis were a model case of early Asian assimilation into the English Midlands – idealistic and hardworking, and as good-hearted (or naïve) as some of Sherlock Holmes's more credulous clients. One of the most affecting parts of the whole case is how the Edaljis themselves somehow retained their essential faith in the British system even in the face of appalling personal hardship.

Although sometimes portrayed as of peasant origins, they were an impressively literate family. While in his early twenties, Reverend Edalji had published a series of scholarly dictionaries and grammars enquiring into the Indo-Aryan language Gujarati, and had used the proceeds from these to pay for his passage to England. On arrival there, he wrote a commentary on St Paul's Epistles to the Galatians that was widely accepted as the definitive work on the subject. Its success made it possible for Edalji to find a living within the Church, and in June 1874 he married 31-year-old Charlotte Elizabeth Stuart, herself the daughter of an Anglican vicar and the niece of three others. She, too, privately published several theological papers, making almost intelligible the fantastic complexity of the Book of Leviticus, which she summarised as 'God's true and perfect contract with mankind'. The couple had three children: George Ernest Thompson, born in 1876, Horace, born in 1879, and Maud, in 1882.

George Edalji was a shy, academically gifted boy who stared up at the world through bulging brown eyes. When he was 8 years old he volunteered to share a bedroom with his father, who was suffering a variety of health problems, in order to be able to help in the event of a medical emergency. At the same time, Charlotte Edalji moved in to her infant daughter's nursery. These same sleeping arrangements continued for the next twenty years, and in time led to the rumour that the family indulged in unnatural practices.

Meanwhile, Reverend Edalji would find himself embroiled in several long-running disputes with members of his church council (then as now, something of an occupational hazard), largely over his insistence on personally supervising the religious education of his school-age parishioners. The reverend's Bible readings apparently only strengthened his belief in the scripturally sanctioned bond he felt existed, in descending order, between God, himself, and his congregation. It was said that when local people sometimes spoke of the 'zeal of the convert', they had him in mind.

In August 1888, the first of the poison letters arrived at the Great Wyrley vicarage. Rather oddly, it asked that Reverend Edalji order a particular local newspaper, and suggested that his windows would be smashed if he failed to comply. A second letter contained the specific threat to shoot the reverend, and resulted in the first appearance of the police in the case.

On New Year's Day 1889, 12-year-old George Edalji reported finding a letter on the table of the hall in the vicarage, the gum on the envelope still wet. Three more such letters appeared in the same week, all of them written on paper apparently torn from George's school exercise book. As noted, the police eventually arrested the Edaljis' 17-year-old servant girl Elizabeth Foster, who pled guilty to a reduced charge of using threats and was given probation. By all accounts, the young offender showed no contrition in the dock, and subsequently claimed she was innocent of a crime to which she had confessed only on her lawyer's advice. A renewed outbreak of anonymous letters from 1892–95 actively championed Foster's cause. She was said to have moved around the Birmingham area in the meantime, eventually settling with a maiden aunt, using 'cunning, corruption and seductiveness' to advance her way in life, which was reportedly distinguished by 'a sexual need as blatant as her perfume'.

George Edalji, meanwhile, enjoyed a conventional middle-class education at Rugeley Grammar School, about 8 miles to the north of Great Wyrley. Again, he seems to have been quietly independent and self-willed. Perhaps he had to be. He was on his own. George was a Christian, an Asian and a bit of a swot. One of his contemporaries remembered him as 'eager and deep, inclined to be a tad smug, [his] hand always up first in class'. He was an avid reader. When he turned 13, George's great-uncle Compson, vicar of Hillesley in Gloucestershire, gave him a leather-bound copy of Thomas à Kempis's 60,000-word biblical treatise Of the Imitation of Christ, and the next morning George came downstairs announcing he had read it from cover to cover.

As a teenager, he was known to write long and warmly affectionate letters to his family members, even when they were living together under the same roof. He was also soft-spoken and scrupulously polite, always tipping his school cap when he passed a lady in the street. And he was a meticulous dresser. Despite all these attractive qualities, George had few close friends and no known girlfriends. His mother later observed that her elder son was 'never one to travel in crowds'. In later life, George neither drank nor smoked (although he was known to gamble), and for many years chose to share a home with his adult sister. He was an odd bird, and in the final analysis, it seems, probably a lonely one.

Beginning in July 1892, when George was 16, the Edaljis were subjected to a second and even more virulent anonymous mail campaign. It has never been successfully established why their persecution should have resumed after some three and a half years' silence, although Conan Doyle later theorised that Reverend Edalji's role in the 1892 British general election, and his outspoken views on more narrowly parochial affairs, may have played a part.

Much of the abuse was addressed to the Great Wyrley vicarage, although some was sent to a W.H. Brookes, a local grocer and church warden, and showed a distinct turn to the psychotic. One of the Brookes letters, for instance, included a vivid account of his adult daughter sexually molesting her 10-year-old sister. The writer went on to allege other practices in the Brookes household less refined than this. Often written in two distinct hands, one seemingly educated, the other bovine or childish, the letters increasingly came to focus on the Edalji family, and on George in particular. 'The blackman will die … I swear by God that I will murder George Edalji soon. The only thing I care about in this world is revenge, revenge, revenge, sweet revenge,' read an early example:

> Every day, every hour, my hatred is growing against George Edalji … And your horrid little girl … That damn cunt … Bloody blasted dam bloody currst buger bleeding blasting kid … I will descend into the infernal regions showering curses upon you all.

… and so on.

Seeming to refute the idea that he was somehow responsible for the threats to his own family, Reverend Edalji went to the trouble of arranging to reproduce some of the letters in the Staffordshire press in the hope that a reader might help to identify their writer or writers, but to no avail.

By late 1892, the correspondence had come to loosely revolve around a group of Walsall youths including Fred Brookes, son of W.H. Brookes, and the impressively feckless 12-year-old Royden Sharp. Sharp was later expelled from the local grammar school for 'fighting, lying, cheating, forging his end-of-term report' and, climactically, 'knocking down the Head of House with a clout to the jaw'. Another figure mentioned in the letters was 14-year-old Fred Wynne, a local tough and intimate of the Walsall-based gang that often travelled to and from school in the same railway carriage. George Edalji sometimes shared part of their journey, although, as usual, seems to have kept his distance from the other boys.

An unsigned letter in December 1892 boasted that the author and his friends had 'reely wrecked' their train compartment on a recent journey, while 'the blackman Edalji' had merely looked on at the vandalism. A second note later that month contained the threat to break the legs of a named railway porter if he failed to leave money for the writer, before suggesting both that Fred Brookes was enjoying sexual relations with the 10-year-old Maud Edalji, and that George was engaged in similar practices with Brookes's sister. Although the English secondary school system was not then troubled, as it was later, by counsellors, if it had been they surely would have found the young passengers regularly embarking on the Stafford to Wolverhampton branch line that winter to be suitable cases for concern.

Meanwhile, the police again intervened. On or about 7 December, a Sergeant Upton of the Cannock station called at the Great Wyrley vicarage to take statements from Reverend Edalji and his family. After 16-year-old George had finished his story he turned to go back upstairs to his room, at which point Sergeant Upton put his hand on the boy's shoulder and said, 'I have been given orders to ask for your assistance in order to eliminate you from our enquiries'. His orders were to obtain by whatever means necessary a sample of George's handwriting, to see if it matched the letters. The teenager, who seems not to have realised what was happening, said, 'I will be glad to help'.

At Upton's direction, George then wrote out several phrases such as, 'Unless you run away I'll murder you and your slut wife' and 'The grocer's kid will cop it from the blackman', but according to the sergeant's report of 8 December none of these struck him as being obviously similar to the hand of the anonymous writer. It has to be said that the gruffly capable but stolid Upton is one of several authority figures in the case to have seemingly stepped direct from the pages of a Sherlock Holmes story.

The letters continued to arrive at the Great Wyrley vicarage following his visit, and Conan Doyle would later record that some of them were strong stuff, even for a man like him, accustomed to working among the worst slums of Victorian Portsmouth, or for that matter to have practised as a surgeon in an army field hospital in the depths of a typhoid epidemic. One communication accused Reverend Edalji of 'gross immorality with persons using Vaseline in the same way as Oscar Wilde'; while another attested that he kept a number of ladies, their physical charms explicitly stated, for the amusement of himself and his friends. No one who read this correspondence, including Sergeant Upton, was left in any doubt that the writer was personally familiar with both Reverend Edalji and his family; or that given the letters' mixture of juvenile bravado and obsession with the female body at its most immodest, it was likely that a teenaged boy was involved.

In time, the anonymous party or parties added physical pranks, or harassment, to a campaign that had previously existed only in written form. On 12 December, a key was discovered lying on the Great Wyrley vicarage's back doorstep. Reverend Edalji passed it to Sergeant Upton, who in due course determined that it had been removed from Walsall Grammar School. Two days later, excreta was found daubed on the outside of the vicarage's upstairs windows. Sergeant Upton again investigated, and decided that this was an inside job – no one could have accurately thrown the matter from outside, he reasoned, as most of the soiled windows were shielded by the branches of a large yew tree.

Another new twist to the campaign involved a series of hoax advertisements in the local newspapers. In one, the Edaljis' home was said to be available for rent. According to another, the family would be hosting an open house on a certain date, and the dress code for this was stated to be unusually relaxed. Soon, tradesmen began arriving at the vicarage from all parts after apparently being summoned by Reverend Edalji, only to find themselves the victims of a practical joke. Eventually, a boxed notice appeared in the *Birmingham Gazette* and several smaller papers. 'We, the undersigned, G.E.T. Edalji and Fredk Brookes,' it read, 'do hereby declare that we were the sole authors and writers of certain offensive and anonymous letters received by various persons during the last twelve months.' This, too, was later revealed as a fraud. Like Reverend Edalji's decision to publish some of the hate mail in the hope that it might help identify its source, George's faked confessions would seem to refute the idea that the family were somehow responsible for harassing themselves.

Even so, official suspicion now increasingly fell on George Edalji, who it's possible to speculate may have secretly enjoyed at least some of the attention. One elderly man who had known George in his seventies told me that the latter had once stunned him with an 'outpouring about the stupidity of the police compared to himself fifty years earlier', although this had fallen short of an admission of guilt. The individual added that, in his quiet way, the teenaged George had apparently 'always risen to a good challenge', and found it 'exhilarating' to trade wits with the forces of law and order. They were his adversaries, but they were at least halfway worthy adversaries. 'George enjoyed jousting with the officers who came to the vicarage,' I was told. 'It was a chance to perform.'

So the game was on. On 7 January 1893 the Chief Constable of Staffordshire ordered his force to 'watch the[se] accursed Edaljis in the least of their doings.' At one point, Sergeant Upton claimed to have seen George furtively posting a letter in a pillar box at the gate of Wyrley and Church Bridge Station, as it was then called. Not only that, but the sergeant had been able to note the colour and size of the envelope, and these had exactly matched one subsequently delivered to W.H. Brookes, the grocer, containing a prank letter.

Referring to the incident of the grammar school key that had appeared on the vicarage doorstep, Sergeant Upton wrote to Reverend Edalji on 23 January 1893:

> Will you please ask your son George from whom the key was obtained? It was stolen, but if it can be shown that the whole thing was due to some idle freak or practical joke, I should not be inclined to allow any police proceedings to be taken in regard of it. If, however, the persons concerned in the removal of the key refuse to make any explanation of the subject, I must necessarily treat the matter in all seriousness as a theft. I must say at once that I shall not pretend to believe any protestations of ignorance which your son may make about this key. My information on the subject does not come from the police.

There are two possible explanations for Sergeant Upton's suspicions, and why they should have assumed so much importance later.

The first and official explanation was that the sergeant and his colleagues diligently followed proper procedure throughout, drawing upon truly Holmesian powers of observation and reason. Immediately on first entering the vicarage, Upton had 'gained a sense' of what was going on, he later said. There was a 'strained and melancholy' atmosphere about the place (hardly surprising, given the circumstances), and the 'Hindoo lad' had seemed to him to be curiously evasive. Even separating the objective facts from their automatic and intuitive subjective interpretation, as Holmes would surely have done, there was the matter of George's motive and opportunity. It was widely acknowledged that he was a precociously intelligent but inward boy, of the kind who might conceivably have enjoyed sparring with the forces of officialdom;

and he, of course, had access to the vicarage at all hours. According to this reading of events, George was a sort of functioning teenaged sociopath who had developed a bitter and contemptuous attitude towards the world under the carefully preserved façade of a mother's boy.

The other and more likely explanation is that the average semi-rural English police force of the 1890s all too often substituted selective experience and guesswork for true scientific deduction, and that in this case there was the powerfully aggravating factor of race, the miscegenation issue, and the family's unorthodox domestic arrangements as a whole: all enough to trigger a provincial copper's preconceived notions of what an imaginative 'Hindoo lad' like George might get up to.

On 17 March 1893, the anonymous correspondent wrote to tell Reverend Edalji, 'Before the end of this year your kid will be either in the graveyard or disgraced for life'. There was some more in this vein, and then in closing he added, 'Do you think that when we want we cannot copy your kid's writing?' It was, in fact, ten years before the 'kid', George Edalji, was ruined for life, but in every other respect the letter was chillingly prescient. As Conan Doyle later noted, 'It is difficult after this to doubt that the schemer of 1893 was identical with the [maniac] of 1903'.

In coming to compile a list of alternative suspects who might have wished to cause harm to his family or himself, Reverend Edalji found that he was somewhat spoilt for choice. There was Elizabeth Foster, for instance, who had 'form' as an anonymous letter writer, then still living in the area and possibly seeking revenge for her original 1889 conviction. The reverend also expressed doubts about one Daniel Cotton, who some years earlier had left his position as the St Mark's church organist after an 'almighty row' with the parish council. In time W.H. Brookes, the grocer, added the names of two local men whom he had publicly accused of theft from his shop, and who thus might have borne him — and by association, the Edaljis — a grudge.

We've touched on some of the enigmatic young gang of travellers on the daily school train, who as a rule seem to have been unusually preoccupied by the female sex in general and that of the blameless young Maud Edalji in particular. In addition to these, there were at least half a dozen other individuals who were thought to be nursing a grievance of one kind or another against the 'Hindoos' in their midst.

Was it all something to do with Reverend Edalji's sometimes outspoken politics? Did he have enemies, as he long suspected, even within his own party affiliation? One day, the former local MP Edward Holden, a Liberal, dropped by the Great Wyrley vicarage to 'offer support and see how the Reverend was faring'. Shapurji Edalji met him at the door with a piece of paper and asked him to write the words 'Bitch wife' on it. This and samples from other friends were then sent off to a handwriting analyst in Birmingham, who charged Edalji £30 for his services but never conclusively identified a suspect.

In the spring of 1893, a new name joined the list of candidates under consideration as the anonymous letter writer. This was 50-year-old James Morgan, a university-educated Birmingham man who was known to possess an imaginative and florid prose style. Were he in fact guilty, it seems likely he acted out of personal rather than narrowly political or theological motives. He was a misfit who had failed to keep a job in high finance to which he believed he was entitled, and had been reduced to working as a Walsall insurance agent and occasional newspaper stringer. As a result, he had conceived a deep hatred of authority, and, the theory went, chose to harass his local vicar as a protest against the injustice of which he believed he was the victim.

On or around 28 April Morgan went, by invitation, to the Great Wyrley vicarage, an appointment he described rather tartly as 'a commandment from his Holiness the Pope of Wyrley to attend his chateau'. The subsequent interview was not a success. Reverend Edalji promptly accused Morgan of composing the hate letters and Morgan denied this, but then added the curious flourish of boasting that he *could* have done so by sitting down to demonstrate various handwriting styles in an essay which included a number of sexually charged insults of the Edaljis. From then on, the two men conducted their exchanges through a spirited correspondence in the pages of the *Cannock Advertiser*.

Morgan seems to have been one of those plausible lunatics who enjoy a public controversy. At one point, he sent the paper a detailed account of a recent confrontation between himself and the Edalji and Brookes families, a report embellished with lively passages of direct speech and a frustrated novelist's descriptive touches. Alas, no such meeting ever occurred. It's possible Morgan had convinced himself intellectually that he was a criminal mastermind, but both Reverend Edalji and the police came to discount his claims. Successive charges and counter-charges in the pages of the *Advertiser* continued during 1893, though these often wandered off from the specific point and into lengthy biblical digression on the one side and wholesale denunciations of the local community on the other. Morgan wrote in one letter that he had 'powerful nemeses' in the area, and it was they who wished to demean him in:

… the eyes of these vile, lazy, pettifogging, ignorant collier folk of which there are a sight too many in Wyrley Bonk [*sic*] for my liking … Even the dirty, defiled, unwanted children of these vulgar, ignorant fools, the miners, make fun of me.

The full truth about the hate letter campaign may never be known. But as in the case of another mystery – Conan Doyle's 1892 'The Adventure of Silver Blaze' – what matters most is not so much the beginning of the story but its escalation into the realm of animal maiming and the mindset of the criminal behind it.

In the meantime, the abuse, whether appearing in epistolary or more tangible form, continued to rain down on the Edaljis' home at regular intervals until December 1895. The letters arrived roughly once a month, often couched in apocalyptical language, typically composed in red ink and apparently written in short bursts of manic energy around the edges of the paper, so that one had to turn the page through 360 degrees to read all of it. Much of the correspondence had a sexual component. A number of striking combinations were suggested: one letter addressed to the Edaljis' new maid, Nora, dwelt on her employer's penchant for seducing young girls and initiating them into bondage, flagellation, bestiality and other, less easily classified debauches. Another letter invited Nora to flush the family cat down the toilet. The same young woman was later instructed to 'put shit with anything you may cook for the [Edaljis] and save all your piss and put it to boil potatoes'.

Perhaps just as striking a characteristic of the 1892–95 correspondence was its untiring acclaim for the heroic figure of Sergeant Upton. He was eulogised this way in one letter, 'Ha, ha, hurrah for Upton! Good old Upton! Blessed Upton. Good old Upton! Upton is blessed! Dear old Upton!' The author increasingly focused on the universal knowledge, peerless wisdom, and exquisite professional subtlety of the Cannock Police in general, which was not entirely the impression Conan Doyle came to form of that force. 'Cretinous' was his private assessment. Such was the praise consistently heaped on these same guardians of public order in the anonymous letters, quite apart from their other obsessions, that it is hard not to believe there was a vein of real derangement in the writer.

At this point it seems fair to introduce Captain the Honourable George Anson, the imposing new Chief Constable of Staffordshire. The second son of the Earl of Lichfield, Anson had served twelve years as an army officer before retiring to join the police. It was said that he had beaten sixty-seven other candidates to become chief constable at the early age of 31, although against this precocious record of achievement it's only fair to note that his family, based at the nearby 900-acre Shugborough Hall, enjoyed a certain prestige in the area.

Anson has been widely portrayed as a prime representative of the late Victorian English landed Establishment, imperialistic, vain, personally bigoted in his attitude to 'foreigners' like the Edaljis, and displaying some of the less attractive qualities of an Inspector Lestrade in his unimaginative police work. It's a caricature, if one with a grain of truth. At the time, Anson, a small, dark-haired man habitually dressed in a long white raincoat and a trilby, was generally seen as a hardworking, conscientious administrator who preferred to keep his name out of the papers. Although his family had a stake in several local news organisations, Anson himself never bothered to meet with the press or establish any relationships with the opinion-making elite. He genially assured his officers that he had the confidence of 'Matthew' (Viscount Ridley, the Home Secretary), which was all that mattered, and thus pandering to the likes of the *Walsall Gazette* was silly. When criticisms of him or his force were raised, Anson could almost invariably reckon with his minister's backing. 'The captain was a man who chose to serve in the police instead of lounging around on his estate and was not looking for ways to stir a controversy,' I was told by one of his descendants.

On the other hand, Anson was quite capable of delivering a blunt and critical assessment of a situation or individual if minded to do so. He seems to have taken an instant dislike to the 'Hindoo vicar', Reverend Edalji, and to have quickly determined that there was a case to be made against the reverend's son George. In time, Conan Doyle wrote that he personally met with 'nothing but frankness and courtesy' when coming to interview Anson, who happened to be a fan of Sherlock Holmes. But even this relationship eventually broke down under the strain of their differing interpretation of the strange events at Great Wyrley. In 1911, Doyle wrote to Anson, 'Your letter is a series of innuendos mixed up with a good deal of rudeness.' Anson in turn jotted a note in his police book, 'Is Conan Doyle mad?' 'The matter is a personal one between Sir Arthur and myself,' he remarked later.

In a startling 1920 appendix to his official report on the Edaljis, marked 'confidential', Anson would admit to fabricating evidence for Conan Doyle to chase, apparently designed to distract and discredit him. Among other things, he had created an elaborate ruse to suggest that the young Walsall thug Royden Sharp had travelled to London to deliver a poison pen letter to Doyle's door.

In fact, Sharp never made such a journey. The whole thing was a 'practical merriment' on Captain Anson's part (not entirely different to the sort of pranks once visited on the Edaljis) although, to be clear, it was one meant to confound what Anson saw as a meddling amateur detective rather than directly pervert the course of justice. As Harry Houdini and several other leading anti-spiritualists would attest, Doyle in his later years could be querulous and dogmatic, working himself up into a nervous state which found expression in outbursts of rage, blame and apparent derangement, resulting in dire predictions brought to him through a 7,000-year-old spirit agency called 'Pheneas' that a named individual would suffer eternal damnation after death. Such was the fate he would come to promise Captain Anson.

✳ ✳ ✳

In December 1895, the second wave of anonymous correspondence to the Edaljis ceased as abruptly as it had begun. The last two letters in the sequence were posted at Stafford Station, which later suggested to Doyle that the writer had been travelling to or from the area by rail. Like Holmes, he was a great enthusiast for all manner of train timetables. It was thought highly significant that Royden Sharp had reported for duty that week on a ship leaving Liverpool, which could be reached by a direct service from Stafford. Captain Anson was not impressed by the coincidence of these events. He had come to believe that George Edalji was at least complicit in his family's harassment, and that the reason for this was that he had been mistreated, if not sexually abused, by his father. 'The boy was possessed with a blind fury,' Anson wrote confidentially. 'He had no friends and associates, and no doubt would suffer chaff at school for being a semi-oriental and I imagine could not forgive his father.'

It's easy to dismiss this as the pseudo-psychological babblings of an aristocratic policeman, but there were others, too, who broadly endorsed Anson's theory. George Edalji's own solicitor believed that his client had been involved in some of the anonymous letter writing. George's younger brother Horace, later to leave the area and change his name, gave the police a statement saying the same thing. Other speculation included a story about the consumption of mind-altering drugs on the Great Wyrley vicarage premises, turning it into a sort of prototype 1960s commune with sinister Manson family-like undertones.

In later years there were reports, never substantiated, that George had run up a series of gambling debts, and embezzled £200 to pay them. The psychiatric factor again surfaced in 1905, when a senior Scotland Yard officer, Neville MacNaughton, compared aspects of the Edalji case to that of the late Dr Neil Cream, a predatory killer who had been hanged in 1892 for poisoning prostitutes. 'There is no doubt that the fellow who perpetrated the [Great Wyrley] outrages is a sexual maniac,' MacNaughton wrote to a colleague in the Home Office:

… and if physionomy goes for anything, Mr Edalji junior has the face of such an individual … Dr Cream was a man of good education, but morally perhaps the worst specimen I have ever come across … Having poisoned his victims, Cream invariably wrote letters to any public men whose names were at that time appearing frequently in the papers, accusing them of murdering the women. He also found great pleasure in discussing the case with police officers, and it was by reason of these imprudent actions that suspicions were primarily attached to him. History seems therefore to have repeated itself.

✳ ✳ ✳

Many who knew him have described George Edalji as keeping a certain remove between himself and others, as though he had his guard up, or as though for sheer diffidence he preferred not to mingle unduly with his fellow man. Others simply described him as aloof. He was unquestionably intelligent, bookish and a bit intense, with a habit of fixing the huge headlamps of his eyes on those he met, while his nose and lips twitched slightly, as if betraying the inner strain of the occasion. Edalji's conversational technique was once described as:

Long periods of silence, punctuated by sudden bursts of direct, almost embarrassing questions about the state of one's health, or marriage, for instance, of a kind both intrusive and completely divorced from any interest in the answer. At the end of each cross-examination he would abruptly fall back into coma again. Small talk was not his forte.

Nonetheless, George Edalji made significant progress in life between the ages of 18 and 25. On graduating from Rugeley Grammar School, he entered Mason's College in Birmingham to study law, travelling the 20 miles to and from the vicarage by foot and train. Edalji proceeded to win the Birmingham Law Society's first prize in three successive years. He qualified at the age of

23; set up his own solicitor's practice in Birmingham at 24; and at 25, perhaps reflecting his already long experience as a commuter, published a well-received book on railway law.

As usual, he seems to have restrained himself when it came to his social life. Edalji never drank, appeared to have no interest in women, and continued to share a modest attic bedroom with his father. As a hardworking young solicitor, commuting in and out by train, he was up at 6 most mornings, returning home around 7.30 in the evening and then often making it his habit to see clients at the vicarage for an hour or more each weeknight. Keeping the hours he did, he could have been forgiven had he chosen to simply relax at the weekends, but characteristically Edalji did the opposite, setting up a regular Saturday morning law clinic where anyone was welcome to come to Great Wyrley to consult him without charge.

While George's calm, scholarly manner proved an asset professionally, it also offended certain people whose aversion to him was perhaps further excited by his skin colour. To such individuals, it seemed he was 'putting on airs' and 'getting above himself'. There was an incident in December 1900 when two local youths accosted him when he was out walking in the fields around Snareshill, a village about 3 miles from Great Wyrley. For once, Edalji had 'blown up', a court later heard, shouting at his assailants that they were no better than animals, vowing 'to see them caged up'. A Walsall magistrate agreed that George had been the victim of an unprovoked assault, and fined the two men £5 each. The following year, a clerk to the same Walsall court, C.A. Loxton, publicly accused Edalji of painting 'immoral and offensive' comments about him and his fiancée in various public spaces. Loxton was unable to substantiate the charge, however, and was eventually removed from his post to the Stafford County Lunatic Hospital.

A more serious professional challenge came in June 1900, when Edalji's law partner absconded with some £900 (about £65,000 today) of their clients' funds. George himself made good the losses, falling heavily in debt as a result. Threatened with a judgement of bankruptcy, he took the simple if rather un-English expedient of writing letters to prominent citizens – Conan Doyle among them – requesting donations. When later reviewing the Edalji case in the House of Commons, the Conservative MP and future Lord Chancellor F.E. Smith remarked that George was:

> A man of studious habits, with a good character … The only circumstance which had been or could be alleged against him was that at the age of 25 he was in

pecuniary difficulties – a not uncommon circumstance in the case of men of his position in life qualifying for an expensive profession.

✳ ✳ ✳

On the morning of 2 February 1903, a work horse belonging to Joseph Holmes, a Great Wyrley shopkeeper, was found to have been disembowelled during the night. There seems to have been relatively little attention paid to the crime until later in the spring, when in quick succession three more horses, three cows and a sheep met the same fate. At that stage it became clear that a serial maniac was loose in the community. Following another outrage on 6 June, Captain Anson of the Staffordshire Police assigned four of his men to patrol the fields around Great Wyrley at night. Despite this precaution, two more horses were soon found gored in a manner that the local newspapers were unable to fully report; it involved the use of a sharp knife with a curved, scimitar-like blade. The wretched animals had evidently bled slowly to death.

Clearly, whoever was responsible for the attacks was unusually strong, proficient in his butchery work, and sadistically minded: during the course of his rampage, a succession of farm animals were stabbed, slashed, tortured and sexually mutilated. Another of Holmes's horses was found with a knife embedded in one of its buttocks. When Captain Anson came to decide on his prime suspect as the mad ripper, there were not many candidates, and the verdict was quickly reached. Anson reported to his superiors at the Home Office that George Edalji had been seen 'prowling about' the area late at night, an emotive choice of words that may have owed something to the officer's pre-existing animus towards the family. George himself insisted that what the police saw as 'prowling' was really no more than his habit of innocently strolling around the nearby lanes in the hour before going to bed.

Meanwhile, the campaign of anonymous letters and mocking advertisements resumed after a seven-year silence, with most of the more choice abuse now directed at George rather than his father. 'Edalji the lawyer' had carried out the maimings at full moon to give the impression there was 'a looney' afoot, one note insisted. In another, the police were tipped off to watch for a passenger with 'eagle eyes and ears as sharp as a razor and fleet of foot as a fox' who would be travelling on the evening train from Walsall to Great Wyrley. 'He crawls on all fours up to the poor beasts, an' fondles them a bit, and then he pulls the hook smart across 'em, and out their entrails fly, before they guess they are hurt,' the writer elaborated:

> You want 100 detectives to run him in red-handed, because he is so fly, and knows every nook and corner. You know who it is, and I can prove it; but until £100 reward is offered for a conviction, I shan't split no more.

The phrasing of this letter, and more specifically the use of the semi-colon, later led Conan Doyle to believe that it had been co-authored by a 'blithering lunatic' working in league with an educated man. A third note warned chillingly that Edalji and his associates were planning to 'do 20 wenches like the horses before next March'.

While most of the correspondence was unsigned, some purported to come from a 'Greatorex', which was the surname of a graduate of Walsall Grammar School who happened to be a cousin of the seafaring Royden Sharp, a former butcher's apprentice. Sharp had just returned to the area after several years' service on the Atlantic ships. The actual Wilfred Greatorex later testified that he had known George Edalji by sight 'for three or four years', and that they had quite often travelled around on the same train. He denied all knowledge of the letters.

Most of them were to the effect that George was the leader of a cut-throat gang that was roaming the fields at night for the purpose of molesting cattle – 'there will be merry times when they start on little girls,' the writer warned:

> Mr Edalji, mean[time], is going to Brum on Sunday night to see the Captain, near Northfield, about how it's to be carried on with so many detectives about, and I believe they are going to do some cows in the daytime instead of at night.

Another 'Greatorex' letter reached the police on 7 July 1903, and named several young men in addition to George Edalji as engaged in certain imaginatively detailed atrocities. Among the group's past or intended activities were animal sacrifice, witchcraft, and the wholesale rape of Great Wyrley's juvenile female population. One letter taunted the police that they would never 'gess' the writer's identity, and another seemed to suggest that 'Irish Fenians' were behind the carnage. What strikes the reader now is the sheer variety of the perversions said to be about to engulf Great Wyrley, which went well beyond the normal rural vices. (Several American newspapers such as the

New York Times would later insist that the Edaljis had lived in a community of irreproachable public morals, and completely immune to the temptations of drink and sex, but this was merely to confirm their ignorance of English country life.)

A series of further notes and letters followed during the summer, climaxing in a postcard addressed to George Edalji at his Birmingham office. It accused him of unusual sexual conduct with a local young girl and concluded, 'Rather go back to your old game of writing anonymous letters and killing cows and writing on walls'. At trial, the police maintained that Edalji had written this card himself, apparently in an attempt to finally convince them that he was the victim of a demented prankster. Another note arrived on 23 July. Admitting to not caring much for 'natives' like Edalji, it nonetheless advised him to quickly leave the area in order to provide himself with an alibi when the next slashing occurred. It was signed, 'Lover of Justice'. Edalji, who came to believe that his disgraced former law partner might be involved, now offered a £25 reward for information leading to an arrest in the case; another brazen ruse, the police believed, to draw suspicion away from himself.

※ ※ ※

On 17 August 1903, a wet and blustery Monday, George Edalji arrived home from his day's work in Birmingham at about 6.30 p.m., followed his usual practice of entertaining some neighbouring clients for an hour or so, and then changed from a light linen jacket into a blue serge overcoat and a pair of stout boots in order to walk around the village before his supper was ready at 9.30. After that he sat in the parlour and chatted to his 21-year-old sister Maud before retiring around 11 p.m. to the bedroom he shared with his father. The elderly reverend later testified that he had then locked the door of their room as he always did, before abruptly waking up at around 4 a.m. with one of his regular bouts of lumbago. His son had been 'completely motionless' in his own bed within a few feet of him.

There was a fresh wind rattling the vicarage windows, and the five or six policemen posted by Captain Anson around the garden and nearby fields were exposed to a monotonous, drenching rain. They saw no one leave the house. While the officers commendably trudged to and fro all night in the summer squalls, 27-year-old George Edalji apparently slept soundly in the same child-sized iron bed he had used since the age of 9. He had no way of knowing that it would prove to be his last night of freedom for more than three years.★

Shortly after 6 on the morning of 18 August, a young colliery worker named Henry Garnett crossed a field about a mile from the vicarage and found a pit horse slashed across its stomach. 'It had a cut on the side,' Garnett testified. 'The blood was trickling from the wound. It was dropping pretty quickly.' The police arrived promptly and apparently discovered blood smeared on the nearby grass – the attacker's attempt to wipe his hands clean, they believed – as well as several pairs of footprints leading to and from the scene. Over the course of the morning, it became clear that no logical method was to be applied in preserving either the bloodstains or the footprints, with up to fifty policemen and curious passers-by successively strolling up to peer at the evidence and offer an opinion. A veterinary surgeon, Dr Robert Lewis, was summoned and reported that the horse had been assaulted at some time between 2 and 6 that morning. The wretched animal itself was humanely destroyed.

Conan Doyle later tended to find fault with the overall professionalism of the police investigation of the Edalji case, and their approach to the initial forensic analysis of the scene gives some backing to that judgement. The area was later described in court as a 'shambles' in every sense of the word. Captain Anson happened to have just left on a shooting holiday in Scotland, and in his absence the investigation was led by an Inspector Campbell from the Hednesford station. Around 7 that morning, Campbell dispatched a constable to intercept George Edalji as he caught his usual train to Birmingham, with the request that he return to answer a few questions. Edalji, thinking it all had something to do with the receipt of another anonymous letter, rather than a case of sadistic animal slaughter, politely declined to accompany the officer, citing the amount of work awaiting him at the office, and continued on his way. Edalji later remarked in court that this struck him as being entirely consistent

---

★ There is some doubt about whether the police had mounted a specific watch on the vicarage that night, or merely assigned men to the local area. Captain Anson later testified, 'It was found impossible, owing to the nature of the surroundings, to make absolutely certain that no one could come in or out of the house without being observed.' Conan Doyle, by contrast, wrote of the case, 'The outside of the vicarage was watched by constables … By the police evidence there were no less than twenty men scattered about waiting for the offender.'

with the attitude of an innocent man who merely wanted to get on with his day's business, and that had he anything to hide he would have surely returned to the vicarage to dispose of any incriminating evidence. Nonetheless, in the weeks ahead the story grew that George had somehow fled from arrest at his local station – 'A response that cast suspicion on the accused and apprised us that there must have been precisely such anxiety and guilt on his part as had manifested itself throughout,' Captain Anson later remarked, on his return from the grouse moors.

At 8 a.m. that same morning, Inspector Campbell and his men called at the Great Wyrley vicarage, where they quickly relieved the Edaljis of George's linen house coat from the evening before. According to the inspector, this bore clear traces of bloodstains and horse hair, an opinion the family hotly disputed. It was never fully explained why the police believed that Edalji might have ventured out into a raging storm wearing what was essentially a smoking jacket rather than his heavy topcoat. Campbell then asked to see any 'knives' or 'daggers' on the premises, but had to content himself with a small gardening trowel belonging to Maud. Five minutes after the police left one of their party returned, seemingly as an afterthought, to remove a pair of George's damp boots with worn-down heels, allegedly a match to some of the footprints found at the crime scene.

Boasting as it did an Indian cleric, a bolted room, and an attacker who evidently armed himself with an oriental sword, it was all a plot intricate enough to qualify as the basis for a Sherlock Holmes story. At 11 that morning, Inspector Campbell and two other officers arrived at George Edalji's office and placed him under arrest. The accused, who seems to have remained calm throughout, merely remarked that in his opinion it was Loxton, the clerk of the Walsall Court, who was behind the recent outbreak of anonymous letter writing. At 1.30 p.m., Edalji was taken by train to Cannock Police Station and formally charged under the Malicious Damages Act of 1861 with deliberately wounding a horse. Staring ahead, the young solicitor stayed doggedly on theme as he spoke about his family's harassment by Loxton and others over the course of the previous fifteen years. 'I am entirely innocent,' George repeated.

✻ ✻ ✻

If the Edalji case seems to show the dark side of Edwardian society at work, Conan Doyle's progress in these same years represents a model of upward assimilation. The author born in poverty, son of a mentally fragile and fitfully employed alcoholic, would present himself at Buckingham Palace in October 1902 to receive a knighthood. In short order, he also found himself Deputy Lieutenant of Surrey and the organiser of a 300-strong private militia he called the Undershaw Rifle Club. Now in his mid forties, Doyle was to report feeling at the 'absolute top' of his energies and earning power.

There had once been a time when he had been floundering around as a 'feckless young hack', and there was to come a moment when that same writer metamorphosed into an elderly occult propagandist, irascible and dogmatic and open to widespread ridicule. But in between there was a wonderful golden late summer. Doyle was not a man who, having found a winning formula, was content to practise it with little or no variation for the rest of his life, any more than he could stand to be idle for more than a few minutes at a time. He continued to ski at breakneck speed and to play competitive tennis, golf and billiards, enthusiastically strummed the banjo, and in 1902, when he was 43, ascended some 6,000ft in a hot air balloon, an experience that 'thrilled' him and in turn led to his taking to the air in a rickety biplane.

Doyle was also something of a pioneer motorist, paying 400 guineas for a 10-horsepower navy blue Wolseley, in which he bowled around the Surrey countryside dressed in tweed plus fours and a yachting cap, collecting various speeding tickets and once crashing the car as he rounded a corner, leaving his brother Innes and him trapped upside down ('Well, dear boy,' Doyle observed, 'I'm afraid this means a late luncheon') until help arrived. His one obvious disappointment on the games field – and a non-sporting one – came in June 1901 when he appeared for the MCC side in a series of cricket matches at Lord's. Strolling around the ground arm in arm with Jean Leckie in the tea interval, he encountered his younger sister Connie and her husband, the *Raffles* author 'Willie' Hornung. They were not amused that Arthur would choose to parade his mistress while his wife lay gravely ill at home. A subsequent clear-the-air interview at the Hornungs' flat ended acrimoniously. Doyle was left to write to his mother protesting that his own family had behaved 'monstrously' in the matter.

Doyle was equally prolific on the professional level, publishing a new series of Brigadier Gerard adventures in 1902, joining a spirited debate on European free trade (he was against it) in the pages of the *Spectator*, and shooting off some suitably chilling gothic horror stories that combined a working knowledge of medieval torture techniques with a taste for the occult. Sherlock Holmes had also been revived (with a plot apparently suggested by Jean Leckie), though for once *The Strand* had editorial reservations about the new stories, two of which, 'The Norwood Builder' and 'The Solitary Cyclist', got by with no actual crime for Holmes to solve. Certain critics would later carp churlishly that Jean had assumed a creative role in her partner's work not wholly dissimilar to that played by Yoko Ono some sixty-five years later.

In early 1904, Doyle was once again to apparently call 'time' on the Holmes franchise. 'I am tired of [the detective]', he told the *New York Times*:

> I want to do some solid work. Sherlock and [Brigadier] Gerard are all right in their way, but after all, one gets very little satisfaction from such stuff afterward. Nor do I think I shall write any more short stories for some time to come.

Doyle's most ambitious work of the period was his historical novel *Sir Nigel*, a prelude to *The White Company*, which won him mixed reviews but a handsome $25,000 for American serialisation rights. The money would have been welcome, because in May 1906 Conan Doyle's theatrical agent Addison Bright shot himself after it was discovered that he had systematically embezzled some £27,000, most of it from Doyle and James Barrie.

When Louisa died that July, Doyle sank into another period of depression. He began waking at 4 in the morning, unable to sleep, his mind turning over one seemingly insoluble problem after another. It was a compulsive form of torture. 'He afflicted himself for months,' Barrie observed to a mutual theatre colleague:

> Had he done all he could [for] the poor woman? What would become of the children? He became impatient and irritated because of the slowness with which the next phase of life can unfold. He made himself quite unhappy.

It's not beyond the bounds of reason to speculate that Doyle suffered some form of temporary mental impairment during this period. At the very least, it seems fair to say that he would have been unusually receptive to the sort of moral and professional challenge offered by the tragedy of the George Edalji case.

✳ ✳ ✳

Much has been written on whether or not Conan Doyle experienced a full-scale spiritual crisis at this time, and came to lose his religious belief as a result. Most of it concludes that he did. As we've seen, as a young man he was a devout if not strident Roman Catholic. But like many others in the years around the First World War he came to regard the Orthodox Church as repressive and corrupt, and only a few years later he was tearing into the 'Papist tyranny' for its opposition to spiritualism, apparently convinced that he, personally, was being persecuted by 'agents' from Rome. At the same time, Doyle always believed – more so as he immersed himself in the occult – in the concept of an afterlife. In July 1913, he wrote to Hubert Stansbury, the author of a book debunking the idea of man's immortal soul, telling him that he 'trusted utterly' in a spirit that survived the decomposition of the body.

Doyle's wasn't so much a lack of belief in God as a lack of belief in organised religion. There were clearly some specific milestones on his path away from the established Church. Doyle's experience of his Jesuit schoolmasters, and his more inflexibly Catholic relatives; his father's ordeal; and then Louisa's long and wrenching decline can only have fuelled what was already a marked aversion to accepting most forms of received moral wisdom. This process was well on its way by 1907; a decade later it would accelerate as a direct result of the appalling toll taken by the war on his extended family, and led to his final embrace of the worlds of psychic phenomena such as slate writing, spirit photography and fairies. Perhaps it's little wonder traditional Sherlock Holmes fans later wished to say little of Doyle's activities at this time.

When Doyle interested himself in the Edalji affair, therefore, it wasn't necessarily in a way that was larded over with 'religion' or false piety. Nor was he primarily rallying round what he saw as a case of egregious racial prejudice. The author's sympathies could certainly be aroused by, for example, the 'repugnant' way in which he found many black people treated during his visits to the United States. Major James Pond, the promoter of Doyle's American lecture tour in 1894, remembered that his client 'often talked about these things while sitting on a racially [segregated] train running from one city to the next, holding a cigar in one hand and a constantly replenished tumbler in the other'.

Over the years, Doyle frequently spoke out on a range of such issues that engaged his finely tuned senses of honour and justice. In October 1909, for example, he published his 50,000-word booklet *The Crime of the Congo*, railing at conditions in that slave state, and later sat on the London committee of the General Jewish Colonising Organisation as well as several other broadly pro-Zionist groups. But while Doyle was prepared to adopt controversial and often deeply unpopular causes – including a crusade against the execution of his friend Roger Casement following Casement's wartime attempt to run German guns into Ireland – it wasn't always from the perspective of seeking to 'advance universal rights [and] the multicultural ideal', as one later progressive account of his life puts it.

A careful examination of Doyle's major campaigns shows that he had a highly developed social conscience, but not one expressly based on the burning conviction that black people were invariably treated like second-class citizens and suffered an existence wholly separated from their white contemporaries. Reflecting towards the end of his life on the Edalji case, Doyle wrote:

> George … was the son of the Parsee vicar of the parish of Great Wyrley, who had married an English lady. How the vicar came to be a Parsee, or how a Parsee came to be the vicar, I have no idea. Perhaps some catholic-minded patron wished to demonstrate the universality of the Anglican church. The experiment will not, I hope, be repeated.

✳ ✳ ✳

When Captain Anson returned from his holiday to visit the scene of the crime in Great Wyrley, he immediately impressed his authority on the proceedings, allowing reporters and sightseers to inspect the field where the poor horse had been assaulted, pointing out bloodstains on the grass, making statements, inserting himself into photographs, and generally parading around 'to issue instructions [with] an effortless, natural condescension, looking down his prominent nose at men physically taller than himself'.

It's somehow tempting to caricature this society policeman as a sort of Edwardian grandee buffoon, stumbling around the English countryside quaffing port and oppressing the proletariat – like a character out of *Brideshead Revisited* crossed with Inspector Clouseau. But in fact, Anson proved to be a rather diligent investigator by the standards of the day, whatever one makes of his ultimate conclusions. Applying himself to a microscopic study of George Edalji's house coat, he soon announced that there were 'numerous' horse hairs (twenty-nine, in some accounts) to be found concentrated around the left shoulder, although conceding that these were very short and 'not readily seen without a close inspection'. Similarly addressing the point about the myopic George Edalji threading his way through muddy fields to surgically molest livestock in the dead of night, Anson hit on the expedient of covering his own eyes with a thin gauze bandage and retracing the same route. His official report to the Home Office of 22 December 1903 remarked that he had found it 'a curiously easy walk, and especially to anyone who knows the ground'.

Doyle was unconvinced. Anson had shown none of Holmes's forensic acuity and passion for detail, either in properly securing the crime scene or later. As a result, the field had quickly become a kind of 'combined carnival and picnic ground, [where] onlookers came for a pleasant summer day's outing,' Doyle complained. The disputed jacket should surely have been handed to a 'referee – the police doctor, or any other doctor,' he added, and samples of the alleged hair sealed in an envelope for analysis by both prosecution and defence experts. Instead of this elementary precaution, Edalji's clothes had simply been carried off by the police, who then wrapped them in the same brown paper package as a strip of the dead animal's hide on their way to the laboratory.

Although the coat showed 'two stains in the centre of the right cuff, each about the size of a three-penny bit,' and the police doctor determined these to be mammalian, Doyle countered that 'not even the most adept operator who ever lived' would be able to rip up a beast of that size without being liberally drenched in blood. 'The idea is beyond argument,' he announced definitively. Much of the other physical evidence could be equally quickly disposed of, even by the technology available at the time. During their search of the Great Wyrley vicarage, Inspector Campbell and his men had seized a set of straight razors belonging to Reverend Edalji. 'Some were said to be wet – a not uncommon condition when a man has recently shaved,' Doyle noted witheringly. 'Dark spots' were observed on the back of one of the razors, but even the police were forced to conclude that these were nothing more sinister than rust stains.

* * *

Sherlock Holmes is a master of the specific. Time and again, the detective's case book shows that under sufficiently intelligent examination, the facts of a crime, far from being meaningless, will inescapably assemble themselves into a revelatory pattern; sheer, accumulated detail gets him there in the end. But Holmes is also quite adept at the broader art of profiling a criminal. More often than not, he's able to recognise and identify various telltale habits or characteristics of the guilty party before actually bringing him to justice. Like his author, Holmes clings to the notion that life has purpose – the perpetrators of most outrages aren't normal men and women somehow temporarily driven out of their minds, but inherently corrupt, venal or demented social misfits acting out their twisted moral concept of life.

Here, then, was Doyle seeking to establish the true identity of the culprit in the Edalji case:

> I have no doubt at all [he] is a lunatic, and his destination should be not a prison, but an asylum. The religious mania … is the index of a family weakness which becomes a diabolically mischievous madness … He will be found, when exposed, to be a man of eccentric life and character, with periodic accessions of actual madness, during which he loses all prudence and control … Such a man is a danger to the community in which he lives, as no one can say what turn his destructive propensities may take. That he still lives in the Midlands [here Doyle, as Holmes, reverts to the detail] is made feasible by the postmarks of two of the [recent] letters. I trust that it will not be long before he is under medical supervision.

A cliché now, when it's routine procedure for the FBI and other investigative agencies, this sort of psychological analysis shows Doyle's originality at the time. Like Holmes, he realised both the necessity of getting into the criminal's mindset, and the danger of proceeding from there without adequate evidence. In this respect, at least, we can say that there was scarcely any distinction at all between 'the doll' and its maker.

✳ ✳ ✳

On his way to Birmingham Station after his arrest, George Edalji turned to Inspector Campbell and said, 'I am not surprised at this. I have been expecting it for some time.' The police made some play of this remark at Edalji's trial, preferring to interpret it in the light of a guilty man confessing his crime, rather than of a completely blameless party acknowledging their own preconceived bias. Similarly, Edalji later told officers, 'I won't have bail, and when the next horse is killed, it won't be by me'. The prosecuting counsel also quoted this remark at trial, with the suggestion that 'the prisoner knew perfectly well what he was about when he said it' – the inference being that some accomplice of Edalji's would commit a fresh outrage while his friend was incarcerated, thus clearing him of the crime. Oddly enough, something similar did happen: another horse was found disembowelled, although the prosecution quickly accommodated itself to this development by claiming that George Edalji was the mastermind of a gang of maniacal local animal-rippers.

Confronted with these same facts, Conan Doyle had a very different perspective on them. 'Edalji believed that there was a strong conspiracy against him,' Doyle wrote:

> In the face of the letters he had every reason to believe so. So long as he was in his cell he was safe, so he thought, from this conspiracy. Perhaps another crime would be committed, and in that case, he thought, in the innocence of his heart, that it would clear him … In his wildest dream he could never have imagined that such a crime would be fitted in as a link in the chain against him.

Doyle was equally unmoved by the fine detail of the police inquiry, which he characterised as conducted 'not for the purpose of discovering the truth, but for the purpose of accumulating evidence against George Edalji'.

Among other defects in the Crown case, Doyle pointed to the significant absence of bloodstained razors, or weapons of any sort, at the Great Wyrley vicarage; the hotly disputed matter of the late appearing twenty-nine alleged horse hairs; and the fact that the mud scraped from Edalji's clothes and boots was of a completely different type of soil than that found at the crime scene.

There was also the issue of sheer physical practicality. As we've seen, the best expert opinion was that the horse had been assaulted at some stage between 2 and 6 a.m. on the morning of 18 August, a time at which Reverend Edalji swore his son had been sleeping in his bed just a few feet away from him. It's true that the reverend testified that he himself had been asleep until around 4 a.m. So, in theory, George could have risen at some point between 2 and 4 that morning and, succumbing to a sudden atavistic frenzy, dressed and armed himself, unlocked the bedroom door, tiptoed undetected out of the house and into the storm, made his way in the dark through half a dozen fields, crossed over the main London and North Western Railway line, expertly mauled the horse, and then retraced his steps, all without being seen by the policemen stationed around the vicarage, or its immediate grounds, specifically for the purpose of watching him. This is exactly what the prosecution alleged had happened, and Edalji paid the full penalty of the law as a result. But for the critical fact that this was real life, it all resembled the sort of classic 'locked door' mystery beloved of Sherlock Holmes.

✳ ✳ ✳

On Monday, 24 August, George Edalji arrived for his preliminary hearing at Cannock Police Court, although 'arrived' somehow fails to convey a progress that combined elements of a municipal street party with the overall atmosphere of a lynching in the American south. Most of the local mining community was on its summer leave (in those days, taken at home), which only added to the general melee. By 8 that morning, 200–300 people had massed tightly at the courthouse door for a glimpse of the accused, who eventually drew up in a four-wheeled police cab with a clutch of excited small children clinging to the rear.

Local opinion appeared divided between the curious or obsessed on the one hand, and the unappreciative or vocally hostile on the other. As Edalji alighted, the mob pressed forward and somehow wrenched the cab door from its hinges, although most contemporary reports note the generally 'high-spirited' and 'festive' nature of the occasion.

The hearing itself was brief, and largely concerned with the question of bail. Captain Anson had some objection to this, so Edalji was returned to the jail in Stafford. Outside the courtroom, Reverend Edalji told waiting reporters, 'You may as well live in Turkey', which might have the resonance today of 'North Korea'. Both then and now, there was some misconception about the nature of the charges against the accused. Despite several exaggerated newspaper reports, there were just two initial indictments: one accused Edalji of wounding a pony, and the other of writing a single threatening note to the police. The Crown quickly decided to drop the latter, although in the event the whole fifteen-year saga of the anonymous letters, and their authorship, would prove a central part of the trial. It remains debatable whether or not it was legally proper for the prosecution to offer quite as much evidence as it did about an offence which was not at issue.

At the subsequent hearing of 31 August, Edalji surprised both the court and, apparently, his own family by refusing bail when it was offered to him. Here, to Captain Anson, was the first telltale sign of a prearranged conspiracy to fabricate an alibi. On 21 September, the crime was duly committed: another work horse was found maimed, the property of a local farming family named Green. Nineteen-year-old Harry Green, the farmer's son, eventually confessed to the offence. He and Edalji were acquainted, although there was no evidence that they were particularly close, or for that matter had colluded together.

A week later, young Green changed his mind and declared that he was innocent; the confession had been 'bullied out of [him] by the law'. Perhaps he had tried to kill the family's horse, he conceded, but only because it had previously been injured and he wanted to put it out of its pain. Curiously enough, the Greens had also received a number of anonymous letters following the assault. Some threatened further attacks, while others offered to identify the members of the 'Great Wyrley gang' for a consideration of £20 paid in cash. The correspondence was shown to Inspector Campbell, who thought the writing closely resembled George Edalji's, though even he admitted to 'practical concerns' when asked how Edalji could have dispatched the letters from his jail cell.

On 23 October 1903, George Edalji was convicted at Staffordshire Quarter Assizes of the crime of cattle mutilation. The jury took only forty-eight minutes to reach its verdict. Three minutes later, the assistant chairman of the sessions, who presided at the trial, returned from the room where he and his four colleagues had gone to give 'full and due' deliberation to their sentence. 'You have been found guilty of this very serious charge, and as we think, very properly,' he told Edalji, who stood facing him at attention between two warders:

> Now we have to consider what punishment to award you. On the one hand, we take fully into consideration your position and what this means to you; on the other hand, we have to consider the state of the county of Stafford and the neighbourhood of Great Wyrley, and the disgrace which has been inflicted on us and that neighbourhood by the condition of things.

'Your sentence is penal servitude for seven years,' he then informed the prisoner. On hearing this, Edalji shuddered slightly, raised his eyes to the ceiling, and said nothing. It was reported that he had nodded respectfully to the bench as he was then led out to begin his sentence, which was served first at Lewes and then at Portland prison.

In the days ahead, several newspapers would go on to speculate about Edalji's lack of outward emotion on learning his fate. According to the *Birmingham*

Gazette, it was all a case of oriental inscrutability – or 'a vain mind couched in mystery' – while to the comparative religion experts at the *Lichfield Mercury* the prisoner at the bar had simply gone into a 'typically Hindoo hypnotic trance' on hearing the news. It was left to the *Daily Mail* to add the anthropometric detail that Edalji was plainly a 'degenerate of the worst type. The shape of his jaw and mouth are those of a man of very debased life.'

5

'YOU NEVER FORGET THE FIRST NICK OF THE RAZOR'

Investigative journalists, historians and at least one world-renowned contemporary novelist have all focused on the flawed nature of the evidence presented against George Edalji at his trial. There is no absolute proof of any conspiratorial intent – whether involving the police, the prosecution, the Home Office, or what's broadly termed 'the Establishment' – but there are certainly signs of what Doyle called 'extraordinary conduct' and 'stupidity' by the various authorities. That there was a rush to judgement is obvious to any unbiased observer; arrested on the same morning as the maiming occurred, Edalji was already serving his lengthy sentence for the crime nine weeks later. Many critical witnesses were overlooked, many paths were not explored and alternative suspects not pursued, and glaring discrepancies in the physical evidence either missed or deliberately ignored.

Those responsible for these decisions would say the right man was nonetheless convicted. Yet the irony of the hurried investigation and ensuing verdict against Edalji is that they allowed the case to rumble on for years to come, with Conan Doyle leading the charge for the defence. It's clear that he felt a strong personal engagement with the accused, who aroused not only his professional interest but also the very real sympathy he characteristically reserved for the underdog. While some of his reasoning may seem slower, and his forensic abilities less refined, than those of the icily logical Sherlock Holmes, in the end Doyle proved to be the superior mind of the two.

※　※　※

On 8 September 1903, Edalji had returned to Cannock Police Court for his committal hearing on the charge of wounding a horse. Even this relatively routine procedure provided one of those flashes of sudden insight or recognition beloved of fictional crime dramas. According to the *Wolverhampton Star*:

> Edalji came up fresh and cheerful from a night in the police cells, and walked briskly into court. He was greeted affectionately by his father, the Vicar of Great Wyrley, and also by his mother.
>
> The prisoner's favourite attitude, leaning back with arms folded and legs crossed, revealed very plainly the curious wearing down of the heels of his boots, which forms an important link in the chain of evidence against him …
>
> A constable named Cooper described the curious footprints found near the wounded horse and [leading] towards the vicarage. The heel-marks, he said, were noticeably broad and very short. He took the left boot of the pair obtained from the vicarage – identical to those now worn by Edalji in court – and made impressions in the mud next to the footprints. The two sets of impressions corresponded exactly in size, shape and in the heel peculiarity.

Under cross-examination, Constable Cooper acknowledged that a number of people had walked randomly around the crime scene before he had been able to make his impressions in the mud there, but that nonetheless he remained confident of his findings. There had then been some discussion of the anonymous letters, which were not part of the criminal complaint, apparently in order to establish an atmosphere of moral turpitude around the Edaljis.

Inspector Campbell took the stand to describe a visit to the Great Wyrley vicarage, during which the defendant had seemed to him 'more interested in the malicious communications than would appear natural for any purely innocent young man'. Since George had by then been on the receiving end of the hate mail for fifteen years, on and off, it might be argued that for him not to have been curious about it would have been the stranger reaction. At that stage, the prosecution introduced its star witness – one Thomas Gurrin, the same Treasury handwriting expert whose courtroom evidence in 1896 had helped convict the innocent Adolf Beck of allegedly swindling a series of women out of their valuables. Unabashed, Gurrin now testified that a number of the anonymous letters he had examined in this case 'show the same peculiarities as those which the police had received in Edalji's own script. [He] was of the opinion they were written by the same hand.'

At the conclusion of the prosecution case, Edalji had risen from his table, said simply, 'I am perfectly innocent and prefer to reserve my defence', and then sat down again.

Of the subsequent trial it's perhaps enough to say that the prosecution skilfully rehearsed its theories about the state of the defendant's coat, trousers and boots as they appeared on the morning of 18 August; again raised the matter of his wet razors, allegedly freshly wiped clean of blood; and revisited the long history of the poison letters. Conan Doyle would not be the only one to later wonder whether it was proper under English evidence law for Edalji's presumed role in the mail-writing campaign to be used to help convict him of the maiming, which was the sole offence he was tried for.

The prosecuting counsel neatly pre-empted the argument that the defendant had been in custody at the time of the assault on the Greens' horse, and thus was innocent of all other such offences. Edalji was merely the lynchpin of a gang of ruthless conspirators 'go[ing] about the countryside looking for prey', the court heard, although, when asked, Captain Anson couldn't immediately say when, if ever, the police might make further arrests in the case.

Edalji's defence, it has to be said, lacked some of the polish and self-assurance of the prosecution side. There was a spirited rebuttal of the bloodstain evidence, and the accused, called to the box, vehemently denied any knowledge of the maiming or of the anonymous letters. But no mention was made of Edalji's poor eyesight, which Doyle, the former oculist, would insist rendered him unfit to commit the crime he was accused of.

In later testimony, the jury was asked what possible motive the young lawyer might have had for periodically abandoning his 'irreproachable and scholarly' attitude to life for that of the homicidal fiend. It was a valid point. The defence's frequent references to the corruptibility of the police were, however, perhaps counter-productive. There might well be 'occasional excesses and individual lapses', the *Star* admitted, but in 1903 public confidence in the British judicial system, and in uniformed authority as a whole, remained high among all classes of society. It would be at least another generation before the catastrophic shock of the Great War began to undermine some of the certainties of the age.

However procedurally diligent they may have been, and notwithstanding Doyle's later tribute to their 'most amicable, refined and accomplished chairman', it has also to be said that the Stafford Quarterly Assizes were not ideally suited to the challenge of trying George Edalji. The small downstairs courtroom, more used to serving as a forum for disputes involving matters of poaching or petty rural theft, rapidly took on some of the characteristics of a particularly animated county fair combined with those of a circus sideshow. A large crowd of would-be spectators gathered each morning outside the front door, and to service them street vendors marched briskly to and fro bearing trays of refreshments. Early on the first day a scuffle broke out, and two otherwise 'reputable individuals attire[d] in bicycling garb' plunged through a plate-glass window in a debate about their respective positions in the queue which had formed on the courthouse steps.

Meanwhile, local opinion appeared divided on the specifics of the case. One middle-aged lady arrived wearing a straw hat customised with a slogan indicating how positively she would respond to George Edalji's acquittal, while others in the crowd shouted, 'Lock him up!' and its coarser variants. It all had the makings of a first-class tabloid celebrity frenzy, so far as one could ever be said to have existed in the typical English provincial market town of 1903.

In fact, there is a mass of evidence from contemporary newspapers and other accounts of the trial that the great majority of local people, not only those who crowded around the assizes, but ordinary residents as well, believed that Edalji, either acting alone or as part of a conspiracy, was guilty as charged. It could hardly have been otherwise. The maimings were still fresh in everyone's memory, and many of those jostling for admission to the courtroom had personally witnessed the gory crime scene. It was not difficult for them to imagine the peculiar-looking young Asian committing the outrage for some obscure reason presumably rooted in the sadistic traditions of the East. The folk tales of the murderous Thuggee gangs active for centuries in India, and the more recent history of terrorist attacks on British officials there, gave substance to the popular belief that the 'Hindoo' was intrinsically more predisposed to maniacal and savage acts of violence than the white man.

Even so, Edalji received at least a passably fair hearing within the constraints of the law. The presiding judge, Sir Reginald Hardy, had by then had a long and distinguished legal career spanning nearly thirty years. Born in 1848 (a direct descendant of the vice admiral of 'Kiss me, Hardy' fame), he'd taken a first-class degree at Oxford before qualifying as a barrister at London's Inner Temple. After marrying Lucy Gladstone, the prime minister's niece, Hardy had been lucky enough to successively hold office as the High Sherriff of Staffordshire, a JP, and more recently as presiding magistrate of the quarterly sessions. He was also a church warden, a charity commissioner, and a lieutenant colonel of his county's yeomanry.

With a few rare exceptions, Hardy is agreed to have been knowledgeable and personally unassuming – in other words, exactly the sort of conscientious public servant and imperial conservative Conan Doyle might normally have warmed to. In one popular account of the Edalji case, Hardy is depicted as a 'legal lightweight' whose control of the trial alternated between incompetence and flagrant prejudice against the defendant. This is not quite fair. When, for instance, the prosecution came to quote Edalji's remark that he had been 'expecting [his arrest] for some time', Hardy was at pains to point out that this was more consistent with innocence than guilt. Regarding a possible motive for the crime, he made the eminently sane assertion that, 'We may never know why some offences occur'. Just as there was such a thing as the inexplicable suicide, he added, so there was the unaccountable need of a 'small but dangerous few' to inflict harm on others.

When the time came for his summing-up, Hardy told the jury that there had been failures on the part of the police to protect the crime scene, or to properly use the footprint evidence that resulted, and that they were to carefully consider whether or not the handwriting expert had been entirely convincing. On retiring, they would be provided with writing samples to compare for themselves, as well as with detailed maps of the Great Wyrley area. There were other remarks that seemed to favour the prosecution case, too, but taken as a whole this was not the summation of a 'red-faced old county buffoon sputtering bile against the accused' as he's been called. It's true that Hardy and his colleagues took only minutes to consider Edalji's fate once the guilty verdict against him had been returned. It's also true that their sentence of seven years, while not lenient, was just half the maximum total allowed by law.

✳ ✳ ✳

There was an immediate and sustained, if not universal, campaign which presented Edalji as the victim of an appalling miscarriage of justice, and demanded that he be given a pardon. An early advocate was the maverick figure of 58-year-old Roger Dawson-Yelverton (hereafter 'Yelverton'), a Welsh-born former deputy judge of the West London Courts and Chief Justice of the Bahamas, and now – following his removal from the latter post for malpractice – a colourful if not always professionally successful barrister. Yelverton's specialty was the wrongly convicted, for whom he perhaps felt an affinity; his own dismissal from the bench drove him into 'ill-paid exile, drink, despondency and a belief in the occult', it's been said.

He was soon able to organise a petition for Edalji's freedom, which attracted more than 10,000 signatures. *The Times* reported that an 'impressively high percentage [were] those of eminent jurists'. Yelverton in time presented this document to the Home Secretary, who from December 1905 was none other than Herbert Gladstone, son of the late premier and thus a cousin by marriage of Edalji's trial judge. Senior civil servants reviewed the case, but concluded that there were no compelling grounds for exercising the royal prerogative, which remained the only available means of a pardon prior to the establishment of a unified Court of Criminal Appeal in 1907.

Among other things, Yelverton pointed out that there had been at least three further animal maimings carried out following Edalji's conviction, 'but that in each case, every injury is said by the police to be accidental and attributable to barbed wire or some concealed danger'. Meanwhile, the London barrister Sir George Lewis, a more orthodox champion of seemingly lost causes (and the model for Sir Robert Morton in Terence Rattigan's play *The Winslow Boy*) also wrote to the Home Secretary protesting Edalji's innocence.

One of the case's most engaging moments came when Lewis and Gladstone later found themselves discussing the matter over a glass of mulled wine while dressed respectively as the prophet Moses and an Egyptian pharaoh, as gold-painted servants fanned them with large feathers, during the course of Lewis's annual Christmas costume ball at his home in London's Portland Place. Even this singular line of attack failed to secure Edalji's release. The barrister and Liberal MP Robert More also made representations in the case, but these broke down following More's unexpected death in November 1903 at the age of 67.

Early in 1904, Charlotte Edalji sat down to send a letter to some 300 of Britain's leading public figures. She told those among them who had already expressed their misgivings about George's conviction, 'My husband, daughter,

THE MAN WHO WOULD BE SHERLOCK

and I are deeply grateful to hear that you are kindly enquiring into the matter of what we feel to be a cruel, and unjust sentence on one who is innocent.' (There was no mention of the views of the Edaljis' younger son Horace on his brother's imprisonment.) George was 'thoroughly fond of his profession', she continued:

> I am an English woman, and I feel that there is among many people a prejudice against those who are not English, and I cannot help feeling that it is owing to that prejudice that my boy has been falsely accused.

Mrs Edalji concluded by asking that the letter's recipients 'help us with your influence, and that our son may be restored to us soon'. Although the family's heartfelt appeal went out to a 'very wide section of the great people in England … concerned with the structure and fate of society … and informed or wishing to become informed about grave matters of justice', there is no evidence that Doyle himself received a copy.

Meanwhile, the subject of this plea would go on to serve just less than three years of his seven-year sentence. Edalji spent his first ten months of confinement at the Victorian red-brick Lewes Jail, which he later agreed was 'not pleasant'. In August 1904, he was transferred to Portland, off the Dorset coast, although unlike Adolf Beck before him he was at least spared the worst horrors of the local rock quarry. Instead, possibly as a sardonic commentary on his crime, Edalji was engaged for ten hours a day patching up feeding bags for horses, before eventually being assigned 'light duties' which mainly consisted of picking threads of coir fibre out of a large pile and passing these to a fellow inmate to sew into doormats. At some stage it was discovered that Edalji's eyesight was poor, and as a result he slept in a medical ward at night.

During his time in custody it also emerged that he had left behind certain debts in civilian life, including an unpaid bill of £340 (£22,000 today) from a London stockbroker. The magazine *Outlook* would speculate that Edalji had undergone a sort of metamorphosis, something like that in a modern-day werewolf film, in order to commit his crimes. Had this 'seemingly innocuous [and] blinking little man' become 'for a few hours paganised and returned to the Orient?' they wondered. Set against this was a series of barnstorming editorials starting in early 1905 in the weekly *Truth*, the *National Enquirer* of its day, which not so much defended Edalji as roundly attacked the police and trial proceedings.

The Home Office eventually relented and in 1906 ordered the prisoner's transfer to Pentonville, followed by his conditional release. It was noted that Edalji had put on weight during his time in custody, and looked a little flabby. His regulation dark suit was buttoned tightly at the waist. Now aged 30, Edalji emerged to announce that the prison officials, at least at Portland, had been 'kindness itself'. During the previous three years, his mother and sister had managed to visit him at roughly monthly intervals; his father and brother never did.

✳ ✳ ✳

Following his wife's death in July 1906, Conan Doyle is generally thought to have simply vanished from sight, resurfacing only after several months of solitary introspection. There is no doubt that he underwent a period of deep and prolonged mourning, but recent research questions whether he did so entirely alone.

As early as 3 August, Doyle felt able to meet his mistress Jean Leckie for a weekend at the well-appointed Ashdown Forest Hotel, about 40 miles east of Hindhead on the Kent–Sussex border. Four days later, he joined in a vigorous debate in the pages of the *Daily Express* about whether Britain was becoming a more or less religious society; taking a progressive view of the matter, his verdict was that 'men of all creeds should be [free to] live in amity and charity'. On the 10th of the month, Doyle drove over to join Jean Leckie for dinner at her family home in south London. Writing to 'the Mam' on 6 September, Doyle remarked that he had just received a note from Jean's mother 'which gave me much pleasure', that he felt drawn to writing a sequel to his prizefighting novel *Rodney Stone*, and that in the meantime he would be on holiday at a Scottish country hotel where 'there is good air and golf & cricket – all of which I need'.

Even so, there's no doubt that Louisa's death triggered one of the rare periods of relative sloth in a life of otherwise iron self-discipline and constant industry. 'Nothing could exceed his energy when the working fit was upon him,' Conan Doyle had written of Holmes in *A Study in Scarlet*, 'but now and again a reaction would seize him, and for days on end he would lie upon the sofa in the sitting-room, hardly uttering a word or moving a muscle from morning to night.' This broadly fits the pattern of Doyle's own life as he cast about for a new project to throw himself into in the autumn of 1906.

And now the game was afoot. Within days of reading of George Edalji's release from custody, Doyle had extracted and reviewed the trial records and arranged to meet Edalji himself in London. Striding through the lobby of the Grand Hotel, Charing Cross, for their appointment, the one-time eye specialist extended a 'bear-like hand' and greeted his guest with the Holmesian observation, 'You suffer from astigmatic myopia, I see'. It was as dramatic an opening gambit as anything in Doyle's fiction, and his subsequent investigation was equally assured in its demolition of the police case.

Just as Holmes cannot 'live without brainwork', we're told, so his author now sprang back to life with his familiar mixture of cold, scientific logic and warm, chivalric sympathy on behalf of the underdog. Convinced that 'I was in the presence of an appalling tragedy', which in all likelihood owed more to the victim's race than any compelling evidence against him, Conan Doyle went public on 11 January 1907 with the first of a two-part, 18,000-word dialectical blast against the stupidity and shortcomings of the official investigation, called simply, 'The Story of Mr George Edalji'.

Both then and in the months that followed, Doyle dwelt at length on the matter of Edalji's physical unsuitability to commit the crime he was convicted of. It formed the opening argument of his articles, which were initially published in *The Daily Telegraph* and widely reprinted by other papers before being collected into a pamphlet. 'I had been delayed and he was passing the time by reading the paper,' Doyle wrote of his meeting Edalji:

> I recognised my man by his dark face, so I stood and observed him. He held the paper close to his eyes and rather sideways, proving not only a high degree of myopia, but marked astigmatism. The idea of such a man scouring fields at night and assaulting cattle while avoiding the watching police was ludicrous to anyone who can imagine what the world looks like to eyes with myopia of eight diopters.

So far so good for the logical, self-confident approach to the case, but perhaps the eyesight evidence was less compelling than Conan Doyle first thought. In the following days, the *Telegraph* hosted a lively debate on the issue. 'I must take exception to the statement that eight diopters [of myopia] is a very extraordinary amount,' an optician named James Aitchison wrote:

> On reference to my record of 1,000 cases of short sight I find that nearly 200 equal or exceed that amount, and probably in an ophthalmic surgeon's casebook,

dealing as he would mostly with diseased conditions, the percentage would be greater ... There are many persons wearing concave lenses of from ten to 15 diopters power, and getting almost full visual acuity.

There was considerably more in this vein. A doctor in Hove named I.A. Barry concurred with Mr Aitchison. He wrote:

I personally happen to have the misfortune to suffer from myopic astigmatism in a degree which is actually greater by about one dioptric than Mr Edalji's, and yet with correcting glasses my vision is brought up to almost exactly normal. If mine, why not Edalji's?

Similarly, a Mr A.H. Henderson-Livesey of London chided Doyle and suggested that he 'apply to the case more accurately the methods of "deductive analysis" of his great creation'. Edalji might be weak-sighted now, Mr Livesey allowed:

But what proof is advanced that [he] was in that condition when the crimes were committed? A man with slightly defective eyesight may well become blind in the space of three years, especially when those years are passed in confinement ... Why was this evidence not called at [Edalji's] trial? Because, whatever may be the condition of the man's eyes now, he certainly was not blind, or nearly blind, three years ago.

There followed a deluge of correspondence – from, among others, a Mr Lestrade and a Mrs Watson – that battered the letter pages of the *Telegraph* and other papers like a particularly violent tornado. To Sydney Stephenson, editor of *Ophthalmoscope* magazine, 'Assuming that Edalji was familiar with the countryside, and active in his movements, it seems to me that the short-sight from which he suffered would handicap him but little in his errand'. Meanwhile, Captain Anson, writing direct to the Home Office, moved from optometry closer to the realm of the supernatural. Edalji, he informed his civil service colleagues, possessed 'a panther-like gait and eyes that [come] out with a strange sort of glow, like a cat's, in a low light'.

This was far from the end of the whole protracted debate about George Edalji's eyesight and his physical health generally. Much of the public correspondence on the subject rang with the thrill of the writers' own 'self-deluded cleverness,' Doyle remarked. There was such a thing as being too sure of yourself, his critics replied. 'Whereas Sherlock Holmes realise[d] he needed to always be learning, his author assumes no such obligation,' Captain Anson later told a reporter.

After acquainting himself with Edalji, on 3 January 1907 Conan Doyle took the train to Cannock, where over the course of the next two days he visited the scene of the crime, met with most of the principals involved in the case and arranged to interview Captain Anson. 'That brings me to what is the most painful part of my statement, and the one which I would be most glad to shirk were it possible for me to do so,' Doyle wrote in the *Telegraph*:

> No account of the case is complete which does not deal with the attitude taken up by Capt. Anson against this unhappy young man … I have no doubt [he] was quite honest in his dislike, and unconscious of his own prejudice. It would be folly to think otherwise. But men in his position have no right to yield to such feelings. They are too powerful, others are too weak, and the consequences are too terrible.

As proof of this pre-existing bias on the part of the police, Doyle quoted an officer, who may have been either Captain Anson or Sergeant Upton, as having remarked to Reverend Edalji as long ago as 1892, 'You may tell your son at once that I will not believe any profession of ignorance', and 'I will endeavour to get the offender a dose of penal servitude'.

Anson, publicly denying any impropriety, privately expressed doubts about Doyle's sanity. For the three hours of their meeting, he had 'never ceased issuing instructions, making demands, requesting papers, calling in [my] sergeant and giving him orders'. It was as though his visitor had been the king himself, rather than merely a famous writer. Anson was a Sherlock Holmes devotee, and he seems to have struggled hard to make allowance for the character's author. As a result, we can question the captain's professional judgement, but not his manners. 'Since I took up the case I have myself had a considerable correspondence with Anson,' Doyle wrote later:

> The letters are so courteous to me personally that it makes it exceedingly difficult for me to use for the purpose of illustrating my thesis – viz, the strong opinion which Anson had formed against the Edalji family. One odd example of this is that during fifteen years that the vicarage has been a centre of debate,

the captain has never once visited the spot or taken counsel personally with the inmates.

… although perhaps Doyle had forgotten Anson's role in investigating the school key that had mysteriously appeared on the vicarage doorstep one night in December 1892, in the course of which he closely interviewed both Reverend Edalji and his son.

A curious incident occurred at about the time Conan Doyle was writing his articles for *The Daily Telegraph* and preparing to submit a petition to the Home Office. There was another outbreak of mischievous letter writing in Great Wyrley. Signed by a 'Martin Molton', the new correspondence displayed considerable familiarity with daily life at the vicarage, and suggested that George had colluded with a family member in perpetrating the hoaxes of 1892–95 – a campaign, it will be remembered, that had included a flurry of faked newspaper advertisements, as well as unflattering printed references to the reverend's sex life. 'Molton' was also intimate with the details of George's debts, and referred cryptically to Charlotte Edalji having once sought a divorce from her husband. Taken as a whole, it was agreed that the letters, most of which were addressed to Captain Anson, showed a high degree of knowledge about the affairs of many of those closely connected to the case over the previous two decades. Some eighty years later, a June 1907 memo by the then Home Secretary Herbert Gladstone was discovered, and revealed that a member of George Edalji's own legal team had wondered if his client might have 'played some role' in the various letter campaigns, as opposed to the horse maimings. On reading the Molton correspondence, the lawyer in question is supposed to have remarked, 'He is at it again'.

In the following weeks, Captain Anson addressed himself to the source of these latest letters. He came to believe that the 24-year-old 'spinster Maud Edalgi [*sic*]' was the likely culprit, if only to the extent of taking down her elder brother's dictation. In time, Molton offered to meet the police if £2 was left for him in an envelope at a post office box in central London. This was done, and a plain-clothes detective assigned to keep watch and arrest anyone who showed up for the money.

On 19 January 1907, George Edalji, accompanied by Roger Yelverton, duly appeared at the post office and tried to claim a separate letter in which they insisted Molton had promised to reveal the name of the pony assailant of 1903. The police heard out this story and released the pair without charge. The Molton letters then ceased.

* * *

Conan Doyle's visits to Great Wyrley in the winter of 1907 mixed elements of a conventional Sherlock Holmes field trip with the author's own 'fiery conviction', as he put it, that an innocent man had been persecuted largely because of the colour of his skin. Doyle's investigation thus proceeded with a combination of deductive talent and moral outrage. Holmes himself would have recognised the latter trait, if only to dismiss it from his mind. 'It is of the first importance not to allow your judgement to be biased by personal qualities,' he admonishes Dr Watson in *The Sign of the Four*:

> A client is to me a mere unit, a factor in a problem. The emotional qualities are antagonistic to clear reasoning. I assure you that the most winning woman I ever knew was hanged for poisoning three children for their insurance-money, and the most repellent man of my acquaintance is a philanthropist who has spent nearly a quarter of a million upon the London poor.

It must be said that Doyle himself sometimes fell short of this objective ideal, but otherwise proved an able and determined investigator, compensating for any technical shortcomings by using his narrative gifts to present the case for Edalji in a clear, methodical, and, to many, convincing argument.

As if to emphasise his emotional commitment to the case, there are at least two accounts of Conan Doyle's investigation giving way to significant displays of anger. Both outbursts were the result of being contradicted. The first came when Doyle walked the route between the Great Wyrley vicarage and the scene of the pony slashing of 1903, and as a result informed Captain Anson that George Edalji would have been 'physically unable to grope about there' after dark. The captain replied that a Home Office specialist who examined Edalji's eyes had found nothing much wrong with them – and besides, he, Edalji, had 'had plenty of practise roaming those same fields at night'. At that, Doyle had turned 'beet red', Anson recalled. 'Let me tell you something about the condition of astigmatic myopia,' the one-time doctor began. The rebuke that Anson endured, according to his later account, was no ordinary one. It was epic, delivered by Doyle 'in such a way that a schoolteacher might have chastised a wayward or unusually tiresome child'. Doyle himself was the competent authority here, was the gist of it, and the official policeman 'merely a foot soldier', if that, in the campaign to learn the truth.

A second hour of fury that lived on in Anson's mind came when the two men had found themselves discussing the sleeping arrangements that prevailed at the Great Wyrley vicarage. The captain repeated the remark that he had made in a private letter a few days earlier. 'The father had his son sleep in his room for many years, with the door locked,' Anson factually noted, before adding, 'The reason has not been given'. Conan Doyle replied that there was nothing mysterious about that, and Anson again contradicted him, saying, 'We can only guess at the motive'. Doyle seems to have interpreted this as a veiled accusation of sexual impropriety involving the Reverend and George Edalji. In any case, it caused him to again flush bright red, and to turn furiously on his host. According to Anson, Doyle, 'his eyes flaring', then remarked that he would prefer 'not to again hear such a vile canard', and 'would not be entirely responsible for his actions' were it repeated.

As a rule, Doyle tended to do better in the role of the absolute master of events rather than any lesser capacity. He acknowledged this fact when, a few years later, trying to enlist for active duty on the outbreak of the First World War. 'I should love the work,' he told his brother Innes, 'and would try to be subordinate – which is my failing.' It was characteristic, then, that on his arrival in Great Wyrley Doyle should promptly grill the local police on a whole series of procedural shortcomings and technical oversights on their part. Why had they not taken precise casts of the footprints leading to and from the crime scene on the morning of 18 August? What precautions had been made to protect the area from being trampled underfoot by curious onlookers? How could it ever have been thought proper to wrap George Edalji's coat together with a piece of the dead animal's hide in the same package, prior to sending them off for analysis? Had the word 'contamination' occurred to anyone?

This was the sort of direct, Holmesian line of attack that represented the material side of Doyle's investigation. He simultaneously made the most specific of allegations of official misconduct (some of which extended to accusing the police of tampering with evidence) and sketched out a broader vision of events in which 'the Establishment', as personified by Captain Anson, had covered its own systematic failings by persecuting an innocent young man. In so doing, Doyle mastered the art of the rhetorical campaigner for justice by appearing at once concerned about individual lapses on the part of the authorities, and attentive to the larger drama that cast Edalji as the victim of a monstrous conspiracy.

Conan Doyle thus became a particularly active investigator, striding briskly around the muddy fields of Great Wyrley, 'a tall, broad-shouldered man, tweed-clad, energetically smoking a cigar,' in one account. There is no mention of him ever specifically wearing a deerstalker cap or an Inverness cape, but at least one report suggests that at some point Doyle had leant down in the presence of several bystanders to study the grass underfoot with a magnifying glass, thus giving the onlookers instant visual gratification: this was what they had come to see. While in the area he also called on several local residents to canvass their opinions about the whole affair.

Although there was no shortage of alternative suspects, he appears to have been struck by the frequency with which Edalji himself was named as the guilty party. One woman remarked that 'the Hindoo' had for years marched confidently around the place, often at night, routinely travelled in and out of Birmingham by train, qualified as a lawyer, and had even written a book – none of them activities associated with a man who could barely see his hand in front of his face. More than one of those he interviewed told Doyle that the maiming of animals was more common in rural counties than he might suppose. Such things happened, he heard, when a certain kind of young man 'overdid the Bacchic rites on a Saturday night'. (As Doyle was quick to point out, the crime had occurred on a Tuesday.) The speculation was that the animal ripper was neither a psychotic sadist per se, nor some kind of freakish hybrid out of the pages of a vampire tale, loping across the fields on a moonlit night, but just some drunken adolescent acting out a dark impulse, for a reason concealed somewhere back among the shortcomings of his brutal home life.

Such theories still did not fully explain the new round of letters that arrived following Conan Doyle's first visit to Great Wyrley. Variously signed by 'Molton', 'The Nark' and 'Lew Is', they were more cryptic than actively deranged. Several contained intimate details of Captain Anson's prior investigations of the Edalji family. Some included specific quotations and private remarks of the captain's that suggested the author had at some time personally interviewed him. Anson seems to have rapidly concluded that Doyle himself had written at least one of the notes, perhaps as a way to intimidate him.

Curiously, Doyle soon received letters of his own, largely a combination of threats and bizarre religious occultism. Could Britain's most distinguished living author and the second son of the Earl of Lichfield really have been exchanging vitriolic mail designed to drive the other party off his head? There's anecdotal evidence that a pockmarked young man had also confronted Doyle one night in a Great Wyrley pub and warned him off the case in tones of 'agricultural bluntness'. Doyle had held his ground. The man then added enigmatically, 'You never forget the first nick of the razor.'

On 15 January 1907, Conan Doyle went by appointment to visit the Home Secretary, Herbert Gladstone, whom he knew socially. Doyle took the opportunity to demand a public inquiry be convened into the Edalji affair, before mentioning his own belief that the local police had failed dismally to arrest the real culprit in the case, whom he named as Royden Sharp. It was agreed that the existing libel laws discouraged his publishing this accusation. When Doyle emerged from the meeting, he told waiting reporters that everything had gone well, and that his esteemed friend the minister would soon act in the matter. This ability to swiftly navigate the political corridors of power, dealing on equal terms with men of prominence and wealth, was perhaps more redolent of Mycroft Holmes than his brother Sherlock.

Just ten days later, Doyle announced that Gladstone was to appoint a 'special committee to confer and deliberate', although in the event this was to prove more of an in-house exchange between civil servants, who concluded that George Edalji was possibly insane, and had very likely written at least some of the anonymous letters over the course of the previous twenty years.

Meanwhile, in two other developments, Doyle quickly disassociated himself from the official Edalji Support Committee, largely the creation of Roger Yelverton, accusing it of extremism; and, in an unusual twist, the *Police Chronicle* greeted the news of an Edalji inquiry with almost audible church bells and cannon fire, publicly welcoming a 'fresh eye' to review the evidence and 'immediately correct any errors of judgement'.

By the spring of 1907, therefore, two separate and sometimes opposing investigations were underway to conclusively determine the identity of the mad slasher of Great Wyrley. In a classic Sherlock Holmes adventure, the same general storyline would portray the detective as rigidly pursuing a line of strict scientific inquiry, stripped of any accompanying emotion and conjecture, and the official force as plodding stolidly ahead in the face of their own technical shortcomings and personal prejudices. It's a caricature when applied here, but one that has a grain of truth.

In fact, Conan Doyle soon found himself fighting on two fronts: there was the mystery of the criminal case to be solved, and then the need to draw together publicly all the different bodies that had contrived to put George Edalji in prison, the police, lawyers, judges, civil servants and politicians, and present them as branches of a single conspiracy. In otherwise conventional middle age, Doyle thus found himself cast as a radical judicial agitator and general anti-Establishment zealot, and his opponents as a corrupt and effete aristocratic elite with no real moral convictions beyond the desire to protect their own privileged status.

George Lewis, the pro-Edalji barrister, shrewdly assessed the tension between Doyle and the official investigator, Captain Anson:

> There is certainly a most serious schism dividing Sir Arthur and the competent police authority; and a schism quite incurable, because founded in the breasts of both is the absolute and unshakable certainty of the rightness of their cause.

By then Anson had already served thirty-one years successively as an army officer and as Chief Constable of Staffordshire. Neither instinct nor experience had equipped him as one of life's docile other ranks. Unburdened by self-doubt even then, Anson had once written in his school yearbook, 'It is not so much brilliance as effort that secures the prize – determination to accomplish something'. Gaunt and austere, yet with an air of languid amusement, habitually clad in an exquisite, dark suit, his signature raincoat and trilby to hand, he seemed to embody a kind of patrician hauteur that could repel as well as attract. Anyone familiar with Anson's descendant, Patrick Lichfield, the society photographer, need only think of that same character with a more severe haircut to get some of the flavour. When such a man meets an ambitious middle-class Scot like Conan Doyle, and each is convinced not only that he alone is right but that his opponent is mentally deficient, drama generally ensues.

No one could ever question the passion and intensity with which Conan Doyle pursued the Edalji case, both as an investigator and a tireless author of articles and petitions on the subject. It consumed him throughout 1907, and at intervals for the rest of his life. On 15 September of that year, he wrote to Captain Anson about a fresh outbreak of horse slashings in the Great Wyrley area, vehemently denying that George Edalji could have been personally involved in the crime as he was 'resident in a home 150 miles away, in the presence of witnesses'.

Three days later, Edalji was a guest of honour at the reception that followed Doyle's wedding to Jean Leckie in London.

It remains arguable, however, whether Doyle's unflagging loyalty, peerless narrative skills and undoubted moral commitment to the cause of Edalji's innocence were matched by equally acute gifts as a forensic detective. We've seen that he perhaps made too much of the eyesight evidence, to the extent that the ensuing public debate about myopia and diopters and other such esoteric data began to overshadow more important arguments for the defence.

In time, Doyle also descended into the thicket of a long and convoluted newspaper exchange in which he presented himself as an expert in handwriting analysis. Holmes, of course, is able to interpret documents with consummate skill, once concluding in 'The Norwood Builder' that a murder victim had previously written his will while riding on a train. By comparing facsimile copies of the Great Wyrley letters, Doyle now deduced that there were two or possibly three authors involved, conceivably brothers, and that one of them was a 'rude and foul-mouthed' Walsall boy, by inference Royden Sharp.

Captain Anson, increasingly relaxing his self-imposed ban on press interviews, soon replied through the pages of the *Staffordshire Sentinel* to deny that the police had ever been in any way prejudiced against Edalji. 'Various persons were indicated as being conceivably implicated in the offences, but as time went on any grounds for suspecting them disappeared one by one,' he declared. On the specific matter of the handwriting, Anson noted that the seated Home Office committee agreed with his own conclusions, 'so there is nothing new in the decision that Edalji wrote the letters'.

Conan Doyle was on more solid ground when he attacked the police's handling of the chain of evidence on the morning of Edalji's arrest. There were two distinct strands to this campaign. First, Doyle pointed out that there had been what could be charitably called honest mistakes in procedure:

The outrage had occurred just outside a large colliery, and hundreds of miners going to their work had swarmed along every approach. The soft wet soil was trampled. Yet eight hours after the seizure of [Edalji's] boots, we have Inspector Campbell endeavouring to trace a similarity in tracks. The particular boot was worn at the heel, a fairly common condition, and some tracks among the multitude were down at the heel, and why should not the one be caused by the other? No cast was taken of the tracks. They were not photographed.

Fully twenty-nine of the sixty Sherlock Holmes stories include footprint evidence. The detective has even contributed one of his periodic monographs on the subject. In this particular case, we can almost hear Holmes's rebuke of Inspector Lestrade from 1891's 'The Boscombe Valley Mystery':

> 'Oh, tut, tut! I have no time. That left foot of yours with its inward twist is all over the place. A mole could trace it, and there it vanishes among the reeds. Oh, how simple it would all have been had I been here before they came like a herd of buffalo, and wallowed all over it. Here is where the party with the lodge-keeper came, and they have covered all tracks for six or eight feet round the body.' He drew out a lens, and lay down upon his waterproof to have a better view … 'What have we here? Tip-toes, tip-toes! Square, too, quite unusual boots! They come, they go, they come again …'

Doyle went considerably further than this when it came to questioning the findings of the police surgeon who examined George Edalji's topcoat on the evening of his arrest. At eight o'clock that morning, Inspector Campbell had confiscated the coat after telling the family – who disputed his claim – that he could see a single hair on it. Ten hours later, this had become twenty-nine hairs. 'It would be sad indeed to commit one injustice while trying to correct another,' Doyle wrote in the *Telegraph*, 'but when the inevitable inquiry comes this incident must form a salient point of it.' Later in the article he added:

> Since writing the above I have been able to get the words of Dr Butter's evidence. They are quoted, 'Numerous hairs on the jacket, which were similar in colour, length, and structure to those on the piece of skin [cut] out from the horse.' In that case I say, confidently – and all reflection must confirm it – that these hairs could not possibly be from the general body of the pony, but must have been transferred, no doubt unconsciously, from that particular piece of skin. With all desire to be charitable, the incident leaves a most unpleasant impression upon the mind.

In other words, Doyle was accusing the police of, at best, colossal procedural incompetence in wrapping up Edalji's coat in the same bundle as the dead animal's hide; or, at worst, of wilfully fabricating evidence by planting horse hairs wholesale up and down the jacket's sleeves. Captain Anson preferred not to address the hair issue, at least in public, although he denied that there had been any significant flaws to the crime scene investigation as a whole. George Edalji could easily have left the vicarage undetected on the night of 17 August, Anson insisted, for the simple reason that:

> The house had not been particularly watched [on] this date ... Inspector Campbell, who gave general directions, and Sergeant Parsons, who actually detailed the men for duty on the vicarage side of the road, both stated positively that no one was watching the vicarage, but the [inquiry] has by an extraordinary blunder, converted Campbell's words, 'I gave general directions; no one was watching the vicarage that night' into 'I gave general directions to one watching the vicarage'.

There had been nothing improper about the subsequent seizure of George Edalji's coat, Anson added, nor had the police ever claimed to have found blood on Edalji's razor. Everything had been done according to the book. There had been no more anonymous letters from 1903 to 1906, Anson later informed his brother Thomas, 'because their author was sitting in prison at the time'.

Reviewing the various proceedings today, one is again struck by the speed with which it all happened. Conan Doyle first immersed himself in the case around Christmas 1906. His magisterial two-barrelled blast in *The Daily Telegraph* appeared the following 11 and 12 January. The Home Office seated a 'full and final consultative panel' (including the Chief Magistrate of London, Sir Albert de Rutzen, who happened to be a cousin of Captain Anson) later in March, and this reported back on 23 April. (The reader may wish to compare this to the more measured pace of certain recent inquiries.)

The Crown in turn exonerated Edalji of the animal attacks, but not of the twenty-year campaign of anonymous letters. 'He has, to some extent, brought his troubles upon himself,' the Home Secretary wrote. As a result of this compromise, Edalji received both a pardon and the return of his previously suspended law licence, but no compensation. At that, the venerable English poet George Meredith wrote to Conan Doyle to tell him, 'I shall not mention the name which must have become wearisome to your ears, but the creator of the marvellous Amateur Detective has shown what he can do in the life of breath.' The *New York Times* was more succinct, 'Conan Doyle Solves a New Dreyfus Case', ran its headline. 'Creator of "Sherlock Holmes" Turns Detective Himself.'

And still the letters came. One could almost be left to wonder if there had ever been such a thing as a completely innocent communication sent anywhere in the Great Wyrley area. In the spring and early summer of 1907, both George Edalji and Captain Anson were on the receiving end of a varied and lively correspondence, though once again it was hard to identify a single unifying theme beyond the obvious psychosis of the writer. Long, rambling prose essays were followed in turn by lacerating, unsigned poems asserting, in earthy terms, that the sworn representatives of the law were engaged in a whole series of unsavoury activities and sexual misdeeds around the West Midlands.

There were letters to Royden Sharp, too, including one sent from London on 17 April, telling him, 'They can't arrest you yet until Edalji's cleared. Someone preached on you … Doyle setting watch on you. Your wife has told out of spite.' Since Sharp was a bachelor, this last detail only added to the mystery. A Home Office official named Stanley Blackwell, who examined the Sharp correspondence, came to the conclusion that Doyle himself, or at least one of his associates, was behind it. Blackwell wrote to his minister to tell him that the letters were presumably a ploy to somehow trick Sharp into saying or doing something incautious and thus incriminating himself.

If so, the first part of the strategy seems to have worked. Early in May, Sharp appeared in Cannock Police Station late one Saturday night to lodge a complaint. The gist of his remarks was that, since he had received another anonymous letter that morning, it occurred to him that the authorities might now enter into a more active phase of their investigation and seek to identify the author or authors of all the calumnies against him. (The actual choice of words appears to have been more colourful.) The desk sergeant on duty replied only that enquiries were being made, and that there was nothing more he could presently add. Still dissatisfied, Sharp brought his fist down on the counter in between them and challenged the man to a duel. The matter seems to have ended with the arrival of several of the sergeant's colleagues from a back room, at which point the fight suddenly seemed to go out of Sharp altogether, although as he retreated he is said to have shouted back over his shoulder, 'I could have split him from end to end!'

There were several more letters for Doyle, too. One read:

We are narks of detectives, and know Edalji killed the horse and write [sic] the stuff. Edalji is not the right sort nor is Greatorex who killed horses too. Gladstone has proof of his guilty deeds. I so worship Sherlock Holmes I would lose my life to save his neck.

Doyle put some stock in the fact that this letter was posted in London, where Sharp, according to the head porter at Cannock station, had been just the day before. When Inspector Campbell subsequently went to interview the porter, however, he retracted his statement. Doyle was informed of this development. Then the porter in turn received an anonymous letter, in which the writer politely suggested that he search his memory once more and tell the police that his original account had been correct.

Another line to Doyle in May expressed the view that Edalji 'along with his dad and all black and yellow faced Jews' best belonged behind bars. There was a good deal more in this same vein. Barely bothering to conceal his inside knowledge of the case, the author of another note to Doyle boasted that the police were now examining the possibility that a sailor or traveller of some sort was behind all the letters, and possibly also the rippings, and that 'Sharpe' was the leading candidate.

'It is quite a three-pipe problem, and I beg that you won't speak to me for fifty minutes,' Sherlock Holmes remarks to Dr Watson in 1891's 'The Red-Headed League', before falling into a tobacco-fuelled reverie. Holmes's author was equally as absorbed by the Edalji affair as it unfolded through 1907. The temperature of public debate and interest in the case as a whole was such that the newspapers continued to prominently feature it on their front pages for many months after Edalji himself had quietly returned to his law practice. Doyle was consumed by the belief that the police had botched their original investigation, whether through malice or incompetence, or a 'noxious compound' of both, and his relations with Captain Anson in particular soon reached a degree of mutual antipathy rarely seen outside marriage.

It might not be going too far to speak of an obsession. Writing almost daily, sometimes twice a day, over the summer (with a short break during his honeymoon with Jean Leckie), Doyle bombarded his adversary with a characteristic variety of forensic detail and moral indignation. A long letter of 2 September, barely a fortnight before his wedding, discusses the exact properties of the weapon used in the maiming of August 1903, and how 'the weight of the [horse's] bowels helped to break an opening in it'. Several other notes made precise allegations against Royden Sharp and his three brothers. 'Colour prejudice may have been enough to prompt them to bait the Edalji family in the cruel way they did,' Doyle wrote at one point. Occasionally the author exercised his gift for satire, once enquiring of Anson if he believed Edalji had somehow seeped through the walls or windows of his locked bedroom on the night of 17 August, before 'lop[ing] around the countryside in a diabolical frenzy?' Anson wisely declined to trade literary barbs with one of the world's most commercially successful authors, but stoutly denied that he had any interest in the matter beyond finding the truth. 'No doubt several persons have at different times been mixed up with writing forged and anonymous letters in the Wyrley district,' he wrote to Doyle in October 1907, 'and the more done to clear it up the better.'*

The more personal attacks infuriated the aristocratic policeman, and his anger only intensified when his family name seemed to be publicly smeared by Doyle's allegation of racism. 'Is he mad?' Anson once again privately enquired.

Although Doyle continued to see Royden Sharp and one or more of his brothers as principally responsible for the crimes Edalji was supposed to have committed, they were far from his only suspects in the case. Among several others, there was, for instance, Harry Green, the local farmer's son who allegedly killed his own horse while it was paddocked in Benton's field, the same area where George Edalji was said to wander abroad late at night, more than a month after Edalji himself had been taken into custody; Fred Brookes, a feeble-minded Walsall youth whose grocer father had been one of the recipients of the second wave of anonymous letters in 1892–93; and a married, middle-aged, one-eyed local pit worker named Thomas Farrington. Judged to be an inoffensive man, if of irregular habits, Farrington later testified in court that he had spent the evening of 24 March 1904 in a pub before settling for the night in a nearby pig sty, where he had slept soundly until the 'bull' (siren) blew to signal the start of the work day. The police alleged that he had in fact risen some hours earlier, stolen into an adjacent field, and slit the throats of two sheep pastured there. A jury subsequently took just

---

* Doyle's rebuke of Captain Anson is well taken, although within only a few years the same author was convinced that there were those, like Harry Houdini, who in fact possessed some miraculous dematerialising power that allowed them to pass through solid objects and reassemble themselves on the other side.

forty minutes to find Farrington guilty, and he was sentenced to three years' imprisonment. Since Edalji himself was then already in custody in Lewes Jail, the police had suggested that the pair had been part of an animal-ripping ring active in the area, although no evidence was ever presented that the men actually knew each other.

Finally, there was one Jack Hart, a young Cannock man who had at one time practised in the butchery trade. Convinced that he was part of the criminal conspiracy against Edalji, Doyle wrote to Hart on at least four occasions in June and July 1907 to encourage him to turn king's evidence against the Sharp brothers. On 18 August, Hart travelled to London for an interview with Doyle and his own brother, Innes, a scene that presents some of the tragicomic potential of a country ruffian being confronted by Sherlock and Mycroft Holmes in the Diogenes Club. Little of substance emerged: Hart freely admitted that he knew and loathed George Edalji (whom the Doyles had secreted in the next room), but denied any direct knowledge of the maimings. Captain Anson heard about the meeting, and for once agreed that his rival had taken a useful line of inquiry. 'I would not be a bit surprised to know that he [Hart] helped Green to kill his own horse, or anything of the sort,' Anson wrote to Blackwell at the Home Office. 'He is not a man to be treated as above suspicion.'

With his impassioned commentary about Edalji being a scapegoat, and the police evidence against him 'open to the gravest doubt, and contradicted at every point by reputable witnesses', Conan Doyle became more than just a popular author with a social conscience. He entered the broader tides of history. In the harshly polarised environment surrounding the case, and at a time when the officially approved man of letters rarely strayed into anti-government rhetoric, Doyle's continuing articles and speeches flaying the authorities fixed him in the public eye as something close to a radical. Doyle not only lent his name to the judicial reform camp, and thereby put it in the mainstream; he made an honest scepticism about the way Britain as a whole was governed not just respectable, but necessary and patriotic.

Writing later on the Edalji case, Doyle likened the corruption of the 'Staffordshire and Whitehall elite' to the cabal of French military officers and politicians who had conspired against Alfred Dreyfus in 1894. Convicted of treason, the young (and Jewish) artillery captain had spent nearly five years imprisoned in medieval conditions on Devil's Island in French Guiana. Just as France had its 'Dreyfusards', so there were those whom the British press now described, sometimes mockingly, as 'Edaljiites'. 'The parallel is extraordinarily close,' Doyle wrote:

> You have a Parsee, instead of a Jew, with a promising career blighted, in each case the degradation from a profession and the campaign for redress and restoration, in each case questions of forgery and handwriting arise, with [Major Ferdinand] Esterhazy in the one, and the anonymous writer in the other. Finally, I regret to say, that in the one case you have a clique of French officials going from excess to excess in order to cover an initial mistake, and that in the other you have the Staffordshire police acting in the way I have described.

Thanks to Conan Doyle, the unfolding Edalji scandal became a daily news staple for millions of ordinary Britons, and, in Doyle's hands, a highly dramatic and strongly moral one.

✳ ✳ ✳

On 12 May 1907, Conan Doyle spoke on the Edalji affair at a specially convened meeting of the Crimes Club in London. He told his fellow members that the 'eyesight evidence' alone made it 'inexpressibly absurd' to agree with the verdict of the original trial jury. 'Any impartial man,' he added, 'must do violence to his reason to think otherwise.'

Whether later speaking of occult matters like spirits and fairies, or as he did here of a more material miscarriage of justice, it was the obvious conviction Doyle brought to his remarks that generally won his audience. In the hands of a lesser speaker, the message might have been ineffective, absurd even. Time and again, Doyle's indignation captured exactly the sense of bitterness, resentment, and pent-up anger of the 'Edaljiites' as a whole.

Doyle was particularly scathing about his rival, Captain Anson, who had again made the most 'vile of insinuations about the Edalji family': namely that the father and his elder son slept together for the purpose of sodomy, and that the relationship between the mother and her daughter had also been 'unconventional, in some moral sense of the word'. Anson himself denied making any such allegation, or having ever suggested the least sexual impropriety about the sleeping arrangements at the vicarage. But Doyle told his Crimes Club audience that this was 'quite disingenuous' – that the captain had allowed himself these 'base aspersions [was] quite certain, and there was no room for doubt whatever'. He proceeded to give some account of his recent discussions with Herbert Gladstone at the Home Office. There was some cause for cautious optimism, Doyle noted, following the committee of inquiry's report. It had been announced that a formal ministerial statement would be made in the near future. Regrettably, he added, there was also some lingering official misapprehension about the identity of the anonymous letter writer involved. 'The balance of proof is enormously against George Edalji having ever put his pen to the paper,' Doyle concluded, although who knew what 'blinkered politicians' might make of the matter?

Just three days later, the Home Secretary did indeed pardon Edalji, but, as we've seen, fell short of offering him either a public apology or financial redress. Not one to relinquish a fight, Doyle waited less than a week to reply. He wrote:

> Let me ... consider the theory which I believe still obtains at the Home Office that the bad boy of 1892–95 was actually George Edalji reviling his own people, and writing furious letters to those who had never offended him ... At that date Edalji was 19 years of age, an excellent scholar, who had finished his grammar-school education, and had already started that course of legal study at which he was to win such distinction. Can anyone believe that he is responsible for this barbarous writing and more barbarous spelling and grammar? It is impossible to suppose such a thing.

This was perhaps an instance where Doyle's need to see the ultimate moral truth of the story blinded him to some of its contradictory detail. Might Edalji have deliberately roughened his language and disguised his handwriting, for instance, or, as the police believed, had he dictated at least some of the vitriol to an accomplice? Sherlock Holmes would have been more incisive on the subject, as he shows in 1891's 'The Man with the Twisted Lip' when analysing a letter sent to the wife of a missing businessman:

> 'Coarse writing!' murmured Holmes. 'Surely this is not your husband's writing, madam.'
>
> 'No, but the enclosure is.'
>
> 'I perceive also that whoever addressed the envelope had to go to inquire as to the address.'
>
> 'How can you tell that?'

'The name, you see, is in perfectly black ink, which has dried itself. The rest is of the greyish colour which shows that blotting-paper has been used. If it had been written straight off, and then blotted, none would be of a deep black shade. This man has written the name, and there has then been a pause before he wrote the address, which can only mean that he was not familiar with it. It is, of course, a trifle, but there is nothing so important as trifles.'

The difference between Holmes and his author in this case is that one operated as a forensic detective, and the other as an idealised campaigner for justice who, once having formed an opinion of a man's good character, never allowed for the possibility that there might be many facets, some pure, others murkier, struggling for pre-eminence in the same individual.

Doyle's crusading instincts were by no means satisfied by the government's compromise in the Edalji case. He fired off increasingly incendiary letters to the Home Office at regular intervals for the next twenty years. At one point, he found himself engaged in a three-way correspondence involving Captain Anson and their mutual friend the new Home Secretary Winston Churchill, each man attempting to convince the others of his deep and lifelong sympathy with the oppressed. Doyle wasn't quite the first world-famous writer to take issue with the police. But he brought the intellectual versus authority figure friction to radioactive levels. More practically, he also helped to raise over £300 (£20,000 today), by public subscription, for a George Edalji compensation fund. A Court of Criminal Appeal became part of the English legal system in August 1907, partially as a result of the case. Edalji himself was re-enrolled as a solicitor that November, although, perhaps understandably, he chose not to practise in the greater Birmingham area.

Doyle never lost his sense of indignation at the way the authorities seemed to have colluded against Edalji. 'After many years,' he wrote in his 1924 autobiography, 'I can hardly think with patience of the handling of the case.' For all that, when considering the long record of professional misconduct and procedural shortcomings that characterised the story as a whole, it's worth remembering that in late 1905 Gladstone's predecessor as Home Secretary, Aretas Akers-Douglas, had acted on his own initiative to reduce Edalji's sentence to one of three years' imprisonment, not seven, and that he did so well before Conan Doyle entered the fray. There were several subsequent parliamentary debates on the issue, notably in July 1907, not distinguished by their restraint in criticising the original conviction. This led in turn to

Captain Anson arranging for his friend and local MP, Lieutenant Colonel Henry Staveley-Hill (Conservative), to ask the Home Secretary on the floor of the Commons 'to say that there is no ground for the very grave charges made against the Staffordshire police in the Edalji case'. The minister was 'delighted' to give the assurance asked of him.

✳ ✳ ✳

Determining whether George Edalji was a scapegoat, a superficially innocuous young man with a psychotic streak, or perhaps a bit of both, is no easy task. Yet we have clues. They include the opinion not only of the Home Office and the Staffordshire Police, but of Edalji's own brother and counsel, that the Crown's case was essentially sound in its conclusions about the authorship of at least some of the anonymous letters. Even Conan Doyle appeared to concede the possibility that the authorities had managed to successfully separate the issue of the hate mail from that of the animal attacks when he wrote in May 1907:

> I have purposely said nothing of the outrages themselves and confined my remarks to the letters, since these are the only things for which Edalji is now held responsible, and it is on account of that alleged responsibility that compensation is refused him.

Of course, for the most part the writing of such letters, or the placing of hoax advertisements, however misguided, falls short of a serious criminal offence. Even in the climate of 1903, it's not a matter that would normally have merited a sentence of seven years' hard labour. Edalji may have pondered in his cell the bitter irony of his being convicted of a crime of which he was innocent, but of having sown the seeds of his downfall by a protracted, and singularly ill-advised, campaign of adolescent mischief.

The most striking thing about Conan Doyle outside of his printed works is his lifelong sympathy with the vulnerable or minority members of society, coupled with his zeal for total immersion in whatever cause happened to capture his attention. His diatribes in *The Daily Telegraph* and elsewhere remain models of controlled literary aggression – as even Captain Anson was later to admit, 'You could delight in his sheer energy, and find yourself applauding every so often as the sweet arrow of one of his sentences hit its mark'. But a social crusader doesn't usually succeed merely by being colourful. Setting aside his obvious narrative gifts, Doyle's claim is forensic – it's as a detective that he asks to be judged.

The corkscrew plot of the Great Wyrley outrages, as it unfolded over the years, could certainly have done service as a sixty-first and final Sherlock Holmes tale. It includes a number of ingredients from the existing Holmes canon: the graphology that plays a part not only in 'The Twisted Lip' but in cases as varied and far-flung as 'The Stockbroker's Clerk' (1893), 'The Missing Three-Quarter' (1904) and the detective's fourth and last novel-length appearance in 1914's *The Valley of Fear*, which opens with the arrival of a mysterious cipher message from a man who writes under the alias 'Fred Porlock', an agent to Professor Moriarty.

As we've seen, there's also an episode in 1892's 'Silver Blaze' that hinges on an attempted night-time mutilation of a racehorse in an open field. Footprints and bloodstains are both staple components of Doyle's fictional stories and his real-life investigation. There was even the question, seriously raised by the local police, of whether George Edalji had made use of a trap door or secret passage of some sort in order to make his way to and from his locked bedroom on the night of 17 August 1903, a plot device similar to that in the Holmes tales 'The Norwood Builder' and 'The Golden Pince-Nez'. The verdict of admiring Doyle biographers is that a mind capable of such sustained imaginative feats, and the creator of an alter ego endowed with the ability to perceive and interpret clues baffling to the official flatfoot, would likely not have found himself at a disadvantage in any battle of wits with the rural Staffordshire Police.

It's possible, however, that in the particular case of George Edalji it was Captain Anson whose stubborn concern with matters such as motive and opportunity aligns him with Holmes's rationalist approach to detection, and Doyle whose own rush to judgement, based on a mixture of subjective impressions and strong moral instincts, more obviously suggests a Dr Watson. Anson, it's true, doesn't always make an immediately sympathetic figure. When contemporaries came to reminisce about the titled army officer-turned-detective, the word 'humility' would often colour their accounts. They say he was extremely sparing with it. We know that Anson was well bred, irrepressibly proud of his family, responsible and honest, but also that he was gruff, high-handed, and imperious in his judgements (a 'clenched fist', Doyle thought), and thus not one of today's natural community policemen. While competitive to a fault, he was also cautious and realistic.

Although Anson was supremely self-confident, he had no illusions that every criminal offence lent itself to a neat solution. In this case, he made the eminently sane observation that, like most crimes, the horse slashing of August 1903 had taken place without witnesses, 'so we are left with the need to balance the facts and draw the most likely conclusion'. From then on, the captain had reminded Doyle, 'It [was] up to not you or me, but to twelve English jurors to reach the ultimate verdict'. Again, Anson may have had his personal prejudices and limitations as an investigator. But there is still no compelling evidence that he was engaged in a twenty-year long private vendetta against the Edalji family, let alone that he tampered with or planted any evidence. What's more, he delegated freely, which gave him a tactical advantage in his struggles with the fiercely independent Doyle. For all his swagger, Anson valued results too much to be a one-man band.

It remained Doyle's unshakable belief right to the end of his life that one or more of the Sharp brothers of Hednesford, a village 5 miles north of Great Wyrley, were behind both the letters and the assaults that followed. We can only speculate whether Sherlock Holmes would have been similarly persuaded. It's true that the local reputation of Royden Sharp, in particular, stood low: a congenital liar, a cheat and a bully, at one time a butcher's apprentice, described by a contemporary as 'low-browed, crafty, and incapable of truthfully answering an inquiry such as "What did you have for breakfast today?"', he clearly fitted the profile of someone who might casually harm an innocent animal just for the thrill of it.

Whether Sharp had either the wit or even the basic literacy to conceive and carry off a project that involved sending literally scores of letters, in a variety of hands and prose styles, and from dozens of different locations, over a period of some fifteen years, all the while evading the attention of Captain Anson and his men, is another question. Is it possible that the writer of a note accusing Reverend Edalji of 'hypocrisy and humbug' and asking 'How can you preach as you do? I was hungry and you fed me not, naked and you clothed me not, in prison and you visited me not ... God help all the poor souls whom you have accused', was one and the same as the author of another message that advised the Edaljis' maid Nora to save her piss in order to boil potatoes? Such diversity bears the hallmark of a creatively minded misfit more than a monosyllabically imbecilic school dropout.

Doyle's eventual conclusion was that the Sharp brothers had written the letters as a team, each of them bringing his own uniquely warped skill-set to the exercise. 'These guilty [parties], three young adults and a boy, undoubtedly lived under the same roof,' he later reasoned:

> Their epistles are continually on the same paper, and in the same envelopes. In some cases the rude scrawl of the boy comes in upon the very page taken up by the educated writing of the adult. A sheet may exhibit on one side an elaborate forgery of the signatures of the Edaljis, while on the other is a rude drawing (rude in every sense), which could only have been done by a lad. The adults appeared to pride themselves upon forgery, and the results, so far as I have been able to test them, show that they had remarkable powers in that direction. 'Do you think that we could not imitate your kid's writing?' they say exultantly in one of the 1892 letters. They most certainly could – and did.

As a rule, Doyle believed that siblings could often display a wide and sometimes mutually complementary range of genetic skills, as was the case in his own family. But Anson, less scientifically minded, thought the Sharp brothers 'decidedly dim', even in their collective mental candlepower, and 'quite incapable' of the conspiracy Doyle imagined.

On 5 September 1907, the Wolverhampton Police arrested a 22-year-old butcher's mate named Francis Hollis Morgan on a charge of maiming two mares in a field. It was alleged that his cap and a fragment of his pipe had been found at the crime scene. Captain Anson was quick to distance himself from the case, writing to the Home Office on 8 September that the evidence against Morgan was 'very much less than [needed] for a conviction'.

Meanwhile, the arrest seems to have been the spur for yet another outbreak of anonymous cards and letters, posted from different locations around the Midlands but broadly unified in their theme of vowing revenge should Morgan be sent to jail. It was established that George Edalji was then 150 miles away at a holiday resort in Great Yarmouth, which satisfied even the police of his innocence. Just six days later, a magistrate ordered that Morgan had no case to answer and that he be released. It was not a decision to inspire further confidence in the Wolverhampton force, or in the Edalji investigation as a whole. The *London Evening News* saw a 'healthy average of stupidity' among the ranks of Staffordshire law enforcement, and wondered how much longer 'a yokel who is none the less a yokel for being a numbered and lettered official' might continue to command public confidence.

Later that year, George Edalji moved out of his parents' house and left Great Wyrley for good. He was 31. He spent some time in London before settling 20 miles to the north in the new town of Welwyn Garden City. Conan Doyle continued to fight on his behalf, and over the next few years there was a lively correspondence on the case in everything from the *British Medical Journal* to the human-interest weekly, *Tit-Bits*. Doyle particularly ridiculed the idea that the accused man could still be indicted by certain individuals largely because of his 'vacant, bulge-eyed staring appearance [and] dark skin ... in other words, that he looks guilty'. His crusading journalism tailed off only with the outbreak of the war and his own re-emergence as a spokesman and missionary for a new religion.

Roger Yelverton remained perhaps Edalji's most outspoken supporter, although it's possible he may have had the larger agenda of attacking the judicial establishment in general. 'The whole thing is grossly unjust, a terrible stain ... involving such grave consequences that a gentleman was sent to seven years' penal servitude,' he wrote, in the course of a lengthy open letter blasting Home Office officials. Yelverton was undoubtedly motivated in his campaign by a high-minded search for truth and justice. But he was also a masterly self-publicist. In time, he became almost as famous as Doyle himself for his articles and interviews on Edalji's behalf, and was soon leading a glamorous social life, which he later claimed not to have enjoyed. When he rose to speak at one rally, the chairman introduced him as 'the Great Defender', a phrase that stuck because he made such a strong impression, and not one Yelverton himself actively discouraged.

Edalji led a more retiring life, keeping house with his sister Maud until his death in 1953. Maud carried on the fight to clear her brother's name until her own death in 1961. Having begun in an era of hansom cabs and gaslit streets, the Edalji affair had lasted long enough to see a time when human beings were shot into space, and governments possessed weapons that could effectively destroy civilisation in less than sixty minutes.

※　※　※

On 13 July 1930, George Edalji was among the 6,000 spectators who packed the Royal Albert Hall to pay their respects to a man described in the event's programme as 'Our Very Present Friend' – Arthur Conan Doyle, who had died six days earlier. It was a singular scene, part theatrical production, part spiritualist rally, and thus not one Edalji would have recognised from his childhood as a Victorian clergyman's son. A vacant chair was set up on the Albert Hall stage alongside those reserved for the widow and her family. A cardboard sign propped up in front of it read, 'Sir Arthur Conan Doyle'. 'There were many gaudy costumes on display,' the *Empire News* reported, although Edalji himself was 'more formally attired in black, immensely pale in the face, peering distractedly through the thick lenses of his glasses, and answering successive well-wishers with a simple and soft-throated "Thank you"'.

A Reverend George Craze of the Spiritualist Association gave the opening remarks, and then asked the audience to rise for two minutes' silence. Following that, a petite, middle-aged medium named Estelle Roberts was invited up on the stage, where she stood for some time, her eyes closed, swaying back and forth in front of a microphone. From time to time, she punctuated the routine by a sudden, birdlike twitch of her head. After what one report called an 'interminably suspenseful' pause, Mrs Roberts then looked up towards the ceiling of the hall and announced, 'There are vast numbers of spirits here with us. They are pushing me like anything.' Working the crowd like a seasoned vaudeville mentalist, she went on to describe the personal characteristics of several apparitions seemingly hovering above the heads of the audience: 'You, sir – I see by you the spirit of a young soldier … There is a gentleman on the Other Side, named John, looking for his daughter … He has got your mother Jane or Mary with him …'

After some three-quarters of an hour of this, there was a sudden peal of music on the Albert Hall's pipe organ that seemed to galvanise Mrs Roberts's efforts. 'He is here!' she exclaimed, pointing to the empty chair on the stage. 'He is here!' At that, she went across to where Lady Doyle was sitting, told her, 'I have a message for you from Arthur', and leaned forward to speak in her ear. Just then, a second thunderous chord issued from the organ, making it impossible for the audience to hear what was said. Mrs Roberts later told the press that she had first seen Doyle during the two minutes' silence. 'He gave me a message, which I gave to Lady Doyle, but am unable to repeat publicly. I saw him distinctly. He was wearing evening dress.'

According to Mrs Roberts, even beyond the grave Conan Doyle never wavered in his belief in George Edalji's innocence. He was said to have given her this assurance in the course of a 1931 séance also attended by Doyle's widow and two surviving sons. 'Sir Arthur, vigorous, powerful, full of force, very earnest and very grave, came back [and] spoke,' *Psychic News* reported:

Mrs Constance Treloar, President of the Marylebone Spiritualist Association, was present, as was George Craze, Lady Carey, and her great friend Lady Hardinge, Maurice Barbanell and Dr Rust, the brave medical man from Newport … Later Conan Doyle was heard to say, 'Craze, they [the sceptics] can never stem the tide. We are going to deluge the world. Truth is here at last!'

Some twenty years after he first made it, Conan Doyle was then said to have posthumously repeated his remark to the effect that the Edalji case stood 'to the deep disgrace of British administration'.

A Yorkshire medium named Charles Tweedale proved to be the most persistent of those later communing with Doyle's spirit, which once told him:

Well, my dear man, I have arrived here in Paradise. That is not heaven. Oh no! But what we should call a dumping place, for we all come here to rest. Paradise means not heaven, but 'a park' – Persian word.

According to Tweedale, 'Sir Arthur often came through [in] undoubted and direct messages' protesting Edalji's innocence of the animal maiming, though in the course of a lengthy review of the case he apparently declined to finally name the guilty party. Privately, some friends admitted that Doyle's occult remarks over the years had not impressed them. 'Now the late Sir Arthur was an admirable writer of English,' one critic noted. 'If the post-death messages are exact copies of those messages, his knowledge of even the elementary rules of grammar must have suffered woefully since his death.'

✳ ✳ ✳

Despite Conan Doyle's immortal assurances, we can reasonably ask whether his long crusade for justice in the Edalji affair had led him to overlook or disregard certain inconvenient facts that might conceivably have led to a different interpretation of events. Was it all a case of his having first reached a conclusion, and then found the evidence to support it? Did Doyle's unshakable faith in Edalji's good character blind him to the messy truth? As a 1907 editorial in the *New York Times* noted, 'Sir Arthur may have been misled by the literary artist's natural desire to round out his story perfectly. Fact may be stranger than fiction, but in most cases it lacks what is known as "construction".'

The edges of what was real and what was imagined may have started to blur in the Edalji case, but Doyle continued to pursue the authorities on the victim's behalf long after another man might have honourably left the field. 'I have written to the new Home Secretary [Reginald] McKenna about Edalji,' Doyle reported to his mother in November 1911, five years after he first took up the case. 'I'll win that fight yet.' It was the same, in one degree or another, right up to the end of his life, if not beyond it.

A Boston medium called Mina Crandon, who went by the nom-de-séance of Margery, later insisted that she, too, like Charles Tweedale, had received posthumous messages from Doyle, and that these frequently reaffirmed his belief in Edalji's innocence. At various times, she reported Doyle as having appeared to her 'brandish[ing] a flaming sword of righteousness', and 'promising eternal damnation for all those who continue to pervert the course of earthly justice'. In assessing these claims, it's perhaps only fair to add that Margery was known for her habit of holding séances in what were called 'garments of severely spare cut', if not entirely in the nude, and that her most singular achievement while seated around the darkened table was to speak in a 'loud, gruff, masculine' voice said to be that of her late brother. In time, she claimed that Doyle's spirit had even returned in order to name her his literary executor. 'You carry my mantle forward,' he apparently remarked, before encouraging her to write a book with the title *Sherlock Holmes in Heaven*.

* * *

The Great Wyrley outrages reveal a society obsessed, like our own, with instant celebrity, but where in general there was little public sympathy for those who existed outside the commonly agreed idea of what a professional man such as a Church of England vicar should look or act like. In a world where mental illness was untreatable and forensic science in its infancy, seemingly irrational crimes against minorities were bound to happen, and as often as not to go unsolved. Whatever else emerges in the Edalji case, it's clear that the semi-rural English Midlands at around the turn of the twentieth century was not the ideal place for a precocious brown-skinned boy of mixed parentage to grow up.

Was George Edalji, for all that, guilty as charged?

Psychologically speaking, we know that Edalji broadly fits the pattern of the inward child who sees himself adrift in a hostile world, a category responsible for a disproportionate number of history's worst villains. A reading of his available school reports and other testimony of around the early 1890s depicts an adolescent who was by turns gifted, furtive, shy, sensitive to perceived slights and insults, prone to jealousy, charming, yet at times deceitful – in short, who displayed the odd mixture of ego and insecurity often associated with those who grow up feeling themselves to be both more intelligent and more unlucky than everybody else.

As a rule, such individuals consider themselves different from other people, which to a degree they are. Frequently, they judge themselves harshly. And as young adults some of them become adept at learning to deal with what is happening right in front of them while simultaneously maintaining an elaborate fantasy world in their heads. This disconnect between subjective imagination and objective reality should not have come as a surprise to Conan Doyle, who as a medical student had been trained to recognise that there are certain individuals who manage to compartmentalise their thinking to an unusual degree, and that this set of circumstances, allied to the nagging sense of being subject to an isolating, separating and lonely condition such as being a myopic, half-caste teenager in late Victorian Staffordshire, might conceivably produce what we would now call a functioning psychopath.

Of course, these generalisations should be applied with caution to any individual, including George Edalji. Nothing suggests that there was anything untoward about his behaviour until about the age of 13 – as any parent will recognise, traditionally a time when certain strains can emerge between a child's dependency on his elders and a marked aversion to authority figures in general. It was at this delicate transitional point in George's early adolescence that the anonymous letters first descended on the Great Wyrley vicarage.

There seems to be little doubt that they were the work of the maid Elizabeth Foster, and that she wrote them from a mixture of ignorance, malice and disenchantment with her basic terms of employment. In one of the letters she threatened to shoot Charlotte Edalji. Another referred to the reverend as the 'bloody black man', among other unappreciative remarks. At any rate, it seems reasonable enough to conclude that Foster and the Edaljis were not on convivial terms. As we've seen, she pled guilty before magistrates to a reduced charge of making threats, got probation, and retired to live with a mentally ill maiden aunt in the greater Birmingham area.

It's quite true that, as she was at pains to point out, Foster had also received anonymous letters while working at the vicarage. The Edaljis believed that she had simply harassed herself in this manner to deceive the police. Foster later volunteered to appear for the prosecution at George Edalji's trial, although as she proposed to speak primarily of the reverend and his wife's sexual activities her services as an expert witness weren't, in the end, required. There seems little reason to dispute the findings of Cannock Police Court in January 1889 that Foster had sent 'unsigned [and] minatory correspondence to her employers', and it remains within the realms of possibility that she or members of her immediate family may have played some part in the campaign of malicious hoaxes against the Edaljis that began in 1892.

Could George Edalji have taken a leaf from Foster's book and himself written at least some of the letters that tormented his family up to and beyond his imprisonment? Did he smear excrement on his own window, or place a stolen key on his doorstep? If so, might it have been as a way of amusing himself at the expense of a few rather slow country policemen? It's not unknown for a superficially innocuous but neurotic 17-year-old to taunt authority. Thomas Gurrin was far from alone in believing that certain of the anonymous letters of 1892–95 were in the same handwriting as letters admittedly written by George Edalji, with some attempt made at disguise. The jury at Edalji's trial reached the same conclusion, and in time the official committee of inquiry, while not uncritical of the prosecution case, announced that they too were 'not prepared to dissent from that finding'. Horace Edalji similarly believed that his brother had written a number of the second wave of letters as a kind of impish prank. Horace wrote to a friend called Chris Hatton in December 1903:

> Have contacted the mater telling her what I know about George and the [correspondence]. I have asked her to have this agitation against the chief constable [Anson] stopped, and pointed out how serious it is. I don't know what my people will think, but I believe I have done my duty in telling them.

Horace did not have to wait long to learn his family's reaction. Two days later, Mrs Edalji in turn sent her younger son a 'wild' twenty-two-page letter. She 'very warmly' refuted his allegations. In time, Horace came to believe that the key to the second phase of the case, the assaults themselves, lay in George's financial problems as a struggling young solicitor. He wrote:

If he did the outrages, I think he must have done it for the money, considering what desperate straits he was in. There was a bankruptcy petition against him at the end of last January [1903], but he got over it. It is quite possible someone got a hold over him which might explain subsequent proceedings. He paid a mysterious visit to London around the end of February & was away about a week.

Did George Edalji then carry out the slashings because of making some wager in order to clear his debts? The physical evidence strongly suggests he didn't. It will be remembered that he was sleeping in the same locked room as his father on the night of 17 August, and that the surrounding neighbourhood, if not the vicarage itself, was under continuous police watch. Even accepting that Edalji may have written some of the prank letters, quite possibly in league with one or more of those travelling around the area on the same train, isn't to make the case that he also took to stealing out into darkened fields to brutally molest farm animals. 'The value of the letters as evidence that the accused committed the [assault] is quite another question,' even the Home Office concluded. In other words, Edalji may well have been complicit in a sustained juvenile prank, as both the handwriting analysis and the sheer volume of intimate detail contained in the letters about the affairs of the Great Wyrley vicarage strongly suggest he was. It's possible that the animal attacks in some way evolved out of that same ill-judged campaign. But it defies belief that Edalji could have carried out the specific assault with which he was charged, or, for that matter, that his fiercely moralistic father would have willingly participated in a lifelong crusade to clear his son's name had he known him to be guilty.

Royden Sharp, Conan Doyle's own preferred suspect, was by consensus a thoroughly charmless young man with a propensity for violence. The number and frequency of the pub brawls he was involved in would probably cause comment even today. He knew something of the Edaljis' domestic arrangements, and had received enough of an education to qualify him as a writer of reasonably coherent vulgar letters. Were he or his brothers collectively also the mad ripper? That is a harder question to answer. The police never believed that they had enough evidence against the Sharps to bring before a jury, and Doyle thought it best not to publish his suspicions for fear of being sued for libel.

Even so, Captain Anson was sufficiently moved to write to the Home Office for the record in November 1907, acknowledging that Sharp's brother, Walter, 'played pranks in the writing line'. A subsequent police visit to the Sharps' home produced what Anson called 'dirty postcards' similar to those used in the Greatorex correspondence of 1903. There were marked coincidences in timing between Royden Sharp's tours overseas and the sequence in which the poison letters were received. Anson eventually wrote to Doyle to admit that Royden's handwriting 'b[ore] similarities' to some of the hate mail, but that even so 'this [was] no proof of his involvement' in the maimings, a presumption of innocence that would seem not to have been applied quite as strenuously to Edalji himself.

In the looking-glass world of the Edalji case, where nothing was quite as it seemed, all we can now say with certainty is that Conan Doyle, once provoked, was an indefatigable campaigner for justice, and one never afraid to speak his mind. Perhaps he could sometimes seem a little too confident of his position. Writing to *The Daily Telegraph* he offered to 'fully and utterly' convince the Home Office committee of George's innocence within half an hour, and concluded, 'He did not write … those letters. Of that I am absolutely certain, and there is no room for doubt whatever.' But Doyle had a redeeming humour, and was quite capable of deflating his reputation as a detective, as opposed to a fighter for criminal and social justice. 'I am more Watson than Holmes,' he once remarked to Reverend Edalji.

Doyle would continue to worry away at the case until the outbreak of the war that took the life of both his only brother and his oldest son, an ordeal from which he understandably never quite recovered. Doyle and Edalji, between them, are often said to have stung the authorities into finally establishing an English Court of Appeal, although the work to do this had actually begun shortly after the royal pardon and £5,000 compensation awarded to Adolf Beck in July 1904 as a result of his five years of wrongful imprisonment. Perhaps the real credit for this landmark development in British judicial history belongs to Thomas Gurrin, the hapless government handwriting expert who appeared for the prosecution in both cases.

✳ ✳ ✳

In November 1934, Enoch Knowles, a 57-year-old day labourer from Darlaston, a mining community about 8 miles south of Great Wyrley, was sentenced at Stafford Assizes to three years' penal servitude for sending menacing and obscene letters through the post. It was said in court that he had written to 'many prominent or notorious people' over the course of some thirty-five years. Knowles had joined the army in 1916, and from then on 'matters were all quiet', *The Times* reported:

> But in 1931 he got implicated in a county court action, and he apparently had this curious desire again, sending letters to a bailiff who had been in the case. Later he wrote to people on matters that had nothing to do with him at all. On one occasion he wrote a very cruel letter to a member of the Royal Family. The police and the Post Office authorities had been for years trying to find out who was responsible.

At his trial, it emerged that Knowles had been the individual who sent the 1903 anonymous letters to the Staffordshire Police warning them that there was 'a looney' afoot, and that he would 'soon start on little girls'. He was the only person ever to be convicted of the relatively more benign part of the Great Wyrley outrages of 1888–1907. Conan Doyle himself had died before he could see Knowles brought to justice, but George Edalji lived for another nineteen years, continuing to protest his innocence to the end.

6

THE LOST WORLD

Conan Doyle's principal mission in life, at least until he began communicating with the dead, was to 'engage mind and pen for the noblest human purposes', which he saw as distinct from the 'humbler plane' of his detective fiction. Lovers of the Sherlock Holmes canon can be grateful that he had bills to pay.

In October 1909 Doyle embraced another controversial cause when he published his booklet *The Crime of the Congo*, which over time would tragically become something of a perennial crisis. The horrors of Belgian colonial rule in the area had first been brought to public attention in Joseph Conrad's 1899 novella, *Heart of Darkness*, and would still exercise the main protagonists in the Cold War more than sixty years later.

In public, Doyle described the sufferings of the Congolese as 'the greatest crime which has ever been committed in the history of the world'. Privately, he sometimes remarked that it struck him as being much like one of his periodic attacks of gout, 'apparently cured, only to flare up again with renewed vigour'. His book on the Congo took him eight days to write, and sold 60,000 copies in Britain alone. Doyle met with government ministers, lobbied the American President and the German Kaiser, and publicly admonished the Roman

Catholic Archbishop of Westminster for 'falling out of line with the rest of Christian Europe over this scandal'.

His differences with the established Church as a whole increased with time, and aroused furious controversy. Within a decade, Doyle himself would be widely regarded as the spokesman if not the founder of a new religion, one devoted not only to 'irrefutably proving man's immortality', but also to the more secular goal of 'exposing the idiocy that frequently attends our clergy, judges and other men of affairs'. Doyle's fellow doctor-turned-author, Henry de Vere Stacpoole, later wrote of him:

> His motto was that of Theodore Roosevelt, 'Aggressive fighting for the right is the noblest sport the world affords', and he lived up to it ... Conan Doyle was the finest man I have ever met, taking him by and large.

As Doyle himself remarked, there were those who made prisons for themselves out of their 'ignorance or prejudice [towards] Spiritualism's message of hope and comfort'. And there were those whose confinement was of a more material kind. On 18 October 1910 Doyle's attentions again turned to a sensational true-life crime when he travelled up from his new Sussex home, Windlesham, for the opening of the Old Bailey trial of Dr Hawley Harvey Crippen for murdering and dismembering his wife.

Crippen had been born in Coldwater, Michigan, in 1862 and qualified there as a homeopath before moving to London with his second wife, a 22-year-old New Yorker named Kunigunde Mackamotski. Cora, as she preferred to call herself, had ambitions to become an opera singer, but conspicuously lacked both the talent and the training to carry the plan off. One early review in the north London paper *The Clarion* referred to Cora's 'towering nest of auburn hair' and 'Brobdingnagian appearance upon the stage, [which] was not wholly matched by the force of her voice'. There were only a few other public notices over the years, none of them as good as this one. There seems room for disagreement about whether in time Cora had supplemented her income by prostitution. The couple had moved around frequently before settling in 1905 at 39 Hilldrop Crescent in north London's Kentish Town, where they took in lodgers to help pay the bills. Part of the morbid appeal of the eventual trial surely came from the comic disparity between the mousy, bespectacled Crippen and the widely displayed photograph of his well-padded wife, whom the *Globe* correspondent described as 'decked out like a galleon in full sail'.

In early January 1910, Crippen, having been sacked from his job selling Dr Munyon's Patent Medicines, was working under the name 'Cuppen' at Drouets Institute for the Deaf, a quack enterprise located in Finchley, north London, where he befriended an attractive 27-year-old secretary named Ethel Le Neve. The court would hear that they had gone on to 'adopt terms of some familiarity'. Cora, too, strayed from the monogamous ideal with a succession of lovers, some, apparently, of her own sex. She and her husband had struck Le Neve as 'sometimes friendly, often hostile, but strangely inseparable'.

In 1937, a young American psychologist called Abraham Maslow published a paper on sexual dominance. One of his conclusions was that there was an 'alpha female' type, whom he characterised as:

> ... enjoying sexual experimentation, often of a [lesbian] nature, narcissistic, promiscuous, and prefer[ring] a man of equal self-assurance ... When such a woman forms an alliance with a lesser personality, the results can be violent and destructive.

Again, such generalisations should be applied with care to any individual, but, as Maslow wrote, 'they seem to closely fit the known facts of the Crippens' strained marriage'.

When Cora disappeared from her home early in 1910, her husband simply told friends that she had gone back to live in America. It seemed plausible enough to them. Then Le Neve started to appear in public wearing Cora's clothes and jewellery, and the police called on Dr Crippen at Hilldrop Crescent. Chief Inspector Walter Dew of Scotland Yard later remarked that the 'suspect ... had at first been in command of the situation. He kept his apparent good humour, and artfully dodged traps that we set for him.'

They got to him eventually, however, and he referred to 'excessive, vicious, distorted ... loaded, outrageous questioning'. When the inspector next called, he found that Crippen had now also disappeared. A search of the premises revealed a badly decomposed human torso, of indeterminate sex, wrapped in a pyjama top, concealed in the basement. Bernard Spilsbury, the Home Office pathologist and Doyle's fellow Crimes Club member, identified the remains as those of Cora Crippen. She had evidently been poisoned and then dismembered.

On 31 July, in an early use of radio telegraphy, Crippen and Le Neve were arrested on board the liner SS *Montrose* as it docked in Canada. They had passed themselves off to fellow passengers on the Atlantic crossing as a 'Mr Robinson' and his son John, though suspicions had been aroused when the former was seen to be armed with a gun and the latter strolled on the promenade deck 'wearing a stylish blue coat studded with tiny silver stars [while] at his neck was knotted a scarf embroidered in many colours … He was elegant to a fault.'

Ten weeks later, Conan Doyle attended Crippen's trial as the guest of the original defence counsel, Edward Marshall Hall, a 52-year-old barrister who had made his name as a sparkling courtroom performer in the recent 'Camden Town Murder' of a prostitute found naked in a client's bedroom, her throat cut from ear to ear, among several other such high-profile cases. Hall, who parted company with Crippen over their differing opinions about a possible defence strategy, later went down to Doyle's house to discuss his theories on the case. These turned on the fact that Crippen had almost certainly given his wife the anaphrodisiac drug hyoscine, but not necessarily intending it as a lethal dose.

The two men met after dinner in front of the fire in Doyle's upstairs study, without ladies present, so a degree of plain speech was possible. Hall believed that Cora had been a nymphomaniac, and that her inadequate husband had administered the hyoscine to 'dampen that aspect of her ardour'. But the feckless Crippen had miscalculated the dose and his wife had died as a result. Seeing his mistake, he had lost his head. So had the unfortunate Cora.

Crippen would be remembered as a monster, Doyle reasoned, because 'the idea of decapitation plumbs the depths of horror in the human psyche'. However base and repellent it was, he added, the practice at least showed a logical aspect to the murderer's mind, which was otherwise 'not greatly distinguished by any subtlety of judgement' or even 'mean calculation'. Doyle agreed with Hall that in all likelihood Crippen had mutilated the body less in an atavistic frenzy and more in the simple belief that it would prevent identification. In the event, this strategy had nearly succeeded, and Spilsbury's conclusions about the remains would be disputed by DNA evidence nearly a century later.

The fact that Crippen seemed to have taken a week to dispose of Cora's head by dropping it off a Channel ferry indicated to the Crimes Club pair that the killing had not been premeditated. And from there Doyle could reconstruct most of the story:

A pathetically weak man, intimidated by his wife, has a love affair with a young lady at his office. He wishes to subdue the wife, possibly to enjoy an illicit encounter at the marital home. He does this incautiously, to fatal effect. All else that follows is a ghastly series of extemporised deeds which ultimately lead to his flight and arrest.

That left only the question of Ethel Le Neve. Had she been Crippen's partner in crime, or merely his passive companion when subsequently absconding to Canada? It perhaps speaks to Doyle's strong sense of chivalry that he believed the latter.

Dr Crippen was executed at Pentonville Jail on 23 November 1910. The jury had taken just twenty-seven minutes to reach its verdict. At a separate trial, Ethel Le Neve was acquitted of being an accessory to murder.

$$* \quad * \quad *$$

Doyle's fireside talk with Edward Hall was significant for reasons other than the Crippen case. Unusually for a professional man of the pre-war era, Hall was a practising spiritualist. His first wife had died in 1890 following a botched abortion, and he later became convinced that he could communicate with her with the help of a medium. Hall had 'urged Sir Arthur to consider the evidence of posthumous communion' he laid before him, and 'he responded quite favourably'. We know that around 1911 Conan Doyle began attending séances again.

The following year, he wrote to Hubert Stansbury to affirm his belief that a man's spirit survived the decomposition of his flesh. By then Doyle was also in regular correspondence with the physicist Sir Oliver Lodge, whose belief in the paranormal his friend hoped would be 'recognised as a trumpet call for all stragglers' not yet similarly convinced. Doyle also now resumed his experiments in mental psychic feats such as clairvoyance and telepathy. In time, he would write to his sceptical mother, 'I do not fear death … for since I became a convinced Spiritualist death [has become] rather an unnecessary thing'. On the eve of the Great War, Conan Doyle, by now 55, was again beginning to reassess his idea of mortality.

It was typical of Doyle to have increasingly concentrated on the ultimate meaning of life while remaining sharply focused on its material injustices. In the same month that he saw Dr Crippen in the dock at the Old Bailey, he spoke at a dinner given in London for the visiting American civil rights campaigner Booker T. Washington. A week later, he was lecturing on the Congo to a packed house at the capital's City Temple, the so-called Cathedral of Nonconformity wedged under a railway viaduct close to St Bart's Hospital, where Sherlock Holmes first met Dr Watson.

Between times, like most of Britain, Doyle had read of the brutal murder of an old lady of 82 in her Glasgow home one dark winter's night, a case he soon became convinced 'represent[ed] an even more outrageous miscarriage of justice than the Edalji scandal'.

✳ ✳ ✳

The whole concept of premature or violent death was one that was quite familiar to a generation of men (and to a lesser extent women) in the early years of the twentieth century. As well as the series of wars or revolutions everywhere from Morocco to Bosnia to Mexico, few European nations were immune from the heady atmosphere of patriotic fervour that would later be characterised as the 'spirit of 1914'.

There was a widespread sense, if not a universal one, that war was an almost spiritual experience, and that it mattered profoundly how a man behaved when confronted with death. The loss of the *Titanic* was only one, if the most vividly reported, of the individual human tragedies of the era, 'and not one without its uplifting features,' Doyle noted. 'There were many cases of outstanding decency and sacrifice.' It was another stirring example of how Englishmen could die. Doyle took particular cheer from the way in which the ship's orchestra had apparently played on to the last. His poem 'Ragtime', with its climactic lines, 'Shut off, shut off the ragtime! The lights are falling low! / The deck is buckling under us! She's sinking by the bow' went some way to immortalising that classic feature of the tragedy.

Doyle's preoccupation with the *Titanic* was at once moral, spiritual and at least potentially criminal. First, as we've seen, he took violent exception when George Bernard Shaw went into print questioning the crew's judgement and integrity. 'I ask,' Shaw wrote in a letter to the *Daily News and Leader*:

> What is the use of all this ghastly, inhuman, braggartly lying? Here is a calamity which might well make the proudest man humble, and the wildest joker serious.

It makes us vainglorious, insolent and mendacious … The effect on me was one
of profound disgust, almost of national dishonour.

In Shaw's provocative phrase, 'The wreck was nobody's fault, but, on the
contrary, a triumph of British navigation'.

Conan Doyle may have lacked Shaw's coruscating wit, or his undoubted
flair for drawing attention to himself. There was no contest between the two
authors when it came to creative vitriol or quotable aphorism. But Doyle had
the advantage of never thinking himself special, despite all the special things
he had done. He also held an innocent and unshakable belief in the essential
decency of his fellow Britons, notwithstanding the case of the Staffordshire
Police and one or two other notable exceptions to the rule. Doyle again showed
his chivalry and sincerity when he wrote in turn:

As to the general accusation that the occasion has been used for the glorification
of British qualities, we should indeed be a lost people if we did not honour
courage and discipline when we see it in the highest form … It is a pitiful sight
to see a man of undoubted genius using his gifts in order to misrepresent and
decry his own people.

Doyle's final comment in the *Daily News* of 20 May 1912 caught the public
mood skilfully. 'The worst I can say or think of Mr Shaw,' he wrote, 'is that his
many brilliant gifts do not include the power of weighing evidence', lacking
as he did the quality of 'good taste [and] humanity'.

As we've seen, Doyle also had a more personal stake in the loss of the *Titanic*:
his friend, the newspaperman William 'W.T.' Stead, who was 62, was among
the victims. Stead was in some ways as controversial a public figure as Shaw,
with a series of journalistic campaigns on the likes of female suffrage, universal
healthcare and penal reform to his name. In 1885 he had served three months
in prison for the 'abduction' of a 13-year-old girl, an offence he had committed
to draw attention to the scandal of child prostitution.

It's arguable that Stead anticipated Hunter S. Thompson and his school by
nearly a century in adopting the modern journalistic technique of creating a
news event rather than just reporting it. In later years, Doyle spoke at length
about this 'fine and indomitable fellow-fighter', whom he credited specifically
for his lurid exposés of 'life in the meanest slums of London [and] the attendant

horrors of drink', the latter always of particular concern to him. He did not mention that Stead had gone on to publish two pamphlets roundly attacking the behaviour of the British troops in the Boer War, whose appearance he privately called an 'extraordinary outbreak of defamation' of the fighting man. Doyle's own 1902 broadside, *The War in South Africa: Its Causes and Conduct*, was the direct result.

Although Conan Doyle crossed swords with Stead while he was alive, he enjoyed warm personal relations with him after his death. In May 1922, Doyle was in New York to give a sold-out lecture on spiritualism at Carnegie Hall. He brought the performance to a suitably dramatic climax by projecting a series of 'spirit photographs' which appeared to show the presence of 'extras', or ghostly auras, hovering in the background. There were gasps in the room when Doyle then displayed an image of Stead – well known to many in the audience – that he said was obtained by psychic means. 'It was a very clear portrait of a man,' the *New York Times* reported, 'and around the outside was scribbled, in handwriting which Sir Arthur said was undoubtedly his friend's, this line, "I will try to keep you posted".' Stead was as good as his word, because he was seemingly to return to Doyle, either in visual or written form, at regular intervals over the years.

Doyle also briefly considered the sinking of the *Titanic* as an act of individual or state terrorism. Several of the victims' friends and relatives wrote to him following the tragedy to tell him about themselves, their losses, and often their rather fanciful conspiracy theories. 'Over 1,500 souls did not forfeit their lives on the *Titanic*,' one correspondent wrote, 'but on her sister craft *Olympic*.' The two ships had been swapped, apparently, as part of a 'Zionist-backed insurance fraud'.

Other suspects drawn to Conan Doyle's attention included the American financier J.P. Morgan, who cancelled his berth on the *Titanic* at the last moment and 'instead … dispatched his many business rivals on board to the depths of oblivion', and, slightly more plausibly, 'a German (or Austrian) sub-mersible [which] fired an underwater device at the vessel'.

During the period 1910–14 Conan Doyle was as intent as any British statesman on preparing the nation for war with Germany. In November 1912, he gave a public speech on the need for a Channel tunnel (anticipating the authorities by eighty years), which he saw as a vital supply route to the Continent in the event the United Kingdom was cut off by naval action. He went on to publish a cautionary tale called 'Danger! A Story of England's

Peril', a prescient account of the nation being starved into submission by only a small number of enemy U-boats. But although he had no doubt that the submarine would one day be used for commerce raiding, nor any illusions about German military intentions, Doyle discounted these factors in the case of the *Titanic*. There was no 'linear connection' he told the Crimes Club, in terms Holmes might have echoed, and the only way to adopt an alternative theory of the tragedy was to submit to 'circuitous and hypothetical meanderings' of the mind.

In April 1913, Doyle played host at Windlesham to William J. Burns, the 52-year-old private detective whom the *New York Times* had called 'The real Sherlock Holmes' and 'Our Greatest Living Detective Mind', an enthusiasm Burns himself shared. The American brought with him a box-like 'detectaphone', or bugging device, along with other state-of-the-art law enforcement equipment. Doyle was sufficiently impressed to call this a 'real stepping-stone towards [a] definite solution' of a crime. Burns himself, he wrote, possessed 'the easy and polished manners of a diplomat over something else which can be polished – granite'.

Later that month, the two men consulted on a sensational murder case that began in a dank basement room smeared with waste and blood in Atlanta, Georgia. A 13-year-old girl named Mary Phagan had been found strangled and apparently raped in the cellar of a pencil factory where she worked, and the company's manager, Leo Frank, 29, was quickly arrested, tried and given the death sentence. Since Frank was precociously intelligent, hardworking, myopic and Jewish, the case bore a certain surface resemblance, as Doyle noted, to that of George Edalji. As Holmes advises Inspectors Lestrade and Gregson in *A Study in Scarlet*, 'There is nothing new under the sun. It has all been done before.'

Burns investigated the case, and concluded that the real culprit was one Jim Conley, a black janitor at the factory and the state's star witness against Frank. In the Deep South of that time, the Jew typically enjoyed an even less exalted place in society than the African American. Burns based his conclusions on carefully reconstructing the crime scene, and then timing the prosecution's version of events, which meant that Frank would have had to have finished working in his office on the morning in question, gone upstairs, checked on two co-workers, left the building, taken a ten-minute trolley ride home for lunch, returned to the factory, accosted Mary Phagan in the basement, brutally assaulted her, and then walked upstairs to calmly resume work, all within the space of half an hour.

Thanks to Burns and other campaigners, the case became a national issue. In time, the state commuted Frank's sentence to one of life imprisonment. Following that, a lynch mob that included former Georgia Governor Joseph Brown, future President of the State Senate Eugene Clay and several retired or current county sheriffs, removed Frank from jail, drove him for seven hours to Phagan's hometown of Marietta and hanged him from the branch of a tree. Despite having posed at the scene for photographs that were later published and sold as postcards, none of Frank's killers was ever arrested.

Doyle kept a volume full of court transcripts and newspaper cuttings on the case among the files in his crime library. It may have influenced his decision to include a lengthy American flashback in the plot of *The Valley of Fear*, which he began writing later in 1913. Burns subsequently became director of the first national bureau of investigation, predecessor to the FBI, but resigned amidst allegations that his agents had sought to intimidate newspaper editors critical of the bureau's activities. The 29-year-old J. Edgar Hoover took over as acting director, dying in office forty-eight years later. Burns himself moved to Florida and published detective stories until his death at the age of 71.

✳ ✳ ✳

Conan Doyle later wrote that the idea of an acceptable form of public entertainment underwent a 'rude shock' in the years just before the outbreak of the First World War. By now in his fifties, he had abandoned any pretence of sympathy for modernist culture. In particular, Doyle shrank from the more proscriptive plays of Henrik Ibsen, as well as the 'organised din' of Gustav Mahler and the perceived decadence of conceptual painters such as Marcel Duchamp and Edvard Munch. In time, he would go on to support the Conservative Home Secretary's proposals for greater powers of artistic censorship. Doyle's idea of a good writer remained the likes of Thomas Hardy, Winston Churchill or Rudyard Kipling, the last of whom he called 'England articulate'.

To many in pre-war Britain, however, the greatest shock to the established order wasn't the advent of Cubism, or such eye-catching developments as the works of Mondrian and Picasso, or Stravinsky's ballets, or the more kinetic rhythms of black dance bands accompanied by uninhibited young women in Scheherazade skirts. Nor was it the arrival on the London stage of Bernard Shaw's *Pygmalion*, with its scandalous use of the word 'bloody'. The subject of most news comment wasn't a public entertainment at all, though it may be argued that, over time, it became one. Rather, it was a meeting of immaculately dark-suited and apparently sober-minded men held at the Geological Society in London on 18 December 1912, when a 48-year-old lawyer and amateur palaeontologist named Charles Dawson claimed to have discovered bone fragments at a gravel pit near his home at Piltdown, East Sussex, and that these had 'terrific significance' for our understanding of human evolution.

At the same meeting, Arthur Smith Woodward, curator of the geological department at the British Museum, announced that a reconstruction of the fragments had been prepared, and that a resulting 'human-like' skull, thought to be some 600,000 years old, was all but indistinguishable from that of a modern chimpanzee. Dawson and Woodward went on to claim that 'Piltdown Man' represented no less than an evolutionary missing link between apes and humans, and by extension a denial of the biblical story of creation, a thesis much of the more progressive element of the press was happy to accept.

It was to be forty-one years before new scientific dating techniques conclusively proved that Dawson's discovery was a hoax. The Piltdown fossils 'could not possibly form an integral whole,' *The Times* reported in November 1953. Instead, they consisted of a human skull of medieval age, the jawbone of an eighteenth-century orangutan, and several assorted modern chimpanzee teeth. There was also a bone chip determined to have come from an extinct species of elephant unique to the plains of Tunisia. Only a brief microscopic examination was required to show that several jaw fragments presented by Dawson had been filed down to give them a shape associated with that of a human. A sculpted bone found at the original site in Sussex, and thought by Woodward to be 'a wonderfully preserved Neanderthal hunting or sporting tool' – a sort of primitive cricket bat – had been similarly formed with an 'implement like a Swiss army knife'. In short order, Piltdown Man was unceremoniously removed from display and consigned to a metal box in the basement of London's Natural History Museum, where it resides today.

As a part-time archaeologist, Charles Dawson was nothing if not prolific. In addition to what he modestly called his 'supreme discovery' of man's ancestral roots, he also turned up a wealth of flints, vases, tiles, statuettes and assorted hammers and axes, and claimed both to have excavated a large supply of natural gas of 'many inexplicable properties' and personally observed an 80ft-long sea serpent swimming in the English Channel. Even Arthur Smith Woodward, Dawson's champion at the British Museum, allowed that he had 'a restless mind'. A neighbour and fellow archaeologist named Margaret Boycott said, 'Charles was an otherwise obscure, unmarried little man who wore spectacles and a bowler hat'.

Did Dawson lead a Walter Mitty life, which found significance in 'discoveries' that he quite possibly meant as a sort of academic prank, at least up to the moment *Nature* magazine declared the Piltdown fossils 'the most important find of its kind ever made'? Was he perhaps flattered by his subsequent comparison to Charles Darwin? Some researchers have theorised that Dawson had expected his ruse – if only because of the prehistoric cricket bat – to be spotted straight away, but was horrified to see it take root in scientific thought. So he stayed silent. Following Dawson's death from septicaemia in August 1916, no further finds were made at Piltdown.

While Dawson was almost certainly the main culprit behind the twentieth century's greatest scientific hoax, it's long been believed that he had the help of co-conspirators. Could these conceivably have included a nearby resident who was known to be keen to 'adjust the guardrails defining orthodox spiritual teaching', as he put it? Did Piltdown Man provide such a man with the Archimedean point from which to challenge received Christian wisdom? Could the creator of Sherlock Holmes have taken a certain intellectual pleasure from the employment of his skill and cunning at the expense of the religious and political Establishment?

These are the known facts. In 1912, Doyle lived only 7 miles from the scene of Dawson's apparent triumph. He played golf at Piltdown most weekends. A study of his commonplace book, or diary, shows him frequently dwelling on the topic of man's evolution, and describing a whole series of skulls and relics brought to his attention over the years. Doyle also had pretensions as an archaeologist, and one of the characters in his 1912 novel *The Lost World* says, 'If you are clever and know your business, you can fake a bone as easily as you can a photograph'. He knew and apparently admired Charles Dawson, and wrote him an enthusiastic letter in the month Piltdown Man was discovered. Dawson in turn wrote to Smith Woodward to tell him that Doyle, that 'omnivorous reader' on anthropology, seemed 'excited about the skull' and had 'kindly offered to drive me in his motor next week anywhere'.

While it conjures up a vivid image of a caped author in a deerstalker cap paying nocturnal visits to the Piltdown site to scatter assorted bone fragments by the light of a lantern, Doyle's candidacy as Dawson's accomplice should be treated with caution. Although sometimes credulous when it came to the more obvious charlatans of the psychic world, there's little evidence that he ever personally resorted to fabricating data to discredit orthodox religious thought. None of Doyle's own archaeological finds or direct supernatural encounters over the years have turned out to be deliberate frauds on his part. It may well be that, as the *Guardian* writes, 'Sir Arthur's Spiritualism had brought him into conflict with organised Christianity, and he wanted to humiliate its practitioners'. That still leaves the question of timing: Piltdown Man was discovered in 1912, while Doyle underwent his final conversion to the paranormal only in 1916. As in the case of the middle period of anonymous letters in Great Wyrley, we may never know for sure who was responsible and whether, in the end, both offences were nothing more than the activity of an able but emotionally stunted individual who wanted to show off his superior intelligence.

Perhaps the ultimate lesson of Piltdown Man is that, as Harry Houdini once said of Doyle, 'As a rule, I have found the greater brain a man has, and the better he is educated, the easier it has been to deceive him'. Not only did many of the best, and certainly most self-regarding, minds of the early twentieth century rush to embrace the findings of a weekend archaeologist like Charles Dawson; more than a century later, it remains a widespread but lazy assumption that the biblical story of creation and the evolution of the physical universe might not be twin manifestations of a divine act of self-revelation. Doyle himself, for all his aversion to traditional Christian pieties, saw no such contradiction.

✳   ✳   ✳

The annals of criminology reveal that even in the English Home Counties of the early twentieth century, many respectable, middle-class citizens often saw the occult at work. As we've seen, when Conan Doyle moved to the pleasantly leafy village of Hindhead, Surrey, he did so primarily for its presumed benefits to his wife Louisa's health. The house he built, Undershaw, craned out over the spectacular gorge known as the Devil's Punchbowl, the 'loveliest spot in England', Doyle believed, even if one allegedly haunted by the ghosts of highwaymen who had once been hung from a gibbet there. In 1851, a Celtic cross was erected on the site of the executions in response to public unease about it. To one visitor, the view from Undershaw was 'like a scene from a Wagnerian tale', while the house itself offered distinct gothic touches such as 'baronial fires, stained glass [and] a secret chamber built behind a bookcase in the library', and would be steadily enlarged over the years into a 'grandiose manor, suitable for state visits of great artists and other dignitaries'.

As we've seen, by 1913 Doyle and his new family had moved 60 miles away to Crowborough, which at around 800ft above sea level also enjoyed something of a reputation as a health resort. But he returned to his earlier home at least once that year in response to requests that he investigate 'strange phenomena' seen in the area. These included the discovery of a dead cat strung from a tree close to the scene of the judicial hangings, several instances of curious 'stick-like ciphers', similar to those in Sherlock Holmes's 'Adventure of the Dancing Men', daubed on residents' doors, and an anonymous note delivered to the Devil's Punchbowl Hotel which instructed 'Mr H. of Baker Street' to search the nearby woods for a 'sacred chest' containing the meaning of life.

Doyle soon located the 'chest', a badly decayed biscuit tin that was found to hold only a used London bus pass and some ladies' underclothes. He apparently went to the trouble to enquire at Scotland Yard if any women had been reported missing at around the date shown on the ticket, but to no avail. A local lawyer named James Lanyon later thought it:

> Striking [how] this beefy and *sportif* man, who looked like an old rugby player, spoke quite seriously of his belief that there were 'mysterious sprites and entities' at play in the woods, and that the recent phenomena at [Hindhead] were somehow down to them. The condition of his seeming to live in two separate worlds at once was one of the most remarkable achievements of Sir Arthur's mind.

Exercising the more material side of his nature, Conan Doyle also continued to meet regularly with William Melville, the Irish-born former policeman who went on to become the chief of Britain's first Secret Service agency. Since Doyle had once helped raise funds for Melville on his retirement from Scotland Yard, it's possible the spymaster felt himself to be in the author's debt. Perhaps unsurprisingly, there's no known record of their correspondence. But in the darkening European situation of 1913–14 Doyle would almost certainly have spoken to Melville about his recent experience of driving his new gaudy green and red touring car through Germany as part of an international automobile rally organised by the Kaiser's brother. As a goodwill exercise, this particular event counted as only a mixed success. Doyle later regarded the rally as a 'clumsy bit of stage management' intended to draw attention from

German war preparations. 'I came away with sinister forebodings,' he recalled. Melville, who died in 1918, lives on today as the prototype for 'M' in the James Bond franchise.

✳ ✳ ✳

'He did a lot of reading – literature, sports periodicals, and bundles of true-crime files,' Harry Houdini said, suitably impressed at the 'range and quality' of Conan Doyle's mind. By now Doyle had read almost every known work on Napoleonic history. He had read every word that Robert Louis Stevenson and Edgar Allan Poe had ever published. He read and re-read Thomas Macaulay's *Essays* until the cover fell off his original copy and he had to buy another one. Like Sherlock Holmes, Doyle was also a newspaper obsessive, especially the police and court pages and the agony columns. Papers and journals of all sorts are a recurring plot device for Holmes; time and again, he reads an account of a crime in one of the dozen or so London dailies, runs advertisements in them, or consults their personal columns. He's sufficiently familiar with the mass media of the day to immediately identify a letter composed of cut-up newsprint that features in *The Hound of the Baskervilles* as having come from that day's leader in *The Times*. Doyle, too, clearly enjoyed reading for its own sake, but like Holmes also took a keen professional interest in the accounts of the various outrages he pored over at the breakfast table each morning.

Such a case came Doyle's way in a sensational, if not apparently criminal, story published in the *News of the World* on 3 January 1915. It concerned the sorry fate of 38-year-old Margaret Lloyd, née Lofty, a vicar's daughter who had been married only two weeks earlier. Her 42-year-old husband John, apparently a successful land agent, had discovered her lifeless body in the bath of their lodgings at Bismarck Road in north London. The couple's landlady testified that she had been ironing in her kitchen that evening when the sound of splashing came from the bathroom above. This was followed by the 'queer noise of hands rubbing [or] slapping a firm surface', and then by a deep sigh. A few minutes later, she had heard the mournful strains of someone playing 'Nearer, My God, to Thee' on the organ in the Lloyds' sitting room. Mr Lloyd then came down the stairs and went out, only to ring at the front door a few minutes later, explaining that he had forgotten his key. 'I've bought some tomatoes for Mrs Lloyd's supper,' he announced. 'Is she down yet?' Margaret's death was quickly recorded as misadventure, and her widower collected the

£700 life insurance policy he had thoughtfully taken out for her on the day of their wedding.

In retrospect, it might seem that a set of circumstances involving a husband of somewhat dubious background, an inexplicably drowned wife and a sizable insurance policy, all played out to the doleful soundtrack of the last hymn heard on the deck of the *Titanic*, would merit a degree of official scrutiny. Nor was John Lloyd in obvious emotional distress at his bereavement. When the hearse drew up to remove his wife's body, he told the undertaker, 'I don't want any walking, get it over as quick as you can', following which he was heard to say, 'When they're dead, they're dead'. However, the police declined to investigate the affair.

As with the Edalji case, events unfolded with what now seems almost breakneck speed: Margaret Lloyd died on the night of 18 December 1914; the official inquest took place on 1 January 1915; and John Lloyd pocketed his wife's estate in full nine days later.

Although the coroner saw nothing suspect about Margaret Lloyd's death, which was ruled a domestic accident, Conan Doyle immediately made the connection to a similar tragedy he had read about almost exactly a year earlier. This had involved Alice Burnham, a plump and pretty young nurse who, in November 1913, had married a George Smith in Portsmouth. On their wedding day, Smith had taken his bride to a doctor who certified that she was healthy enough to take out a £500 insurance policy, with her husband the beneficiary. The couple had then gone to Blackpool on a delayed honeymoon.

On the evening of Friday, 12 December, Alice had asked if she could have a bath and their landlady, Margaret Crossley, had filled it for her. A few minutes later, Mrs Crossley noticed small drops of water seeping through her kitchen ceiling immediately below the bathroom. At that point, George Smith had called down the stairs, 'My wife can't speak – go for a doctor'. The death certificate was signed at 10.30 that night and the inquest convened at 11 the following morning. It returned the verdict that 25-year-old Alice had 'Accidentally drowned through heart failure when in the bath'. Three days later, after a perfunctory funeral, her husband applied for probate of his wife's estate, which he collected in time for Christmas.

Conan Doyle was not only struck by the coincidence of the two newly married women drowning in the bath with their husbands nearby. As a doctor, he also knew the practical difficulties of a fully grown adult dying in this way – 'in any conventional episode,' Doyle wrote, 'the body would have been convulsed and then pushed up' with the onset of a medical event such as a heart attack. In both recent cases, the tub had simply been too small for the victims' heads to slip below the level of the water. It seemed to Doyle in a letter written in January 1915 to Detective Inspector Arthur Neil of Scotland Yard that 'some degree of coercion' must have been applied.

In time, Alice Burnham's father Charles and Margaret Crossley's husband Joseph both wrote to the police with similar suspicions. Thus began the downfall of George Smith, who was found to be one and the same as John Lloyd, and also presumed responsible for the death in July 1912 of Bessie Munday, a young Kent woman with a £2,500 legacy from her late father. She, too, had drowned in identical fashion after her husband, a man calling himself Henry Williams, had gone to the trouble of visiting a local hardware shop in order to rent a cast-iron bathtub for their home.

On 23 March 1915, George Joseph Smith was charged with the murder of all three women, although he was tried only for that of Bessie Munday. In court it emerged that he had entered into at least six bigamous marriages over the years. The jury took eighteen minutes to find Smith guilty. After his appeal was denied, he was hung at Maidstone Prison on Friday, 13 August. Charles Matthews, the Director of Public Prosecutions, wrote to the Commissioner of Scotland Yard:

I feel I ought not to allow any interval of time to pass without expressing the acknowledgement which, in my opinion, the administration of justice is under to Divisional Detective Inspector Neil, and to the officers who served under him, for their untiring, able, zealous, insightful and intelligent efforts, which played so conspicuous a part in securing the conviction which was this day obtained.

As Doyle has Holmes remark to the callow Inspector Forbes when rebuked for stealing the limelight in 'The Adventure of the Naval Treaty':

On the contrary, out of my last fifty-three cases my name has only appeared in four, and the police have had all the credit in forty-nine. I don't blame you for not knowing this, but if you wished to get on in your new duties you will work with me, and not against me.

Bigamy also played a part in a case brought to Doyle's attention while he was in Chicago for what he modestly called a 'not inconsiderable programme' of forty-two lectures in a ten-week tour of North America. It involved the death of 18-year-old Frank Westwood, who had answered the doorbell of his family's comfortable suburban Toronto home at about nine o'clock one wet Saturday night. Upstairs, his parents had heard a 'sharp report' followed by a thud as their son fell to the floor.

'Mother, mother, I am shot,' he cried. His parents rushed downstairs to find the hallway full of smoke and Frank lying across the doorstep, bleeding profusely, a bullet hole in his waistcoat. At that point, Mr Westwood had fired his own gun in the air, apparently in the hope that it would summon the police. Frank died three days later, having told the detectives who visited him in hospital that he thought his assailant had been a 'dark, slender young man'.

The 'Parkdale Mystery', as the press dubbed it, was as sensational in its way as the case of the serial drowned brides in England. The grounds and the street outside the Westwoods' home were filled with reporters and sightseers on the day of Frank's funeral. The *Toronto World* wrote, 'Half the feminine population of town was present. Young girls, children and mothers of families who came with baby carriages waited in the melancholy drizzle to see the procession.'

Hector Charlesworth, an enterprising young editor at the *World*, sent Conan Doyle some cuttings on the case, adding that Mr Westwood, a wealthy fishing tackle manufacturer, was rumoured locally to be 'excessively uxorious – that is, faithful to three or four wives at once'. There was also the hometown sleuth named W.H. Hornberry, whom the Toronto press referred to somewhat derisively as 'our Sherlock Holmes'. In due course, Hornberry told the inquest into Frank Westwood's death that he had meticulously searched the grounds following the tragedy, seeking clues, and had found a scrap of paper on which was written, 'If you do not – I will'. His Holmesian powers seemed to have deserted him at that point, however, because he had thrown the message away.

Conan Doyle's response to the *World*, though guarded, was enough for it to be splashed by the paper on its front page. 'Dear Sir,' he wrote, 'I shall read the case, but you can realise how impossible it is for an outsider who is ignorant of local conditions to offer an opinion. Thanking you, I am, Faithfully Yours, A. Conan Doyle.'

By the time Doyle arrived to speak in Toronto a month later, the police had arrested a suspect in the case – not a 'dark, slender young man' but a half-caste 32-year-old woman named Clara Ford. Among other unusual habits, she was known to dress in men's clothing, and had once passed herself off as a member of the Toronto Baptist boys' choir. She had apparently become infatuated with Frank Westwood, and shot him after he rejected her. There remained some question whether the police had coerced Ford's confession. Hector Charlesworth recalled that Doyle, though exhausted from his journey, had asked:

> … immediately on his arrival that a reporter be sent to him who could tell him all subsequent developments [in the Westwood case]. When I talked with him he laughingly said that he was the last man in the world to offer answers in murder mysteries, because in the Sherlock Holmes stories he always had his solutions ready-made before he started to write and constructed his narratives backward from that point.

Speaking to reporters after his lecture that night, Doyle added:

> It is a strangely absorbing mystery, and I discussed it at length with my brother after reading it … I can quite understand how, in the first instance, the public may have thought that the family knew something more of the affair than they stated, but I concluded that the father's story was so unusual that it must be true. As to the present prisoner, Clara Ford, I cannot offer an opinion. I never met with such a case as hers. The system of closeting a woman with an officer and cross-examining her for hours savours more of French than English methods of justice.

Doyle was not alone in his misgivings about the police treatment of Clara Ford. At her trial, she withdrew her confession, claiming it had been made in a 'sweat-box' under conditions of extreme duress. Her interrogators had been 'vultures in human form', Ford added. It took the jury just thirty-five minutes to find her not guilty, after which an impromptu municipal street party had broken out. Charlesworth wrote:

> I saw [Ford] proceed in a carriage through town followed by a cheering throng, and in gratitude she asked the jurors to supper at the negro restaurant where she had boarded. The invitation was accepted, and the presiding judge, Chancellor Sir John Boyd, told me later that it was the most disgusting example of the weakness of the jury system he recalled in a long experience.

Clara Ford later toured North America in 'Sam T. Jack's Creoles', a black burlesque show, and was advertised as 'A Damsel who killed a Worm in pursuance of "The Unwritten Law"'.

Conan Doyle would have been familiar with the concept of a woman avenging herself on a man who had seemingly mistreated her. It features prominently in the 1904 Holmes story 'The Adventure of Charles Augustus Milverton', when Milverton is shot by a veiled figure he is attempting to blackmail. Holmes and Watson happen to be hiding behind a curtain, and witness the crime. 'I was about to spring out,' the latter remarks in Doyle's voice, 'when I felt Holmes' cold, strong grasp upon my wrist. I understood the whole argument of that firm, restraining grip – that it was no affair of ours; that justice had overtaken a villain.' Later in the story Holmes declines a police request to investigate the killing, telling Lestrade, 'My sympathies are with the criminals rather than with the victim, and I will not handle this case'.

Strikingly, there's also a certain amount of cross-dressing to be found in Doyle's work: a woman disguises herself as a man in 1891's 'A Scandal in Bohemia', while the reverse formula applies in 1908's 'The Man with the Watches'. Doyle later said that it was 'sometimes almost impossible to view with equanimity the sheer stupidity and cruelty of the police' when seeking to extract a confession from their prime suspect.

※ ※ ※

On Easter Monday, 24 April 1916, Conan Doyle received an unsettling letter from 'an old friend and fellow scribbler on the plight of Central Africa', the Anglo-French journalist Edmund Morel. Morel wrote with the news (which Doyle may already have seen in his daily paper) that their one-time colleague Sir Roger Casement, who was 51 and thought to be either emotionally disturbed or homosexual – in so far as society then made the distinction – had been arrested in the ruins of a Roman fort on the west coast of Ireland, with a German rail ticket in his pocket. The police also relieved Casement of a bag containing 'a green and yellow flag, with a representation of a castle in the centre and some foreign language underneath, some maps, a pair of field glasses, a flash-lamp and forty rounds of ammunition'.

The events that had led the former British consul and distinguished humanitarian campaigner to this pass rivalled anything that Doyle could have conceived in his fiction. Three days earlier, a German U-boat had

landed Casement on the moonlit coast of Banna Strand in County Kerry.
His passage there had not been without incident. There had been engine
trouble and heavy seas, and during the six-day crossing from Wilhelmshaven
Casement had become semi-delirious on his ship's rations of schnapps and
tinned salmon.

Casement had planned to return to the land of his birth to foment an
uprising that would win what he called 'Irish self-determination and manifest
destiny' with the help of a consignment of some 15,000 German rifles and ten
machine guns. In the event, most of the arms were lost at sea. Even if deployed,
they would seem to have been pitifully inadequate to the task. Already doubtful
about his prospects of success, the seasick Casement had been able to stagger
only a few yards onto dry land before being arrested by two police constables
summoned by local villagers. Within hours he was taken to the Tower of
London on charges of treason, sabotage and mutiny against the British Crown
in a time of war.

Casement's trial began at the Old Bailey on 26 June 1916, featured an
Irish cab driver named Moriarty for the prosecution, and ended three days
later in a guilty verdict and the death sentence. It took some courage for
Conan Doyle to publicly support a reprieve for Casement, whom, like the
shoplifting Ella Castle twenty years earlier, he deemed 'more in need of
treatment than punishment'. This was the month of the appalling losses on
the River Somme, and there could be no presumption of public sympathy
for a quixotic Irishman of ambiguous sexuality who appeared to be in armed
cahoots with the enemy.

Doyle shared the widespread distaste for the 'foulest traitor who ever drew
breath', as he was popularly known, but for all that believed Casement could
not be held mentally responsible for his crime. The Irishman's actions struck
him as 'simply inexplicable' from any rational standpoint. 'We would call
attention to the violent change which appears to have taken place in the
prisoner's sentiments towards Great Britain,' Doyle wrote in his petition to the
government, asking that Casement's life be spared:

> We should desire to point out that the prisoner had for many years been exposed
> to severe strain during his honourable career of public service, that he had
> endured several tropical fevers, and that he had experienced the worry of two
> investigations which were of a peculiarly nerve-trying character.

Acknowledging receipt of Doyle's petition, the Home Secretary Herbert Samuel replied:

> As you are good enough to say that you desire to leave it to the discretion of His Majesty's Government whether the appeal should be made public, I am writing to inform you that the Government prefer that it should not.

This was perhaps to underestimate the author's obstinacy and resilience once embarked on a crusade for justice. Doyle soon rallied influential friends such as John Galsworthy, Arnold Bennett, William Butler Yeats, John Masefield and G.K. Chesterton, among others, to Casement's cause, although he seems to have parted from the more broadly pacifist Edmund Morel, whose tactics he called 'a policy of murder'. (George Bernard Shaw characteristically circulated his own rival petition.)

On 2 July, Doyle wrote to his fellow campaigner, the literary journalist Clement Shorter. 'Personally, I believe Casement's mind was unhinged,' he reasoned:

> His honourable nature would in a normal condition have revolted from such an action … I am entirely against his execution. I am sure it is wrong. It seems to me that the line to go upon is to absolutely acknowledge his guilt & the justice of his sentence and at the same time urge the political wisdom of magnanimity. It should be signed so far as possible by men who have shown no possible sympathy for Germany or pacific leanings.

On 13 July:

> Dear Shorter, The summons to the Foreign Office proved to be about Casement. They told me that his record for sexual offences was bad and had a diary of his as proof of it. I had of course heard this before, but as no possible sexual offence could be as bad as suborning soldiers from their duty, I was not diverted from my purpose. None the less it is of course very sad, and an additional sign of mental disorder.

The record shows that Doyle again wrote to the authorities on 25 July, at which point he believed there were still 'some weeks' before the date of Casement's execution. But the prisoner's 'black diaries', as they became known, soon countered any appeals for clemency. Circulated in parliament and the press, no one who read them, according to the *News of the World*, would 'ever mention Casement's name again without loathing and contempt'. He was hung at Pentonville Jail on 3 August 1916.

In his autobiography, Doyle was both generous and not entirely free of authorial pride on the subject. He wrote:

> Casement, whom I shall always regard as a fine man afflicted with mania, has met his tragic end, and Morel's views upon the war have destroyed the feelings which I had for him. But I shall always maintain that they both did noble work in championing the wrongs of those unhappy and helpless negroes … My own book *The Crime of the Congo*, which was translated into all European languages, had also, I hope, some influence towards that end.

Like Holmes, Doyle was not one to let a cognitively demanding role like petitioning the authorities on a matter of life and death prevent him from accepting a variety of other calls on his mental resources. Both characters combined a clarity of mind with the ability, perhaps rarer than it is now, to multitask. In 1915 alone, Doyle wrote comprehensive accounts of the battles of Mons and Le Cateau, both to fall foul of War Office censors; contributed an internationally syndicated article that appeared under the optimistic headline, 'Conan Doyle Sees Victory for England – One Successful Pounce Will Win'; wrote to *The Times* insisting that Britain should retaliate in kind for Zeppelin air raids against civilian targets; busied himself in improving lifesaving armour for Allied soldiers; and tirelessly marched a volunteer force around the Sussex Downs.

He also showed a more distinctly Holmesian touch when he came to develop a secret correspondence with captured British troops held at the prison camp at Magdeburg in Saxony. 'I took one of my books,' Doyle recalled:

> And beginning with the third chapter – I guessed the censor would examine the first – I put little needle-pricks under the various printed letters until I had spelled out all the news. I then sent the book and also a letter. In the letter I said that the book was, I feared, rather slow in the opening, but that from Chapter 3 onwards [the reader] might find it more interesting. [He] missed the allusion altogether, but by good luck he showed the letter to Captain the Honourable Rupert Keppel, of the Guards, who had been taken at Landrecies. He smelled a

rat, borrowed the book, and found my cipher. A message came back to his father, Lord Albemarle, to the effect that he hoped Conan Doyle would send some more books.

This was just the start of a continuing three-year programme of secret communication with captured Allied troops. In time, Doyle provided one of his correspondents with a Bible, a work he felt 'even the Germans' unlikely to forbid. Later variants on this came to include the *Encyclopaedia Britannica* and several volumes of Dickens. Doyle then fashioned his messages by periodically writing a page number, a line number and the number of a word, which he took from an identical edition of the book in his library. His letters were largely composed of seemingly innocuous accounts of the current weather conditions or the result of a local sports event, which allowed him to use the groups of numbers without unduly raising suspicion. Thus, the German censor might think he was reading about the score in a cricket match, while in reality Doyle's letter conveyed news of a recent British offensive, or the intervention of the Americans.

✳ ✳ ✳

'Our household suffered terribly in the war,' Conan Doyle wrote in his memoirs. By the time the deadly summer of 1916 began – with Doyle still lobbying on behalf of Roger Casement – the honour roll already included 'two brave nephews, Alex Forbes and Oscar Hornung, shot down with bullets through the brain' and his 'gallant brother-in-law, Major Oldham … killed by a sniper during his first days in the trenches'.

On 1 July, Doyle's 23-year-old son Kingsley was seriously wounded on the blood-sodden first day of the Allied 'push' at the Somme. 'He is in God's hands,' his father wrote. Although Kingsley was able to return to the front line just two months later, it was an understandably 'profound jolt' to the family, who by then had begun to hold regular drawing room séances under the mediumship of their house guest, Lily Loder-Symonds, a 'sensitive' who had discovered her gift following the loss of three of her own brothers in combat.

Despite these blows, many of Conan Doyle's letters continued to almost exult in the joys and dangers of battle, while his public writings retained their note of patriotic idealism. Donning an outfit 'which was something between that of a Colonel or Brigadier, with silver roses instead of stars or crowns upon the shoulder-straps', Doyle successively visited the Italian, French and British front lines. 'I confess that as I looked at those brave English lads,' he wrote, 'and thought of what we owed to them and to their like who have passed on, I felt more emotional than befits a Briton in foreign parts.' Doyle's faith in the essential merit of the Allied cause survived even a subsequent visit to the front at Saint-Quentin, near the Somme, where he wrote of a scene of almost apocalyptic horror, with a pyre of mangled equipment and dead horses, beside which 'a man with his hand blown off was staggering away, the blood gushing from his upturned sleeve'.

✳ ✳ ✳

Christianity had not been in slow decline for 1,900 years but was 'a vital living thing still growing and working,' Conan Doyle had written in his unpublished 1884 novel *The Narrative of John Smith*, the manuscript of which had been lost in the post. In November 1916, as his family losses mounted in the fields of France and Flanders, Doyle again took up the questions of God and man's relationship to Him in an article published in the psychic magazine *Light*, widely reprinted under the headline, 'Author Says We Can Talk with the Dead'.

Doyle asked:

Are we to satisfy ourselves by observing phenomena with no attention to what the phenomena mean, as a group of savages might stare at a wireless installation with no appreciation of the messages coming out of it? Or are we resolutely to set ourselves to define these subtle and elusive utterances from beyond, and to construct from them a religious scheme which shall be founded upon human reason on this side and upon spirit inspiration on the other?

According to Doyle, this emerging data should be the basis of a new religion 'in some ways confirmatory' of ancient truths and in others a clean break from the past.

Conan Doyle's own spiritual beliefs had been forged in the crucible of experience. As we've seen, he dabbled in psychic activities like clairvoyance and telepathy from his earliest days as a young doctor in Southsea. His famously rational mind had long allowed for the possibility of 'generous amounts [of] non-observable phenomena' at work in the universe. Even then Doyle had been a 'respectful and frequent' visitor to the séance room. Now, as the war dragged on, it would provide him a near daily consolation.

Doyle also consistently sought out intellectual support for his beliefs, perhaps reflecting the nagging sense of insecurity and a need for respect that seem to have set in at the time of his father's long and, to some, shameful decline. Early in his article in *Light*, he cites such men as 'Crookes, Wallace, Flammarion, Barrett, Generals Draycott and Turner, Sergeant Ballantyne, W.T. Stead, Judge Edmunds, Vice Admiral Usborne Moore [and] the late Archdeacon Wilberforce' as corroborating his views. From late 1916, Doyle was to enter into steadily closer correspondence with his 'wonderfully distinguished' friend Sir Oliver Lodge, a pioneering scientist and prolific inventor who ultimately lost out to better funded rivals, among them Hertz and Marconi, when it came to converting his theories on radio transmission into a practical household wireless set. A year earlier, Lodge's son Raymond had apparently spoken to him in a séance, describing his 'supremely comfortable' afterlife in a place he called 'Summerland'.

Soon Conan Doyle was writing to Lodge as a man of science to enquire about the Crewe-based 'spirit photographer' William Hope, who claimed to be able to register images on photographic plates simply by holding them in his hand. Doyle appeared eager to believe, noting that Hope was in 'very poor circumstances' and a deserving case for subsidy. Even so, the creator of Sherlock Holmes clearly hadn't abandoned his analytical faculties entirely. In his earliest discussions with Harry Houdini, Doyle wondered only whether the occult would one day prove useful in solving crimes, and Houdini acknowledged that this might be the case, not mentioning that he himself had once toured the American music halls in a double act with his wife Bess, the climax of which came when Bess fell into a 'trance-like communion' with the soul of some recent murder victim (though never successfully identifying the individual's killer) in each town where they performed. There were other signs, too, that Doyle retained a certain respect for what he called the 'honest, earnest, materialist' approach to life. Writing to Lodge in May 1917, he spoke of having tried to 'scientifically verify' the messages given to him by a medium named Miss Wearne, and that in every case these were 'absolutely wrong'.

Nonetheless, Doyle's life was now 'absorbed in advanc[ing]' the spiritualist cause, and his literary career soon followed suit. Alongside his war history he was to publish works such as *The New Revelation* (1918) and *The Vital Message*

(1919) that understandably came as a surprise to those who knew him only as the author of crime fiction and rollicking Napoleonic dramas. Before *The Vital Message* was even published, letters began to arrive at Windlesham addressed to 'Chief Devil, Spiritualist Church', among other equally unappreciative titles. The saner correspondents contented themselves with remarking sadly that Conan Doyle's recent output was more Watson than Holmes – 'that great man would never have sat down with spooks,' wrote one, a view the author himself evidently shared.

Increasingly, Doyle was once more the preacher that at heart he arguably always had been. On 25 October 1917, he gave a widely reported speech to the London Spiritualist Alliance, chaired by Oliver Lodge, in which he spoke unambiguously about his beliefs. Several well-attended public lectures followed. Meanwhile, readers of *The Strand* magazine, who had long enjoyed a privileged first appearance of Conan Doyle's Sherlock Holmes stories, would come to find themselves puzzling over articles entitled 'The Absolute Proof' and 'The Evidence for Fairies', contributed by the same author.

Doyle's sense of mission also took more earthly form. As by the cases of George Edalji and Roger Casement, his crusading instincts were roused by the 'tragic human consequences' of alcohol, and the distressing prospect of thousands of battle-hardened soldiers returning on leave to 'harlot-haunted' London.

Perhaps no single event shook Doyle's public reputation as the creator of English literature's greatest human calculating machine quite as much as the long, often tragicomic, saga of the Cottingley fairies. When the young Elsie Wright and her cousin Frances Griffiths returned from their photographic expedition behind the Wrights' home that hot Saturday afternoon in July 1917, it was recalled that they did so 'in high spirits', having had 'wonderful fun' with their camera. That this particular account of their adventure was true cannot be doubted. In time the photographs they claimed to have taken came to the attention of first *Light* magazine and then Conan Doyle, who was not slow to pronounce on them as proof of a 'primitive missing link' in the evolutionary chain. 'I have something far more precious [than spirit photographs]', Doyle wrote to Houdini:

Two photos, one of a goblin, the other of four fairies dancing in a Yorkshire wood. A fake! You will say. No, sir, I think not … The fairies are about eight inches high [and are] beautiful, luminous creatures. Yes, it is a revelation.

There were to be several further twists and turns to the story, to which we'll return in a later chapter, but the ultimate result was that Doyle went into print in a December 1920 front-page article entitled 'The Evidence for Fairies'.

The reaction to this was mixed. The newspaper *Truth* expressed a widely held view when, on 5 January 1921, it wrote, 'For the real explanation of these fairy photographs, what is wanted is not a knowledge of occult phenomena but a knowledge of children'. Even this was mild compared to some of the popular jokes that made the rounds, including the one where Doyle was said to have appeared at the climax of his friend Barrie's *Peter Pan* to lead the audience in a chorus of 'I do believe in fairies!' Other wisecracks were less elevated.

It was a credit to Doyle, never one to abandon his position lightly, that he persevered in his beliefs even when much of the spiritualist world took issue with him. In March 1922, he published his full-length book, *The Coming of the Fairies*, which laid out the story of the photographs, their supposed provenance, and his conclusions about this 'subhuman' and 'miraculous' life form. It remains his most notorious literary act, not excluding his killing of Sherlock Holmes. It's arguable that Doyle's public reputation never quite recovered from the controversy. As Houdini noted in a letter to their mutual friend Orson Munn, owner of the *Scientific American*:

> The authority of an evangelist such as Sir Arthur is like that of a trainer in a wild-animal act. His mastery depends on never being challenged, [and even if] he survives an assault, his aura of invincibility is gone forever.

✳ ✳ ✳

In September 1918, Conan Doyle paid his brief but indelible visit to the British lines at Saint-Quentin. Describing his experiences there to the public was hardly a cheerful task – his image of an incarnadine shambles of men and animals is among his most vivid writing – but at least it appeared that the tide was finally turning in the Allies' favour.

But then he learnt that Kingsley, who had eventually been posted home, both due to his original war wound and to complete his training as a doctor, had been taken to St Thomas's Hospital in London, suffering from influenza. He died there on 28 October, just two weeks short of the Armistice and of his own twenty-sixth birthday. His father saw him in the mortuary, 'looking his brave steadfast self', and oversaw the arrangements to bury Kingsley next to his mother in the village churchyard near Undershaw.

Barely twenty-four hours after receiving the 'stunning' news, Conan Doyle went on stage to deliver a spiritualist lecture in Nottingham. Composing himself, he told the audience that his oldest son had 'survived the grave, and there was no need to worry'. Less than four months later, on 19 February 1919, Doyle's younger brother, Innes, organising relief supplies in Belgium, also succumbed to the influenza epidemic that would eventually account for some 60 million victims worldwide. Innes, who was 45 at the time of his death, had long ago been his brother's perennially cheerful companion and boy Friday in Southsea, making the years of struggle bearable and forging a real-life relationship that foreshadowed that between Holmes and Watson. It was another 'terrible, shattering' blow.

On 7 September, 1919, Conan Doyle shared a platform at a spiritualist rally in Portsmouth with a 38-year-old Welshman named Evan Powell, a colliery clerk who was also a 'very powerful' medium. After several spirits had been summoned, the speakers agreed to hold a more private session. Around midnight, Doyle, his wife and five friends adjourned to a room in a nearby hotel, where they searched Powell, tied him to a chair, and turned off the lights.

'We had strong phenomena from the start,' Doyle wrote to Oliver Lodge:

> The medium was always groaning, muttering, or talking, so that there was never a doubt where he was. Suddenly I heard a voice.
> 'Jean, it is I.'
> My wife cried, 'It is Kingsley!'
> I said, 'Is that you, boy?'
> He said in a very intense whisper and a tone all his own, '*Father!*' and then after a pause, '*Forgive me!*'

Conan Doyle, who assumed Kingsley was referring to his earlier doubts about the paranormal, concluded his account by saying that he had then felt a strong hand pressing down on him, followed by a kiss on the forehead. 'I am *so* happy,' his dead son assured him.

7

A CASE OF IDENTITY

The murder of the 82-year-old spinster Marion Gilchrist in the dining room of her home on the rainy midwinter night of Monday, 21 December 1908 was savage even by the most depraved standards of Edwardian Glasgow.

At around 7 that evening, the victim's young maidservant Helen Lambie stepped out from the middle floor flat they shared at 15 Queens Terrace, West Princes Street, close to the city centre, to buy groceries and a local paper. She left her mistress sitting in a chair drawn slightly away from the dining table, her back to a coal fire, reading a magazine. A court later heard that the home had been dimly lit, 'the gas in the kitchen turned down, and that in the hall half-on', and that 'all the windows were fastened except that in the kitchen, which was open two or three inches at the top'. No one else was on the premises.

Lambie testified that she had closed both the door of the flat and the street door behind her, and then briskly made her way to the shop around the corner. Ten minutes later, she returned to a scene of 'the most sanguinary and appalling carnage'. Hardened Scottish police officers blanched at the sight.

It was the beginning of a criminal case that included a manhunt that would lead across the Atlantic to the Tombs Prison in New York, touched upon some of the most prominent families in Glasgow, sent a man to jail for nearly nineteen years, ruined the career of a probably honest policeman, and came to obsess Arthur Conan Doyle, who believed it would 'remain immortal in the classics as the supreme example of official incompetence and obstinacy', for the rest of his life.

This was Doyle's description of the crime scene:

> The poor old lady [was] lying upon the floor by the chair in which the servant had last seen her. Her feet were towards the door, her head towards the fireplace. She lay upon a hearth-rug, but a skin rug had been thrown across her head. Her injuries were frightful, nearly every bone of her face and skull being smashed. In spite of her dreadful wounds she lingered for a few minutes, but died without showing any sign of consciousness.

The official police report was more graphic:

> There were wounds on the right cheek extending from the mouth, wounds on the right forehead, and of [sic] the right side of the head. There was a deep hole on the left side of the face between the eye socket and the left ear … The left eyeball was entirely missing, having been driven into the cavity of the brain or having been gouged out. The right eye was partially torn out of its socket by the deep fracture of the right side of the brow. There was much blood on or among the hair of the head. On the carpet rug beneath the head on both sides was a considerable amount of clotted blood, and fluid blood had soaked into the substance of the rug. Between the head and the fender of the fireplace a piece of brain tissue weighing about three-quarters of an ounce, as well as smaller pieces, and several pieces of bone covered with blood were found. Two of these pieces were retained.

This was 'ghastly enough for anyone's taste,' Doyle admitted. But there were also several curious circumstances surrounding the crime that added to its air of Holmesian intrigue.

In December 1908, the flat below Marion Gilchrist's was occupied by a young musician named Arthur Adams, his mother, and three of his five unmarried sisters. They were on somewhat formal terms with their upstairs neighbour. One of the sisters, Rowena, testified that shortly before 7 on the night of the crime she had noticed a man:

… leaning against the railing [outside] … I only saw a dark form, [but] I took in the face entirely, except that I did not see his eyes. He had a long nose, with a most peculiar dip from here [pointing to the bridge of the nose]. You would not see that dip amongst thousands.

A few minutes later, Arthur Adams, sitting in the dining room of his flat, heard a sound 'like a thud, [followed by] three distinct knocks, as if wanting assistance up above'. Alarmed at this, he had gone upstairs and repeatedly rung the doorbell of Miss Gilchrist's flat, but received no answer. He recalled:

After I had been standing at the door for half a minute or so I heard what I thought was the servant girl breaking sticks in the kitchen. It seemed as if it was someone chopping sticks. At that time I did not know whether Miss Gilchrist's maid-servant was out or not. I waited fully a minute or a minute and a half at the door.

At that, Adams, who was of the view that 'the best neighbour [is] the one who leaves you alone, rather than always calling at the door', had returned downstairs to his own flat and reported his findings to his family members waiting for him there. His sister Laura was unconvinced. At her urging, Adams 'once again ascended to Miss Gilchrist's door, where [he] rang the bell for a fourth or fifth time'. As he was standing there, uncertain of what to do next, he suddenly heard footsteps coming up behind him. 'This was the servant girl, Helen Lambie,' Adams related. 'When the girl came up I told her I thought there was something wrong, or something seriously wrong. She told me that it was the pulleys in the kitchen that I had heard.'

According to the evidence at trial, Lambie had then unlocked the front door of the flat and passed into the faintly lit hallway. Or at least that was Adams's account. In what was to be the first of several eyewitness discrepancies in the case, Lambie herself remembered that she had remained 'frozen' on the landing beside her neighbour. Both parties agreed that a moment later a slim, early middle-aged man wearing an overcoat had suddenly appeared from inside the flat and come towards them.

Since Lambie had looked straight at this individual and said nothing, Adams 'did not suspect anything wrong for the minute'. Whether Lambie then spoke at all was never fully clarified, but the evidence suggests that she remained calm as the man passed by her. Adams recalled:

I thought he was going to speak to me, till he got by me and ran off, and then I suspected something wrong, and by that time the girl ran into the kitchen and put the gas up and said it was all right, meaning her pulleys. I said, 'Where is your mistress?' The girl went into the dining-room. She said, 'Oh! Come here!' I just went in and saw this horrible spectacle.

At that point Adams and Lambie both ran downstairs, the former now thinking to give chase to the man they had seen leaving the flat. It was already too late. He had disappeared 'as if swallowed up by the night'. Abandoning the search, Adams was at least able to alert a passing police constable.

Lambie, for her part, also ran into the street – not in pursuit, but to knock furiously at the nearby door of Miss Gilchrist's niece, Margaret Birrell, and tell her what had happened. It was the beginning of a night of terror for Miss Birrell as she listened to the 'ghastly lore' the maid sobbed out. Her long-suppressed account of their conversation would eventually provide one of the case's most sensational twists. Writing three years after the fact, Conan Doyle was left to conclude that Lambie's 'whole reasoning faculty had deserted her' from the moment she had first come home to find her downstairs neighbour waiting anxiously on her doorstep.

In particular, there was the curious incident of Lambie's attitude to the shadowy figure seen leaving Miss Gilchrist's flat. Like the dog in the night, she had done nothing. Lambie 'did not gasp out "Who are you?" or any other sign of amazement,' Doyle remarked, 'but allowed Adams to suppose by her manner that the man might be someone who had a right to be there'. Even on entering the flat, Lambie, who was then aged 20, and of modest education, had unhurriedly inspected the kitchen and spare bedroom rather than rushing to check on her employer. 'She gave no alarm,' Doyle wrote:

> It was only when Adams called out, 'Where is your mistress?' that she finally went into the room of the murder … It must be admitted that this seems strange conduct, and only explicable, if it can be said to be explicable, by great want of intelligence and grasp of the situation.

When the police came to investigate the crime scene they found no obvious sign of a murder weapon, although the attending doctor speculated that the victim may have been struck by a 'few, heavy swinging blows from the back leg of a wooden chair, the assailant while wielding it stamping upon the body and thereby fracturing the ribs'. There was little pretence beyond this of any worthwhile forensic examination of the premises. Similarly, the fire irons and the furniture near where the body lay were seen to be spattered with blood, but again the authorities avoided the sort of chemical or microscopic analysis that might have suggested itself to Sherlock Holmes.

Miss Gilchrist's set of gold false teeth was found lying on the floor beside her. Her magazine and reading glasses were next to each other on the dining room table, as if she had laid them there before greeting a visitor. John Glaister, Professor of Forensic Medicine at Glasgow University, later testified, 'My view is that the old woman when she saw a stranger entering her room stood to her feet, that she was struck with something, and was knocked down'. Asked how many blows might have been inflicted, Glaister replied:

> There must have been several – a very large number I should say, to give a rough guess, judging from the wounds and the size of them, anything between twenty and forty … It must have been a furious assault, a continuous assault, [done] with almost lightning rapidity.

The Glasgow Police officers who attended the scene may have lacked Holmes's powers of deductive reasoning, or in some cases even the more basic gift of observation, but their search of the premises still yielded up certain unmissable clues. A wooden box, for instance, lay on the ground in the middle of the flat's spare bedroom. It had been prised open and its contents, piles of legal documents, were strewn around the floor. There was no blood to be seen either on the papers or anywhere nearby. The intruder had evidently lit the gas lamp in the room, and left the matchbox (the 'Runaway' brand) behind him when he fled.

Helen Lambie later testified that a single crescent diamond brooch, worth some £50, was missing from the flat. The balance of Miss Gilchrist's sizable jewellery collection was untouched. It comprised sixty-two individual pieces and was officially valued at £1,875 6s 3d, or roughly £140,000 ($200,000) today, though some estimates put these figures significantly higher. Most of the valuables were kept hidden among the dresses in Miss Gilchrist's wardrobe. Perhaps understandably, she had often expressed concern about the possibility of being attacked and robbed. Nothing else had been taken. There was no sign of a forced entry.

On the morning after the attack, a police inspector searched the small backyard of Queens Terrace and found a 'piece of an old broken auger' (or drilling tool) lying there. Professor Glaister told the court that he had examined this and 'detected a number of grey hairs attached to it', but could not swear that these were the victim's. Nor could the professor conclusively say whether stains on the auger were blood or merely rust. This particular weapon 'might have been used in the commission of the crime, [but] could not have produced all the wounds we found,' he testified.

There were several other aspects of the Gilchrist case that seemed to qualify it as the plot of one of the more gothic Sherlock Holmes mysteries. Had it all been a premeditated killing, the police wondered, or a burglary that had gone wrong? If theft was really the intruder's primary motive, as the authorities came to believe, it was curious that he had contented himself with a single item. How had the solidly middle-class and never-married Miss Gilchrist been able to afford a collection that was worth ten times more than a professional woman's average annual salary in the first place? Had she herself, as local rumour had it, been a criminal receiver?

Then there were the singular circumstances of the victim's family history. Miss Gilchrist appeared to be on poor terms with many or most of her immediate relatives, and had taken extraordinary precautions concerning her personal safety, another plot device familiar to several Holmes stories. In recent years, she had had no less than four locks fitted on her front door, and had installed a lever that worked much like a buzzer might today in order to control access to her flat from the street. An apparently 'ferocious' Irish terrier watchdog joined the household in December 1907, but was seemingly poisoned just three months before its owner's death.

Miss Gilchrist had made out her will in May 1908, and revised it again six months later. The main beneficiaries were a 44-year-old former maidservant named Margaret Ferguson (née Galbraith) and Ferguson's family. It has been suggested that this individual was in fact Miss Gilchrist's illegitimate daughter, although there are no clear-cut records to that effect. Whatever its true nature, the couple appear to have enjoyed an unusually warm working relationship. In general, Miss Gilchrist was said, even in middle age, to be a 'difficult, and sometimes impossible, mistress', who later in life developed into a 'distinctly quarrelsome' character who believed 'agents' were on her trail, and, more plausibly, that the local shopkeepers were systematically cheating her. By her early eighties she seems to have become a somewhat regal but generally fair employer, if not one untouched by the sort of self-indulgent dottiness that sometimes accompanies old age.

As Conan Doyle later noted, there was also the matter of the 'enigmatic, and often contradictory' eyewitness descriptions of Miss Gilchrist's suspected killer. Rowena Adams testified that she had seen a tall, long-nosed man wearing an 'ordinary cap' and a heavy tweed coat loitering in front of 15 Queens Terrace a few minutes before the crime. The figure who then passed Arthur Adams and Helen Lambie in the hallway also had a hat and coat, but had shrunk in size. A few days later, a 14-year-old shoemaker's apprentice named Mary Barrowman came forward to claim that she had seen someone 'in a dark suit of clothes, Donegal hat [and] dark brown boots' sprinting away from the house that evening before disappearing into the crowd. 'I was at the lamp-post when he ran up against me,' she testified. 'It was quite bright there [and] I had a good look at him coming towards me.' (Here some discrepancy exists with Arthur Adams's memory that the street was both dark and completely empty when, in turn, he had run out of the front door in hot pursuit of the fugitive.)

Meanwhile, Agnes Brown, a 30-year-old schoolteacher, remembered two men tearing from the scene a few minutes after the murder. One wore 'a three-quarter length grey-coloured overcoat' and 'had both hands in his pockets as he ran away' – a curious detail. The other seemed to be more heavily set, wore a navy blue overcoat with a velvet collar and carried something in his left hand – 'it might have been a walking stick, but I thought it looked clumsier than that'.

Although there were certain inconsistencies in the accounts of all five eyewitnesses, taken as a whole their testimony was enough for the police to publish a more particular description in the Christmas Day editions of the Glasgow newspapers. This led them to their man. Early in the morning of Saturday, 2 January 1909, a party of six American detectives boarded the RMS *Lusitania* as she lay off New York Harbour after a stormy Atlantic crossing and arrested a second-class passenger who gave his name as Otto Sando, a dentist on his way to Chicago, and ultimately San Francisco.

This was only the latest of the various instances of mistaken or disputed identity that came to characterise the Marion Gilchrist case. 'Sando' was in fact a 36-year-old German Jew who had been born Oscar Joseph Leschziner in Opole, one of those marginal towns batted around between Prussia and Poland at regular intervals throughout the nineteenth century, where his father was a baker. Having left Germany to evade military conscription, he would eventually come to settle in Glasgow under the assumed name of Oscar Slater.

When detained on the *Lusitania*, Slater was found to be in possession both of a pawn ticket for a diamond brooch of about the same size as the stolen one, and, perhaps just as damning for his prospects in the eyes of a typical Edwardian Scots jury, a 23-year-old travelling companion named Andree Antoine, popularly known on the streets of Glasgow as Madame Junio, who was not his wife.

Slater was then a solid, barrel-chested figure, hard-faced, with rapidly receding dark hair and a noticeably crooked nose. It had long ago been broken in a bar fight. Despite or because of this blemish, he generally impressed people as someone who could look after himself. More than one of Slater's acquaintances would remark that there was something a little frightening about him – 'You thought he would stop at nothing to get what he wanted,' a family friend recalled of him even in his older age.

When the police returned him to Glasgow in February 1909 Slater said only:

I am a native of Germany, married, a dentist, and have no residence at present. I know nothing about the charge of having assaulted Marion Gilchrist and murdering her. I am innocent.

Slater did not speak during his subsequent trial, evidently because he thought that his heavy foreign accent might prejudice the jury against him. In the event, the first they heard from him was when he rose to his feet immediately following their verdict to spontaneously address the court. 'My Lord, what shall I say?' Slater enquired in his broken English:

I came over from America, knowing nothing about the affair, to Scotland to get a fair judgement. I know nothing of the affair, absolutely nothing. I never heard the name. I know nothing about the affair. I do not know how I could be connected with the affair. I know nothing about it. I came from America on my own account. I can say no more.

The trial judge, Lord Guthrie, made no direct comment on this outburst, but instead slowly assumed the traditional black cap and sentenced Slater to be hung in Duke Street Prison, Glasgow, three weeks from that date.

✳ ✳ ✳

When Slater first arrived in Glasgow at the age of 28 in March 1901, he had some money left from his days as a bank clerk and unlicensed bookmaker in Opole, and he managed to keep his head above water for a year by gambling and occasionally trafficking in small amounts of stolen jewellery. He seems to have avoided any contact with the law and, up to a point, led a comparatively respectable life, marrying a local woman, playing billiards most afternoons at the Crown Hall rooms near his lodgings in Sauchiehall Street, and strolling around town dressed in an immaculate dark suit and a bowler hat.

By early 1902, however, Slater's funds had dried up and his marriage had fallen apart. He left his digs without paying the rent he owed, or troubling to formally divorce his wife, and spent the next few years living off his wits as far afield as London, Brussels and New York. It was alleged that during this period he had managed the affairs of several prostitutes and that one of them, the young Frenchwoman Andree Antoine, had become his common-law wife.

Conan Doyle, although typically robust in his criminal defence, never concealed his personal distaste for Slater, whom he described as 'a disreputable, rolling-stone of a man' and thus quite different to the subject of his earlier public campaign. 'In one respect,' Doyle wrote in his memoirs:

> The Oscar Slater case was not so serious as the Edalji one. Slater was not a very desirable member of society. He had never, so far as is known, been in trouble as a criminal, but he was a gambler and adventurer of uncertain morals and dubious ways – a German Jew by extraction, living under an alias.

Slater appears to have left and reconciled with Antoine several times during these years, in which he described himself variously as a gym instructor, an impresario and a commodity trader, moving around between various cheap hotels, often leaving no forwarding address, and in general living a life not dissimilar to the fictional Arthur Daley, if conspicuously lacking that character's comic flair. There is no evidence that he ever seriously practised as a dentist.

Some doubt exists as to Slater's whereabouts in September 1902, when 30-year-old Patrick Leggett fatally stabbed his estranged wife Sarah in her Glasgow home. Rapidly tried and convicted, he was executed in the grounds of Duke Street Prison the following November. Several anonymous letters later came into Doyle's possession that accused Slater of being an accomplice to the crime, allegedly by handling the victim's jewellery, although this was never proven. We know that he was back in Glasgow in mid 1905, when he befriended a bookmaker's clerk named Hugh Cameron, who went by the nickname of 'Moudie' or 'Mole'. Cameron later confirmed the generally poor impression people had of Slater's character when he told a court, 'He was a gambler [and] he lived on the proceeds of women'.

When difficulties arose for him in Glasgow, Slater spent several months in lodgings around central London, with rooms, or at least accommodation addresses, at 33 Soho Square and 36 Albemarle Street. The latter was only a few doors away from Doyle's publisher John Murray and adjacent to Brown's Hotel, where the author often stayed when visiting town. Although the two men moved in different circles, they shared a London pastime: both liked to attend the nearby theatre, and Slater later spoke of his 'high feeling of excitement [as] the lights went down and another performance was set to begin'. Those nights in the dark were probably the closest he had yet come to his benefactor.

* * *

On 29 October 1908 Slater took the train back to Glasgow, where his mistress Antoine joined him a few days later. After moving between several modest hotels, they settled in a rented flat at 69 St George's Street, where Slater advertised himself as 'A. Anderson, Dentist'. A fellow German émigré named Max Rattman later told a court of this period:

> I saw him nearly every day … I met him generally in Gall's public-house, and I met him at various clubs in the evening, sometimes in the Mascot Club, in Virginia Street, and sometimes in the Motor Club, in India Street, and I met him in Johnston's billiard saloon, opposite the Pavilion, in Renfield Street.

Rattman added that Slater had frequently been in dire financial straits due to his gambling habit. 'Some of his debts were [incurred] at the Mascot or the Motor,' he recalled, 'although the bulk of his money was lost at the Sloper Club', an establishment Rattman did not personally frequent and which was closed by the licensing authorities a year or two later.

Several other witnesses spoke both of Slater's precarious finances during the autumn of 1908 and of his stated plans to return to America as a result. Another member of Glasgow's German community, first coming across him

A CASE OF IDENTITY

181

that November in the Sloper Club, remembered his countryman as 'neatly dressed and almost clean shaven, with a high domed head and a stubbly moustache'. Photographs taken of Slater at around this time show a seemingly respectable individual with a passing resemblance to the actor Sir Ben Kingsley. 'He looked you in the eye and spoke in a level voice,' his compatriot noted. Only when Slater offered his 'slightly moist and deathly cold' hand did his new acquaintance realise that he was 'face-to-face with a frightening human being'.

✳ ✳ ✳

The instinctive belief of the Glasgow Police that here was a German Jew of dubious morals fleeing to America with a French fancy woman in his bed and a pawn ticket for a diamond brooch in his pocket, and thus that he had savagely assaulted Marion Gilchrist, never quite fitted the hard facts of the case as Conan Doyle and others later established them. The brooch, for instance, had never at any time belonged to the murder victim. Oscar Slater had owned it on and off for several years, and had frequently pawned it when funds ran low.

Nor was his departure on the *Lusitania* as sudden and unpremeditated as was initially thought. Doyle's lifelong dread of moral irregularity met with a matching ability to rise above any personal prejudice and simply marshal the evidence of a case when he wrote:

> In the Bohemian clubs which [Slater] frequented – he was by profession a peddling jeweller and a man of disreputable, though not criminal habits – it had for weeks before the date of the crime been known that he purported to go to some business associates in America. A correspondence … showed the arrangements which had been made, long before the murder, for his emigration.

Antoine, he added, was 'just an attractive little thing, in whom, in spite of her wayward and feather-brained outlook, or perhaps in consequence of it, he found the type of gratification he sought'.

Doyle later established that Slater had received two letters on the morning of 21 December 1908, the day of Miss Gilchrist's death. One was from a friend in London, telling him that Slater's abandoned wife was enquiring after him and wanted money. The second was from John Devoto, a former business acquaintance, inviting Slater to join him in San Francisco. 'It was the spur,' Doyle noted. Between them, the two communications served as a sudden call to action, converting Slater's latent desire to move further afield into a definite plan. Since both the sea voyage and the brooch were thus false clues, the only logical conclusion to be drawn by the prosecuting authority in the case was that the police had by pure chance arrested the right man. As Doyle remarked with some understatement, 'The coincidence involved in such a supposition would seem to pass the limits of all probability'.

Nor did the police ever convincingly reconstruct the events immediately preceding Marion Gilchrist's death, leaving this to the diligence and tenacity of the unofficial investigators. Doyle's timeline established that Slater had, in fact, spent much of 21 December preparing for his imminent Atlantic crossing. He dismissed the maid who worked at the St George's Street flat, telling her after breakfast that morning that 'I could go away some[where] to find another situation'. Later that afternoon, he wrote both to a post office in London to extract some money he had on deposit there, and to a jeweller urgently asking them to return the watch they were repairing for him.

Witnesses testified that Slater was in Johnston's Billiard Hall between about 6.15 and 6.30 that evening, and both his mistress and his servant testified under oath that he had dined at home as usual at 7 p.m., just as Marion Gilchrist was being brutally attacked in her flat some quarter of a mile away. A local shopkeeper saw Slater standing 'quite calm' outside his front door in St George's Street just after 8 that night, and thought nothing more of it until he read the next day's newspaper. As the two men casually nodded to each other, an ambulance wagon had raced past them on its way to the murder scene.

At 9.45 p.m. Slater was attempting to raise a loan from the management of the Motor Club on India Street, a not uncommon activity on his part. The dismissed maid, who had no logical reason for perjuring herself, swore that she had seen 'no change in [her] employer's ordinary habits' either on the evening of 21 December or in the days that followed as she worked out her notice and he prepared to leave for America.

It is not immediately easy to see the logic for such a violent attack as transpired in West Princes Street that night being committed by a complete stranger who had already decided to emigrate. It was never established that Slater had at any time known of Gilchrist's existence during the seven weeks they lived in the same Glasgow neighbourhood, and at best he only partly fitted the description provided by Arthur Adams, Helen Lambie and the other eyewitnesses. Moreover, it was an odd sort of burglary for an outsider to have pulled, as the police strongly suggested had been the case. As Doyle noted:

> When [the murderer] reached the spare bedroom and lit the gas, he did not at once seize the watch and rings which were lying openly exposed upon the dressing-table. He did not pick up a half-sovereign which was lying on the table. His attention was given to a wooden box, the lid of which he wrenched open [presumably the 'breaking of sticks' heard by Adams]. The papers in it were strewed on the ground. Were the papers his object, and the final abstraction of one diamond brooch a mere blind?

Around 6 p.m. on the evening of Christmas Day 1908, a Sloper Club regular named Allan McLean entered the Glasgow Central Police Station and made a statement. He had read Mary Barrowman's description in the afternoon paper of the man 'about 28–30 years of age, tall and slim build, no hair on face, long features, nose slightly turned to the right', whom she claimed had rushed past her in the street on the night of the murder. McLean told the authorities that this sounded broadly like his acquaintance Oscar Slater, and that what was more Slater had recently been trying to sell a pawn ticket for a valuable diamond brooch that had come into his possession. As a result of this information, a Detective Inspector Powell went to the St George's Street flat, where he found only the dismissed maid, Catherine Schmalz, packing her bags. Schmalz told him that 'Mr Oscar' and 'Madame' had left just hours earlier, taking all their belongings with them. She thought they might have gone to London.

Early on 26 December, the Glasgow Chief Constable wired his colleagues in Scotland Yard with the request that they apprehend Slater, who could be easily identified by his travelling companion – 'a woman about 30, tall, stout, good looking, dark hair, dressed dark costume, sable furs, large black hat', another administrative slip since Antoine was slim and 23.

There was still some doubt as to the fugitives' destination, however, because the following morning a cable arrived for the Chief Constable of Nottingham, asking him to keep a watch for 'Slater, alias Anderson, who left here hurriedly with a woman on Friday last, and may have gone to your city as two single railway tickets were issued for passengers by the 9.30 p.m. train'. At some stage, late on 27 or early on 28 December, Schmalz then suddenly remembered that her former employer had in fact gone, under an alias, to Liverpool en route to America. The Glasgow Police in turn cabled New York, 'Arrest OTTO SANDO second cabin *Lusitania*. Wanted connection with the murder of Marion Gilchrist here. He has a twisted nose. Search him and the woman who is his travelling companion for pawn tickets.'

The events that followed in some way foreshadowed the dramatic sea chase that served as the climax to the arrest of Dr Crippen eighteen months later. In both cases, the suspect was detained while travelling incognito in the company of a mistress as their ship completed its Atlantic crossing, and in due course both men were returned home for trial. In the meantime, Slater was taken to the Tombs Jail in New York (despite its uncompromising name, actually an eight-storey tower block in French chateau style, if with no pretensions to comfort), which would remain his home for the next six weeks. The official cable confirming his arrest remarked that he had made 'no trouble' on his capture, and that he had had the grand sum of 40 cents on him in local currency.

The police in Glasgow were evidently satisfied that they had got their man. The proceedings to extradite Slater began almost immediately. Subsequent attempts to suggest that the German Embassy in Washington might intervene, or even offer sanctuary, were to no avail. The official consensus was clearly that Slater had murdered Marion Gilchrist in the execution of a burglary.

A series of anonymous letters, however, questioned whether the thrust of the Glasgow investigation might not be better directed towards the victim's own family members. The first such note reached the police as early as Christmas Day 1908 and read, 'Regarding the murder of the old woman, if you look for a relative, you will I think come out on top'. Another note, dated 5 January, suggested that the writer had a friend who had known Miss Gilchrist, and that 'on her last visit to deceased [this person] was shown a box by deceased who told her that it contained papers her nephew was very anxious to get from her'. There was considerably more in this vein over the coming weeks.

As in the Edalji case, there were significant differences in the handwriting and phrasing of the various letters, and more particularly in the violence of their language, but taken as a whole the correspondence seemed to point squarely towards the idea that Miss Gilchrist had known her assailant. Another note of 5 January teasingly told the police that the author knew 'something about the broch [*sic*]', and that he or she was 'willing to come & give you the details in the first place, only I don't want my name put in the papers'.

On 12 January 1909, William Warnock, Chief Criminal Officer of Glasgow's Sherriff Court, and Detective Inspector John Pyper of the city's Western Division set sail for New York on board the SS *Baltic*. They were accompanied by Arthur Adams and Helen Lambie, the two witnesses who had seen a man brush past them in the hallway of Marion Gilchrist's flat, and by Mary Barrowman, the young teenager who had been walking up West Princes Street on the night in question.

Some discrepancy exists in the account of what happened when the Glasgow party arrived in Manhattan's federal building in order to identify Slater. Lambie remembered plainly enough:

> When I went into the courtroom I found a number of people there. I sat in a chair. I saw the man in the room that I had seen in the lobby of my house; I recognised him and I identified him.

Mary Barrowman was similarly convinced. 'I remember standing in a corridor or passage to the law court,' she testified:

> There were three men coming along the corridor and in between the [outer] two men I saw this man, the man I had seen on the night of the murder. I told Mr Pyper that this was him coming. I had no difficulty in telling that he was the man.

Another version has Barrowman saying in New York, 'That man here is something like him,' which she amended at Slater's trial to 'very like him'. Arthur Adams, who was near-sighted, recalled at trial only that 'I pointed out Slater, but I did not say that he was the man. I said he closely resembled the man.' When asked by the police commissioner in New York if he positively recognised anybody in the courtroom as the individual he had seen in Glasgow, Adams replied, 'I couldn't say definitely. This man [Slater] is not at all unlike him.'

Significantly, Slater himself did nothing to prevent his extradition back to Scotland. Given the chance to contest the writ for his removal, he said only, 'I will go home'. Slater told his Glasgow friend Hugh Cameron of his intention to return in a scribbled note dated 2 February 1909, and this letter, half craven, half defiant, captures some of the essence of the man:

Dear friend Cameron – To-day it is nearly five weeks I am kept here in prison for the Glasgow murder. I am very down-hearted to know that my friends in Glasgow like [Motor Club manager] Gordon Henderson can tell such liars about me to the Glasgow police … I don't deney I have been in his place asking him for mony because I went brocke in the Sloper Club. Only I will fix Mr Gordon Henderson. I will prove with plenty of witnesses that I was playing there mucky, and I am entitled to ask a proprietor from a gambling house when I am broke for money … He would not mind to get me hangt and I will try to prove that from a gambling point, I am right to ask for some money. *I hope nobody propper minded* will blame me for this …

I shall go back to Glasgow with my free will, because you know so good than myselfs that I am not the murder.

I hope my dear Cameron that you will still be my friend in my troubel and tell the truth and stand on my side … I really was surprised I don't have seen your statement because I think you was too strait forvard for them. They only have taken the statement against me and not for me …

Keep all this quiet because the police is trying hard to make a frame up for me. I must have a good lawyer, and after I can proof my innocents befor having a trail, because I will prove with five people where I have been when the murder was comitted.

Thanking you at present, and I hope to have a true friend on you, because every man is able to get put in such a affair and being innocent.

My best regards to you and all my friends – I am, your friend

Oscar Slater
Tombs, New York.

On Slater's return to Glasgow later that month, the police examined the seven pieces of luggage that had accompanied him on both his recent Atlantic crossings. Among other items, they discovered what was described in court as a 'small hammer', about 1ft long, weighing less than ½lb, which the maid Catherine Schmalz had used for breaking up the coal into suitably sized pieces for the fireplace at the St George's Road flat. Conan Doyle was unimpressed by the Crown's later suggestion that this was the implement that had bludgeoned Marion Gilchrist to death:

The [hammer] was clearly shown to have been purchased in one of those cheap half-crown sets of tools which are tied upon a card, was an extremely small and fragile instrument, and utterly incapable in the eyes of commonsense of inflicting those terrific injuries which had shattered the old lady's skull.

Even if one accepted the prosecution thesis that this was indeed the murder weapon, Doyle wondered why it was that the pockets of Slater's overcoat, also impounded by the police, showed no trace of bloodstains. John Glaister, the forensic medicine expert, was asked about this latter point during the trial. He admitted that there was 'no definite sanguin[ary] residue' to be found anywhere on Slater's clothes (the more you study the state of prevailing Edwardian criminal investigation techniques, the more you appreciate Sherlock Holmes), although some twenty-five 'brownish-red marks' microscopically detected on the sleeves of the accused's coat struck him as suggestive.

'To my mind,' Glaister testified:

These stains had been subjected to the influence of water. When a waterproof coat gets wet with rain, the water keeps on the surface of the cloth. I do not know whether it was rain that got on the stains or whether they had been subjected to washing, but they were not stains [as] I should have expected them to be after immediate effusion on the cloth. They were paler in colour. We could not tell whether the coat had been actually scrubbed or whether there had simply been rain upon it.

Although there was a certain amount of further give and take in the matter of the physical evidence, the central police contention that Slater, an acknowledged lowlife, had gone to Marion Gilchrist's flat armed with his coal hammer, had used this to kill her when interrupted in the commission of a robbery, if not at the outset, and had then fled with his morally equivocal lady friend to America, where he was apprehended and positively identified by three unimpeachable eyewitnesses (one of whom, Helen Lambie, may or may not have previously fallen prey to his animal lusts) proved sufficient for a Scottish jury. After a four-day trial, in May 1909 at the High Court in Edinburgh, the panel of fifteen voted nine for 'Guilty', five for 'Not Proven', and one for 'Not Guilty'. In England, this same division (with 40 per cent not satisfied by the Crown's case) would have resulted in a new trial, but was enough here for the judge to impose the death penalty, at least until modified by subsequent events.

Doyle again betrayed his personal misgivings about the accused, which several of the jurors seem to have shared, when he wrote in a book-length article on the case published in August 1912:

> Oscar Slater might conceivably have committed the murder, but the balance of proof and probability seems entirely against it. One cannot feel the same burning sense of injustice over the matter [as with Edalji]. And yet I trust for the sake of our character not only for justice, but for intelligence, that the judgement may in some way be reconsidered and the man's present punishment allowed to atone for those irregularities of life which helped to make his conviction possible.

Doyle was characteristically confident of his position in a letter he wrote later that month to his mother:

> You may rely upon it that I have made no mistake over the Slater book. He is as innocent as you or I … You must refresh your memory about the facts. No connection of any kind was ever proven between him and the old lady and maid. Your woman's wit will tell you that the maid would not have eagerly sworn his life away if he had been her lover. Trust my judgement.

Certainly, the trial evidence as a whole showed that both the police investigation, and the testimony of the expert witnesses, fell some way short of the ideal Sherlock Holmes methodology. Neither Professor Glaister nor Edinburgh University's distinguished forensic scientist, Harvey Littlejohn (son of Doyle's old lecturer, and partial model for Holmes, Henry Littlejohn) thought to remove the head of Slater's coal hammer and test it for bloodstains. Nor could they agree whether the hammer was of sufficient size and weight to have inflicted such damage in the first place. Opinion of the auger, or drill bit, found in Marion Gilchrist's backyard was similarly divided. Professor Glaister thought this 'gave no indications of the presence of blood', and dismissed it as the murder weapon, while William Robertson, a doctor of medicine and science at Edinburgh University, felt it 'more likely to have caused the wounds than the hammer'. Neither man could say with any certainty how the auger had come to be smeared with 'irregular dark blemishes' like bloodstains, or to be covered in matted grey hair, nor could they give an opinion as to whether the hair and alleged blood had even belonged to the victim. 'We are in the region of speculation,' Glaister admitted.

The prosecution rapidly gave up the idea of presenting an airtight scientific case against Slater. A more general hypothesis, along with the Crown's continual aspersions on the defendant's character, would have to suffice. The one witness to show a modicum of Holmes's technique of assessing the clues, or 'trifles', and deducing from them what might have happened was William Warnock, the sheriff who had accompanied the Glasgow identification party to New York. He later claimed in court that 'I made it a point to observe the prisoner's mode of walking, and did so observe it', a key factor, he believed, in establishing Slater as the man who had hurried past Lambie and Adams on the night of the murder, but not one that impressed itself with anything like the same force on the eyewitnesses themselves.

Taken as a whole, the trial showed that the state of scientific criminology in 1909 still lagged far behind the level Doyle had routinely described in the Sherlock Holmes stories over the course of the last twenty-two years. Although Holmes is known for having anticipated actual developments in fields such as toxicology, ballistics and crime scene investigation in general, he's as adept at interpreting the psychological clues in a case as he is at observing the material evidence. The detective's first appearance in a short story, 1891's 'A Scandal in Bohemia', contains the plot device of Holmes (or, technically, Watson) crying 'Fire!', and thus tricking the female protagonist, Irene Adler, into rushing to save her most prized possession – an amorous photograph of her and the king.

As a rule, Holmes wasn't a man to be easily shocked. So he would have been fully alive to the possibility that Marion Gilchrist might have met her end at the hands of a family member, and that the motive for this, if not narrowly financial, lay concealed somewhere back among the riddle surrounding the paternity of her alleged illegitimate daughter some forty years earlier. Had there been more than one such child born out of wedlock, as several anonymous letters suggested? Slater's counsel, Alexander McClure, alluded to the matter of the deceased's 'obscure [and] recondite' past in the course of a courtroom exchange with a Glasgow Police officer named John Trench:

Q: Have you heard that [Miss Gilchrist] was the mother of the servant girl
Lambie?

A: No.

Q: But of another?

A: Yes.

Q: Have you heard that she was the mother of Slater?

A: No.

The exchange continued:

Q: Have other men been in custody with this case besides Slater?

A: I believe there were several men arrested shortly after the murder.

Q: And a number of witnesses failed to identify these men?

A: Yes.

Q: Have a number of witnesses failed to identify Slater?

A: There have been a number of people who have seen him who did not know
him at all.

The whole question of proper identification loomed large at Slater's trial, and
a more spirited defence counsel might have made something of the obvious
discrepancies in the eyewitness testimony. Apart from the mixture of coats,
hats, caps, complexions, walks and noses variously described in court, there
was the evidence of Annie Armour, a Glasgow Subway booking clerk who
had been on duty at the nearby Kelvinbridge Station on the night of Marion
Gilchrist's murder.

Armour recalled that an 'excited looking' man had appeared at her booth
sometime between 7.30 and 8 that evening. Instead of the normal transaction,
this individual had 'come rushing in, flung down a penny, [and] ran clattering
downstairs' to jump on a departing train. The Crown's clear implication was
that the agitated man had in fact been Slater fleeing the scene of the crime.
Armour was vague about the matter of the passenger's trousers, boots and hat,
but testified that she was 'quite certain he had no moustache at all'.

By contrast, Arthur Adams told the court that the man who had pushed
past him in Marion Gilchrist's hallway roughly half an hour earlier might
have been clean shaven or, equally, might have had a 'very little' moustache,
while no fewer than four members of the McHaffie family, who lived directly
opposite Miss Gilchrist in West Princes Street, testified that they had seen a

Slater-like figure loitering outside on several occasions prior to the murder, and that this individual had been 'dark hued' and 'moustached'. A Glasgow police constable named Christopher Walker corroborated these last points when he described a man he had noticed on the street not long before the murder, 'looking in a slanting direction' towards Miss Gilchrist's flat. He had subsequently identified the watcher as Slater. Constable Walker told the court, 'He was of dark complexion, and with a moustache.'

Slater's trial at Edinburgh before the austere figure of 60-year-old Lord Guthrie has been portrayed as a miscarriage of criminal justice which resulted from a pre-existing and pervasive animus towards the accused that approached the worst excesses of the People's Court under the notorious Nazi judge, Roland Freisler. It's true that Guthrie refrained from bellowing and gesticulating at the prisoner, shouting down the reasonable pleas of the pathetic figure standing before him in the dock. Several misleading statements on the part of the prosecuting Advocate General went uncorrected, but so, too, did those of the defence witnesses. A letter Slater had written in German to his friend Max Rattman, for instance, was rendered in court as, 'Dear Max, Having left Glasgow suddenly, I am very sorry I was not able to say goodbye', while to some experts the better translation would have been not 'suddenly' but 'unexpectedly' or 'surprisingly', which was perhaps to convey less of the sense of a man making last-minute business arrangements and more that of a fugitive from the law. Similarly, in his final address to the jury, the judge was rightly at pains to point out that the material evidence against the defendant was 'weak', and that 'It is not for him to disprove the charge, but for the crown to prove it'. Conan Doyle himself wrote, 'In his summing-up of the case [the judge] recapitulated the familiar facts in an impartial fashion.'

When it came to Slater's character, however, Lord Guthrie left the jury in little doubt of his true feelings. 'He has maintained himself by the ruin of men and on the ruin of women, and has lived a life that many blackguards would scorn to live,' Guthrie thundered:

> That is an illustration of what I mean when I talked of evidence being double-edged. It is nothing remarkable to find a man of that kind taking a wrong name, telling a lie about his destination, going by different names, murder or no murder … If you or I had told false stories about where we were going, if we were to travel under an assumed name, there would be a strong inference that we had been doing something of a serious kind that we wanted to conceal.

Left: 'The Langham Hotel will find me,' Sherlock Holmes's client remarks in 1911's *The Disappearance of Lady Frances Carfax*. The building played a significant part in Conan Doyle's own detective life. (Author's photo)

Below left: After Conan Doyle dedicated *The Adventures of Sherlock Holmes* to his old Edinburgh University lecturer Dr Joseph Bell, Bell wrote to tell the author: 'You are yourself Sherlock Holmes and well you know it.' (Wikimedia Commons)

Below: William J. Burns (1861–1932), the pioneering midwest detective who enjoyed the title of 'America's Sherlock Holmes' before retiring to write mystery stories in Florida. (Wikimedia Commons)

George Edalji's police mugshot. A leading daily newspaper took one look at the young solicitor and called him 'a degenerate of the worst kind'. (Staffordshire Record Office)

Geo. E. F. Edalji   3460   30·9·03

George Edalji in court where he was sentenced to seven years' hard labour. (Staffordshire Record Office)

The Edaljis' vicarage, where George allegedly let himself out of the back bedroom he shared with his father in order to disembowel local cattle. (Staffordshire Record Office)

Dr Crippen, the superficially mild-mannered homeopath who was tried for murder in October 1910 and executed the following month. (Wikimedia Commons)

The Daily Mirror

END OF THE ATLANTIC CHASE: "DR." CRIPPEN, WHO WAS ARRESTED AT FATHER POINT, CANADA, YESTERDAY.

Right: Crippen's wife and victim Corrine Turner, seen here in her stage guise as Belle Elmore. (Library of Congress)

Below: Arthur Conan Doyle in 1914, still a materialist but on the edge of the 'great unknown'. (Wikimedia Commons)

Bottom right: Oscar Slater. (Wikimedia Commons)

The victim's room in the Oscar Slater case. (Wikimedia Commons)

West Princes Street, Glasgow, seen today. (Alex Holmes)

Right: Albemarle Street, London. Slater used an accomodation address at No. 36, the semi-derelict building on the left, just a few yards away from both Doyle's publisher and the hotel where he often stayed when visiting town. (Author's photo)

Nov 13th/27.

15, Buckingham Palace Mansions,
S.W.1.

Dear Mr Baldwin,

I am so sorry to trouble you, for there are few men for whom I have a greater respect. I am however very much in earnest over this Oscar Slater business, and it cannot remain as it is. It will surely develop into a big political issue unless there is some inquiry into the scandal connected with the man's conviction. I regret that I cannot believe in the "thorough invest-igation" by the Scots office alluded to in your former letter. There are limits to human stupidity and this is beyond them. I have twice stood as Unionist candidate in Scotland but none the less I would make it my business to put justice before politics and I hold Oscar Slater meetings in any contested election & show that it is a U government which with full knowledge which their predecessors did not have refused fair play because the man was humble & his persecutors powerful.

Left: Conan Doyle's letter of 13 November 1927 to the Prime Minister, Stanley Baldwin, about the Oscar Slater case. Slater walked free from prison the next day. (Mitchell Library, Glasgow City Archives)

Conan Doyle's cousin Arthur Vicars, the man at the heart of the case with a Holmes-like plot involving stolen jewels, miscarriages of justice and murderous revenge. (Wikimedia Commons)

Arthur Conan Doyle statue inscription. (Wikimedia Commons)

Above: Arthur Conan Doyle supposedly being visited by a spirit – as seen by the medium Ada Deane. (Wikimedia Commons)

Right: Sherlock Holmes statue in Picardy Place, Edinburgh, close to the site of his author's birth. (Wikimedia Commons)

Roger Casement, the former
diplomat who despite Conan
Doyle's intervention went to the
gallows as a traitor.

Agatha Christie in younger
life, already with an enigmatic
expression. (Wikimedia Commons)

Harry Houdini demonstrating a 'faked séance'. (Wikimedia Commons)

MARGERY GENUINE, SAYS CONAN DOYLE; HE SCORES HOUDINI

MEDIUM AND HER NEW CHAMPION

CRITICIZES THE
EXPERT BODY IN
SEVERE TERMS

DOYLE GETS MESSAGES FROM DEAD RELATIONS

He Declares Two Letters Sent to Him by Medium in Toledo, Ohio, Are Genuine.

CHICAGO, May 21.—Sir Arthur Conan Doyle, who arrived in Chicago today accompanied by Lady Doyle and their three children, exhibited two letters he received from a medium in Toledo last night which, he said, were from his son Kingsley, who was killed in the war, and from his mother, who is also dead.

DOYLE SAYS GHOSTS MAY USE THE RADIO

Tells Psychical Institute He Expects Aerial Messages From Spirits in Four Years.

SEES PERIL IN INTELLIGENCE

Calls Psychic Researchers Spiritualism's "Worst Enemies," Then Gives Them $250.

Psychical researchers are the spiritualists' worst enemies: they operate only with a scalpel and they lack a heart, according to Sir Arthur Conan Doyle, who spoke yesterday at a reception in his honor at the American Psychical Institute and Laboratory, 40 West Fifty-seventh Street.

Above: Selection of newspaper cuttings on Conan Doyle's spiritualist activities. 'Is he mad?' one headline enquired.

Spirit writing made by Lady Conan Doyle in the words of Harry Houdini's late mother, Atlantic City, June 1922.

In the case of a man like Slater, whose life has been a living lie, that inference does not necessarily arise. The man's life has been not only a lie for years, but is so to-day …

'The Lord Advocate,' Guthrie concluded:

… founds on the prisoner's admittedly abandoned character as a point in support of the crown. He is entitled to do so, because a man of that kind has not the presumption of innocence in his favour which is a form in the case of every man, but a reality in the case of the ordinary man.

Following this summation, the jury members returned an hour and ten minutes later to record their verdict. Several observers, among them the Edinburgh lawyer William Roughead, remarked that at the word 'guilty' a palpable shock had run through the courtroom. Abandoning the air of studied composure he had shown throughout the previous four days, Slater himself had then leapt to his feet and made his pitiable appeal to the judge. 'A scene more painful it is fortunately the lot of few to witness,' Roughead wrote, 'and none who did so on this occasion is likely to forget it. The prisoner was then removed, and the court rose.'

✳ ✳ ✳

In a stone-walled cell at Glasgow's Duke Street Prison, Slater slept fitfully on his first night as a condemned man. The threadbare blanket provided little comfort against the cold of an early spring thunderstorm. In the next cell, another inmate taunted him as a 'dirty Jew' and graphically outlined the fate that awaited him in less than three weeks' time.

Early the next morning, a slot in the door scraped open, and through it appeared a tiny portion of bread and jam on a tin plate. Slater would hardly recall the next years with fondness, but those first few days of confinement had driven him 'closest to the edge', he later admitted. His fellow convicts were not sympathetic to the cold-hearted German who stood condemned of bludgeoning an elderly Scotswoman to death. The prison staff in turn addressed him as 'Fritz', 'animal', 'scum' and 'swine'. Slater was not allowed books, newspapers or tobacco; he could not write letters. There was no Court of Criminal Appeal in Scotland in 1909, and the condemned man's only hope was that someone on the outside such as a public-spirited (or circulation-conscious) newspaper editor would raise a petition on his behalf.

This was essentially what happened. Summarising Slater's recent trial, the *Glasgow Herald* wrote, 'The first emotion caused by the news of this verdict in the case of nine out of every ten who read the evidence closely, must have been one of intense surprise'. A deluge of letters and notes soon came in to the paper to support this belief. Slater's solicitor Ewing Speirs also rallied support on his client's behalf, and on 17 May, just eleven days after the guilty verdict, presented the Secretary of State for Scotland, Lord Pentland, with a petition containing over 20,000 signatures. That same week, Lord Guthrie wrote to the Scottish Office with his own thoughts on the trial. Although he 'resolutely believed' Slater was guilty, he wondered if it might not be an occasion when 'the prisoner could be respited [reprieved]?' There were, however, limits to this apparent show of official compassion. In the event of any such relief, the Secretary of State noted, 'The case would not be one for release under the ordinary practice at the end of twenty years'.

The ambivalence about Slater's proper punishment was finally resolved in a scribbled note from Lord Pentland to his principal assistant. On 25 May, less than forty-eight hours before he was due to hang, Slater was told that his sentence was being commuted to one of life imprisonment. It was noted that he had stood rigidly to attention to receive the delegation that brought him the news, and that he broke down in tears on hearing it.

Within a year, William Roughead published his bestselling *The Trial of Oscar Slater*, a transcript of the proceedings which included both a critical commentary on the original police investigation and a possibly sardonic dedication to the trial judge, Lord Guthrie. As a result, several other well-placed commentators in turn took up the case. What was compelling in Slater clearly wasn't the moral fibre of the man himself, nor any particular sense of gratitude he showed to his many supporters. It was the fact that the police had never put forward one single piece of hard evidence, or a link of any sort, to connect him with Marion Gilchrist. It was enough, apparently, that Slater bore a general resemblance to the man described by some of the eyewitnesses, and that shortly after the crime he had fled to America under an assumed name, accompanied by a French whore.

Provocative as this last point was to the sensibilities of an Edinburgh jury, one has to ask the question: did Slater receive the same treatment he might have expected if he had not been a German-Jewish immigrant of admittedly lax morals? If a respectable young Scot of roughly the same physical type had hurriedly gone off on a Christmas visit to New York with his fiancée, would it have been thought right to bring him back in handcuffs and charge him with the murder? Would it also have been thought right to convict him on the evidence, knowing that he could hang as a result?

❋ ❋ ❋

It would be three years before Conan Doyle became actively involved in the Slater case. He had politely declined when originally approached by the defence team to write about the trial. Doyle's interest seems to have been stirred by a new edition of Roughead's work that appeared in May 1912, as well as by the more practical consideration that he had just sent off his own latest book, *The Lost World*, an adventure yarn that brought dinosaurs back to life three generations before Steven Spielberg did, and thus had a certain amount of time on hand.

The result was the 18,000-word, sixpenny pamphlet *The Case of Oscar Slater*, which led to a renewed public debate on the convicted man's trial and sentence and, in time, to heated questions in the House of Commons addressed to the Home Secretary. 'It will make a huge uproar,' Doyle had confidently predicted of his own contribution to the case. It did, although as he also foresaw, the officials involved in Slater's prosecution simply denied or ignored his central thesis that Miss Gilchrist's murderer had been interested not in her jewellery but in family papers kept in her flat. Doyle wrote:

> What confronts you is a determination to admit nothing which inculpates another official and as to the idea of punishing another official for offences which have caused misery to helpless victims, it never comes within their horizons.

It was the beginning of an eighteen-year struggle. Swallowing his personal distaste for the convicted man, Doyle displayed much the same mixture of crusading zeal, occasional forensic acuity and undoubted persistence once embarked on a cause familiar from the Edalji case. As we've seen, he was not a man to be easily deterred, nor one to dwell unduly on any opposing point of view.

There were certain general similarities, too, between the mystery surrounding Marion Gilchrist's death and the plots of several Sherlock Holmes tales. The core premise of a man wrongly accused of murder, which it turns out actually involves another party altogether, with contributing motives including thwarted love, greed and blackmail, lies at the heart of 1891's 'The Boscombe Valley Mystery'. In 'The Adventure of the Blue Carbuncle' (1892), the police, investigating the theft of a fabulous jewel, wrongly arrest a character with a lowlife reputation, while in 'The Priory School', published in 1904, suspicion in a kidnapping case falls on a 'silent and morose' German named Heidegger, only for Holmes to unravel a thread again involving bitter family intrigues over a disputed inheritance.

Beginning with the semi-mythical 'Mam', his confidant from the time he was sent to boarding school in 1867 until her death fifty-three years later, Doyle's relations with women would be consistently deferential and respectful, if perhaps more a matter of chivalry than real affection. He was known to defend female virtue to an almost unnatural degree, as when his 18-year-old son Adrian once incautiously described a girlfriend as 'ugly', and received his father's 'vicious back-hander across his face' by way of rebuke. But Doyle, even so, came to first question and eventually to mock the reputation of a key witness in the Slater case, the maid Helen Lambie.

Not only had she displayed 'great want of intelligence' on the night of the murder. There were subsequent grounds for believing that Lambie had lied repeatedly, under oath or not, and in her later years, having moved to America, she seemed to routinely give interviews that contradicted at least part of her sworn testimony, only to then retract what she had said and revert to her original story. Among other small but telling details, Doyle – in a move Holmes would have appreciated – pointed out that Lambie had once told the authorities that she recognised Slater at an identity parade because he was wearing his 'own coat'. It was later established that he was not then wearing his own coat, but one supplied to him out of a police lost-and-found storage locker.

The extraordinary thing that emerges in Conan Doyle's pursuit of justice, even more pronounced in the case of Slater than Edalji, is the sheer tenacity he exhibited once roused to action. Despite profound changes in his own circumstances in the years 1912–30, including his full-scale religious conversion, he never wavered from what he called his 'unshakable belief in the fact that [a] serious scandal had arisen', and that 'a full and unstinting pardon [was] due the convicted man' as a result. To most of Slater's supporters, such a prospect must have seemed a remote one once the initial furore of the trial had died down and he was shut up in Scotland's notorious Peterhead Prison to serve his whole-life sentence. Yet, despite the fact that the Great War intervened, that the public and press inevitably found other causes for concern, and that many of the key witnesses died or emigrated or simply lost interest, Doyle himself showed no signs of doubt that justice would eventually prevail.

Meanwhile, Slater was left to smuggle out a series of scribbled notes that sought desperately to identify the real killer or killers, such as the one he wrote in 1910:

> My firm opinion is that the murder was one of [the family] or a other sweethearth of Lambie … A[n] old story and allwise true, is when murder is committed and the reason was robbery, and a servant was staying in the house like Lambie, knowing so many boys, the murder is most times the sweethearth, or a friend of the sweethearth.

Slater's pathetic note, which contained more than a grain of both common sense and insight into the criminal mind, did him no good. It was the last word anyone on the outside would hear from him for over four years.

8

'AS BRUTAL AND CALLOUS A CRIME AS HAS EVER BEEN RECORDED'

'The creator of "Sherlock Holmes" may be excused if he now and then turns away from the literature of invention and directs his detective talent upon real crimes and real problems of criminality,' *The Times* reported on 21 August 1912. 'Some time ago he did this in the Edalji case, and to-day Messrs. Hodder and Stoughton publish a little sixpenny book from his hand under the title "The Case of Oscar Slater".'

As we've seen, Conan Doyle entered the fray only after some hesitation. Although it's true that he signed off on *The Lost World* in March 1912, he was far from idle that spring and early summer. Among other duties, Doyle found himself in a spirited public correspondence on everything from the continuing question of Irish Home Rule to the desirability of finishing Khartoum cathedral, before entering the thicket of his long and vitriolic exchange with George Bernard Shaw on the loss of the *Titanic*.

So Doyle's first contribution to the renewed Slater debate was neither inevitable nor planned in detail in advance. If anything, he seems to have reacted poorly when initially approached at the time William Roughead's book was published. 'Very soon after my marriage, having just got clear of the Edalji case, I became entangled in that of Oscar Slater,' Doyle later wrote, not exactly seething with enthusiasm at the memory:

> I went into the matter most reluctantly, but when I glanced at the facts, I saw that it was an even worse case than the Edalji one, and that this unhappy man had in all probability no more to do with the murder than I had. I am convinced that when on being convicted he cried out to the judge that he never knew that such a woman as the murdered woman existed he was speaking the literal truth.

The Case of Oscar Slater was not only a popular success, but strengthened that identification with lost causes that had begun as long ago as Doyle's support of the kleptomaniac Ella Castle in 1896. It was as much a searing indictment of the Slater investigation as it was a triumphant vindication of the convicted man. Doyle's central complaint was that the Glasgow Police had moved, like an institutional Inspector Lestrade, straight from suspicion to conclusion, without any intervening process of objective reasoning. What was needed was to step back and reflect on the case with a more detached attitude. Here was the 'not unimportant' matter of the criminal's motive, for instance. 'One question which has to be asked was whether the assassin was after the jewels at all,' Doyle wrote:

> It might be urged that the type of man described by the spectators was by no means that of the ordinary thief ... Why did he go straight into the spare bedroom where [the family papers] were kept? Any knowledge gathered from outside (by a watcher in the back-yard, for example) would go to the length of ascertaining which was the old lady's room. One would expect a robber who had gained his information thus, to go straight to that chamber. But this man did not do so. He went straight to the unlikely room in which [the papers] were kept. Is not this remarkably suggestive? Does it not presuppose a previous acquaintance with the inside of the flat and the ways of its owner?

Here Conan Doyle spoke in the authentic voice of Sherlock Holmes. It was all a matter of perspective. The police had spent so much time confirming their suspicions of Slater that they never stopped to ask a basic question: how did the murderer get in to Marion Gilchrist's flat in the first place, if Helen Lambie was right in insisting that she had shut both the doors, and there was no sign of a forced entry? The conclusion (obvious now, but not at the time) was that he had had a duplicate key. 'In that case all becomes comprehensible,' Doyle reasoned:

> … for the old lady – whose faculties were quite normal – would hear the lock go and would not be alarmed, thinking that Lambie had returned before her time. Thus, she would only know her danger when the murderer rushed into the room, and would hardly have time to rise, receive the first blow, and fall, as she was found, beside the chair upon which she had been sitting.

Doyle wrote contemptuously of the narrative the Glasgow Police put forward to explain the crime. He was particularly unimpressed by the theory that the killer had simply rung the downstairs door bell, that Marion Gilchrist had used the lever in her front parlour to let him in, and then, without checking who was coming up the stairs, had obligingly opened her own front door and returned to her chair and her magazine, calmly awaiting her caller. 'This is possible,' Doyle wrote:

> … but is it not in the highest degree improbable? Miss Gilchrist was nervous of robbery and would not neglect obvious precautions. The ring came immediately after the maid's departure. She could hardly have thought that it was her returning, the less so as the girl had the keys and would not need to ring. If she went as far as the hall door to open it, she only had to take another step to see who was ascending the stair. Would she not have taken it if it were only to say: 'What, have you forgotten your keys?' That a nervous old lady should throw open both doors, never look to see who her visitor was, and return to her dining-room is very hard to believe.

But either way, whether the murderer was admitted by his victim or already had a key, there was the troubling matter of how, exactly, he had then killed Marion Gilchrist.

Doyle might never have created Holmes at all were it not for his own medical background – time and again, he has the detective assessing the clues in a case before objectively concluding what had happened, much like any prudent doctor noting a patient's symptoms as an aid to diagnosis. Some of the same spirit of rational inquiry applied here. Doyle called on fifteen years as a 'struggling and actual medic', as he put it, in coming to address the physical characteristics of the murder weapon. 'My first choice would be a burglar's jemmy, bifurcated at one end,' he wrote:

> … while the blow which pushed the poor woman's eye into her brain would represent a thrust from the other end. Failing a jemmy, I should choose a hammer, but a very different one from the toy thing from a half-crown set of tools which was exhibited in court. Surely commonsense would say that such an instrument could burst an eyeball, but could not possibly drive it deep into the brain, since the short head could not penetrate nearly so far. The hammer which I would reconstruct from the injuries would be what they call, I believe, a plasterer's hammer, short in the handle, long and strong in the head, with a broad fork behind.

Doyle's working hypothesis was that someone had gone out equipped with this weapon in order to extract the personal papers from their hiding place in Miss Gilchrist's spare bedroom, and had then been forced to improvise horribly with it when she intervened, either before or during the actual burglary. 'But how such a thing could be used without the user bearing [blood] marks is more than I can say,' he admitted:

> It has never been explained why a rug was laid over the murdered woman. The murderer, as his conduct before Lambie and Adams showed, was a perfectly cool person. It is at least possible that he used the rug as a shield between him and his victim while he battered her with his weapon. His clothes, if not his hands, would in this way be preserved.

Doyle's public broadside on behalf of Slater proved to be both successful and divisive. It was successful in that it led directly to a high-level inquiry, if not to a retrial; and divisive because it further polarised opinion about the man now known officially as 'Inmate 1992' in Peterhead Prison.

The most obvious rift was between those who believed Slater to be a scapegoat, and others who thought him guilty not only of murdering Marion Gilchrist but of a whole series of other violent crimes. In September 1912, for instance, a 'J. Buyers Black', describing himself as a 'technical expert of the Scottish Insurance Bureau', wrote to tell Doyle that there was apparently irrefutable proof pointing to 'the Jew' being the real killer in the case known as the Whiteinch Murder, in which, as we've seen, Patrick Leggett was convicted of fatally stabbing his wife Sarah. Other correspondents in turn leapt to Slater's defence. The Glasgow *Daily Record* published an open letter to Doyle from a member of the original 1909 jury, who said he had not been convinced by the evidence: 'I had the feeling all through the trial that there was a missing link somewhere.' The paper added that many local people believed that Miss Gilchrist's murderer was still among them, 'walking the streets, perhaps tortured by his conscience'.

Over the years, Doyle rarely complained about his unpaid duties as a de facto court of last appeal, and apparently enjoyed corresponding with a wide range of people around the world, replying sympathetically when they wrote to tell him about their various lines of investigation, their resulting deductions, and even sometimes their slightly dotty criminal conspiracy theories. Even so, he admitted, his postbag in the weeks and months following publication of *The Case of Oscar Slater* was:

> ... rich stuff, [with] a wide array of offences laid at the wretched man's door ... If Slater, as an adolescent, had not actually committed the Whitechapel Murders, that must have been the sole outrage of the past 25 years he had failed to perpetrate.

✳ ✳ ✳

It would be hard to exaggerate the impact Conan Doyle's intervention of 1912 had on the Oscar Slater case, and, more especially, in helping launch a concerted campaign for Slater's release. It's often been said that he took broadly the same role as Émile Zola, a generation earlier in the Dreyfus affair. Doyle, it's true, avoided both the more heated tone and direct accusations of Zola's rhetorical blast, and stopped short of publicly naming those responsible for the conspiracy against the convicted man. Nor was he himself put on trial, or forced into exile, for his views. But Doyle nonetheless spoke persuasively about the shortcomings and contradictions of Slater's prosecution, and ended with a lofty moral appeal both to the police and the public at large that justice be allowed to prevail.

Doyle wrote:

I am aware that it is easier to theorise at a distance than to work a case out in practice whether as detective or as counsel. I leave the matter now with the hope that, even after many days, some sudden flash may be sent which will throw a light upon as brutal and callous a crime as has ever been recorded in those black annals in which the criminologist finds the materials for his study. Meanwhile it is on the conscience of the authorities, and in the last resort on that of the community that this verdict obtained under the circumstances I have indicated, shall now be reconsidered.

Among those apparently moved by Doyle's appeal was 44-year-old Glasgow Police Detective Lieutenant John Trench. Trench, who joined the force in 1893, had played a significant part in the original investigation of Marion Gilchrist's death, and appeared as a witness for the prosecution at Slater's trial. He had shown a Holmesian attention to detail in describing to the court the way in which a lookout might have familiarised himself with Miss Gilchrist's flat.

'The close [entry] to No. 46 West Princes Street is on the opposite side of the street from the close leading into the deceased's house,' Trench testified in 1909:

Directly opposite. The stair leading to the houses there begins immediately behind the close door, and takes a turn. It is a spiral one, and is continuous until the first flat is reached ... Six steps down from that landing there is a staircase window fronting West Princes Street, and the sill of that window is six feet from the steps of the stair. By getting up to the landing at the first flat you can see through this window, and you can see to the door of the close of Miss Gilchrist's house. When I went up [to] the second flat I found a staircase window there. That staircase window is only two-and-a-half to three feet above the stair. That window looks directly into the room of the house where Miss Gilchrist was murdered ... The stair begins just immediately from the door, and if the door is pushed back there is a recess formed between the outside wall and the door. The recess is of considerable size. A man could quite easily stand behind it.

Three years later, however, having read Conan Doyle's account, Lieutenant Trench's mind had fastened on another aspect of the investigation altogether. This was the visit he, Trench, had made two days after the murder to the home of Miss Gilchrist's niece, Margaret Birrell. During the course of their interview, Miss Birrell had told him that on the night of the crime Helen Lambie had run to her house and, in her shock, had positively named the man she had seen fleeing her employer's flat just a few minutes earlier. It was not Oscar Slater.

According to Trench, in a statement he gave to the Slater inquiry in 1914:

> I say positively that Miss Birrell said to me that Helen Lambie on the night of the murder told her that the man she saw leaving the house was A.B. Notwithstanding I am told that both Miss Birrell and Helen Lambie emphatically deny the whole story and express astonishment at it, I adhere to my statement that that was what Miss Birrell told me.

Conan Doyle could hardly have invented a more dramatic episode or startling revelation in his detective fiction. Although the libel laws prohibited Trench from publicly identifying 'A.B.', his name soon emerged in exchanges between Slater's supporters. It was Francis James Charteris, who at the time of the murder was a 33-year-old family doctor and visiting lecturer at St Andrew's University. Charteris was the victim's nephew by marriage. He was also familiar with the interior of Marion Gilchrist's flat, and could conceivably have had an interest in the contents of the papers kept there.

Charteris had actually visited the scene of the crime only minutes after the murder, apparently alerted by Margaret Birrell, and had offered to help the first police and medical orderlies to respond. Although his professional services weren't required – Miss Gilchrist had already been pronounced dead – it raises the chilling image of a cold-blooded assassin returning to insinuate himself into the investigation of his victim's death. Francis Charteris lived until 1964, when he was 88, having long since become aware of Trench's allegations against him. He could hardly have avoided them, since by then several major newspapers had also drawn the same conclusion. At the very end of his life Charteris spoke to a journalist from the *Scottish Daily Mail* and told him:

> When I got to the [victim's flat] the police superintendent was interviewing the servant-girl, Nellie Lambie. She was very excited, I remember. Her eyes were practically jumping out of her head. The police were trying to get a description from her of the man she had seen leaving the flat. She was very vague, almost incoherent, and I remember remarking to myself that they could hardly rely

on anything she had to say. Then quite suddenly she blurted out, 'He was like Dr Charteris there'.

Although the elderly Francis Charteris dismissed this remark as 'nonsense', for once Lambie may not have been entirely wide of the mark in her description. In all probability, the man she saw hurriedly leave Marion Gilchrist's flat following the murder was indeed 'like' Dr Charteris. He was in fact his elder brother, Archibald. We'll return to the troubled relations between the members of the Gilchrist and Charteris families, and what precisely may have happened on the night of 21 December 1908 as a result. For the time being, it's enough to note that Doyle's involvement in the case proved to be the turning point for Lieutenant Trench, and that Trench's statement in turn led to an extra-judicial inquiry (to which Slater wasn't invited), held in Glasgow from 23–25 April 1914.

Among other things, Trench told the inquiry:

> On 3 January 1909, I visited Nellie Lambie at 15 South Kinning Place, at the house of her aunt. She was lodging there. I had with me a sketch of Oscar Slater which I had received from Superintendent Ord. I showed the sketch to Lambie. She could not identify. She said she did not know him.

Trench had gone on to ask Lambie if she was confident that Francis Charteris was the man she had seen fleeing Marion Gilchrist's flat on the night of the murder. She replied, 'It's gey [or 'very'] funny if it wasn't him I saw.' Trench added:

> My conclusion after meeting Lambie was that if she had had any one to support her she would have sworn to [Charteris]. So much impressed was I that I mentioned the fact to Superintendent Ord the next morning, asking if he thought that [Charteris] might not be the man. His only answer was, '[Superintendent William] Douglas has cleared up all that. What can we do?'

Against this, there was the inquiry testimony of Margaret Birrell, her lodger Fred Cowan, and Helen Lambie herself, all of whom denied that Lambie had so much as breathed the name of Francis Charteris, either on the night of the murder or at any time in the future. Mary Barrowman, in turn, repeated her story from the original trial about a man much like Slater running past her on the street outside Marion Gilchrist's house, and Barrowman's employer came forward to deny having ever told Trench that he doubted the girl's word. Superintendent Ord also contradicted his subordinate officer's account:

> I did not on 3 January, 1909, instruct Lt. Trench to visit Helen Lambie at the house of her aunt. I did not give him a pencil sketch of Oscar Slater. I never saw such a sketch. I have no recollection of Lt. Trench reporting to me anything of a conversation in which Helen Lambie is said to have told him with regard to [Charteris] being the man she saw: 'It's gey funny …' and followed on with other remarks to the same effect. I can say positively that no such statement was ever made to me.

Superintendent Douglas added, 'I saw Miss Birrell [on the night of 21 December], and she did not say that Helen Lambie made any such statement [about Charteris] to her.'

According to Chief Detective Inspector John Pyper of Glasgow Central Division, neither Birrell nor Lambie had 'ever [said] anything then or since that would cast the slightest suspicion on [Francis Charteris]'. He concluded, 'I have carried on a good part of the [investigation] and from all I have heard I have not a shadow of a doubt that [Charteris] had nothing to do with the murder.' When James Millar, the inquiry's presiding officer, came to report his findings to the Secretary of State for Scotland, he added his opinion that Margaret Birrell, Helen Lambie and Mary Barrowman seemed to be honest and trustworthy witnesses, and that both they 'and certain of the attending police officers exhibited signs of great surprise when Trench's statements were read to them'.

Lieutenant Trench is often held up today as an intrepid fighter for justice who knowingly put his own career at risk in order to blow the whistle on the lazy and unscrupulous detective work that had characterised the Slater case so far. It may be a caricature, but if so, it's one with a grain of truth. That he was generally perceived as more rational and reasonable than the gruff, bullet-headed John Ord (and for that matter, Ord's superior and near-namesake, Chief Superintendent John Orr) doubtlessly enhanced Trench's credibility as a champion of the convicted man, and thus also his present-day appeal. His outward appearance – solid and jovial – together with the fact that he was a holder of the King's Medal, and was widely regarded as a conscientious and diligent investigator during his first twenty years on the force, contributed to his image of respectability and competence. In any event, he seems to have been a model police officer, if not one who was strikingly gregarious or sociable towards his colleagues.

In November 1912, Trench had been largely responsible for preventing a miscarriage of criminal justice in a case popularly known as the Broughty Ferry murder, which bore certain similarities to the Marion Gilchrist affair. An elderly spinster named Jean Milne had been found battered to death in her Dundee home, and suspicion quickly fell on one Charles Warner, a Canadian-born drifter who moved around the area, generally sleeping in the open if the weather held, intruding on someone's barn or shed when conditions forced him indoors.

Trench, who was seconded to lead the investigation into the murder, soon concluded that the victim had known her killer, and that her death had very likely been the result of an argument about money. A half-smoked cigar found in the dining room fireplace suggested that Miss Milne had had a male caller on the day in question, an impression strengthened by the open bottle of whisky and two glasses on the sideboard.

Meanwhile, the nomadic Warner had made his way to Maidstone, in Kent, where the local police arrested him. Trench interviewed the prisoner, who told him that he had been in Antwerp on the day of the murder. Although Warner had no hotel or restaurant receipts to support his story (he'd slept rough when travelling), he produced a ticket to indicate that he had pawned his waistcoat while abroad. Trench went to Antwerp, located the pawnshop, and confirmed the alibi. Warner was released without charge.

Although Jean Milne's murder remained unsolved, it was widely acknowledged that an innocent man had at least been spared a trial and a possible capital conviction. When the Glasgow papers reported on the case, several of them published pictures of Lieutenant Trench being welcomed back to the station house by his commanding officer, Chief Superintendent Orr. Within a short time, the two would engage in a bitter professional struggle, with Trench the loser.

This benign impression of John Trench may not always hold up to closer scrutiny, however. In January 1914, he had decided to enlist the help of a Scottish lawyer and author named David Cook to publicise the Slater case. Trench's numerous critics on the Glasgow force suggested that in doing so he had been motivated less by a selfless quest for truth and justice and more by his ambition to position himself as the best-known of the contestants to succeed Superintendent Orr when the time came. If so, his strategy for professional advancement failed spectacularly. On 14 September 1914, the Glasgow Magistrates' Committee recorded:

> After full and careful consideration of the case … the Committee unanimously found [Trench] guilty of the charge on which he was suspended by the Chief Constable, viz communicating to a person who is not a member of the Glasgow Police Force, namely Mr David Cook, Writer, information which he had acquired in the performance of his duty, and copies of documents from the official records in the case of Oscar Slater, [and] the Committee, in respect of said finding, and in terms of Section 78 of the Glasgow Police Act, 1866, dismissed Dt. Lt. Trench from the Force of that City.

This was not the end of former Lieutenant Trench's troubles at the hands of his sometime employer, the Glasgow Police. In August 1915, both he and David Cook were sent for trial (in the same courtroom where six years earlier Slater had been condemned to death) in a somewhat bizarre case brought against them for handling stolen goods. The charge arose from the January 1914 burglary of a Glasgow jewellery shop, and the police contention that Trench and others had subsequently tried to swindle £400 out of the insurance company covering the loss. The judge quickly brought an end to the proceedings when he told the jury, 'I direct you that there is no justification at all which would enable you to return a verdict of guilty against the defendants'.

Although Trench walked from court a free man, it was said that he was broken by his experiences. After fighting overseas with the Royal Scots Fusiliers, he returned to Glasgow and died there in May 1919, aged 50. Seventy years later, the Scottish Office conducted a full review of Trench's dismissal from the police and concluded that this had been 'harsh'. However, according to then Secretary of State Donald Dewar, 'There is no statutory authority to issue a pardon or posthumous rehabilitation of this officer. He should have contested his original treatment in a court of law.' It remains unclear how, exactly, Lieutenant Trench could have effectively mounted a challenge to his expulsion from the police in September 1914. By the time the official letter confirming the magistrates' decision reached him, he was already in advanced training with his battalion for overseas duty, a service he could easily have avoided had he so wished because of his age.

This is not necessarily to endorse Trench's eventual view of the Oscar Slater case, however. The scenario he outlined of corruption and treachery involving literally dozens of brother officers may well be plausible, given the laissez-faire approach which we know many police officers of the time took to their investigations. What more compelling proof could there be of this conspiracy than Slater's trial itself, in which no positively incriminating physical evidence was presented, but where the judge informed the jury that the defendant did not warrant the presumption of innocence?

At the same time, to believe Lieutenant Trench's narrative in its entirety is to accept not only that the Glasgow Police colluded as one to frame Slater, but that, in time, their conspiracy reached down into the local community as far as the likes of the bootmaker Colin Maccallum, Mary Barrowman's employer, who emphatically denied making the remarks Trench attributed to him, and 32-year-old businessman James Howat, who told the 1914 inquiry that he was 'quite sure' Barrowman had come to his home on the night Marion Gilchrist was murdered, a story Trench insisted was totally fabricated.

Reading the transcript of the inquiry today, it's hard to see what practical grounds the civilian witnesses like Maccallum and Howat might have had for lying quite as brazenly as the believers in a conspiracy think they did. As the generally sympathetic William Roughead wrote:

> Mr Trench was an able and experienced officer whose promotion from the ranks was earned by 21 years' meritorious service. That any man with a record such as his should have invented the whole story is well-nigh incredible ... He had nothing whatever to gain by persisting in his statement, he stood to lose and in fact lost everything – prestige, place, and pension. On the other hand, it seems almost beyond belief that these respectable witnesses would state deliberately what they knew to be false. Both stories cannot be true.

Although the complete text of the Slater inquiry remained secret for the next seventy-six years, a partial transcript was published on 29 June 1914. It happened to be the day on which the world awoke to the news that the schoolboy terrorist Gavrilo Princip had shot the Archduke Franz Ferdinand and his wife at Sarajevo, setting in train the reflexive diplomatic steps that led to war.

Conan Doyle, who was then visiting Canada, was not impressed by what he read of the Glasgow proceedings. 'No one who has mastered the facts can read this account without amazement,' he wrote in the *Spectator* later in July:

> It appears to completely cut away point after point which told against Slater at the trial. How the verdict could be that there was no fresh cause for reversing the conviction is incomprehensible. [It is] the supreme example of official incompetence and obstinacy.

Fortunately for Slater, just as Trench and Cook left the field, and Doyle himself increasingly turned to his twin preoccupations with the war and spiritualism, the campaign for justice was strengthened by a new recruit who promised to bring to it qualities of tenacity and aggression possibly accentuated by his taste for strong drink.

William Park, a Glasgow-based freelance writer and an early proponent of investigative journalism (or 'muckraking', as it was known then), came of an old and wealthy family from western Scotland. He was a tall, striking figure, with a love of fast women and slow horses to match his fondness for the local malt. At the same time, he was widely read and partial not only to Sherlock Holmes but also the socialist effusions of the Scots-born MP, Keir Hardie, whose public eulogy on Karl Marx he used to quote with enthusiasm. The author Peter Hunt later referred to Park as 'that strange, self-tortured fanatic, whose avowed intent it was to disembowel the Glasgow Police'.

On 23 September 1914, Park wrote to Conan Doyle to point out several 'discrepancies' and 'rank fabrications' in the recent Slater inquiry. Two days later, another letter arrived. In it Park wondered if Doyle might care to write to the Secretary of State for Scotland, though he, Park, agreed that little could realistically be done for Slater until after the war – 'and he may be dead by then, as several ex-convicts have told me that he is off his head'. The correspondence continued on a roughly weekly basis during the remainder of 1914. On 8 October, Park wrote to tell Doyle that he considered the Secretary of State:

> A hopelessly stupid man … He is simply a promoted man in the street. It is our view … that the Trench business should only come in as an episode to the main story of the sham inquiry and humbug report.

A fully organised campaign for Slater's release was still incomplete at the end of 1914. By then Doyle was heavily involved in writing on behalf of the

War Propaganda Board, as well as training his own home-defence militia, and had less time to devote to what he called 'pacific affairs' as a result. He seems to have politely acknowledged Park's letters without actively encouraging them. 'In spite of the shocks and strains which each day brought,' Doyle later remarked, 'I did not grudge the many hours of concentrated thought [the Park correspondence] demanded', language that perhaps suggests the opposite was true. Another letter, of 7 December, told Doyle of Park's intention to proceed with a book on the Slater case, and more particularly 'to expose the police conduct, show how they prepared their prosecution, [and] illustrate the discrepancies between statements at trial and those given secretly to police'.

By the following spring, Park's focus had turned to the criminal case brought against John Trench and David Cook. 'I shall be glad of any suggestions from you,' he wrote to Doyle on 20 May. 'Your keen acumen and experience of police methods may throw light on the mystery of the arrests.' A civil but noncommittal response ensued. The previous autumn, Conan Doyle had published his fourth and final Sherlock Holmes novel, *The Valley of Fear*, while retaining his usual ambivalence about his 'poor hero of the anemic printed page'.

'If I had a good competence, I would devote myself to some serious literary or historical work,' Doyle told his editor at *The Strand*, before adding, 'I have large commercial interests and if they took a good turn (as they may well do) I should be in that position.' Doyle had spent some seven weeks in 1886 creating Holmes and, it could be argued, the rest of his life regretting it. He did not actively investigate the Slater case between 1914 and 1925, although he frequently went on record lobbying for an inquiry, or supporting the pleas of Park and others for a new trial. Nor did he forget the convicted man. 'From time to time one hears word of poor Slater from behind his prison walls,' Doyle wrote, 'like the wail of some wayfarer who has fallen into a pit and implores aid from the passers-by.'

About the war itself, Doyle was unambiguous. Every Briton should give tirelessly to the cause, he said, and before long he was drilling his volunteers, writing the history of battles almost before their outcome was conclusively known, and agitating for everything from the issue of proper body armour to the commissioning of a special badge for any soldier suffering a wound.

The conflict also marked the point where he came to finally reconsider his spiritual beliefs. As both the nation's and his own family's losses mounted, Doyle increasingly turned to the séance room for comfort. In the spring of 1916, he contributed two letters to the psychic journal *Light* on the theme 'Where is the Soul during Unconsciousness?' Together, they addressed the question of 'life's ultimate purpose' and the 'inchoate yearning for meaning' Doyle saw all around him. The strands of theory and experience he wove together in *Light* would help form the basis for the new spiritualist movement which emerged in the early 1920s, and that led millions of people who had never read a word of his detective fiction to take serious note of him.

By early 1917, Conan Doyle was talking about the importance of applying the 'psychic line' to certain miscarriages of criminal justice. 'There was a Spiritualist circle which used to meet in Falkirk,' he later wrote:

> … and shortly after the [Slater] trial messages were received by it which purported to come from the murdered woman. She was asked what the weapon was which had slain her. She answered that it was an iron box-opener [or crowbar]. Now I had pondered over the nature of certain wounds in the woman's face, which consisted of two cuts with a little bridge of unbroken skin between. They might have been caused by the claw end of a hammer, but on the other hand, one of the woman's eyes had been pushed back into her brain, which could hardly have been done by a hammer, which would have burst the eyeball first. I could think of no instrument which would meet the case. But the box-opener would exactly do so, for it has a forked end which would make the double wound, and it is also straight so that it might very well penetrate to the brain, driving the eye in front of it.
>
> The reader will reasonably ask why did not the Spiritualists ask the name of the criminal. I believe that they did and received a reply, but I do not think that such evidence could or should ever be used or published. It could only be useful as the starting point of an inquiry.

It was not, as it turned out, the last such paranormal investigation into the Oscar Slater case. Starting in the winter of 1917–18, Doyle himself made regular attempts to summon the spirit of Marion Gilchrist, and once claimed that he had 'seen the lady with great clarity' during a séance held by candlelight in his Sussex dining room.

Nonetheless, Slater remained a prisoner at Peterhead for some nineteen years. This was not a time when a German convicted of murder could presume on the goodwill of the British public. The author Thomas Toughill writes in his magisterial account of the case:

> Slater … was not a model prisoner. He protested his innocence from the outset and openly resented the treatment he received. There were, it is said, occasions when his attitude led to the exchange of blows. Any hopes he had that he would have his sentence reviewed after fifteen years, in effect 1922, came to nothing.

Visitors were shocked by Slater's appearance. 'I found him sitting like a frozen thing at the barred window of his cell,' one lady, who was not his wife, recalled. Slater had refused to take anything but bread and water for almost a month, and a doctor warned the woman that the prisoner would die if the fast continued.

✳ ✳ ✳

Following John Trench's death in 1919, his widow provided Conan Doyle with a copy of his last will and testament. It reaffirmed the obsession of Trench's life and career by 'adhering again to my statement of 23 April 1914', in which Helen Lambie was said to have positively identified her employer's killer. Attached to the will were some of the former detective's private notes on the Slater case.

Later that year, Francis Charteris was appointed Professor of Materia Medica at Glasgow University, a position he held for most of the next three decades. Lieutenant Trench's allegation against Charteris and his family was never legally substantiated, and would seem to have relied, as much as anything else, on Trench's quotation from memory of witness statements of which no record existed and which the individuals themselves denied were ever made. There must still be a suspicion that he harboured a grudge of some sort against his superior officers. Nonetheless, Trench's evidence to the 1914 inquiry was among the most courageous demonstrations of opposition to what he called 'the whole foul edifice' of the police investigation into Marion Gilchrist's murder. Conan Doyle would come to remark that 'this officer showed commendable fibre', and not a little of the Holmes technique, in his overall contribution to the case.

Late in 1919, Doyle again signalled his support for Slater by putting his name to an open letter calling for his release.

During the next eight years, Conan Doyle struggled to reconcile his pragmatic and materialist approach to life with his escalating crusade on behalf of spiritualism. Doyle's attitude to the Slater case mirrored this internal conflict. His famously rational 'Sherlock Holmes' side continued to worry away at the problems of the physical evidence and witness testimony presented at the trial. In time, Doyle came to the brink of obsession in his repeated musings on the exact nature of the weapon that had been used to kill Marion Gilchrist. Was it a box-opener? A chair leg? An antique fire iron?

The 'puny hammer' nominated by the police struck Doyle as:

Ludicrous… It was said by the prosecution to bear some marks of having been scraped or cleaned, [but] the police do not appear to have pushed the matter to the obvious test of removing the metal work, when they must, had this been indeed the weapon, have found some soakage of blood into the wood.

Doyle wrote this in 1912. More than twelve years later, in his memoirs, he was still drawn to the hammer. 'A case [against Slater] was made up in the most absurd manner,' he wrote:

The frail hammer was evidently the instrument which had beaten in the woman's skull. The handle might have been cleaned. Then surely there had been blood on it. The crown got a conviction, and the wretched foreigner was condemned to death.

Some of Doyle's repeated examination of the effects of a blunt object being driven into a human eyeball showed the same unflinching approach (with a similar, shudder-inducing result) of the notorious razor-slicing scene in Luis Buñuel's 1929 surrealist film *Un Chien Andalou*. It was this same attention to physical detail that largely helped to sustain the story until – fifteen years and a world war later – Slater was freed and Doyle ascended into investigative Valhalla as the pattern for all time of the hero crusader for criminal justice.

But there was more to Doyle's campaign than just the anatomical fixations of a former oculist. He also continued to fire off letters on the affair to a variety of friends, editors and politicians. He made public appearances, and put his name to successive petitions for a retrial. He encouraged, and in some cases subsidised, other campaigners, notably William Park, on Slater's behalf. 'I became very obstinate at a certain point in my life,' Doyle reflected when he was 70. 'I knew I was confronted by official incompetence and wickedness, and I was determined to do all I could for [Slater], not just for his sake but to establish a principle.'

While continuing to follow the traditional route of writing letters and signing appeals, Doyle also increasingly adopted the 'psychic line' in the Slater investigation. He seems to have had a particular rapport with the Falkirk Spiritualist Society and its secretary, John Stoddart, who had once known the murder victim. Stoddart wrote to Doyle in February 1925, '"Stephanus" (a medium) has informed our circle about a missing document from Miss Gilchrist's papers, named the real criminal, can reveal where the murder weapon is, and insists that Oscar Slater will not suffer the death penalty.' Doyle thought this a notable feat of 'mediumistic prophecy' – the weapon was apparently a burglar's jemmy, subsequently dumped in the river Clyde – although as Slater had been officially reprieved more than fifteen years before Stephanus made his prediction, and this fact had been splashed over every British newspaper, there may also have been more material means at work.

In the same week the spiritualists met in Falkirk, a convicted house-breaker named William Gordon was released from Peterhead Jail. Unbeknownst to the authorities, concealed in his dentures he carried a message written on waxed paper which had been given to him by his fellow inmate, Oscar Slater. It was a direct appeal for Conan Doyle's help. Slater had little new to say in his brief note, but something about the sheer desperation of its author's plea stirred Doyle to act. It was 'literally a case of word of mouth,' he observed.

The campaign for Slater's release gathered renewed momentum as a result. Doyle again wrote to the Secretary of State for Scotland, but received only the reply that 'This Office has considered your representations, but does not feel justified in advising any interference with Slater's sentence'. It appeared to the editorial writer of the *Glasgow Herald*, whose headline read 'Case Closed', and to others, that that concluded the affair. Such observers again underestimated Doyle's obstinacy and resilience. Throughout 1926 he continued to furnish William Park with both money and technical advice for the latter's long-delayed account of the Slater affair.★

★ A slightly surreal photograph exists of Conan Doyle, dressed in tweed plus fours, sitting over some correspondence at his garden table in Sussex. The caption reads, 'Portrait of the famous author writing his 440th letter to William Park about Oscar Slater, 1927'.

Published in July 1927 by Doyle's own Psychic Press, Park's book was an instant success. As a contemporary reviewer said, 'It has the fortitude to ask questions about a miscarried case at a time when the problem is not that people just don't know better, but that people just don't care.' No less a figure than Edgar Wallace, the prolific mystery author (and future creator of King Kong) wrote in a starred review in the *Morning Post*, 'Slater has served 18 years for a crime of which anybody but a fool might know that he is guiltless'. The mass-market *Daily News* in turn ran a series of front-page articles both on the book and the Slater case in general. Questions were again asked in parliament, to which the Scottish Lord Advocate replied that he would be 'very much surprised' if the government saw fit to release the prisoner. As William Roughead later sardonically noted, 'His lordship was destined to experience that sensation.'

Park's book, to which Doyle wrote an introduction, can lay claim to being a forerunner of the sort of literary forensic reappraisal of notorious criminal cases that the writer Ludovic Kennedy popularised some forty years later. Commonplace now, the genre barely existed in the 1920s. Park was also a pioneer of the 'factional' narrative widely used to this day by thriller writers to establish verisimilitude.

Along with the page-turning style, the book contained one or two genuine revelations. The Glasgow Police, for example, had apparently misrepresented the testimony of Slater's acquaintance Allan McLean about the diamond brooch being hawked around the Sloper Club in the days following Marion Gilchrist's murder, and had done so 'to make a case against the suspect where none otherwise existed'. ('This may explain why McLean hanged himself,' Park wrote to Doyle in November 1927.)

There was also a question of whether Judge Guthrie had edited his final address to the jury when it came to publishing the official transcript of the trial. 'The old rascal re-wrote the speech [and] introduced wholesale paragraphs and sentences he never said,' Park confided to Doyle, although for compelling legal reasons he tempered these remarks in print. But the book's one true bombshell, which was found in the papers forwarded by Lieutenant Trench's widow, was a page Trench had torn from the police files at the time of the 1914 inquiry. This showed that Superintendent Ord had originally written in a departmental review of the case, 'The clue when first received against Slater was very much less strong than against other suspects'. However, somewhere between Ord writing this in 1909 and it being presented to the inquiry five years later, the crucial phrase had been doctored to read '*not stronger* than against other suspects'. 'You will be the hero when this comes out,' Doyle generously wrote to Park while preparing Park's book for publication. He added, 'I was told from spirit séances a little while ago that it was all about to be cleared up.'

Spurred by the success of *The Truth About Oscar Slater*, the weekly *Empire News* (formerly *The Umpire*, the paper which had once alerted Doyle to the Edalji affair) went to the trouble of tracking down the now 39-year-old Helen Lambie, who had emigrated to Peoria, Illinois, after the war. She had since had an unhappy married life that had produced two daughters, both of whom she named after Marion Gilchrist. Historians of the Slater case have tended to find fault with Lambie's testimony, which seems to them to be inconsistent on certain key points, and her interview with the *News* gives some backing to that view. The headline read, 'Why I believe I blundered over Slater'. In the story that followed Lambie apparently recanted her statement given at the time of the trial, and instead remarked:

> It is quite true that I [recognised Marion Gilchrist's killer], because when I returned from buying the paper that night and encountered the strange man coming from the house he did not seem strange to me … When I told the police the name of the man I thought I knew they replied, 'Nonsense! You don't think he could have murdered and robbed your mistress!' They scoffed so much at the notion of this man being the one I had seen that I had allowed myself to be persuaded that I had been mistaken.

On reading this, Conan Doyle, who had never been impressed with Lambie's evidence, fired off a syndicated article on the case. When it was published, he sent a copy of it to Park. But before doing so, Doyle crossed out the paper's 'anemic' headline and wrote in the more direct, 'Confession of Lambie. End of the Slater case'.

However, on closer examination, Lambie's *Empire News* interview may not have been the 'incontestable' and 'definitive' statement Doyle believed. In a letter home to her mother, whom she presumably had no reason to lie to, Marion Gilchrist's former maid offered yet another account of the events following her employer's death. 'No one [from the press] has come here,' Lambie wrote on 13 November 1927:

... so we will see how far they will go. I can see plainly now all is a frame-up, and Conan Doyle has no statement from me in my handwriting. He says he has a copy, so Conan Doyle knows he is working on a false statement. The Government will not allow themselves to be fooled by falseness, and if I come forward on my own accord no one will pay [my] expenses ... Conan Doyle may give up, [as] falseness will never clear or get Slater free. He should have got hanged years ago. They should hang him yet, as he is the man and no other man. Conan Doyle is only aggravating and causing an agitating in the papers to get the public on his side.

This contradiction did not sit well with the Slater purity narrative, and in time Lambie, whom Doyle now called 'a woman hungrily alive to the sound of her own righteousness', went to the trouble of swearing out a statement which she had notarised on 18 December 1927. It read:

I wish to put a denial to the statement recently [*sic*] published in Newspapers. There is no truth in that statement. Connan [*sic*] Doyle used a false statement. I would not blame another man. Slater is the man that I saw coming out of the house of Miss Gilchrist. I am as strong and of the same mind as I was at the trial.

Meanwhile, the *Daily News* enjoyed a scoop of its own when it tracked down 34-year-old Mary Barrowman, whom it found living in distressed circumstances in Glasgow. On 5 November 1927, she had this to say to the paper about the events of nineteen years earlier:

Regarding the proceedings in New York, where I was confronted with the prisoner for the first time as far as speaking to his identification was concerned ... I only said that Slater was very like the man I had seen [on 21 December 1908].

It was when I returned to Glasgow that the question of Slater being positively the man was brought before my notice. This was done by Mr Hart, the Fiscal.

This gentleman was most severe in his treatment of me as a witness. He made me appear at his office day after day to have a meeting with him.

It was Mr Hart who got me to change my statement from being 'very like the man' to the emphatic declaration that Slater was the man.

✳ ✳ ✳

It was a remarkable development, and it further galvanised Conan Doyle. From the summer of 1927 onward he was increasingly prepared to advise the Slater camp, to sit on boards and committees, contribute articles, and above all to win over those in a position of authority. As we've seen, he was not a man to be easily swayed from his position, nor to dwell on any possible opposing point of view. On 2 November, Doyle wrote to the editor of the *Manchester City News* in reference to Lambie, 'What a story! What a scandal! She says that the police made her say it was Slater. Third degree! What a cess pool it all is!' There was a similar note of outrage (if one tinged by ego) when he told another editor:

> I was up against a ring of political lawyers and others who could not give away the police without also giving away themselves … Oscar Slater never knew that Miss Gilchrist existed … The faked police persecution of their own honest Inspector [Trench] was a shocking business.

But perhaps the one imperishable contribution Conan Doyle made to the outcome of the Slater case was to send a copy of Park's book, and some accompanying notes from Trench's papers, to the Scots-born former prime minister, Ramsay MacDonald. MacDonald in turn took up the sword and wrote to the Scottish Secretary, Sir John Gilmour, demanding a 'handsome and generous' resolution to the case in which 'the authorities strove for [Slater's] conviction by influencing witnesses and with-holding evidence'.

MacDonald went on to invite Gilmour to 'minutely inspect' the page torn from the Glasgow Police log, in which the line 'very much less strong' had been 'sexed up' to read 'not stronger than'. Shortly after this, the government suddenly decided that perhaps there had been some irregularities to the Slater case after all, and on 7 November Gilmour informed the House of Commons, 'The prisoner has now completed eighteen and a half years of his life sentence, and I feel justified in deciding to authorise his release on licence as soon as suitable arrangements can be made'.

Even this seeming capitulation, which left a good deal unsaid, failed to satisfy Doyle. The Slater business 'will surely develop into a big political issue unless there is some inquiry into the scandal,' he wrote to the prime minister, Stanley Baldwin, on 13 November. 'I regret that I cannot believe in the "thorough investigation" by the Scots Office alluded to in your former letter. There are limits to human stupidity and this is beyond them.'

Shortly before noon the following day, Oscar Slater walked free from Peterhead Jail and after lunch in a nearby hotel boarded a train back to Glasgow. It was eighteen years, ten months and twelve days since he had first been taken into custody. In his fulsome letter of thanks to Doyle, Slater revealed that he had 'meant to take Peterhead for twenty years, [and] then if no help came to end my life'. He was accompanied on his homecoming journey by a rabbi and a reporter from the Glasgow *Daily Record*. The next morning's paper described Slater as 'looking remarkably fresh … his face was wreathed in smiles as he accepted congratulations on his freedom, [although] he allowed his nerves just now are a little on edge'. He had been breaking rocks in the Peterhead prison quarry until 11 a.m. on the morning of his release.

There were extraordinary scenes on Slater's arrival that evening at Glasgow's Buchanan Street Station, where a crowd of some 300 spectators had gathered to get a look at the notorious figure. A reporter perched on a stepladder asked him if he was going out to celebrate. 'No, I'm going to bed,' he replied. Slater spent his first night of freedom at the rabbi's home in Kelvingrove Street, less than a mile away from the scene of Marion Gilchrist's murder.

So happy was he when he heard the news, that Conan Doyle sat down at Windlesham to consult with the spirits, and more particularly with Pheneas, the 7,000-year-old sage from the Mesopotamian city of Ur. Speaking through Lady Doyle's mediumship, Pheneas predicted that Slater would be completely exonerated from the charge of having murdered Marion Gilchrist, but that in time he and almost everyone else on earth would perish in a global apocalypse that might take the form of a great flood or earthquake. To protect themselves, Pheneas urged Doyle and his family to buy a large house at Bignell Wood, on the edge of the New Forest, as this would afford at least some degree of shelter in the coming crisis. (It may be purely coincidental to find the spirit proposing this particular beauty spot in southern England, which had long been a favourite retreat of Lady Doyle.)

While Doyle dutifully did this, in time also publishing the starkly titled essay, 'A Warning', that he distributed to friends and fellow believers to prepare them for the worst, Slater himself moved into a modest home in Ayr on the west coast of Scotland. He would live there for another twenty penurious years, during which he fell into ill health, wrote an unpublished memoir, remarried, and spent much of his spare time whittling driftwood. Although the government never deported him as they once threatened to do, early in the Second World War he was briefly interned as a German national.

Meanwhile, many of the papers again took up the mystery of Marion Gilchrist's death. If not Slater, then who was responsible? The *Daily Record* and the *Sunday Chronicle* were among those to actively campaign for a full judicial inquiry, while others, like the *Citizen Herald*, continued to insist that the real crime was that the 'Jewish-born brute' had escaped the gallows in the first place.

Doyle himself used the pages of the *Empire News* to try to establish 'who [were] the guilty parties of the whole episode'. He again disparaged Helen Lambie as a witness, and took the opportunity to warmly salute the late Lieutenant Trench, but apparently for legal reasons fell short of naming the actual killer. Doyle was less squeamish in his private letter to Stanley Baldwin. 'A note as to who *did* do the crime may interest you,' he told the prime minister, before recapping the salient facts of the case and explaining that it had all been prompted by the contents of Marion Gilchrist's will.

In the days that followed, Doyle sent a circular letter to all 615 British MPs demanding a public inquiry. Among those to receive this was 50-year-old Brigadier General John Charteris, the Unionist member for Dumfries, whose brother Francis was the man Doyle, taking Lambie at her published word, believed had battered Marion Gilchrist to death. As a result of this petition, a special bylaw was passed to allow the new Scottish Court of Criminal Appeal to retroactively hear Slater's case.

Doyle also wrote direct to the released prisoner:

Dear Mr Oscar Slater,

This is to say in my wife's name and my own how grieved we have been at the infamous injustice which you have suffered at the hands of our officials. Your only poor consolation can be that your fate, if we can get people to realize the effects, may have the effect of safeguarding others in the future.

We still work in the hope of getting an inquiry into these iniquities and eventually, as I hope, some compensation for your undeserved suffering.

Slater replied effusively:

Sir Arthur Conan Doyle, you breaker of my shackels [*sic*], you lover of truth for justice sake … My heart is full and almost breaking with love and gratitude for you and your dear wife lady Conan Doyle and all the upright men and women, who for justice sake (and that only) have helped me, me as an outcast.

Till my dying day I will love and honour you and the dear Lady, my dear, dear Conan Doyle, yet that unbounded love for you both, makes me sign plainly

Yours,
Oscar Slater.

Doyle had no way of knowing that this was to be perhaps the last fully friendly exchange he would ever have with Slater, whose correspondence from then on dwelt increasingly on financial matters rather than the technicalities of his guilt or innocence. As a result, there was some noticeable cooling of the 'unbounded love' so freely expressed in the heady days of November 1927. Soon Slater was writing to ask Doyle's advice about which lawyers to appoint to pursue his claim for compensation. In time, the monetary aspects of the whole affair became something of a mutual preoccupation. Doyle generously guaranteed £1,000 of his own funds to help pay for Slater's future defence, while launching a petition for additional contributions in the pages of the *Jewish Chronicle*. The intended beneficiary was not entirely happy with these initiatives. On 7 December, Slater (rarely at his most confident with the written word) wrote to tell Doyle that he was aware of his fundraising efforts on his behalf, but disappointed by some of the response. 'I thought that half a dozen influential Jews … would have paid the bill like sportsmen,' he complained:

> Dear Sir Arthur, it makes me *sick absolutely sick* to think on such actions. If [need be] I will *pay it all* … All collected money must go back to the Jews and we will thank the few who have given for their kindness.

Two weeks later, Slater wrote again to ask Doyle to accept a present which 'although of no great value is dear, dear to my heart because I have handled it daily for more than ten years'. This may have been Slater's homemade cigarette case; the following summer he sent Doyle a silver cigar-cutter in lieu of the £300 he had been asked for, and Doyle returned this with a curt note saying he would prefer the cash instead.

New Year's Day 1928 brought another exchange about smoking materials. Thanking Doyle for the gift of a pipe, Slater wrote, 'Yesterday I went down to the shore to have a quiet puff and except a little burning at the tip of my tongue I have enjoyed it imensely [*sic*].'

But even this congenial mood was soon to pass. In March, Slater wrote to furiously deny having given an interview critical of Doyle in the *Daily Express*, and to tell him:

Your pipe, sir, is dear to me, as a gift – but to use it, it is a failure, then only by touching it my tongue starts to nip, and any attempt to fill the pipe makes my stomach heave up and down.

Thanks largely to Doyle, Slater was able to engage the eminent Scottish barrister Craigie Aitchison, a future Lord Advocate, to represent him at his appeal. The lawyer charged £80 a day for his services. Although Slater's correspondence in this period shows flashes of feeling for Doyle and his other benefactors, it makes them out as unreasonable about money. 'Sir Arthur still makes me beg for my capitol [*sic*],' he complained.

Slater's petition was submitted to the Secretary of State for Scotland on 2 March 1928. Its first five numbered paragraphs spoke about the flawed eyewitness testimony presented at trial, while the sixth and critical one contended 'that the presiding Judge in said charge animadverted on the character of your petitioner to his prejudice'.

There were further pained exchanges about money throughout the spring. 'Sir Arthur! I never have failed my friends yet!' Slater protested on 2 May, admitting that a recent letter from the author had upset him greatly. Slater's rabbi friend later described him as behaving ungraciously in this period. After receiving a cheque, 'It was rare that he took note of the amount without complaining it was too little, or that others were benefitting from funds which he felt were his'. On 5 May, Slater wrote to tell Doyle that he was grateful to William Park, as well he might be, but 'this great worker makes mistakes also'. He added that he was prepared to pay the immediate expenses for his appeal, 'but nothing later'.

Meanwhile, the Lord Justice General, Lord Clyde, had agreed that Slater might have his day in court, but not be allowed to personally testify there. This was not well received. On 13 June, Slater informed the press that he was withdrawing his appeal. When a reporter from the *Ayrshire Post* went to his home to ask him about his reasons for doing this, 'Slater got so upset that we fell into a noisy row in the sitting room. I terminated the interview.' A few days later, Slater relented and agreed to pursue his claim after all. 'I think that I have hurt you, my faithful friend,' he wrote to Doyle on 17 June:

But I am not sorry that I have acted as I did, because I only behaved, as any other animal would behave, who is free, yet lying bleeding and wounded on the ground, using his last strength, to lash furiously out again, when painfully treated.

On 9 July, Slater's appeal hearing opened in front of Lord Clyde and four other judges. They sat in the same Edinburgh courtroom where the criminal trial had taken place nineteen years earlier. It's a curious detail that other than his shocked outburst on hearing the original verdict against him, Slater himself failed to say a word at either of the proceedings, and had not even attended the 1914 inquiry. Explaining his decision, Lord Clyde remarked that the petitioner in this case clearly had nothing new to say, and thus 'it would be quite unreasonable to spend time over his examination now, and the court therefore is not prepared to allow his evidence to be received'.

In July 1928, Conan Doyle was 69 years old. He still spent long hours every day at his desk, reading a constant flow of letters and reports about often outlandish paranormal activities (the claims of a woman to have levitated from one part of London to another, for example, or of a man who reported pieces of coal mysteriously falling from his ceiling), and keeping up his own prolific output on both spiritual and material matters. Although Doyle's reputation had been made with his invention of Holmes over forty years earlier, and he was by now a wealthy man, the words just kept on coming. For him, writing was like scratching an endless itch. During that summer, Doyle contributed articles on everything from the true meaning of life to the correct way to bowl a cricket donkey drop. Among other time-consuming projects, he took up the case of the missing transatlantic flier Walter Hinchliffe, whose disappearance he speculated had been caused by transportation to a parallel universe, rather than bad weather. The ridicule of much of the press, the opposition of the Church, and the refusal of the government to relax the witchcraft laws saw Doyle increasingly content to distance himself from the Establishment he had once seemed to embody.

In September 1928, Conan Doyle also brought out a new edition of *The Coming of the Fairies*, in which he reaffirmed his belief that the events eleven years earlier at Cottingley were of greater significance to mankind than Columbus's discovery of the New World, and soon went on to offer not only a fresh warning about the impending global cataclysm, but also a detailed geological account of how it would happen. This boiled down to a complicated formula involving the tilting of the polar axis and the consequent cracking of the earth's crust – another example, perhaps, of the author's twinned faith in science and the occult.

In the middle of these various commitments, Doyle took the time to return to the city of his birth to attend the Slater appeal, both as an act of moral support and to cover the proceedings for the *Sunday Pictorial*. That the world-famous and now physically ailing author would drop everything on his behalf was something Slater himself took in his stride. 'The old man puffed about here like a noisy train,' he remarked. It was their first personal meeting.

Doyle in turn found little to modify his unfavourable opinion of Slater's character. Nonetheless, his published report of the proceedings showed that he could be warmly sympathetic towards the victim of a miscarriage of justice without assuming any personal liking for him. 'One terrible face stands out among all those others,' Doyle wrote in the *Pictorial*:

> It is not an ill-favoured face, nor is it a wicked one, but it is terrible nonetheless for the brooding sadness that is in it. It is firm and immobile and might be cut from that Peterhead granite which has helped to make it what it is. A sculptor would choose it as the very type of tragedy. You feel that this is no ordinary man, but one who has been fashioned for some strange end. It is indeed the man whose misfortunes have echoed around the world. It is Slater.

After four days of evidence, the judges took another week to reach their decision. They found little with which to take issue in the testimony presented at the original proceedings. However, the trial judge on that occasion had failed to warn the jury to put out of their minds any prejudice they might have had about Slater's personal lifestyle, and more particularly 'his disreputable relations with the female members of his household'. As a result, Lord Clyde announced, 'We think that the instructions given in the charge amounted to misdirections in law, and that the judgement of the court before whom the appellant was convicted should be set aside.'

This was still very far from a ringing declaration of Slater's innocence. Rather than announcing that he had been the victim of a ghastly miscarriage of justice, the tribunal had quashed his conviction on what amounted to a technicality. It wasn't that Helen Lambie or anyone else had lied under oath at the original trial, but that Lord Guthrie should never have uttered the fateful phrase in his summing-up, 'A man of that kind has not the presumption of innocence in his favour'. Nonetheless, it was vindication of a sort. Cheers went up in the courtroom as Lord Clyde concluded his judgement, and *The Times* remarked that the crowd outside was 'ecstatic … it was not the logic but the nature of the ruling which was so startling'. There were cries of 'He's a jolly good fellow!' and 'Dear old Oscar!' Spectators waving hats and arms crowded around Slater on the steps of the courthouse, and the general air of festivity continued long into the warm summer's night both in Edinburgh's streets and pubs.

Slater himself 'very calmly' returned to his hotel, where he later sat down to write Doyle a letter with his impressions of the whole affair. He was not entirely satisfied with the outcome, he admitted. Welcome as the verdict was, Slater wrote:

> They went to [*sic*] far in throwing muck at me in a open court … This cruel five judges, this judges, *who knew the frame up of my case*, should have limited themselves a little and in not doing so, even the lay man in the street know now that my character was the staff for the Crown to lean on. I will fight and expose the all – *all them who I know have taken my confidence and have betrayed me.*

That night, while the normally staid town of Edinburgh celebrated, the hero of the hour retired early to bed.

❊ ❊ ❊

Showing his Scots good sense, Conan Doyle took the pragmatic view that the verdict was the best they could reasonably hope for, and that the priority now was to press the government for financial redress. 'You will get not a penny if you do not apply for it,' he wrote to Slater on 1 August. This was timely advice, because that same morning the British Cabinet met in Downing Street, and as part of their discussion (immediately after a debate on armed forces' pensions, and before one on the regulation of 'reconstituted and synthetic cream') considered:

> … how best to compensate the appellant Slater … After review, [it] was agreed that the Secretary of State for Scotland should endeavour to secure a settlement of the question on the basis of an *ex gratia* payment of £5,000 to Slater, but, if necessary, should have authority to give up to £6,000.

In time this latter sum was accepted.

Conan Doyle then began his long campaign to have Slater reimburse the defence funds Doyle and others had raised on his behalf. 'Will you now relieve those who supported you of their costs?' he enquired on 9 August, requesting a 'clear and direct' reply. One was never forthcoming. Throughout what proved to be the last two years of his life, Doyle was regularly obliged to break away from his spiritualist ministry to squabble with the man who had once professed his 'unbounded love [and] honour' about relatively minor sums of money. It seems fair to say that at the heart of the problem lay not so much a dispute about cash as a fundamental difference in moral values. Doyle simply assumed that Slater would wish to immediately clear his debts to his supporters. In his position, this is what Doyle himself would have done. But Slater took the view that he should never have been put on trial, nor had to mount a defence, in the first place, and thus was not liable for the expenses incurred. This offended Doyle's code of honour. 'You seem to have taken leave of your senses,' he wrote to Slater. 'If you are indeed responsible for your actions, then you are the most ungrateful as well as the most foolish person whom I have ever known.'

The Doyle–Slater relationship went steadily downhill from there. By 1929, it had achieved total dysfunctionality. 'These bills have to be met now … I beg you will send me a cheque by return for £300,' Doyle wrote in one letter; and in another he spoke to their mutual friend William Park of this 'tiresome man'. There is relatively little in the later correspondence about the fate of Marion Gilchrist. Slater clearly saw himself as the principal victim of the whole affair, and Doyle was increasingly forced to act more as an accountant than an avenging detective. His files on the case document his out-of-pocket disbursements, his travel expenses and the sales figures for Park's book, but the actual crime is elided. Doyle carefully preserved a letter written to him by a P.E. Baker on 13 September 1929. In it, Baker refers to a clipping from a local newspaper, and says:

> … that in using the term 'ungrateful dog', you really flatter Slater. As the owner of a well-bred dog, I cannot conceive how even a mongrel would be as undeserving as this. As I believe the common rat has yet to be proven of any real value to humanity, whereas dogs have, it might be more appropriate to use the term, 'Dirty Rat'.

In time, Slater himself wrote direct to the Scottish Office to express his opinion that 'the [authorities], in common fairness, ought not to expect me to bear the costs of this case'. Though most of his letter was low-key, he ended sharply, invoking the principles of humanity, justice, freedom and 'British fair play' cruelly denied him over the past twenty years. He got a 'Dear Slater' letter back from a civil servant indicating that the £6,000 was the full and final settlement, though in theory it could be reduced on review, and that the appellant's further comments on the matter were not actively encouraged. That concluded the government's direct interest in the case.

Slater continued to trade epistolary barbs with one of the world's most accomplished and personally tenacious authors, however, and eventually he and Doyle took their dispute to court. This was perhaps the least edifying part of the whole saga that followed in the wake of Marion Gilchrist's death. Doyle's friend Anthony Clyne, a religious sceptic, wrote to him on 14 September 1929 with the hope that his squabbles with Slater would not be allowed to blunt his enthusiasm for truth and justice. 'That I disagree so flatly with your views on various subjects should make my assurance more convincing,' he added.

Two days later, Leopold Greenberg, editor of the *Jewish Chronicle*, wrote to tell Doyle that he was 'very perturbed' to hear he was taking action against Slater, which he considered a 'sorry ending to what [had been] something of a noble and successful endeavour'. The following week, Doyle's lawyers wrote to Slater's regarding the date of a possible civil hearing in Edinburgh. The respondent's ill health delayed this, however, leaving Doyle to make more unappreciative comments about his adversary in the press. In one of several vitriolic notes with which he bombarded the author in 1929 on the 'vile stuff and abuse pouring from your pen', his erstwhile comrade, now thorn in his flesh, Slater, complained of 'unbelievable lyes [*sic*] in the newspapers'.

On 11 October, Slater's agent wrote to Doyle to say that his client was now prepared to pay £250 towards his costs, but that Doyle's published comments about Slater being 'an ungrateful dog and a liar' raised the prospect of a countersuit for libel. An apology was in order, the agent believed. By then Doyle was on a tour of Scandinavia as part of his mission to bring the psychic gospel to the world, but he wrote to a mutual colleague:

Dear Mr Reade
    It would be as well that Slater should be warned … [to] be careful what he says or writes. If he repeats the string of lies which he has told, such as that I received

£400 for articles from Scotch papers, that I made as much as he did, that I took up his case to gain personal credit … I shall have to declare him once more to be what I consider him to be.

There was more wrangling between the opposing sets of lawyers throughout October, leading Doyle to write to an intermediary from Copenhagen:

Do what you can to prevent this perverse and misguided man from plunging into litigation, [for] it will most surely end in his losing that competence which I have gained for him.

This final estrangement was all the more tragic given the fact that Doyle's own health was now failing so badly. He broke down several times during his speaking tour, privately complaining of acute breathing difficulties, but refused all offers to curtail his schedule. He had to be carried off when his ship returned to Dover on 7 November.

Four days later, Doyle gave back-to-back Armistice Day speeches to packed houses, telling his audiences of a recent séance with Einer Nielsen, a Danish medium, and assuring them there was 'no final death'. As a result, he insisted he felt 'happier and clearer' than he had for years. Although Doyle had to postpone a subsequent talk after collapsing in a London taxi, he was able to contribute a long, valedictory piece to the *Sunday Graphic*. He wrote:

I have been pronounced to be suffering from a complaint – angina – which is certainly painful and hardly at my age curable, and yet, owing to my psychic knowledge, I am conscious of a profound inward serenity and a deep peace of mind … God does not throw us upon the scrap-heap.

Something about Doyle's published remarks – if not the threat of further legal action – apparently stirred even Slater, because later in November he swore out a statement:

I hereby undertake not to raise any suit against you for damages on account of alleged slander prior to this date.

Signed
OSCAR LESCHZINER (Slater)

※ ※ ※

Although the Slater case ultimately descended into a morass of public recriminations about legal fees and expenses, the search for Marion Gilchrist's killer, or killers, wasn't entirely abandoned. Conan Doyle came to believe that the prospect of bringing the guilty parties to justice was 'well-nigh hopeless', but felt duty-bound to continue to press the police to reopen the case even though 'this could not be more than a gesture'.

Doyle's own conclusions about the affair followed on those of William Park, who died not long after Slater won his appeal. Park had come to believe that the key to the case lay somewhere among the three Charteris brothers, Archibald, Francis and John, and Marion Gilchrist's three nephews, James, George and Wingate Birrell. One or more of these individuals had been in league with Helen Lambie, the theory went, and Lambie herself had later disappeared to America so as not to be available to Slater's defence. Park told Doyle in a letter of 2 November 1927 that Lambie had let the killer into Miss Gilchrist's flat before going out 'for the pretended paper' on the night of the murder, and had entered into this fatal arrangement for 'romantic or financial reasons, and possibly both'.

As Doyle later privately remarked, it was a cast worthy of a Sherlock Holmes tale: a superficially respectable extended family of soldiers and lawyers that was inwardly teeming with mutual jealousies and resentments. Helen Lambie had evidently believed that her mistress would be relieved of her jewels but not physically harmed, Park told Doyle. But something had gone wrong in the execution of the robbery. Perhaps the old woman had struggled with the intruder, fallen, and hit her head. If her visitor was indeed Francis Charteris, a doctor, he would have been quickly able to assess the extent of her injury. At the very least, presuming Miss Gilchrist revived and identified him as her attacker, he would be ruined for life. If she then subsequently died, he would be charged with her murder. In William Park's view, one he shared with Doyle, Charteris, having swiftly reviewed his options, had plucked up the nerve to finish the old lady off where she lay and then to walk brazenly past Arthur Adams and Helen Lambie before disappearing into the street. Lambie's eventual departure for America was 'the most complete sign that Charteris is the man,' Park wrote.

※ ※ ※

Wealthy, elderly spinsters who are attacked in their homes by complete strangers are far rarer than those assaulted by their own family members or acquaintances. Why should that be so? The obvious answer is that the insider has the all-important knowledge about the victim's circumstances denied the casual intruder, and, as often as not, the access required to successfully carry off the crime in the first place. It's difficult, if not impossible, to read the transcript of Oscar Slater's trial today and not conclude that it was a travesty of justice that sent Slater to prison for nearly twenty years. The whole case against him really began with the misapprehension that the brooch he had been trying to sell on spec at various intervals during 1908 was in fact the same one that was removed from Marion Gilchrist's flat on the night of her murder. As Allan McLean, the young cycle dealer and habitué of Glasgow's faintly sinister Sloper Club later testified:

> I remember a man visited the club whom I only knew as Oscar ... I heard, in the month of December, that he was offering a pawn ticket for a brooch to a friend of mine named Anderson. I heard of the death of Miss Gilchrist on the 21st. I noticed that [Slater] did not return to the club after that, [and] on Friday, 25th instant, went to the Detective Department, Central Police Office, and reported the matter.

This was commendably civic-minded on McLean's part, but the case against Slater suffered a serious blow − or at least it should have done − when the police subsequently discovered the pawn ticket still in the suspect's possession, recovered the brooch, and conclusively determined that it was not the one missing from the room of the murdered woman. As Conan Doyle wrote, 'The case of the police might well seem desperate after this, since if Slater were indeed guilty, it would mean that by pure chance they had pursued the right man.' To Doyle, the only remaining question was whether the 'Establishment', in the form of the senior ranks of the Glasgow detective bureau, the Lord Advocate, the procurator fiscal's office and others at different levels of the judicial branch and local government had then swiftly come together in a like-minded alliance to protect the real killer, or if the official investigation was distinguished more by sheer lethargy and ineptitude on the police's part.

Inheritance being one of the most obvious motives for a family crime, it's perhaps worth noting Marion Gilchrist's circumstances on the day she met her death. Miss Gilchrist had signed her will on 28 May 1908, and added a codicil to it the following November, just a month before her murder. The police examined this document, and thus would have known that the deceased left provision for her sister Jane Birrell, for her putative daughter Margaret Galbraith Ferguson, and other members of the Ferguson family, as well as a lump sum of £5,000 (some £360,000 today) for an individual listed only as 'James Johnston, residing at Shanghai, China'. It's been speculated that Johnston was the father of Marion Gilchrist's illegitimate child.

There was a married Glaswegian vicar of that name who officiated at the city's Free Church of Scotland until 1877, when Margaret Ferguson was a girl of about 13, after which he moved to London before serving as a missionary. The will made no reference either to the three Charteris brothers or to Miss Gilchrist's three Birrell nephews. There was, however, some talk about the family unit in general, and the deceased's apparent belief that the state would ultimately become the benevolent 'parent' for all people, regardless of their individual background or circumstances – further evidence that the 82-year-old lady at the heart of the tragedy was not always the quiet, conventional figure sometimes supposed.

As we've seen, Helen Lambie later reportedly disclosed the name of the man she saw leaving Marion Gilchrist's flat on the night of the murder, and that individual was Dr Francis Charteris. Charteris was then 33, and steadily building up a private medical practice which he combined with lecturing duties at Glasgow University. In April 1907, he had married a wealthy young local woman named Annie Kedie, and Marion Gilchrist and Helen Lambie had both attended the wedding. Charteris was three years younger than Oscar Slater, of the same general build and, like him, had a somewhat prominent nose. It's not beyond the realm of belief that a spectator could have mistaken one man for the other if glimpsed on a wet midwinter's night.

Charteris then lived at 400 Great Western Road, less than half a mile from the scene of the murder, and by his own admission he had no compelling alibi for the night in question. Speaking more than fifty years later, he told the *Scottish Daily Mail*:

> I was working alone all afternoon in my laboratory. I had seen no one before the [police] called me, and my surgery was just beside the subway station – the next one to that for West Princes Street. For all that I could prove to the contrary, I

might have gone to Miss Gilchrist's flat, done the deed and returned without being seen.

To establish a motive, or indeed any real connecting link between Dr Charteris and Marion Gilchrist is another matter, however. It's true that Helen Lambie said in her disputed October 1927 interview with the *Empire News*, 'I knew [Miss Gilchrist] had papers to which she attached far more importance than to anything else in the house'. Commenting a month later in the same paper, Conan Doyle wrote of his belief that 'there was some romance, some tragedy in [Marion Gilchrist's] life, dating perhaps far back, but having consequences now which were becoming manifest in her old age,' another plot twist readily familiar from the Sherlock Holmes stories. Although Doyle failed to develop his point, he seems to have imagined that Dr Charteris, perhaps with Helen Lambie's collusion, had gone to the victim's flat on the night of 21 December to purloin these 'papers' – presumably containing details of Miss Gilchrist's illegitimate heir – with a view to subsequently challenging her will. The crime thus had nothing to do with money and valuables per se, and Doyle assumed that the single brooch had been removed as a blind to throw the police off the trail.

To accept this theory, however, is to believe that a particularly concerted and unusually durable conspiracy had then sprung up virtually overnight to protect the reputation of a largely unremarkable family doctor, and that it continued in effect for the remaining fifty-six years of Charteris' life, and indeed thereafter. At the very least, the man who assaulted Marion Gilchrist was a reasonably proficient house-breaker, if not a cold-blooded murderer. No evidence of such a spirit was ever shown in the life of this rather shy, retiring doctor, who, full of honours, spent his declining years largely haunting the bar of the Royal and Ancient Golf Club.

In later life, both Helen Lambie and Arthur Adams flatly denied that Charteris was the man they had seen leave Marion Gilchrist's flat on the night of her death. An eminently reliable and well-placed witness, if one who prefers anonymity, adds, 'The doctor always believed that Slater was innocent, and that members of the household were involved. If he knew anything more about it than that, he took it with him to his grave.'

Although some sort of family involvement seems the most likely explanation, there's also a second possibility: that Marion Gilchrist's death was the tragic result of a common burglary by a gang of thieves, none of whom was the least interested in the contents of her will or private papers. The author Richard Whittington-Egan later gave some credence to this theory in his book *The Oscar Slater Murder Story*. According to this version of events, a Glasgow hoodlum named James Inglis later confessed that he and three accomplices, Craig, Wilson and Jamieson, had heard about Miss Gilchrist's jewel collection from a woman who worked as her cleaner, cased the premises, and subsequently took advantage of Helen Lambie's brief absence on the night of 21 December to let themselves in with a skeleton key and go about their business.

Jamieson, described as a 'moral degenerate' who sometimes worked as a chemist's assistant, was the one who had committed the actual murder. He had probably been drinking before Miss Gilchrist had stood up to confront him; some deep frustration suddenly exploded into psychopathic violence, the theory goes, after which he had swiftly left through the front door while his associates, forced to abandon their plan by Helen Lambie's return, made their own escape by climbing out the kitchen window and dropping the 10ft onto the grass at the rear of the flat. They were never seen again.

A close variant of this story also followed Oscar Slater's death in 1948, when the *Sunday Express* published an interview with an anonymous 58-year-old man who said, 'I know who committed the murder. I wish now to tell the tale that would have saved Slater and sent two men to the gallows.' Essentially, this was the same burglary-gone-wrong scenario as later emerged in Whittington-Egan's book. While a man named 'W' had kept watch, another man named 'J' had rung Marion Gilchrist's bell. Apparently thinking it was Helen Lambie returning with her evening paper, the old lady had pulled the lever to open the front door, before again settling in her chair by the dining room fire. According to the paper's informant, 'J' had then quickly walked upstairs, where 'he struck at Miss Gilchrist, but did not knock her out as he expected. So he followed her, striking again and again with his jemmy, until she collapsed.'

'By this time,' the story continued:

… the people underneath had become alarmed, and were making for Miss Gilchrist's. 'J' had no time to hunt for money or jewellery. He may have snatched a piece or two hurriedly before he was disturbed, but to the best of my knowledge the two men gained nothing by the murder.

At the time of the trial, a Miss Agnes Brown, a schoolteacher, told the police that two men rushed past her in West Princes Street. One, she said, had his arm pressed close to his side.

That was 'J', supporting the jemmy under his jacket.

Over the years, there would be no shortage of other suspects proposed as Miss Gilchrist's killer. A recurring figure near the top of this list of possible assassins was the dead woman's maid, Helen Lambie. Lambie, it was known, had stepped out for the paper on the evening of 21 December taking the only set of keys to the Gilchrist flat with her. Could she then have passed these to one Paddy Nugent, her married lover, who had come upstairs from the street and committed the crime while Lambie established her alibi by ostentatiously going off on her errand?

Little is known of Nugent except that he operated as an unlicensed bookie in Motherwell, and that he broadly matched the description given by Rowena Adams, the victim's downstairs neighbour, of the man she had seen lingering at the door of the Gilchrist close minutes before the murder. This individual 'had a long nose, with a most peculiar dip,' she testified. 'He had a very clear complexion, not sallow nor a white pallor but something of an ivory colour … He was clean shaven, and very broad in [the] head' – just one of many eyewitness statements that could be said to have eliminated Oscar Slater as much as incriminated him. (Some Slater scholars have speculated that 'Nugent' was one and the same as Hugh Cameron, or 'Moudie', the Glasgow bookie's clerk who befriended Slater, and that the two men had run a small but locally popular Cambridge Street brothel catering to a clientele that included several judges, and whose staff were known to impersonate historical figures such as the late Queen Victoria in 'highly unorthodox costume', but this last detail has proved impossible to corroborate.)

Lambie, in one published account:

… got away with it simply because, being a maid, she was generally accepted to be stupid. After hours of the most detailed examination in the witness-box in New York, she still had her wits about her sufficiently to stop [Slater's agent] Gordon Miller dead in his tracks. Miller never had any doubt about the fact that the girl was guilty, nor that she was very clever.

Even if you accept that, however, it's still hard to see how Lambie can be said to have personally gained from her employer's murder. After returning from her long, impoverished exile in America, she lived in equally straitened (and mostly solitary) circumstances in the north of England, and died there in 1960, aged 72.

✳ ✳ ✳

When introducing Sherlock Holmes to the public in *A Study in Scarlet*, Conan Doyle wrote of his detective's investigation of a crime scene:

> He whipped a tape measure and a large round magnifying glass from his pocket. With these two implements he trotted noiselessly about the room, sometimes stopping, occasionally kneeling, and once lying flat upon his face. So engrossed was he with his occupation that he appeared to have forgotten our presence, for he chatted away to himself under his breath the whole time, keeping up a running fire of exclamations, groans, whistles, and little cries suggestive of encouragement and of hope. As I watched him I was irresistibly reminded of a pure-blooded, well-trained foxhound, as it dashes backward and forward through the covert, whining in its eagerness, until it comes across the lost scent.

It has to be said that Doyle himself fell short of this model of forensic precision and acuity in his own investigation of the Oscar Slater affair. He neither visited the scene of the crime nor personally interviewed any of the principals. He took an instant dislike to Slater himself. Later, Doyle told a spiritualist meeting, 'Instead of thanking me for my efforts … he recited to me his material grievances, a list that was as varied as it was long.' As we've seen, the two men continued to argue about financial matters right up to the time of Doyle's death.

Set against this, however, was the author's sheer tenacity in pressing Slater's case in the pages of books and newspapers, and his numerous direct appeals to members of successive British governments. Over the years, even the most senior ministers would prove less fastidious about meeting him than might have been the case for a purely anonymous petitioner seeking redress on behalf of a convicted murderer. A working relationship with Doyle often brought with it a social component. At the time Ramsay MacDonald wrote to the Scottish Secretary in October 1927 to demand Slater's release, for example, he sent a second, more personal note, thanking Doyle for the recent gift of several signed first editions of his books. This was the sort of connection that few other campaigners could ever hope to enjoy with the ranks of the political or judicial Establishment.

Doyle's name lent instant credibility to a cause such as Slater's, which otherwise might never have come to the point of an inquiry, let alone a full appeal. It should also be remembered that he published William Park's book on the case, often considered to have been the turning point in Slater's fortunes, and that he did so contrary to the advice of his wife and many others who believed he was risking his own reputation as a result. Doyle later described Park as 'hav[ing] within him that slow-burning, but quenchless, fire of determination which marks the best type of Scotsman'. This was equally true of Doyle himself. He may not have been the world's greatest forensic detective, but no one was better at stubbornly pursuing the facts of a case and exposing them to the proper audience – which is what good investigative journalism, like good police work, is based upon.

✳ ✳ ✳

There is another compelling theory of what happened to Marion Gilchrist on the evening of 21 December 1908. This version of events also turns on the contents of the victim's will, but it involves the Birrell as much as the Charteris family. The reputation of Wingate Birrell, in particular, stood low in the Glasgow of this period. Aged 40 at the time of Miss Gilchrist's death, stocky and dark complexioned, he was a British Army veteran who had since been reduced to earning a precarious living by hawking pin cushions, a role he allegedly combined with shop-breaking and other petty crime.

Birrell had apparently spent some time in Australia, but by 1908 was living in digs at Woolwich, south-east London, from where he's known to have regularly travelled home to Scotland. A January 1909 Glasgow Police file on the Gilchrist murder refers to Birrell as being 'of bad character', which suggests he had come to their attention before the murder. A second official report quotes a relative describing him as 'a wild young man [who] has been on more than one occasion sent abroad by his family but always turned up again'. This would seem to echo the contents of the anonymous but impressively detailed letter someone sent to the Scottish Secretary on 20 May 1909, at which point Oscar Slater was scheduled to die just seven days later.

'My Noble Lord,' it began:

I am so frightened you are going to hang Slater – *He never committed the murder* – Nelly Lambie was engaged to Birrell, Miss Gilchrist's nephew. He was a very wild chap – and none of his family would have anything to do with him as he was always borrowing money from them & kicking up rows. But Nelly said she did not care as she would be far grander than anybody in the street someday … On the night of the murder she had a man in the kitchen – at 6.30. When she went out or was expecting anyone she put a piece of coal between the doorstep and the door, *then a slight push opened it* … Well, after the murder the man went over the kitchen window, crossed the street into the Crescent, saw the crowd around the close and walked away – he left that night for London, *sold the brooch to a dealer in Little College St and left for New Zealand* before anyone knew.

✳ ✳ ✳

Did Wingate Birrell kill his aunt? The author Thomas Toughill, a highly respected researcher into the Slater case, is one of those who believes Miss Gilchrist's death was the result of a simmering family feud about the old lady's will that finally boiled over into homicidal violence on the night of 21 December. Birrell may conceivably have been in league with Helen Lambie, and very possibly have recruited Francis and Archibald Charteris, or been recruited by them, in the commission of the crime. (The third Charteris brother, John, was serving with the army in India at the time of the murder.)

Strange things had begun happening in West Princes Street during December 1908. Several local residents believed that someone was keeping watch outside the Gilchrist flat, and Rowena Adams's testimony about the man she saw loitering there shortly before 7 on the night of the 21st could have fit Francis Charteris just as easily as it did the mysterious Paddy Nugent. At that point, it's said, Archibald Charteris and Wingate Birrell had slipped into the flat while Helen Lambie went out to buy the newspaper and establish her alibi.

'Whatever the plan was,' Thomas Toughill writes:

… it did not take into consideration Wingate's temper … When Miss Gilchrist started to harangue and insult him, he saw red and beat her to death. He then left the house by climbing over the kitchen window. Archibald, who was still in the bedroom looking through his aunt's private papers when Lambie and Adams entered the flat, summoned up the necessary composure and calmly walked past them in the hallway. In the street, he met up with his brother and the two rushed off down West Princes Street, almost colliding with Agnes Brown in the process … Birrell was told he had to flee the country, which he did via Kelvinbridge underground station, just across the road. He was in such a state when he reached the station that he attracted the attention of the booking clerk, Annie Armour, who testified at trial that she believed the man she saw was Slater.

We've seen that Francis Charteris went on to a distinguished medical career, and his brother Archibald eventually rose to the heights of the Glasgow legal profession as a solicitor, author and lecturer. Before emigrating to Australia, he had frequent dealings with James Neil Hart, the chief law officer who prosecuted Oscar Slater. Wingate Birrell, who sometimes called himself William Gilchrist, and claimed to be the murder victim's illegitimate son, died on 4 March 1909, of tuberculosis, at a charity hospital in London.

At the end of the day, there are two possible variants of what really happened, and why Marion Gilchrist's murder should have assumed so much importance both to Conan Doyle and others. The first and now most popular explanation is that members of the Charteris and Birrell families were engaged in an internecine feud of almost Shakespearean dimensions, had wished to read or extract certain of the old lady's papers and entered her flat to do so, and that the actual murder was a ghastly but unintended consequence of this intrusion. This theory seems to broadly fit the contours of a classic inheritance crime, of the sort quite often seen in the Holmes stories and elsewhere, and it in fact occurred to several people even before Oscar Slater went on trial in May 1909. The suggestion that one of Miss Gilchrist's relatives had wielded the bludgeon that killed her and had then stood by while another man was convicted in his place was not new. Something of the sort had been rumoured ever since it emerged that Helen Lambie had supposedly run straight from discovering her employer's lifeless body to the nearby home of Margaret Birrell and told her, 'Oh, Miss Birrell, Miss Birrell, Miss Gilchrist has been murdered, she is lying dead in the dining-room, and oh, Miss Birrell, I saw the man who did it', and gone on to name the guilty party as Francis Charteris.

Set against this plot line is the fact that Lambie appears to have been either a congenital liar, or, as Conan Doyle preferred to put it, 'incorrigibly dim', and thus makes an unappealing witness as to whether she in fact said these words. The counter-theory is that the maid had blurted out the names of

Archibald Charteris or Wingate Birrell – Margaret Birrell's brother – as the supposed killer. Lambie would have easily recognised both men, and there's some circumstantial evidence that she was on terms of intimacy with the latter. Wanting to protect her brother, the theory goes, Margaret Birrell had simply substituted 'Francis' for 'Archibald', omitting the name of Wingate altogether, when Lieutenant Trench had come to interview her two days later. Many students of the Slater affair, Conan Doyle among them, would champion this view about one or more of the Charteris brothers being involved, and Francis Charteris himself ruefully acknowledged it when, as an old man, he spoke to the press about the case in 1961.

The problem with this theory is that no one has ever conclusively shown any physical evidence directly linking members of the Charteris or Birrell families to Marion Gilchrist's murder, and none of the alleged conspirators ever admitted to their role in it. In order to accept the 'insider' version of events, it's also necessary to believe that there was a long-running and far-reaching Establishment plot to protect the reputations of a then only modestly prominent group of local doctors and lawyers, and that, Scottish law prescribing the death penalty for anyone found guilty of fabricating evidence in a capital case, those engaged in the cover-up would have been risking their own lives as a result.

A close examination of the purported conspirators' actions on the night of 21 December would also seem to raise questions about their involvement. Could, for example, Francis Charteris have left the scene of the crime at around 7.10 p.m., as has been claimed, then have made his way back to his own home, or at least to a conveniently quiet street corner, conferred there with his brother Archibald and a blood-soaked Wingate Birrell, agreed on a story that would bind all three of them in an intrigue that would last the rest of their lives, taken leave of his confederates, and composed himself sufficiently to then walk back to the murder scene from which he had fled in panic only a few minutes earlier, and present himself as a disinterested doctor and acquaintance of the deceased who was there to help if required? This may or may not be exactly what happened; it is a conceivable, even if it's an implausible, scenario. No one ever proved that Francis Charteris did all this, however, and at the very end of his life he told a reporter, 'I am no more a murderer than you are'.

The other explanation, which still refutes much of the case presented by the Crown in 1909, is that someone curious about the contents of Marion

Gilchrist's will, presumably but not necessarily a family member, had entered her flat on the night in question, and that this individual had previously enlisted Oscar Slater as an accomplice. Once again, it has to be said the supporting evidence is purely circumstantial. Slater lived in the general vicinity. His drinking haunts lay close by Wingate Birrell's. He was known to deal in stolen goods. He had an alibi, but not exactly an airtight one, for the time in which the murder was committed.

Had he acted as a lookout, or as a straightforward burglar on the night, perhaps as a blind while others ransacked the old lady's papers? What still strikes anyone reading the full transcript of the trial is the sheer number and variety of witnesses prepared to identify Slater, whatever the individual discrepancies in their accounts. Marion Gilchrist's neighbour Margaret McHaffie, for example, told the court that she had seen someone 'loitering about' for several weeks before the murder, and subsequently 'had no difficulty' in recognising the man as Slater. Annie Armour, the local station booking clerk, similarly testified that she had 'no trouble in picking the prisoner out' from among the dozen or so men shown to her at a police line-up. A Glasgow tram conductor named William Sancroft remembered that he had been discussing the murder with some of his passengers on the evening of 23 December, that 'all of a sudden a man who was sitting on [a] seat got up in a hurry and passed by, pushing me to the side', and that this, too, he later recognised as being Slater.

What emerged in the statements of various neighbours and transport workers ensued also in those of local businessmen, schoolteachers and beat policemen. In addition to these, there were several other witnesses to Slater's presence on the scene, quite apart from the disputed but insistent accounts of Helen Lambie and Mary Barrowman. It's true that the unimpeachable Arthur Adams, Miss Gilchrist's downstairs neighbour, swore only that Slater 'closely resembled the man' he had seen leaving the victim's flat, but it's possible that Adams acted more from an abundance of caution, and his stated opposition to the death penalty, than any real doubts about the killer's identity. A correspondent named G.M.A. McChlery wrote to the *Scotland Herald* in December 1993, 'My father told us on many occasions that Arthur Adams had told him that he was sure Slater was the man, but he would not swear to it in court as that would have meant the rope.'

The full truth about Marion Gilchrist's brutal murder may never be known. But there must remain a suspicion that the police stumbled on to at least part of the story, that having got their man to their own satisfaction they simply ignored any additional or contrary evidence, and that they did so more as a result of institutional sloth and incompetence than in support of any well-oiled municipal conspiracy. We can say with some conviction that Oscar Slater wasn't the lone assassin in this case, and thus not guilty of the crime as it was presented to the jury in May 1909. Whether he was completely innocent of any involvement in Marion Gilchrist's death is another matter.

※　※　※

Instead of doggedly following the trail of evidence in the Slater case, Conan Doyle took the polemic approach with a series of indignant pamphlets and articles. As a result, his role was closer to that of Dr Watson than Sherlock Holmes. Even if falling short as a forensic detective, however, Doyle was incapable of supporting a cause half-heartedly, and over the course of eighteen years he contributed hundreds of pages of editorials and reports, petitions to officials and legislators, and legal notes and letters to fellow sympathisers in Britain and overseas. Slater owed him a significant debt of gratitude for his eventual release.

We've seen how their relationship still cooled. In later years, Slater came to discount or ignore Doyle's part in securing his freedom, and answered occasional interview requests on the subject with a brief, pre-printed card which read, 'Publicity not desired'. With his compensation from the Crown, Slater maintained a small flat in Glasgow as well as his seaside bungalow in Ayr, where he eventually came to retire with his second wife. His funds exhausted, he was destined to end his days on parish relief.

In 1946 Slater applied for naturalisation as a Scottish citizen, but a final decision on the matter was still pending when he succumbed to an apparent stroke two years later. He was aged 76 at the time of his death, and it was just over twenty years since he had walked through the gates of Peterhead Prison into freedom. Among the many obituary notices published around the world was one in a Glasgow newspaper which read, 'Oscar Slater Dead at 78, Reprieved Murderer, Friend of A. Conan Doyle' – a statement that contained both an error of fact and a highly debatable matter of opinion.

9

IS CONAN DOYLE MAD?

Like many late nineteenth-century rationalists inspired by scientific discoveries, the young Conan Doyle always seemed to be searching for an earthly detachment. He wished, in other words, to be engaged as a scientist with the physical world, and yet apart from it. He knew that he wasn't alone in this. When, in 1893, the 34-year-old Doyle applied to join the Society for Psychical Research (SPR), he'd already attended dozens of séances, toured haunted houses, and conducted experiments in mesmerism and mind control with eminently solid citizens like his friend Henry Ball, a society architect, and Alfred Drayson, the retired major general who believed in spirits.

The president of the SPR who approved Doyle's application was no less established a figure than Arthur Balfour, a former Conservative Leader of the House of Commons and future prime minister, whose friend Annie Marshall had at one time regularly brought him letters written to her from the Other Side. Marshall had once predicted her own death in 'Neptunian – that is enigmatic – circumstances, in which water will play a part' (she drowned herself at the age of 31), and added, 'Our great spiritual thinkers will always face a dubious public reception'.

Among the SPR's other prominent members at around the time Doyle joined it were the naturalist Alfred Russel Wallace, Darwin's peer in the theory of natural selection; the physicist and radio pioneer Oliver Lodge; Lodge's fellow scientist William Crookes, a commercially successful inventor and founding editor of *Chemical News*; and the crusading Fabian author, Frank Podmore. The list isn't exhaustive.

In its prospectus, the SPR made it clear that it sought to bring what it called 'pure scientific logic' to its activities, which then ranged from its meticulous census work enquiring into the prevalence of 'spiritual hallucinations' (of the 17,000 British adults canvassed in one survey, 1,684 said that at some time they had been physically 'embraced' or 'kissed' by an unseen force, among several other less conventional liaisons), to a perhaps more engrossing paper on a Holmes-like case given the name 'The Spectre Dog of Peel Castle'. It was an approach that seemed to combine coldly Holmesian observation and analysis with an underlying belief in the reality of paranormal communication, and thus one that would have appealed to a young medical man with an open mind on basic theological issues.

In other words, Conan Doyle united the qualities of a rational thinker with a lifelong and deepening interest in the intangibles of human existence. He himself saw no contradiction between the popular author of neatly constructed detective stories and the occultist who sat down around the baize table to summon the spirits. Rather, the one was the logical evolution of the other. Speaking of the 'psychic question' in his 1924 memoirs, Doyle wrote:

> It is the thing for which every preceding phase – my gradual religious development, my books, which gave me an introduction to the public, my modest fortune, which enables me to devote myself to unlucrative work, my platform work, which helps me to convey the message, and my physical strength, which is still sufficient to stand arduous tours and to fill the largest halls for an hour and a half with my voice – have each been an unconscious preparation. For thirty years I have trained myself exactly for the role without the least inward suspicion of whither I was tending.

Even so, Conan Doyle's full-scale conversion to spiritualism was an unusually protracted one. In January 1880, when he was 20 and struggling as a medical assistant in Birmingham, he attended a public lecture with the title 'Does Death End All?', writing afterward that it was 'a very clever thing ... though not convincing to me'. Doyle later reported that he had 'had the usual contempt which the young educated man feels towards the whole subject which has been covered by the clumsy name of Spiritualism', a subject he then saw as a litany of fraudulent mediums, spurious phenomena, and other 'bogus happenings' that had duped the public.

During the 1880s, Doyle published a number of stories that took a light-hearted, if not openly sceptical view of the supernatural. In his 1883 'Captain of the Pole-Star', he allows his fictional hero, like him a young doctor, to refer mockingly to 'the impostures of Slade', a popular American medium who claimed to receive paranormal messages on a small slate blackboard he held in his hands. Later that year came Doyle's story 'Selecting a Ghost', in which a wealthy shopkeeper seeks to audition prospective spooks to haunt his mansion. This was 'rank comedy', he perhaps unnecessarily informed his editor.

When Doyle started his first Holmes story, *A Study in Scarlet*, in March 1886, he had several goals, both artistic and material, but psychic instruction wasn't among them. Some thirty-five years later, Doyle was still at pains to keep his personal beliefs separate from those of his fictional detective. 'This agency stands flat-footed upon the ground, and there it must remain,' Holmes remarks in the somewhat macabre tale of 'The Sussex Vampire'. 'The world is big enough for us. No ghosts need apply.'

Gradually, however, Doyle was moving towards a new and unorthodox belief in the powers of mind over matter. We've seen that he engaged in apparent displays of table-tapping, clairvoyance and telepathy while still a young doctor in Southsea. In 1887 Doyle underwent an early spiritualist epiphany when a medium advised him not to buy a particular book, as he was then privately thinking of doing, which he took as proof of some 'profound power' at work. Less than a month later, Doyle published a letter in *Light*, one of the then half-dozen popular British psychic magazines. Acknowledging that he was a 'novice and inquirer' in the field, he noted, however, it was 'absolutely certain that intelligence [can] exist apart from the body'. The message from the local medium had apparently convinced him of life's ultimate meaning. With his characteristic gift for the lucid phrase, and his boundless self-confidence, Doyle assured the readers of *Light* of the 'unimpeachable logic' of his position. 'After weighing the evidence,' he wrote, 'I could no more doubt the existence of the phenomena than I could doubt the existence of lions in Africa, though I have been to that continent and have never chanced to see one.'

This was also the period in which the seemingly conventional author, with his superbly cognitive fictional hero, was exploring the laws of karma and reincarnation, among other aspects of Eastern philosophy, and closely following the time travel theories of Madame Blavatsky and her fellow Theosophists. As a doctor, Conan Doyle made no secret of his interest in the uncharted potential of the human mind. In fact, as we've seen, a degree of spiritualistic belief was de rigueur for many late Victorian scientists, including another of the leading lights of natural selection, Professor Thomas Huxley.

Huxley may have been the man to coin the term 'agnostic'. Although believing in the Bible's 'core moral teachings [and] uplifting use of language' – and the possibility that 'Christ's etheric body' had become visible to the disciples after his crucifixion – Huxley 'unequivocally endorsed' several mediums. The idea that such men somehow actively threatened the established Christian Church, which promptly saw its theological authority replaced by a blancmange of pantheism, mysticism, and greeting-card sentimentality has not stood the test of historical inquiry. Even the writings of a self-confessed 'spookist' like Huxley contain affirmations of the 'palliative' and 'universal' aspects of organised religion, such as divine protection, infallible justice, and, of course, life after death. The later nineteenth-century obsession with angels, which influences Christmas cards to this day, seems to have broadly satisfied both religious traditionalists and those seeking a more occult meaning of life.

Conan Doyle's early researches into the paranormal weren't, therefore, an unheard of or illogical activity for a young doctor whose recent family history seemed to imply a distressing connection between religious fervour and insanity. Nor had Doyle yet abandoned – if he ever did so – his more rational and conventionally reasoned approach to life. An 1883 exchange of letters in the *British Journal of Photography* suggests that he was still fully alive to the possibility of mediumistic fraud. In reply to a W. Harding Warner, who wrote to advance his claim that certain men have 'radiating from them a light [that] can be photographed', Doyle replied:

Will Mr Warner consent to throw a 'photosphere or luminous halo' round this Delphic utterance of his? From so-called facts he draws inference which, even if they were facts indeed, would be illogical, and upon these illogical inferences draws deductions which, once more, no amount of concession would render tenable.

Ten years later, Doyle began work on a novella he called *The Parasite*, which featured several passages juxtaposing reason and the occult. That he still reserved judgement on the supernatural as a whole can be seen when a character in the book attends an obviously rigged séance. 'I like none of these mystery-mongers,' he remarks, before going on to denounce the sort of medium who gulls her customers by 'slapping a surreptitious banjo'.

Well before the First World War saw Doyle's final leap of faith, therefore, he had already critically explored many of the boundaries of human perception. Though not yet ready to embark on the last and most controversial of his public crusades, nor was he a man to ignore new theories or beliefs about God's purpose, any more than he was an author content to stick with a winning formula to the end of his career. Writer, physician, ferocious moralist, provocateur, an associate of both royalty and underworld lowlifes, the animating force behind major changes to the judicial system in England and Scotland, Doyle was one of the great progressive minds of the late nineteenth and early twentieth centuries, a dynamic figure linking the disparate worlds of crime, the arts, social reform, British nationalism and, increasingly, the enigmatic practices of the séance room.

Doyle's metaphysical researches took different forms over the years. In January 1887, even before *A Study in Scarlet* appeared in print, he'd enrolled as a Freemason and been inducted into the Phoenix Lodge No. 257 in Southsea. Since Doyle's application for membership came just two days after he sat down with some friends in the darkened dining room of a nearby house, where after half an hour of silence the table had suddenly begun to rap up and down in a code they interpreted as a message from the beyond, it's possible he thought his initiation as a Freemason might in some way contribute to his burgeoning knowledge of the occult. In his first appearance in a short story, 'A Scandal in Bohemia', Sherlock Holmes remarks, 'There is a wonderful sympathy and Freemasonry among horsy men'. In 'The Red-Headed League', published in the same year, Holmes immediately identifies a client as a Mason based on the small pin he wears in his lapel.

There's a more extensive example in 1893's 'The Musgrave Ritual', in which the Musgrave family's eldest son successively undergoes initiation into a cryptic call-and-response routine much like a Masonic catechism. In the spring of 1900, while doing his bit for the British cause in the Boer War, Doyle attended meetings at an improvised Masonic Lodge set up in a field close to the front line at Bloemfontein. He was not the only visiting author to do so. A later issue of *Masonic Illustrated* magazine reported, 'Whilst at the seat of war, Brother Conan Doyle frequented the never-to-be-forgotten scratch lodge in the Free State with Brother Kipling'.

It's been speculated that the Masons' secretive routines appealed to Doyle's sense of mystery, as well as to his lifelong quest for acceptance on his own merits, and not just as an author of popular fiction. The man of real talent who longs to be recognised for something else is a recurring and often endearing figure in the arts. Doyle, who described himself as a teacher to the magician Harry Houdini and came to think of himself as a significant philosopher, would never concede an intellectual argument. It seems fair to say that his Masonic activities were a part of the same restless nature that had long struggled with the conflict between the claims of a conformist society and an intransigent individual. He took nothing mainstream on trust. Doyle eventually branded Houdini's position on the occult a form of 'Catholicism' – a new ideological insult – which implied that the 'little man' (who happened to be Jewish) was in thrall to the reactionary forces of orthodox religion while, by contrast, he, Doyle, espoused the concept of continuous mental revolution.

※ ※ ※

In May 1914, Conan Doyle and his family set sail on the RMS *Olympic*, sister ship of the *Titanic*, for New York. It was his first Atlantic crossing in twenty years. He had chosen this moment in his nation's destiny to accept an invitation from the Canadian government to make a goodwill tour of its national parks. On 28 June, as the visitors were enjoying the view at Niagara Falls (which Doyle thought might be a suitable place to drop Holmes), Gavrilo Princip succeeded in his second attempt at murdering the visiting archduke in Sarajevo. When Conan Doyle arrived home on 19 July, the Austro-Hungarian Empire was in the throes of presenting Serbia with an unconditional ultimatum. The outbreak of full-scale hostilities came two weeks later. Although the military authorities denied his request for an army commission, Doyle was far from idle during the conflict, emerging in 1918 no longer as a potential recruit but as a spokesman and missionary for what he called the 'new revelation'.

While psychiatrist-biographers have written of Conan Doyle's 'identity crisis in middle age', and even his apparent 'male menopause', the best course appears to be to treat any claim to an overall psychological analysis with caution, and instead to study the facts. Doyle was never subject to a blinding light, nor to a single philosophical tipping point in his embrace of the occult. It was not an overnight conversion.

There were several factors at work in finally transforming him from what he termed an 'uncommitted student of the psychic' into a full-time propagandist on the subject. The continuing losses both of family members and of hundreds of thousands of ordinary troops would have preyed on a far less inquisitive mind. 'Where were they?' Doyle later wrote. 'What had become of these splendid young lives? They were no longer here. Were they anywhere? The question was [by] far the most pressing in the world.'

It's arguable that on successive visits to war-torn France, Doyle underwent his own inner desolation among the ruins, and emerged to raise questions about 'the fleeting nature of matter', and 'reveal the eternal values beyond all the shows of time and sense – the things which are indeed lasting, enduring through the ages in a glorious and majestic progression,' as he put it in a public lecture in October 1917, before going on to declare, 'I am now finally satisfied with the truth [of spiritualism], and have not been hasty in forming my opinions'.

On another level, of course, Conan Doyle was on an altogether faster track than he suggested. It's often said that he turned to the séance room only after the war-related deaths of his son Kingsley and his brother Innes. In fact, both these individuals were still alive when Doyle publicly came out as a believer. It's true that he'd involved himself in psychic affairs on and off for some three decades, during which time he grew steadily more antagonistic in his attitude to orthodox religion. But what finally drove Doyle into the occultist camp was neither a climactic revelation following his years of diligent research, nor a breakdown in his normal critical faculties. The trigger-point was both more banal and yet infinitely stranger than that. It came in the form of the Doyles' wartime houseguest, Lily Loder-Symonds, the 'sensitive' who lost three of her brothers in combat and subsequently took to channelling messages sent to her from the spirits of dead soldiers.

'Since the War,' Doyle wrote with characteristic self-confidence in his 1918 book *The New Revelation*:

I have had some very exceptional opportunities of confirming all the views which I had already formed as to the truth of the general facts upon which my views are founded. These opportunities came through the fact that a lady who lived with us, as Mrs L.S., developed the power of automatic writing.

As we've seen, the sickly and widowed Loder-Symonds was at best a somewhat elusive figure who appears to have left little historical record behind her. We know that she was a childhood friend of Jean Conan Doyle, and that she had been one of the bridesmaids at the Doyles' wedding in 1907. A witness to that event remembered her as:

A stout but comely lady in her youthful middle age, bespectacled, her gaze icy blue and penetrating … Mrs Symonds' jaw was firm, with lips tightly locked. Even on an occasion such as this, smiles did not come readily.

Beyond that, it's known only that Lily had once played the harp at competitive level and, like Jean herself, had a mystic outlook on life, apparently believing that the Great War had been prophesied to her as long ago as 1901 by a music teacher known for his psychic abilities. At Windlesham, it was remembered that she knocked on wood, threw salt over her shoulder, and carried a good-luck penny. At a low point in her fortunes, she's said to have begun to read the astrological 'word of the week' in a mass circulation magazine. Increasingly frail from around the middle of 1915, Loder-Symonds came to pass much of her time propped up in bed with her hand poised over a writing pad, then watching – either in detachment or an apparent trance – as the pen moved across the page in front of her, seemingly of its own accord, bringing her and her sitters news from their dead loved ones.

Conan Doyle, it should be noted, did not entirely abandon his critical reserve when first confronted with these startling psychic manifestations under his own roof. 'Of all forms of mediumship,' he later wrote:

… [automatic writing] seems to me to be the one which should be tested most rigidly, as it lends itself very easily not so much to deception as to self-deception, which is a more subtle and dangerous thing … In the case of L.S. there is no denying that some messages proved to be not true. Especially in the matter of time, they were quite imprecise.

If Loder-Symonds truly was taking dictation from forces in the spirit world, they would seem to have been only modestly gifted as forecasters of future world events. Following the May 1915 sinking of the *Lusitania*, for example, Lily's pen had produced the words, 'It is terrible, terrible, and will have a great influence on the War' – particularly, she later added, in drawing the United States into the conflict. While the loss of 1,198 passengers and crew was self-evidently a tragedy of the first order, it could be argued that Loder-Symonds' spirits erred in their conclusions about the event. In fact, it would be a further two years before America entered the war on the Allied side. Could it be that, like many mediums before and after her, Lily was able to take certain facts and then draw plausible inferences from them in an integrated 'prophecy' that was nothing more than reasonably informed speculation dressed up in spiritualistic clothes? While the 'sensitive' continued to speak about current or imminent world events, much of what she predicted also appeared in the newspaper delivered each morning to her sickbed.

On the other hand, later in 1915 Loder-Symonds would sit down with her hosts in the darkened parlour at Windlesham and apparently communicate there with Jean's brother, Malcolm Leckie, who had died at Mons in the early days of the war. Conan Doyle never revealed publicly what had come through on that occasion, but he later wrote of it as 'evidential'. 'I seemed suddenly to see that this subject [spiritualism] with which I had so long dallied was not merely a study of force outside the rules of science,' he wrote, but was 'something tremendous, a breaking down of the walls between two worlds, a direct undeniable message from beyond'.

Of course, it's also true that early death is often seen as a kind of martyrdom, and Lily Loder-Symonds' in 1916, at the age of 42, arguably gave her mediumship an appeal for Doyle it might not otherwise have enjoyed. At around the same time, a claim increasingly argued for a connection between spiritualism and several new scientific philosophies in areas like relativity theory and electromagnetism, which combined to suggest that man's understanding of the universe was far from complete. This particular link seemed to strengthen when Oliver Lodge's son, Raymond, was lost in the trenches. Lodge's subsequent public conversion to the idea of a visible afterlife, on which he wrote a bestselling book, lent an intellectual respectability to a topic that was soon being debated on the front pages of both the British and American newspapers.

Whatever the causes, the result was that at stages over the terrible winter of 1916–17, Conan Doyle finally came out as an apostle of the New Revelation. It was now clear to him, he wrote, that this knowledge was not for his benefit alone, 'but that God had placed me in a very special position for conveying it to that world which needed it so badly'.

✳ ✳ ✳

With the appearance of *The New Revelation* and its sequel *The Vital Message*, Conan Doyle was soon receiving the attention he had hoped for, with headlines and leading articles in everything from *Psychic News* to *The New York Times*. It was clear that he enjoyed the publicity, and equally clear that he would soon come a cropper. He showed his familiar self-confidence and tendency to see even the most complicated issues simply in black and white terms. As a result, Doyle's effusions on spiritualism could sound insufferably pious. 'Psychic knowledge is not a question of proof,' he informed the readers of one American paper. 'I *know* it to be true.' 'Theories of fraud or of delusion will not meet the evidence,' he insisted in a public lecture. 'It is absolute lunacy, or as I am convinced, it is a revolution in human thought.'

Among those who inclined to the former view, there was the anonymous critic in the London *Times*, who accused Doyle of an 'incredible naiveté'. Even this was mild compared to James Douglas, writing in the *Sunday Express*, whose capsule review of *The New Revelation* posed the same question as Captain Anson at the time of the Edalji case ten years earlier. 'Is Conan Doyle mad?' he asked.

In time, even Doyle's mother, now in her eighties but as plainspoken as ever, came to worry that her headstrong son's latest sense of mission would make him a laughing stock – a fear seemingly realised by the *Express* when it gave the headline 'Wines and Spirits' to a report of one of Doyle's psychic speeches where liquor was served.

Why, for all that, did so many people, not all of them believers, sit up and listen to Conan Doyle when he announced to the world that he and others suddenly had the ability to communicate with dead souls, and that this was the greatest spiritual revelation of the past 2,000 years? The answer surely lies in the fact that, however ludicrous he might sometimes seem to be, Doyle possessed one great virtue not in endless supply in British public life as a whole: integrity. Even the sceptical James Douglas conceded this point when he wrote in the *Sunday Express*:

If ever there was a well-balanced mind in a well-balanced body, it is Doyle's …
It is not easy to reconcile these facts with the hypothesis that [he] is stark, staring

mad on the subject of the dead … He has established his right to be heard, and we may be wrong in refusing to hear him. There may be oceans of fraud and folly in spiritualism, but there may be a grain of truth in it.

John Dickson Carr, among the first and most respected of Doyle's biographers, later wrote, 'Did the war affect his judgement? Did it turn him into a moonstruck visionary credulous and incapable of seeing clearly?' It did not, Carr believed, arguing that Doyle's achievements as a military historian and his practical contributions in areas such as the improved design of body armour and the adoption of tactics to counter the U-boat menace to British shipping were hardly the neurotic ravings of a religious maniac. 'He may have been right about Spiritualism. He may have been wrong about Spiritualism. But nobody can say he was far wrong about anything else,' Carr concluded.

In fact, Doyle retained his essentially pragmatic approach both to spiritualism, and to the more extravagant claims advanced by its propagandists, right up to and beyond November 1918. Indeed, he often reprimanded those whose actions seemed to him to compromise the message in the eyes of the general public. A curious example of this came in the weeks and months following the Allied withdrawal from Mons in late August 1914, and the subsequent widespread belief that the British troops had enjoyed some form of divine protection in their retreat. On 5 September of that year, Brigadier John Charteris, chief military intelligence adviser to General Douglas Haig, wrote of a story 'spread[ing] through the 2nd Corps, of how the angel of the Lord on the traditional white horse, and clad all in white with flaming sword, faced the advancing Germans at Mons and forbade their further progress'. He added, 'Men's nerves and imagination play weird pranks in these strenuous times. All the same, the vision at Mons interests me. I cannot find out how the legend arose.'

Most historians now agree that Charteris himself was the man responsible for the myth of the Angel of Mons, which he saw as part of a continuing one-man campaign to spread morale-boosting propaganda and disinformation. A few months later, the same officer transmitted back a report about the Germans having allegedly butchered and cannibalised one of their own men. (In other accounts, it was a Canadian who was eaten.) Charteris passed an adapted version of the story to *The Times*, adding the detail that the unfortunate victim had first been crucified and later returned in spirit to torment his murderers.

Several more such 'rumours, distortions and outright fairy-tales' followed from the same source during the war, *The Times* reported.

Charteris, one of life's inveterate optimists, if one whose military forecasts were to be sorely tested by later events at Ypres and the Somme, has been described as an 'unkempt officer' who 'drank brandies before breakfast'. He was also the younger brother of Archibald and Francis Charteris, who in Conan Doyle's view – an opinion shared by many – had conspired to rob Marion Gilchrist on the night of her death. Doyle thought the professional soldier's tales of heavenly battlefield manifestations 'hogwash', and was still saying as much to Harry Houdini when he entertained him to lunch at Windlesham in April 1920.

Then aged 46, the famous magician was a stubby, Chaplinesque figure, thickening around the waist, with patches of receding grey hair rather too prominently dyed black. He had come to England for a performance tour that combined several of his most celebrated escapes with a critical commentary on the now widespread and often highly lucrative business of contacting the spirits of the dead. Houdini remarked in his diary that in visiting Windlesham he had clearly come to the enemy stronghold. 'The worldwide Spiritist church,' he wrote, was now 'controlled by a single group, and that group controlled by a single man who, in turn, is possessed by a dream'.

Houdini's own disbelief in the occult owed something to the fact that he had known a number of society's most fashionable post-war mediums when, like him, they had been content to operate on the early twentieth-century American vaudeville circuit in the guise of 'bearded ladies, singing clowns, limbless violin players, ape-man hybrids', and, in the case of a latterly popular 'seer' named Madame Thardo, a morbidly obese New York housewife who subjected herself to repeated rattlesnake bites. Houdini's failure to reach his mother Cecilia following her death in 1913 had since served to turn his scepticism about the paranormal into a crusade.

Always drawn to literary figures, he had called on Conan Doyle that April day hoping to make a friend of this 'poetic titan [as] justly famous as myself'. Even at this early stage, there was some spirited intellectual jousting between the two men, neither of them a martyr to false modesty. 'When you say there are 96 volumes on your desk,' Houdini wrote in one letter, 'it may interest you to know that I travel with a bookcase containing over one hundred volumes, and recently, in Leeds, I bought two whole collections on Spiritualism.'

'If you ever index your psychic library, I should like to see the list,' Doyle replied. 'I have 200 now – and have read them too!'

At Windlesham, Doyle had wanted to discuss not so much spiritualism per se, but how the 'little chap' affected his legendary escapes. In particular, he was curious about whether Houdini enjoyed the 'divine' gift of being able to waft in and out of confined spaces. Before long Doyle was convinced that the 'great self-liberator', as his visitor called himself, could arrange and rearrange his molecules at will. 'My dear chap,' he would write:

> Why go around the world seeking a demonstration of the occult when you are giving one all the time? Mrs Guppy [a Victorian mesmerist] could dematerialise, and so could many people in Holy Writ, and I do honestly believe that you can also … Such a gift is not given to one man in a hundred million.

Up close, Doyle was forced to admit, Houdini was 'a little disappointing' when measured against this superhuman ideal. He had appeared for lunch dressed in a typically ill-fitting cream-coloured suit and a frayed straw hat, which he had courteously lifted when ringing the front doorbell. He made a striking physical contrast to his host, who was a foot taller and some 80lb heavier. Later that night Houdini wrote in his diary:

> Visited Sir A. Conan Doyle at Crowborough. Met Lady Doyle and the three children. Had lunch with them. They believe implicitly in spiritism. Sir Arthur told me he had spoken six times to his dead son. No possible chance for trickery.

Even so, it's possible Houdini already had doubts about Doyle's critical faculties. 'Sir Arthur saw my performance Friday night,' he wrote to his friend Harry Kellar a few days later. 'He was so much impressed, that there is little wonder in his believing in [the] mystic so strongly.'

There was justification in this charge, and the gentleman in Conan Doyle was always reluctant to acknowledge that there were those in the spiritualist camp who were more adept at performing certain magic tricks than they were at heavenly communion. As a rule, Houdini was less inhibited in his judgements. All that most mediums were offering was 'stagecraft' rather than any 'supernatural wit', he told one London audience. Much of the 'so-called skill known as mentalism', for instance, was merely a question of bombarding the unsuspecting subject with subliminal messages. If you exposed them to enough pictures of black and white parallel lines, as well as mentioning the words 'striped' and 'animal' several times, 'you might well find that they just happened to be thinking of a zebra'.

Doyle was also convinced that many mediums secreted what he called a 'miraculous stuff', or ectoplasm, while in the throes of a spiritualist trance. 'I have clearly seen it,' he wrote in the *London Chronicle*:

> The room was in darkness, though there was sufficient light to see all that occurred. The ectoplasm, which seemed to cause great pain in its emission, took the form of slightly luminous patches, produced under complete test conditions. They formed on the floor with an inclination to rise and become more clearly defined. They were quite separate from the medium – in fact they were nearer to me than to her.

Houdini, by contrast, thought this 'foul muck' no more than the medium's saliva or her regurgitated food, a routine she sometimes varied by means of concealing foreign objects elsewhere on her body.

'This is how she works,' he wrote of a popular Los Angeles medium who began her séances by standing nude in a bowl of flour so that she was unable to move around without leaving incriminating tracks:

> She has a tube for her vagin [*sic*] in which she stashes a pair of silk stockings … When the lights are out, as it is impossible to quit the floor without leaving footprints, she reaches in and gets the silk stockings, puts them on her feet, steps out of the bowl of flour [and] is able to walk around without besmirching the floor or leaving prints. After the materialization she goes back, takes off her stockings, conceals her load, and – presto! – steps back into the bowl of flour.

Commenting on Doyle's reluctance to believe the worst of a medium, Houdini wrote in his diary that the more academically gifted a man was, the easier it was to fool him. In London, Doyle predicted a 'glorious future for those brave ladies who suffer their indignities for our gospel', while back in New York Houdini and his wife introduced a new double act to debunk 'charlatan mediums and their wiles'. 'When one has a chance to expose such people,' he said, 'one should do so.'

Houdini nonetheless believed that by the autumn of 1921, 'the anti-occultism of recent months may have passed its peak'. Conan Doyle knew otherwise. Undaunted by public reaction to the Cottingley fairies, he had spent much of that year promoting the merits of spirit photography as a 'new and credible' science. Doyle was soon to take a keen technical interest in the practicalities of capturing a ghost on film, and showed an almost Holmes-like obsession in cataloguing the various chemicals and dyes – such as the coal-tar derivative dicyanin – needed to coat the glass plate for a successful result.

He had become convinced that there was something to the business of ghostly 'extras' appearing on film after the Crewe photographer William Hope showed him a picture of his son Kingsley that he said came from the beyond. It was thus something of a further blow to Doyle's prestige when, in February 1922, Houdini's friend Harry Price and a fellow SPR investigator seemed to show that Hope produced his results not by 'spectral manifestation', as he claimed, but by pre-loading his camera with a plate already equipped with the desired image of a dead loved one, or whomever it was the client wished to see. When Hope then developed the film, the 'extra' would be seen apparently floating in the background.

Undeterred by the SPR's attack, Doyle went on to publicly endorse several more spirit images, including one taken (not by Hope) on Remembrance Sunday that seemed to show the ghostly features of dozens of dead British soldiers looming above the crowd observing the annual two minutes' silence at the London Cenotaph. It was later established that several of the faces were in fact those of still-living professional football players torn from the pages of a fan magazine. The *New York Times* was left to remark sadly that by now even Doyle's fiction was 'scarcely more than a pulpit for his propaganda'. George Bernard Shaw felt that 'one might speak almost of mental impairment' in his fellow author.

While Conan Doyle clashed with living writers such as Shaw and H.G. Wells, both of them sceptics on spiritualism, he continued to fraternise warmly with several dead ones. W.T. Stead, for one, still regularly appeared at séances to 'keenly endorse' his friend's paranormal research. Writing in the SPR *Journal*, Doyle went on to reveal that the spirit of Joseph Conrad had materialised to ask for his help in completing *Suspense*, his unfinished Napoleonic novel, and that Charles Dickens had appeared with a similar commission. Doyle later reported that Jerome K. Jerome, author of *Three Men in a Boat*, had also emerged to join the ranks of the unquiet literary dead. 'I was wrong,' Jerome supposedly said, speaking of his earthly materialism. 'We never know our greatest mistakes at the time we make them. Make it clear to Arthur that I am not dead.'

While some speculated about Conan Doyle's mental health, the author himself continued to write accomplished new Sherlock Holmes stories, adding twelve more to the series between 1921 and 1926, each of which was widely reported to be the last. To call the detective the Frank Sinatra of the popular fiction world of the 1920s would be to confer a somewhat flattering sense of consistency on a character who seemed to rest, or retire, and then come back again on roughly an annual basis. It's worth mentioning, if only to refute the idea that Doyle had lost his intellectual faculties altogether as a result of his conversion.

Even in these later years, his analytical powers still spluttered away like a fitful but stubbornly ticking engine. Writing in 1920 to Oliver Lodge, for example, Doyle speaks of a certain medium being 'dead wrong' in her predictions. Occasionally, even Houdini and he seemed to undergo a sort of role reversal on spiritualism. In December 1921, the magician wrote an excited letter enclosing a photograph that purported to show 'something unknown or occult' wafting from the body of a young actress as she embraced Houdini on the set of his latest film. Conan Doyle was unmoved. 'The effect is certainly produced by the whisk of the lady's dress as she rushed into your arms,' he wrote. 'It is certainly not ectoplasm!' A subsequent packet of photographs taken at a Los Angeles séance struck him as similarly 'hollow' and 'very unconvincing … The faces seemed quite absurd.' Doyle went on to denounce those 'hoaxers and frauds' who tried to pervert the course of true psychic knowledge. 'The rotten twigs must come off,' he added.

On 2 April 1922, Conan Doyle and his family set off on the White Star liner *Baltic* to begin a ten-week lecture tour of America. '"I know exactly what I am going to get after death – happiness",' the *New York Times* quoted Doyle as saying on his arrival in the city.

'It is not mere hearsay,' he continued. 'I have talked with and seen twenty of my dead, including my son, when my wife and other witnesses were present …

Spiritualism is the one great final antidote to materialism, which is the cause of most of our recent troubles.'

Taking a less elevated tone, some of the reporters who met him at the quayside wanted to know whether the spirits could tell fortunes or predict the movements of the stock market, and if they had access to sex, alcohol, and cigars in the afterlife. Doyle replied with a convoluted hypothesis suggesting that 'certain familiar pleasures' would indeed be available (though he made clear his own moral distaste for liquor):

> Only the ones we love on this earth [will] be able to meet us in the beyond
> … People who have led selfish, hard lives here will enter that place on a lower
> plane and gradually descend instead of going higher and higher until the spirit
> of Christ is reached.

Synthesising these remarks for its readers, the next morning's headline in the *New York World* read, 'DOYLE SAYS MARITAL RELATIONS OK IN NEXT WORLD. REAFFIRMS BELIEF IN HELL'.

William J. Burns – the self-styled 'Sherlock Holmes of America' – again accompanied Doyle on part of his tour. He remained 'a firm disciple of Sir Arthur', who had come to believe that 'his [was] one of the truly great detective minds of the age'. But he shared some uncomfortable feelings about him. Doyle 'seemed to be much altered [since 1914], and was now guided by an implacable optimism as much as by cold-hearted reason,' he later wrote. Burns may have had in mind a visit they made on 30 April 1922 to the Washington DC home of Julius and Ada Zancig, a husband and wife sometime vaudeville team who now advertised themselves as 'astrologers, tea leaf readers, crystal ball seers, diviners and palmists'. As a result of this sitting, Doyle apparently came away convinced that the couple possessed telepathic powers. 'No word passed at all,' he assured Houdini, 'but Mrs Zancig, standing with her face turned sideways at the far end of the room, was able to repeat names and to duplicate drawings which we made and showed her husband.' In a public testimonial, Doyle wrote, 'I have tested Professor and Mrs Zancig, and I am quite sure that their remarkable performance, as I saw it, is due to psychic causes (through transference) and not to trickery.'

In his book *A Magician among the Spirits*, Houdini demurred. The Zancigs, he wrote:

... have a very clever act. I had ample opportunity to watch [their] system and codes. They are swift, sure, and silent, and I give [them] credit for being exceptionally adept in their chosen line of mystery. Telepathy does not enter into it.

After the first Mrs Zancig had died, Houdini noted, Julius 'took a street-car conductor from Philadelphia and broke him into the team'. Some acrimony had arisen when the young man later defected from Zancig and began offering his own mindreading routine, using a trained monkey as a foil. He was replaced by a magician known professionally as 'Syko the Psychic', who in turn left the act. 'At that stage, Prof. Zancig came to me for an assistant and I introduced him to an actress,' Houdini wrote. 'He said he would guarantee to teach her the code inside of a month, but they never came to an agreement on financial matters.' Where Doyle found Zancig to be a 'remarkable man [who] undoubtedly enjoyed supernatural or telepathic powers,' Houdini saw only an old circus sideshow performer whose new act 'reflects the modern rage for the occult'.

On the morning of 10 May 1922, Conan Doyle and his wife took a taxi from their New York hotel to Houdini's house on West 113th Street in Harlem. After some talk at the lunch table about the phenomena of 'spirit hands' – to Doyle, an irrefutably 'miraculous' feat of spiritualistic intrusion on the material world, and to Houdini a cheap ruse involving some paraffin and a rubber glove – the two men and Houdini's lawyer, Bernard Ernst, retired upstairs to the library. As Ernst recalled:

Houdini produced what appeared to be an ordinary slate, some 18 inches long and 15 inches high. In two corners of this slate, holes had been bored, and through these holes wires had been passed. These wires were several feet in length, and hooks had been fastened to the other ends of the wires. The only other accessories were four small cork balls, a large ink-well filled with white ink, and a table spoon.

Houdini passed the slate to Sir Arthur for examination. He was then requested to suspend the slate in the middle of the room, by means of the wires and hooks, leaving it free to swing in space, several feet distant from anything ... Houdini next invited his distinguished visitor to select one of the cork balls and, by means of the spoon, to place it in the white ink. It was left there to soak up as much of it as possible.

Houdini then asked Conan Doyle to walk out of the house, in any direction he chose, to pause when he was sure he was unobserved, write a phrase on a scrap of paper, put this in his pocket, and return to the house. Doyle did so. Back in the library, Houdini told his guest to fish out the ink-soaked ball and hold it up to the slate hanging in the middle of the room. As Doyle did so, the ball suddenly began to move across the slate, seemingly of its own free will, forming a series of words as it went. When the ball had finished, it just as suddenly dropped to the floor. With his innate sense of showmanship, Houdini then asked Doyle to read out the message on the slate, even though he and Ernst could both plainly see it for themselves. It was the biblical portent of doom, '*Mene, mene, tekel, upharsin*' – the same line Conan Doyle had written down and put in his pocket.

While Doyle pronounced himself 'stunned' by this mystery, which he was certain had been 'contrived by psychic means [and] no other', it seems fair to ask if Sherlock Holmes would have seen matters in a more objective light, without preconception or preformed theories. In particular, might he have perhaps extended a bony hand towards the well-stocked bookcase in his Baker Street consulting room and taken down 'Volume M' (for 'Magicians') from his encyclopaedia of reference? Had he done so, he might have come across an entry for a turn-of-the-century, German-born vaudeville artist named Max Berol. Berol (sometimes working under the name Konorah) had long entertained audiences on both sides of the Atlantic by a remarkably similar trick to Houdini's, which had involved, among other things, the surreptitious exchange of a solid cork ball for one with an iron core, some swift pickpocketing, and a strategically placed assistant holding a magnet at the end of a rod. Holmes might have further read that on his retirement this same performer had gone on to 'sell his entire magical apparatus and all rights thereof' to an anonymous purchaser 'anxious to expand his own not insignificant repertoire'.

Doyle, however, saw none of this, remarking only that it was a 'miraculous effect' that had left him 'breathless with wonder'. Nor was his day's entertainment quite over yet. Houdini was later to remark that his guest had been 'flabbergasted' by a 'lark' he showed him in the taxi as he accompanied the Doyles back to their hotel. To pass the time at a red light, the magician held up his hands, apparently removed the end of his own thumb, and then reattached it. Lady Doyle 'nearly fainted,' Houdini remarked with some satisfaction. 'Never having been taught the artifices of conjuring,' he noted of his day with Conan

Doyle, 'it was the simplest thing in the world for anyone to gain his confidence to hoodwink him.'

The competitiveness underscored Houdini's belief that 'the creator of Sherlock Holmes [is] now in a new line of business, and eaten up with but one subject'. Where Doyle left an impression of 'self-conceit and self-delusion' when in the presence of a medium, he, Houdini, was 'the more methodically-minded detective in [his] spirit investigations'. Later that spring, the magician cut out and scrawled the word '*Ha!*' on a newspaper account of a New York trial in which four defendants – including an Alice Moriarty – were accused of disorderly conduct after holding a series of 'mystic events' at a small apartment on the city's Upper West Side. The four were said to have invited sitters into a darkened room where they would 'twang a clandestine harp' and 'hymn a lusty version of "Some One is Waiting for Me"' while a 'ghostly figure' floated around in a 'robe or drape of the most meager sort'.

It did not go unnoticed in the press that Doyle himself had attended a séance with the defendants, and apparently seen his late mother materialise in front of him. Three days later, undercover officers from New York's 20th Precinct had gone to the room to request a sitting 'like that given to Sir Arthur'. One of the detectives had subsequently leapt up from his seat and rugby-tackled a 'luminous presence' as it passed by him. This was later established in court as being a 29-year-old aspiring actress named Eva Thompson, 'clad in a white sheet, and little else, [her] maternal orbs imperfectly covered by the fabric', a role she was said to have adopted for 'many noted clients'.

After these various curtain raisers, the Doyle-Houdini rivalry finally came to a climax on a hot Sunday afternoon in June 1922, when they met at the Ambassador Hotel in Atlantic City. 'It was a sudden inspiration of mine to invite the little man up to our room and see if we could [summon] his mother for him,' Doyle recalled. 'It was all done at my suggestion,' he added, in *The Edge of the Unknown* (1930), before noting two pages further on in the same book:

> The method in which Houdini tried to explain away, minimise or contort our attempt at consolation, which was given *entirely at his own urgent request and against my wife's desire*, has left a deplorable shadow in my mind and made some alteration in my feelings for him [emphasis added].

But if Doyle was confused about the timing of events that weekend, so was Houdini. Describing the Atlantic City 'miracle' in *A Magician among the Spirits*, he made some play of the fact that 'I especially wanted to speak to my late Mother, because that day, *June 17*, was her birthday [Houdini's emphasis]'. In fact, the séance took place on the eighteenth of the month. Houdini's professional faculties were still sharp enough, however, because:

> … before leaving with [Doyle], Mrs Houdini cued me. We did a second sight or mental performance years ago and still use[d] a system or code whereby we could speak silently to each other … In that manner Mrs Houdini told me all about the night previous [when] she had gone into detail with Lady Doyle about the great love I bear for my Mother. She related to her a number of instances, such as my returning home from long trips [and] spending months with my Mother and wearing only the clothes that she had given me, because I thought it would please her and give her some happiness. My wife also remarked about my habit of laying my head on my Mother's breast, in order to hear her heart beat – just little peculiarities that mean so much to a mother and son when they love one another as we did.

This seems to have been a lot of information for Bess Houdini to have conveyed merely by blinking her eyes and wiggling her fingers, but we have her husband's word for it that he was forewarned 'some business was about to occur' upstairs in the Doyles' darkened hotel suite.

Arranging themselves around a small baize-topped table, lit by a single candle, the three sitters bowed their heads and said a prayer. For some minutes, Jean Conan Doyle continued to remain quite still, gazing down at a pad of paper in front of her, before suddenly turning her head upwards and asking sharply, 'Do you believe in God?' At that, she briskly struck the table three times with her left fist. Then, snatching up a pencil, her right hand began to move rapidly across the paper. 'Oh my darling, thank God, at last I'm through – I've tried so often – now I am happy – Why, of course, I want to talk to my boy – my own beloved boy – Friends, thank you, with all my heart for this,' she wrote, with Conan Doyle swiftly tearing off the finished pages and passing them to Houdini:

> You have answered the cry of my heart – and of his – God bless him – a thousand fold, for all his life for me – never had a mother such a son – tell him not to grieve, soon he'll get all the evidence he is so anxious for – I will work with him – he is so, so dear to me – I am preparing so sweet a home for him which one day in God's good time he will come to – it is one of my great joys preparing it

for our future – It is so different over here, so much larger and bigger and more beautiful – so lofty – all sweetness around one – nothing that hurts and we see our beloved ones on earth – that is such a joy and a comfort to us – Tell him I love him more than ever – the years only increase it – and his goodness fills my soul with gladness and thankfulness. Oh, just this, it *is* me. I want him only to know that – that – I have bridged the gulf – That is what I wanted, oh so much. Now I can rest in peace.

'Houdini had a poker-face and gave nothing away as a rule,' Conan Doyle later remarked. But on this occasion he appeared to be 'profoundly moved', looking 'grimmer and paler' as he read 'each successive page of the message my wife produced, with her hand flying wildly, beating the table while she scribbled at a furious rate'. At the end of the séance, Doyle himself exclaimed, 'Truly, Saul is among the prophets!' and at that, 'gathering up his papers, Houdini hurried from the room'.

✳ ✳ ✳

On 3 September 1922, *Lloyd's Sunday News* of London published the first of twelve instalments of Conan Doyle's book *Our American Adventure*. Among other revelations, the serial went into some detail about the events of the previous June in Atlantic City. Before long, a friendly English SPR officer named Eric Dingwall wrote to ask Houdini, 'Is there any truth in the story of Doyle that you got an evidential message from your mother through Lady Doyle? Also that people say you have become an automatic writer?'

This was too much. Telling Dingwall that he had no intention of becoming known as a 'confirmed spookist', Houdini swore out a statement and had it published in several New York papers. It began:

THE TRUTH REGARDING SPIRITUALISTIC SÉANCE GIVEN TO HOUDINI BY LADY DOYLE

Fully realizing the danger of claims made by investigators of psychic phenomena, and knowing full well my reputation earned, after more than thirty years' experience in the realm of mystery, I can truthfully say that I have never seen a mystery, and I have never visited a séance, which I could not fully explain …

Lady Doyle told me that she was automatically writing a letter which came through her, and was guided by the spirit of my beloved, sainted mother … There was not the slightest idea of my having felt my mother's presence, and the letter which followed I cannot possibly accept as having been written or inspired by her.

It seems not to have occurred to Houdini that this public rebuff might in any way harm what he called his 'warm and kindly' relations with Conan Doyle. Six months later, he was to note serenely that the Doyles had 'attended and certainly enjoyed' a magic performance he gave in Denver. 'We sent them a bunch of violets and five pounds of candy for little Billy, the[ir] tom-boy daughter', he added. Being a pragmatist, Houdini easily overcame his ideological prejudices and continued to speak as if Doyle and he were the 'most cordial of pals' and 'intellectual piers [sic] at that'. He was considerably more outspoken in private, confiding to one friend that he could only wonder why his mother, a Jew, would have communicated with her son under the sign of a cross and in fluent English, a language she had never spoken.

For his part, Doyle was outraged that the 'little man' had seen fit to publicly question his wife's integrity. His deep hatred of any form of injustice, particularly when inflicted on a woman, showed in his rebuke:

I have had to handle you a little roughly in [the press], because they sent me a long screed under quotation marks, so it is surely accurate … I hate sparring with a friend in public, but what can I do when you say things which are not correct, and which I have to contradict or they go by default?

Doyle closed another letter to Houdini by telling him, 'Pray remember us all to your wife. Mine is, I am afraid, rather angry with you.' This was mild compared to the words of the Doyles' spirit guide, Pheneas, when his voice came through to them while they were seated around their living room fire one night in the spring of 1923. Speaking directly through Lady Doyle, Pheneas remarked acidly on the man then busy denouncing the claims of mediums on both sides of the Atlantic. 'Houdini is doomed, doomed!' the spirit shouted. 'A terrible future awaits him … His fate is at hand!'

Soon Doyle found what he called another 'cruelly oppressed' medium to champion. This was a 34-year-old Frenchwoman named Marthe Béraud, who went by the nom-de-séance of Eva C. Blonde and svelte, she often performed in a sheer black body stocking 'which permitted for no possible concealment of substances', and despite this restriction appeared to possess the gift of ectoplasm. 'The Eva controversy is absurd – as if negatives can ever explain anything,' Doyle wrote to the American author Hamlin Garland. 'To me, who have had ectoplasm in my own hand it is all meaningless, save that I am annoyed by the persecution of this woman who has done more for Science than all her critics.'

In time, Doyle would speak of Eva C. as a 'God-given force' and a martyr to the religious Establishment. 'She is a prophet,' he insisted. Houdini was less impressed when he attended one of Eva's London séances. The medium had '"sleight-of-handed" some [foreign] substances into her mouth,' he wrote in his diary, and simply regurgitated them. Only a 'prize boob' would believe in this 'poor deluded female, [who] is probably mad,' he added.

Even so, during one of his public lectures at New York's Carnegie Hall, Conan Doyle, pointer stick in hand, took the opportunity to project a series of graphic illustrations of ectoplasm apparently oozing from Eva's body. One particular image proved so potent that the wife of the city's mayor vomited at the sight, and several other women had to be helped from the room. Undaunted by this reaction, Doyle had brought the talk to a close by stepping forward between two large potted palms on either side of the stage, rapping the stick sharply on the floor, and then raising his hand in a quieting gesture. 'Now I will show you a picture of a ghost,' he announced simply:

A lady was taking a picture at an old English inn. But when she developed the plate apparently something had passed, and she brought it to us in perplexity. It was the image of one of those earthbound spirits called ghosts, a coincidence that might not occur again in 100 years.

As the picture was shown there was a steady crescendo of 'mingled cheers and sobs of excitement,' the *New York World* reported, though a 'few scattered remarks of a skeptical nature' were also heard from the balcony.★

In December 1923, another attractive medium was let loose on Conan Doyle, who arranged a séance for her at his new London flat at Buckingham Palace

★ Houdini later examined the photograph, which he considered to be the result not so much of a supernatural occurrence as of a pre-prepared plate, or double exposure, 'just as anyone with adequate levels of oxygen to the brain would have seen'.

Mansions, near the Houses of Parliament. She was a 35-year-old Canadian-born housewife named Mina Crandon, who went under the alias 'Margery' and was popularly known as the 'Blonde Witch of Lime Street' in honour of her address in the fashionable Beacon Hill neighbourhood of Boston. In 1911, Margery's elder brother Walter, a Massachusetts motor mechanic, had died at the age of 28 after being crushed by a runaway train. She later recalled that following this tragedy she had found solace in the Congregational Church. Margery would go on to tell a *Boston Herald* reporter that her loss had 'cured me of my agnosticism', and also of materialists 'who speak hypocritically of knowing the secrets of our universe'.

In early 1917, Margery had undergone an abdominal operation at the hands of a wealthy Boston surgeon named Le Roi Crandon. At the time of this procedure, later to be the subject of some speculation in spiritualist circles, she was still a practising Congregationalist, and claimed to have 'learned much from the church's skill in deal[ing] with human nature'. The following year, Margery married Crandon; she was 29 and he was 48. After attending a 1923 lecture by Conan Doyle's friend Oliver Lodge, she had gone on to discover a talent for levitating tables, producing flashes of light and manifesting ectoplasm (often from her vagina), among other psychic powers.

On the night of 9 June that year, Margery, her husband and three of their friends had sat down at a table in the attic of their Lime Street home, put a suitably mournful record on the Victrola phonograph, and turned off all the lights. At first nothing had happened. Then, slowly at first, Margery had begun to rock back and forth in her seat with increasing violence, her eyes blazing. At the climax of this frenzy, she suddenly froze in place, paused for a moment, pressed her hand to her forehead, and then remarked in a 'gruff, masculine' tone, 'I said I could put this through!' It was the voice of her dead brother, Walter, speaking.

Six months later, Margery and her husband had embarked on a European tour. She caused something of a stir there by performing in the nude at several Paris séances, before going to England to sit for a photograph by William Hope, which showed an image of Walter unmistakably standing behind her. Even the sceptical *Daily Express* was left to conclude, 'There must be [a] question that some supernatural agency was at work' in her case.

At the séance held at the Conan Doyles' London flat, Margery, dressed for the occasion in a short kimono, was able to make the table rock up and down and a dried flower materialise on the floor, all while her feet remained under close observation, nestling on her host's lap. Doyle later wrote to Crandon, his fellow doctor, fondly remembering his charming wife, whom he believed 'will live in history'. As a woman and a psychic, she had a double claim on his respect. Margery had 'created belief,' Doyle added, not so much in physical phenomena such as the ectoplasm, but in herself as a reputable medium, 'uniquely endowed with superhuman powers to convey the words, and even the distinctive phrasing and idiom' of the dead.

Still unconvinced by any of this, Houdini went to Boston and had Margery sit for him while locked into a large wooden crate of his own design. With holes bored in the device for the medium's head and arms, the general effect was of someone bolted into a steam box in a sauna. Perhaps as a result, Margery failed to manifest any ectoplasm, although she still went on to address both Houdini and the others present in her late brother's voice. The spirit was evidently not pleased at the restrictions placed on his sister's movements. 'Houdini, you God damned son of a bitch!' Walter roared, displaying some of the robust manner for which he was known during his earthly life as a motor man. 'I put a curse on you now that will follow you every day for the rest of your short life. Now get the hell out of here and never come back!'

Houdini did so. 'I charge Mrs Crandon with practicing her feats daily like a professional conjuror,' he wrote in a subsequent article for *Scientific American* magazine, which sponsored his investigation. 'Also that … she is not simple and guileless but a shrewd, cunning woman, resourceful in the extreme, and taking advantage of every opportunity to produce a "manifestation".'

Margery appeared to him to have combined with equal facility the role of femme fatale, ventriloquist, and oracle (she also dabbled in astrology), and her seeming ability to produce objects ranging from rose petals to the occasional small bird released into the air owed less to her powers of divine mediumship than to what he called her 'surgically enlarged vagin'. The Crandons were not pleased with Houdini, whom they continued to predict would come to an untimely end.

In England, the Doyles' spirit guide Pheneas gave a similar verdict. 'Houdini is going rapidly to his Waterloo,' he announced one evening in August 1924, in the course of once again speaking about a future disaster that would overwhelm mankind. 'He is exposed. Great will be his downfall before he descends into the darkness of oblivion!' Two days later, Lady Doyle wrote directly to Margery to tell her:

All you have done is going to have very great results in the future … When the upheaval comes [and] America is stricken, as she will be … you will be a great centre … and they will flock to you and Walter as a bridge of knowledge and hope and comfort … We are also told that Houdini is *doomed* and that he will soon go down to the black regions which his work against Spiritualism will bring him as his punishment.

During the next two years, Walter made several further appearances at which he prophesied the imminent ruin of the sceptics in general and of the 'little kike' in particular. 'He will be gone by Halloween,' he promised at the end of one séance in September 1926.

Meanwhile, Houdini himself had finally moved against Conan Doyle, doing so with his customary aggression – going from lavishly praising his friend to publicly denouncing him without any apparent intermediate reassessment. In July 1924, the *New York Times* quoted Houdini as calling Doyle 'a bit senile' and 'easily bamboozled'. From there, he went on to lampoon the 65-year-old author from the stage. He told one audience in Boston that he felt 'very sorry' for Doyle. 'It is a pity that a man [should] in his old age, do such really stupid things.' Soon all pretence of civility was gone, and the magician remarked that it was his 'sacred duty' to confront 'any such neurotic believer in the occult as Sir Arthur'.

Another chance to do so came early in 1925, when Doyle wrote an article entitled 'Northcliffe Speaks Again!' about the late tabloid press baron. 'Conan Doyle [has been] hoodwinked from New York to San Francisco and back again,' Houdini observed:

I knew Lord Northcliffe when he was plain Harmsworth, and he came to my dressing room in London. I will write something on a piece of paper and seal it, and I challenge the spirit of His Lordship to tell us the subject matter … One must be half-witted to believe some of these things.

In July, Houdini took the opportunity of another public performance in Boston to mock this 'mere scribbler' and 'mental chump' who at the same time was a 'menace to mankind'. 'Sir Arthur Conan Doyle states that I am a medium,' he announced. 'That is not so. I am well done.' After the guffaws had died down, an audience member then stood up to yell, 'I will tell you one thing, you can't fill a house like Conan Doyle did twice'.

'Well, all right,' Houdini shouted back. 'If ever I am such a plagiarist as Conan Doyle, who pinched Edgar Allan Poe's plumes, I will fill all houses.'

'Do you call him a thief?'

'No, but I say that his story "Scandal in Bohemia" is only the brilliant letter [*sic*] by Poe … I walked into his room at the Ambassador Hotel and I saw twenty books, French, English and German, a paragraph marked out of each one of the detective stories. I don't say he used them …' Houdini continued, but the rest of what he said was lost in the ensuing uproar.

Although Houdini's specific complaints varied, in the years ahead he would cling to his essentially hostile view of Doyle as tenaciously as a dog to a trouser leg. Some of the dispute was conducted in person, and some through the pages of the press. 'Houdini, Stirred by Article, May Sue Sir Arthur', ran one headline in the *Boston Herald*. 'I am more saddened than incensed,' the magician noted. 'Conan Doyle believes because he wishes to believe. There is no end to his credulity.'

At one séance held in a central London house, Doyle and some friends apparently made contact with the Russian Bolshevik leader Vladimir Lenin, who had died three months earlier. The revolutionary hero parted from the circle with the cryptic advice, 'Artists must rouse selfish nations'. In time, Houdini addressed the same historical era from a different perspective. 'There is no doubt in my mind that Rasputin was the direct cause of the fall of Russia,' he told a Chicago theatre audience in 1926:

> He was a medium who claimed he could bring back any one of the biblical characters. He held the Czar and more particularly the Czarina in his clutches, and it was through his mediumistic work that he called down vengeance on his own head.

Houdini had been unmoved when told about Conan Doyle's earlier séance. 'I will be elected Pope ere Comrade Lenin returns among us,' he said.

On the Friday morning of 22 October 1926, while lying on a couch in his Montreal dressing room, Houdini was punched several times in the midriff by a 30-year-old amateur boxer and postgraduate divinity student named Jocelyn Gordon Whitehead. Whitehead had previously asked if it were true that the magician had abnormally strong stomach muscles, and had taken his grunted confirmation of this as tacit permission for the assault. Although Houdini made little complaint at the time, three days later he collapsed following a performance in Detroit and was rushed to hospital.

It now seems likely that he had been suffering from appendicitis even before Whitehead's visit, and that the subsequent blows had ruptured his intestine. Peritonitis had set in, virtually a death sentence in the days before penicillin. On the afternoon of 30 October, Houdini dictated a letter to a friend acknowledging, 'I feel none too well at the moment', but insisting, 'I will get over this waviness in no time'.

Around 2 a.m. the next morning, he looked up and told his younger brother Theo, 'I guess I'm all through fighting'. They were to be his last words. Houdini died later that afternoon of what the doctors called 'Diffuse peritonitis [with] complications'. The time of death was given as 1.26 p.m. on Sunday, 31 October – Halloween.

✳ ✳ ✳

Houdini's fate 'was most certainly decreed from the other side,' Conan Doyle wrote to their mutual friend, the author Fulton Oursler. 'The spirit world might well be incensed against him if he was himself using psychic powers at the very same time when he was attacking them.'

Le Roi Crandon later wrote from Boston to tell Doyle of a séance he had held on Halloween night 1926. Both he and his wife had been so 'thoroughly excited' by the timing of Houdini's death that they had wanted an immediate consultation with the spirits. 'The loved one came in,' Crandon wrote:

> … and after greetings [I] said, 'Walter it is apparent that we should not ever take what you say lightly. Houdini passed over today …' Walter whistled more or less in a minor key and said that Houdini would have a long period of acclimatization, that he would be much confused and resistant to the idea of death, and added, 'I am not sure but that I shall have something to do with Houdini and his admission'.

Dr Crandon himself died in December 1939, aged 69, after falling down a flight of stairs. There were allegations that in later years he and his wife had engaged in child sex-trafficking. Following the loss of her husband, Margery seemingly suffered a period of alcoholism and depression. A young *Boston Guardian* reporter named John Hamer would remember calling by appointment at the Lime Street home one morning to find the front door ajar and 'the lady of the house lying on her back in the hall, drunk, dead to the world'. The former society beauty 'cut a pitiable sight, half-clad, her hair matted like Medusa's, snoring as she breathed'. Margery told a researcher who visited her bedside in her final days to ask if she had ever faked phenomena, 'You'll all be guessing for the rest of your lives'. She died overnight on Halloween 1941, fifteen years after Houdini; she was 53.

✳ ✳ ✳

At the heart of Conan Doyle's spiritualism there lay not so much a process of observation and analysis as a need to believe so powerful that it arguably overwhelmed his conscious faculties. Houdini's scepticism only increased Doyle's missionary zeal. Their relationship 'literally defined' him, he noted. Indeed, the general contours of their rivalry continued even after Houdini's death. In January 1928, the magician's widow Bess wrote to tell Doyle something of her current life in New York, and to mention in passing that a mirror had recently broken in her home. Doyle seized on this as a manifestation. He wrote back:

> I think the mirror incident shows every sign of being a message [from] Houdini. After all, such things don't happen elsewhere. No mirror has ever broken in this house. Why should yours do so? And it is just the sort of energetic thing one could expect from him.

Perhaps Conan Doyle accepted the 'new revelation' simply because for the most part it seemed to tell him what he most wanted to hear. His late family members were all blissfully happy in the afterlife. Several had returned to assure him so. There was no death.

Meanwhile, the brave mediums and clairvoyants who brought the world this psychic gospel continued to be ridiculed and persecuted in a way that surely roused his crusading instincts. Doyle told Hamlin Garland:

> The [sceptics] have themselves fallen into the pit that they have dug. I shall bring out a pamphlet to rub it in. The stupidity of these [people] is incredible, but it

comes from the fact that they start not with the question 'Is this thing true?', but rather with 'How is this trick done?'

On 15 August 1929, Doyle and his family were at the New Forest home that Pheneas had urged them to buy as a sanctuary in the coming global apocalypse when a fire took hold of the cottage's thatched roof. By the time the emergency services arrived from Southampton, most of the house's upper half had been destroyed. Doyle later wrote a letter of thanks to the villagers who had rallied round to help drag his furniture onto the lawn, although 'one or two, I regret to say, showed a disposition to remove the goods even further'. In time, the insurance company determined that the fire had broken out in the kitchen chimney, but Doyle wondered whether there might not be a paranormal aspect to it. A few days after the event, Pheneas again materialised to announce that there had been a 'bad psychic cloud' hanging over the burned part of the building. It had been necessary to remove this, the spirit explained, so that what remained could be used for 'high purposes' when Armageddon finally came.

Conan Doyle eventually grew impatient with Pheneas, whose prophecies of doom seemed to him to 'inevitably roll forward from year to year'. He nonetheless continued to believe that the messages his wife wrote down or the voices she spoke in were the authentic words of an Ubanian-era scribe. Doyle told Oliver Lodge that he would not have laboured so long and hard 'to advance a mere hypothesis'. He thought Pheneas as 'vital a presence as any living Pope or bishop', and 'considerably better endowed with divine grace'.

By 1929, an increasingly frustrated Doyle insisted that man's final crisis really must come soon, 'and certainly before the year 1930'. While still 'philosophically convinced' by the spirit's regular pronouncements about the end of the world, he was becoming restive about the precise timetable. Over the course of seven years, this 'infallible guide', as his medium called him, had provided more than 1,000 forecasts about everything from cataclysmic floods and earthquakes to the timing of the best train for Doyle to take from Crowborough to London. Little, if any, of Pheneas' more apocalyptical view of events had materialised. 'I have moments of doubt,' Doyle now admitted:

When I wonder if we have not been victims of some extraordinary prank played upon the human race from the other side … I have literally broken my heart in the attempt to give our Spiritual knowledge to the world and to give them something living, instead of the dead and dusty stuff which is served out to them in the name of religion.

Although Doyle told Oliver Lodge in 1928 that he was considering publishing a sequel to *Pheneas Speaks*, and that this second book would be 'much sterner stuff' than the original, he first delayed and ultimately abandoned the project. The spirit, he noted, explaining his decision, was becoming 'increasingly disinclined' to put a specific date to his ill tidings. In another letter, Conan Doyle told Lodge that he had visited the photographer William Hope in an effort to get a promotional picture of Pheneas. A bearded face had duly appeared, Doyle reported, though 'not of sufficient clarity' for commercial use.

With his public championing of Pheneas, Conan Doyle risked even greater ridicule than had met publication of *The Coming of the Fairies*. Although he went to his grave 'believing implicitly' in this latter miracle, one he added was 'endorsed by witnesses of unimpeachable honesty [among them] my own children', in 1983 the then elderly women at the heart of the affair admitted that 'most' of their original pictures of sixty-six years earlier had been faked. The two cousins had cut out illustrations from *Princess Mary's Gift Book*, a 1914 annual (in which Conan Doyle himself had published a story) and propped them up with hatpins in the grassy banks behind the Wrights' home. Frances Griffiths added that the girls had 'not wanted to embarrass Sir Arthur' at the time, and had been horrified to see the story of the fairies take root for the next sixty years.

We can applaud both Doyle's courage and his tenacity in seeking what he called the 'true, intrinsic and entire cause' of psychic phenomena, and in promoting spiritualism as a whole as 'the first really reasonable system ever given to the world'. The reader alone must judge whether some of the occult's more dramatic narratives appealed to Doyle's adventurous imagination, and perhaps got the better of his rational faculties. It is a question that might fairly be applied in the case of Pheneas, the loquacious Arabian scribe from the ancient city of Ur.

Sherlock Holmes was never bound by the obvious, but at the same time nor was his the sort of mind to ignore the evidence that lay immediately in front of him. Might Holmes have been struck, for example, by the curious coincidence of a story that ran prominently in several British newspapers, and even in the pages of *The Strand* magazine, in the weeks immediately before Pheneas' first appearance at the Doyles' family séance table in December 1922?

It was the gripping account of the 42-year-old English archaeologist Leonard Woolley and his ongoing excavation of the Mesopotamian town of Ur, which he and his colleagues had come to believe was the true site of the flood described in the Book of Genesis, as well as of several other biblical disasters.

10

THE FINAL PROBLEM

The pattern of Conan Doyle's behaviour as a spiritualist missionary had been set by the way he had seen life as a teenaged schoolboy. Despite his own harsh family circumstances, he was a child who tried to find the essential goodness of the world, an optimist about people and nature, and yet one who railed against stupidity and prejudice wherever he found them. This specifically included his religious education. 'Nothing can exceed the uncompromising bigotry of the Jesuit theology,' Doyle wrote over fifty years later:

> I remember that when, as a lad, I heard Father Murphy, a great fierce Irish priest, declare that there was sure damnation for everyone outside the Church, I looked upon him with horror, and to that moment I trace the first rift which has grown into such a chasm between me and those who were my guides.

If Doyle looked upon the organised Church as neither divinely conducted nor infallibly moral, in later years he still made the distinction between those who, like him, were 'in favour of complete liberty of conscience, and others [who put] assertion in the place of reason, giving rise to more contention, bitterness, and want of charity than any other influence in human affairs,' as he wrote in

The Scotsman. Although the circumstances varied over time, it could be argued that Doyle never quite lost the characteristic schoolboy quality of being drawn instinctively to what seemed to him to be honest and forthright and unspoiled in a character, and of being prepared to defend his hero's good name to the end. Perhaps it was this trait of Doyle's that Houdini had in mind when he called him a 'great kid' rather than an altogether serious theological scholar, or that the novelist Hugh Walpole was thinking of when he wrote in his diary on 8 July 1930, 'Conan Doyle dead. A brave simple, childish man. How hard he tried to make me a spiritualist! Very conscious of him tonight.'

In the spring of 1921, while casting around for the plots of new Sherlock Holmes stories, Doyle continued not only to consult the crime pages of the daily press, but also to confer through his wife with the spirits. 'I ought to have trusted your judgement, my own son,' ran a note apparently dictated by his mother Mary, who had died in December 1920. In time, Doyle's late brother-in-law Willie Hornung similarly came through to offer apologies for having ever doubted him while he was alive. Several other such posthumous communications, appearing in either written or spoken form, followed over the years. By contrast, another attempt to reach Marion Gilchrist, the Scottish spinster murdered in 1908, proved only 'partly evidential', Doyle admitted. The departed spirit 'uttered but a few words in uncharacteristically coarse terms' before terminating the séance.

Readers of *The Strand* appear to have had mixed views about the author's subsequent attempts to provide occult solutions to certain historical crimes. For Doyle, however, his wife's successes as a clairvoyant greatly outnumbered her failures. 'I know by many examples the purity of her mediumship,' he told Houdini.

On the surface – the level on which most sceptics treated him – Conan Doyle was by now a sadly deluded old man who spent much of his time sitting around darkened dining room tables talking to dead oriental scribes, while visions of fairies danced in his head. Houdini, for one, characterised the author's later life as 'completely loco', commenting that he had now abandoned his deductive faculties for the 'applesauce' of the séance room. However, Doyle's beliefs were, on a deeper psychological level, an argument within his famously divided self. He reasserted his divine mission even while he remained transported by the 'daily stories of human artifice and deceit' he read about in the newspapers. Both spiritualist and materialist, Doyle continued to turn a coldly rational eye on criminal cases referred to him both by readers who regarded Sherlock Holmes as a real character, and by friends who urged him to exercise his detective skills and stop feeding solipsistically off his infatuation with the occult.

In March 1922, Doyle became involved in a case with a classic, if unusually brutal, Holmesian twist. Three months earlier, a 31-year-old London woman named Irene Wilkins had placed a classified advertisement seeking work as a cook. In due course, a telegram arrived inviting her to take a specific train to Bournemouth, where she would be met by a man named 'Wood' and taken to an interview. Wilkins's parents drove her to Waterloo Station on the afternoon of 22 December 1921 and waved her goodbye. They never saw her alive again. The following morning, a farm labourer found Wilkins's partly clothed body lying face down in a field on the outskirts of Bournemouth. She had been sexually molested, before being repeatedly hit over the head with a hammer, and her bloodied fingers showed that she had fought back against her attacker.

The subsequent investigation by the Dorset Police was not distinguished by its brilliance. Reviewing the sheer number of leads they ignored and clues they missed is again to be reminded of just why the British reading public had so taken to Sherlock Holmes. Eventually the authorities narrowed their search to a 36-year-old soldier-turned-chauffeur, already known to them for his habit of passing forged cheques, named Thomas Allaway.

Allaway convinced investigators that he had been with another woman on the night of 22 December, and, after registering their moral distaste for their suspect, they let him go. At that stage, Conan Doyle's friend Ralph Blumenfeld, the managing editor of the *Daily Express*, wrote to him to complain of the police handling of the case and to ask his advice. Doyle cabled back:

Dear Blumenfeld, I find it hard to think that the letter [a specimen taken from Allaway] is in any hand but that which wrote the telegram. Could not a trap be laid in this way? The man naturally wants to get out of the country. He is a chauffeur. Suppose you put an advertisement in the *Express* and other papers: 'Skilled chauffeur. A gentleman starting on an extended tour in Spain needs services of driver. Steady man over 25 years – for four months. Apply by letter.' The replies would be very likely to contain one from him. All which are like his writing could be interviewed. He could fill up papers for a passport. Then you could see scratches, etc, on hands. Don't you think this is a possible line?

Readers of the Holmes canon will immediately recognise the plot device of 1904's 'The Adventure of Black Peter', where a newspaper advertisement similarly flushes out a maniacal harpoonist named Cairns.

Blumenfeld did as Doyle suggested, although in the end Allaway incriminated himself by continuing to pass bad cheques liberally around the south coast and Home Counties, sufficient for the Reading Police to eventually make an arrest. He was tried at Winchester in July 1922 and found guilty of murder. Blumenfeld later called Doyle's involvement 'undoubtedly the one worthwhile initiative of the whole affair'. Thomas Allaway was hung that August.

Sherlock Holmes's reappearance in 'The Problem of Thor Bridge', published in February 1922, was an unusually self-referential work by an author who normally cast around in the newspapers for his plots, not the recesses of his own life. It seemed Doyle had not so much transcended his infidelity to his first wife Louisa during her final years as been trapped by his attempts to rationalise it when he wrote of the hatred of a woman whose 'own physical charms had faded' towards her husband's younger female companion, and added:

> There is a soul-jealousy that can be as frantic as any body-jealousy, and though my wife had no cause for the latter, she was aware that this girl exerted an influence upon my mind and my acts that she herself never had.

More materially, Conan Doyle revisited some of the scenes that had taken place near his Sussex home in August 1908, shortly after he moved there with his new wife, when it came to the plot of 'Thor Bridge'. A 58-year-old local woman named Caroline Luard, a retired major general's wife, had been found dead on the steps of the couple's beachfront summer home. She had been relieved of her jewellery and her underclothes, and had two bullet wounds to the temple. Her husband had apparently been walking nearby, and he had a curious reaction on first reaching the crime scene. 'The brutes!' he shouted. 'They've killed her!'

Suspicion soon fell on the general himself, and on a mysterious tramp seen in the vicinity, but Caroline Luard's murder remains unsolved to this day. Doyle wondered if the victim might have somehow committed suicide by shooting herself twice through the head in the hope of implicating her husband, much as happens in 'Thor Bridge'. Another possibility was that the general had made murderous enemies during his years of service overseas, and that some sort of vendetta had ensued – a storyline with more than an echo of *The Sign of the Four* to it.

Ralph Blumenfeld thought Doyle's skills as a detective 'entirely true and intrinsic', but agreed that on this occasion his friend had failed to crack the case's 'manifest impossibilities and contradictions'; while a subsequent attempt to raise Caroline Luard in the séance room produced only 'some choice epithets [and] a particularly rank odour' apparently issuing from the medium's womb.

For both Doyle and his fictional alter ego, there were always unsolved, or insoluble, cases as well as those with a clean finish. 'Thor Bridge' opens with a teasing reference to one Isadora Persano, 'the well-known journalist and duellist, who was found stark staring mad with a matchbox in front of him which contained a remarkable worm, said to be unknown to science', among other problems Sherlock Holmes had at one time investigated and abandoned as hopeless failures. It's surely one of Holmes's endearing qualities that, despite the prevailing image, his career never bears the stamp of omnipotence or infallibility – the canon is just as full of his self-reproaches for his own sloth or blindness as it is with the proverbial 'Elementary, my dear Watson'.

Doyle, too, had his shortcomings as a detective. Around 1925 he wrote a note to himself with an overview of some of the cases that had recently caught his attention. There was the 'Queer letter from Australia', for example, or the matter of the 'Wapping Poltergeist', or the riddle of the 'Falkland Island Seer', all of which would remain unsolved on Doyle's desk, much like those failed cases of Holmes's consigned to Dr Watson's battered tin dispatch box held in the vaults of his London bank.

In March 1925, Conan Doyle paid another of his visits to the Home Office, just as he had in the Edalji affair, to raise questions about a recent criminal conviction. This involved a 26-year-old Sunday school teacher turned chicken farmer named Norman Thorne, who happened to be a neighbour of Doyle's in Crowborough. The crime combined a classic love triangle with some of the horrors that characterised the Crippen trial, with Doyle's pathologist friend Sir Bernard Spilsbury again providing the expert forensic testimony that helped secure a conviction.

The clean-cut and outwardly unassuming Thorne had impressed Doyle on first arriving in the area by joining the Band of Hope, a local teetotal society, and by naming his small poultry business after the Methodist Wesley brothers. On the surface, he seemed to be shy and withdrawn – his friend William Latter

(Doyle's chauffeur) called him 'the least demonstrative person I've known', someone who 'sang lustily in church, [but] otherwise said little'.

Despite his apparent show of temperance, the soft-spoken Thorne had a weakness for young women, however. Having left his fiancée Elsie Cameron in London, he had begun to step out with a local Crowborough girl named Bessie Coldicott. In November 1924, Elsie wrote to inform him she was pregnant. Thorne replied, 'There are one or two things I haven't told you for more reasons than one. It concerns someone else as well … I am between two fires.' Elsie appeared not to understand, because she wrote back politely suggesting that they get married. Thorne's next letter abandoned subtlety to announce, 'What I haven't told you is that on certain occasions a girl has been here with me late at night … She thinks I am going to marry her, and I have a strong feeling for her.' This was enough for Elsie to hurriedly buy a third-class rail ticket from London to Crowborough on the morning of 5 December, in what proved to be the last journey of her life.

A month later, Elsie Cameron not having been seen by anyone in the meantime, the police came to visit Thorne at Wesley Farm. He told them he knew nothing about the matter. After Elsie's dismembered body was found buried on his premises, Thorne changed his story. His London fiancée had indeed come to confront him, he admitted, and he had left her alone for an hour or two while he had gone out to visit Bessie Coldicott. When he returned, he found Elsie, dressed in her underwear, swinging from a beam in his hut. She had apparently hung herself in a fit of despair. Thorne had panicked, cut Elsie's body into pieces, and disposed of the remains under one of his chicken runs.

His trial for murder began at Lewes on 11 March 1925. Bernard Spilsbury testified that he had found eight bruises on Elsie's head, arms and legs (described by the defence pathologist as 'trifling, as one might see at Rugby Football every Saturday'), but that there were no scars around her neck consistent with hanging. The accused was asked in the witness box whether he had truly been in love with his fiancée or with her local rival. 'Well,' he said after some deliberation, 'of the two, I suppose I thought more of the other girl.' The jury returned with a guilty verdict after twenty minutes, and the judge sentenced Thorne to death.

After visiting the scene of the crime and minutely examining the beam where Elsie Cameron had supposedly hung herself, Doyle told the *Morning Post*:

I think that there is just one chance in a hundred that Thorne was not guilty of murder, and as long as there is one, I do not think he ought to be hanged. The evidence is strong, but it is circumstantial. Personally, I am against capital punishment except in very extreme cases, and to justify it I think the evidence should be stronger than it was in this case.

For once, Doyle's characteristic sympathy for potential victims of injustice failed to win the day. Thorne, protesting his innocence to the end, was hanged in the grounds of Wandsworth Prison on 22 April 1925. The day before, he wrote a letter to his father declaring himself a 'martyr to Spilsburyism'. Doyle never disguised his personal distaste for Thorne's romantic *ménage à trois*, but clung stubbornly to his belief that a man's life 'should not rest on the accuracy or otherwise' of one individual's disputed technical opinion.

On 3 December 1926, the 36-year-old thriller writer Agatha Christie vanished from her home in Sunningdale, Berkshire. She was despondent following her mother's death that spring and the subsequent discovery of her husband Archie's affair with a younger woman. The next morning, Christie's car was found abandoned at the side of a ditch, its headlights still burning. For the next ten days, as police and thousands of civilian volunteers combed the Home Counties, the press teemed with rumours about the disappearance. Had Christie drowned herself in a nearby, supposedly haunted spring called the Silent Pool? Others suggested the incident was a publicity stunt to promote sales of her latest book, while some clues seemed to point in the direction of murder at the hands of her cheating husband. All the elements of a classic whodunit were there. It was a case that fairly cried out for the attention of Sherlock Holmes.

When the Surrey Police asked Conan Doyle for his help, it was in his dual role as both 'the world's foremost detective mind' and their county's sometime deputy lieutenant, an honorary position he had held for several years while based at Undershaw. Doyle soon added a third strand to his investigative credentials. This was his familiarity with the world of 'psychometric prophecy', and there was some precedent for his use of it in broadly similar cases. In September 1921, the worried parents of a missing 15-year-old London schoolboy named Oscar Gray had appealed to the creator of Sherlock Holmes for his help. To their surprise, Doyle had taken the psychic approach to the problem, turning the matter over to two clairvoyants. 'The results were by no means perfect,' he was later forced to admit in the *Daily Express*, 'but I am sure that Mr and Mrs Gray found consolation in them, and in some ways they were accurate.' (The teenager was found to have merely run away from home and joined the army.)

We've seen that in 1925, just a year before Agatha Christie's disappearance, Doyle had corresponded with a Scottish spiritualist circle about the particulars of Marion Gilchrist's murder. This, too, could be counted only a mixed success. The psychics had confidently predicted that Oscar Slater would escape the death penalty in the affair, although this was only to repeat the decision publicly announced some fifteen years earlier. But Doyle's missionary zeal would never allow him to acknowledge to the public or to himself just how poorly the mediums had performed when measured against Sherlock Holmes's standards. The few such prophetic successes were down to the 'psychic gospel'; the silences and failures were down to something else. So when Doyle now obtained a glove of Agatha Christie's, it wasn't to subject it to the sort of microscopic examination Holmes performed in his fifty-sixth and final short story appearance, 1927's 'Shoscombe Old Place', and in several other adventures before it, but instead to pass it to a bespectacled, 40-year-old London clairvoyant named Horace Leaf.

Leaf took the glove, with apparently sensational results. Doyle later recalled:

> I gave him no clue at all as to what I wanted or to whom the article belonged. He never saw it until I laid it on the table at the moment of consultation, and there was nothing to connect either it or me with the Christie case ... He at once got the name Agatha.

Leaf went on to announce, 'The person who owns it is half dazed and half purposeful. She is not dead as many think. She is alive. You will hear of her, I think, next Wednesday, in a location with connection to water.'

This proved to be another notable feat of what Doyle called 'mediumistic divination' – Christie was found not on Wednesday, but on Tuesday, staying at a spa hotel in Yorkshire, although as the defecting author's name and possible hiding place were already on the front page of every British newspaper by the time Leaf made his prediction, there may also have been more worldly means at work. It remains unclear whether it was a case of Christie having suffered a full-scale mental breakdown; of being in a trance, or fugue state, brought on by trauma or depression; or of contriving her own disappearance as a public revenge on her husband. Recent research suggests that she may have retreated to the hotel simply as a cry for help, if not in a forlorn attempt to save her marriage.

Doyle concentrated less on his fellow crime writer's motives and more on the 'exciting new role' that clairvoyance seemed to play as a cutting-edge investigative tool that would ultimately supersede all other merely 'mortal and subjective' techniques. 'The Christie case has afforded an excellent example of the use of psychometry as an aid to the detective,' Doyle said in a letter to the *Morning Post*:

> It is, it must be admitted, a power which is elusive and uncertain, but occasionally it is remarkable in its efficiency. It is often used by the French and German forces, but if it is ever employed by our own it must be *sub rosa*, for it is difficult for them to call upon the very powers which the law compels them to prosecute.

These hopes for the British authorities to take a more enlightened approach to their criminal enquiries were somewhat dashed by the subsequent remarks of a senior Scotland Yard commissioner. 'We do not keep hopeless lunatics in the police forces of this country,' he announced.

Horace Leaf lived until 1971, often claiming to be in touch with a spirit world where his friend Conan Doyle carried on 'writing books, playing cricket and smoking cigars much as before'. He once conducted a séance where Doyle's signature apparently materialised on a slate, and the author also later appeared to him in the form of a talking cat. Despite these achievements, over the years Leaf would find his services only sparingly required by the official police. Later in the 1960s, he began to experiment with a 'freer, more allusive' form of mediumship that sometimes involved the use of hallucinogenic drugs. Leaf's memoir *Death Cannot Kill* contained the accounts of many more post-mortem conversations with Doyle, who had apparently revealed to him that he was hard at work in heaven writing more Sherlock Holmes tales.

Doyle and Agatha Christie never met, at least in the flesh, and she appears not to have acknowledged his help at the time of her disappearance. Clearly, theirs was not one of those peer relationships based on mutual artistic respect and goodwill. In 1929, Christie published a story called 'The Case of the Missing Lady', which perhaps owes something to Doyle's own 1911 Sherlock Holmes mystery 'The Disappearance of Lady Frances Carfax'. In the Christie version, her sleuth Tommy Beresford seems to be a cross between Holmes and Inspector Clouseau, down to his writing 'a little monograph' and playing the violin excruciatingly badly. Later in the story, Beresford discovers that the lady in question isn't missing at all, but has simply gone to a spa for a rest cure. 'And you will oblige me,' he's left to remark to his Dr Watson figure, 'by not placing this case upon your records. It has absolutely *no* distinctive features.'

✳ ✳ ✳

Conan Doyle's double life as a hard-boiled crime writer and occult visionary had taken on a new complexity when, in May 1924, he published an article in the *Daily Express* describing his recent encounter with the late Soviet leader Vladimir Lenin. As we've seen, Doyle and several friends (including Horace Leaf) had met at around midnight in a darkened London house. Leaf recalled that they had sat down around the dining room table and joined hands, at which point Doyle had cleared his throat and announced, 'This is the most urgent message for the world, and I will carry it, will carry it, will carry it, will carry it, carry it, carry it'. It was like a stuck record. In time his voice became more and more indistinct, and then faded away altogether. For some minutes, the group had sat there motionless, exchanging the occasional nervous remark between themselves. Then, suddenly, the female medium sitting on Doyle's left tightened her grip on his hand and whispered, 'I see him! He is there! He is standing on the stairs looking down at us!'

'In a moment,' Doyle told the readers of the *Express*:

> … the table began to move. It rose and fell in a steady rhythm. My experience of table-sittings, which is a large one, has shown me that undeveloped spirits always make violent and irregular – often circular – movements, and that steady movement is a sign of a deliberate, thoughtful mind.

Having established their visitor's mental state, the sitters had then asked him his name. 'Lenin, the Russian leader,' he announced in a series of Morse code-like raps, transmitted in the darkness. Doyle, who took the Bolshevik's physical presence among them on trust, as he himself could see only his fellow sitters and the material objects around them in the room, then asked, 'Could you spell something in Russian?'

'Yes,' he heard tapped out in the gloom.

'Some lingual tests were then given, but I found it hard to follow them, for spelling out with the alphabet is hard work even in one's own language,' Doyle admitted. However, he was sufficiently impressed to ask the unseen figure in their midst if he had a message for them.

'Yes,' Lenin rapped, before adding his aphorism about the artist's essentially radical role in society. Doyle had absorbed this, and then in turn advised the spirit to reconcile himself to death. Doyle wrote in the *Express*:

> I explained to him the conditions under which he now lived, and the need to turn his thoughts away from worldly matters. I begged him to cease to annoy innocent people, and I told him that he could only work out his own salvation by adapting his mind to the new conditions, by being unselfish, and by striving for higher things.

Perhaps Lenin was suitably chastened, because there was no immediate response to this admonition. In some versions of the tale, the sitters had then heard a soft but climactic '*Spasiba*' rapped out on the table in front of them. At that, the spirit had again withdrawn up the stairs.

It was as though the forces of life and death – a childlike trust in the visions of the séance room, and a Victorian Scotsman's dour belief in rigorous social order on earth (where even a ghost should know his place) – were pitched in unresolved battle somewhere in Doyle's soul. In his favour were a sincere desire for truth, along with courage and admirable persistence. Doyle's critics would have countered with allegations of almost infantile naiveté when it came to his notion of the redemption of mankind. This duality surfaced again in 'The Sussex Vampire', published only weeks before the Lenin séance, in which Holmes explicitly rejects any occult intrusion on his investigations. In 'The Retired Colourman', a story that followed in 1926, Doyle allowed his phlegmatic detective a rare comment on the human condition. 'Is not all life pathetic and futile?' Holmes asks. 'We reach. We grasp. And what is left in our hands at the end? A shadow. Or worse than a shadow – misery.'

In August 1927, Doyle read of the judicial execution at Boston's Charlestown State Prison of Nicola Sacco and Bartolomeo Vanzetti, two Italian-born anarchists who had been convicted of murdering a shoe factory cashier and his guard in the course of an armed robbery seven years earlier. As in the Oscar Slater case, the evidence against the accused seemed to rely on a mixture of conflicting eyewitness testimony and disputed forensics, along with a good deal of character assassination. To their many supporters, Sacco and Vanzetti had been tried less on the basis of the facts of the crime and more as a highly public rebuke of their outspoken political views. As the foreman of the jury commented after announcing the guilty verdict, 'Damn them, they ought to hang anyway'.

'It is impossible to read the facts,' Doyle remarked of the Massachusetts pair, somewhat incongruously in a book entitled *Our African Winter*, 'without realising that they were executed not as murderers but as anarchists'. In particular, Vanzetti, a fishmonger, struck him in near spiritual terms. 'He should not have been [prosecuted] under the pretence that he was an ordinary vulgar criminal,' Doyle wrote. 'Far from this being the case, Vanzetti was a man of such rare and exalted character that one thinks of St Francis of Assisi as one reads his utterances. His personality is likely to grow into a legend.'

Doyle had relatively little of substance to offer as an unofficial detective in the case, although in time he pointed to the fact that Vanzetti claimed to have been peddling eels elsewhere in Boston on the day of an earlier crime of which he had also been convicted. Sixteen eyewitnesses, all of them Italian, had come forward to support his alibi. What was more, Doyle wrote, 'The dusty old invoice had been preserved, and it was shown that on the day before Vanzetti had actually [taken possession] of a barrel of eels. Surely that alone should be enough for any reasonable man?'

The case seemed to fascinate Doyle, and in the weeks ahead he often compared it to the Slater affair, which also reached a climax later that year. More recent ballistics evidence suggests that Nicola Sacco was probably guilty of firing the shots that had killed the two employees at the shoe factory, and that Vanzetti was his passive accomplice. We will likely never know. Doyle was then approaching his seventieth birthday, and there was little reason for him to involve himself in the murky details of a criminal case some 3,000 miles away on the other side of the Atlantic. But just as Holmes sometimes fell into a stupor, staring listlessly out of his window and shooting up cocaine to overcome his lassitude until a new client arrived, so his creator found himself 'terrifically energised [and] roused' by each fresh potential miscarriage of justice to come his way. The Sacco and Vanzetti case may not have been personally relevant, but it was further proof to Doyle that 'police and judicial procedure all over the "civilised" world [was] little better than in the days of the Inquisition'.

✳ ✳ ✳

We've touched on two other international cases whose singular details found their way onto Conan Doyle's crowded desk during the last years of his life. The first involved the brutal murder in November 1927 of 18-year-old Irene Kanthack while out walking her cairn terrier early one evening in the exclusive Zoo Park area of Johannesburg. The local police had quickly determined that 'a native' must have been responsible for the crime, which included the classic mystery writer's conventions of a whimpering, bloodstained dog, a partly clothed body, and a wristwatch on the victim's arm apparently broken to show the time of her death.

Doyle himself was in South Africa a few months later, and consulted with the investigating detectives on the case. Writing about this 'unsolved mystery of first-class importance' in *Our African Winter*, he dismissed the official theory that Irene Kanthack had been abducted by a black man, taken away to be raped and murdered, and then brought back some time later to be lain out in the wood where she was found.

'This is quite inadmissible,' Doyle wrote:

It certainly was not so. The body was hid within a very few yards of the place where the poor girl had been slain, and had certainly never been anywhere else. That being so, we are presented with a curious problem. In a space of time which could hardly have been more than twenty minutes, the criminal had been able to drag the body across, and then cover it with such skill that for three days it lay hid, though Boy Scouts and others were hunting every yard of the wood.

I would venture to draw two deductions from this. The first is that in all probability there were at least two criminals, since from what I saw of the undergrowth I should not think it possible for one man to have collected sufficient boughs and foliage to have covered the body in time. It is a pity that it rained heavily, for those boughs were certainly stained with finger-prints before they were washed off.

My second deduction would be that the criminals were probably Europeans or men of some brain power, who lived at a distance, and wanted time for getting away. A native living in a hut within a few hours journey would naturally have made off and left the body.

Leaving aside Conan Doyle's apparent belief in the superior intellect of South Africa's European settlers, this showed a significant advance on the stalled official investigation into Irene Kanthack's death. Doyle had gone on, it will be remembered, to discover a nearby room rented by a mysterious scarred white man, and that – again in classic crime story format – this had been found to be covered in collages of pornographic drawings and sensational headlines torn from the local newspapers. The police, even so, had declined to visit the premises, or to investigate the scarred man, and there the matter rested.

There were innuendoes that the lead detective in the case, a Colonel Trigger, had himself done away with the victim, and allegations that his colleagues had destroyed the evidence. Although a man named Brown was eventually charged with the murder, the case against him soon collapsed when a magistrate called the evidence presented in court 'tainted beyond all bounds of credibility'. The murder of Irene Kanthack remains unsolved today. Doyle thought it all a 'sorry case of uniformed blindness and obduracy' to rank along with the worst excesses of the Edalji and Slater affairs, and further proof, perhaps, that the Inspector Lestrade type was not one limited to the British force.

The second tragedy to come to Conan Doyle's notice during his African tour concerned a sensational murder in Umtali, part of the present-day city of Mutare in Zimbabwe. A middle-aged Anglo-South African couple of only a few hours acquaintance, Mary Knipe and Job Winter, had gone for a walk in the town's central park on the warm late evening of 6 November 1928. It was a quiet and relatively secluded spot, popular with courting couples, although the local police chief, Major Flintwich, later made much of the fact that there was a 'kaffir hut [with] six or seven miscreants' located nearby. The more you study Doyle's African casebook, the more you find its distinguishing features (apart from the Dickensian names) to have been the violent deaths of a series of attractive white women and the instinctive belief on the part of the authorities that a black man must be responsible.

The facts in this case were that at about nine o'clock a passer-by had heard loud screams coming from a corner of the park and, on going to investigate, found Mary Knipe's lifeless body lying across a path. She had evidently been stabbed several times in her chest and stomach. The horrified passer-by had then heard a male voice say somewhere in the gloom, 'Here I am. I am knocked out.' At that, Job Winter had staggered out from behind a tree, lain down on the grass, and repeated brokenly, 'Who hit me? Who hit me?' It was later discovered that he had suffered a broken jaw, as well as other serious blows to the head, and, to a qualified doctor like Conan Doyle, it was apparent that these injuries were almost certainly not self-inflicted. Winter could remember nothing of any attack beyond the fact that at some stage he had seen 'a native' pass by the bench on which he and his companion had been seated.

There was one other curious point that had immediately struck Doyle when he came to hear the story from a local judge. When Winter was on his way to hospital following the attack, he had said not, 'What happened to Miss Knipe?' or even 'Is she alive?', but, 'I have to catch my boat tomorrow', followed by, 'You're not going to make a case out of this, are you?' Perhaps he was genuinely in shock.

Inspector Bond, who took over the investigation, seemed to Doyle to have:

… acted in an intelligent way … He searched everywhere for a weapon, but found none. He noted that the earth in front of the seat shows signs of disturbance, but could find none at the back or sides. He then traced drips of blood with two small pools of blood along the path to the point where the body was found – about forty yards in all. The woman had evidently backed away down the path screaming, while her assailant had showered blows upon her … She may have fallen at the two points where the pools of blood were. There was no indication of robbery.

The police eventually charged Job Winter with the crime but, as in the Irene Kanthack affair, a judge dismissed the case before trial. Mary Knipe's brutal murder also remains unsolved today.

Doyle visited the scene, and as a result came to believe that it might have been a simple but tragic case of mistaken identity. He wrote:

One conceivable theory is that the attack was not meant for the prosaic and middle-aged couple, but that in the dark the assailant chose the wrong people. It is possible that [another nearby] couple were the real objects of the vindictive hatred of some jealous rival.

According to this reading of events, Mary Knipe had been targeted accidentally – she would have looked similar to any other white woman when seen from behind in the dusk – and following the assault the killer had simply fled into the night taking the murder weapon with him. Notwithstanding his measured praise for Inspector Bond, the case as a whole did nothing to alter Doyle's belief in the 'almost incalculable stupidity and prejudice' of police forces all over the world.

THE MAN WHO WOULD BE SHERLOCK

290

After returning from his African tour in April 1929, Conan Doyle published a 5,000-word 'open letter to all elderly folk' in which he noted matter-of-factly, 'You and I are suffering from a wasting and incurable disease called old age, and there is but one end to it'. He turned 70 the following month. His final literary act was to collect a series of essays on the occult into a slim book called *The Edge of the Unknown*.

Doyle had several health scares, once collapsing during a speech to a London psychic meeting, but he fought on to the end. He began 1930 with guns blazing, not only taking on the Catholic Church and others whom he saw waging an ever-intensifying anti-spiritualist conspiracy, but also starting an internecine war with the SPR, whom he now accused of being 'entirely for evil'.

Conan Doyle's specific bone of contention with the SPR again highlighted some of his strengths and weaknesses as an investigator. Once his mind was made up he was an indefatigable crusader for the truth as he saw it. Set against this, there was the fact that his methods often fell below the exacting standards of observation, analysis and underlying psychological insight that Sherlock Holmes had made his own. Doyle was becoming more dogmatic with age; he refused to read case notes or other documents of more than a few pages, but still insisted that he could get to the truth of a matter by consulting the spirits.

Instead of applying himself as a forensic detective, the art of deduction increasingly consisted of Doyle sitting in a darkened room while his wife Jean practised her automatic writing or channelled their psychic guide, Pheneas. As a whole, these family séances were not notable for their pervasive sense of openness or transparency. Doyle was wary of admitting anyone who might disturb the ascendancy which his wife exercised over their closely controlled circle. The messages that resulted ran the gamut from continuing predictions of man's wholesale doom down to the most trivial details of the children's education or the optimum spot for a summer holiday. Several years earlier, Houdini had been one of those who thought it 'really sad when a great man like Doyle comes to hold his own wife up as a Messiah ... One must be a chump to believe some of these things,' he concluded.

Conan Doyle's final battle concerned a review by the SPR of a book by one Ernesto Bozzano describing the spiritualist activities of an Italian nobleman, Marquis Carlo Scotto, at his Millesimo Castle near Genoa. The marquis had taken solace in the séance room following the death of his son in a flying accident in 1926. He quickly became an occult cause célèbre. At one sitting, he was said to have listened through a brass ear-trumpet to the 'unmistakable sound' of an aeroplane engine, followed by that of the plane falling. There were many other such phenomena as recorded by Bozzano, and later enthusiastically endorsed by both Conan Doyle and his wife. 'It is all in the truest sense of the word a miracle,' Doyle told Hamlin Garland.

The SPR was not impressed. On the whole, the society's researchers took a dim view of the goings-on at Millesimo Castle:

> The sittings were held in complete darkness, for the most part without control and without any searching of those present, [despite which] they are described by Sir Arthur as 'on the very highest possible level of psychical research'.

Conan Doyle responded first by lodging a complaint against the SPR's 'insolence', and then by ending his thirty-six-year membership of the society. It was unfortunate, one Sunday newspaper gloated, that the 'high priest of Spiritualism [had] come down to the earthly plane to squabble', but Doyle was in no mood to compromise. The whole business 'makes one ashamed that such stuff should be issued by a [body] which has any scientific standing,' he wrote in his brusque letter of resignation from the SPR, which, rather disarmingly, the society published in the next issue of its journal.

Despite such controversies, both Conan Doyle and his wife remained remarkably loyal to the spiritualist cause. Both were subject to tests of their faith, and Doyle went through periods of doubt as his health deteriorated. He suffered grievously in his final days.

Arthur Conan Doyle died at home at Windlesham early on 7 July 1930, propped up in his favourite armchair by the window, where he could look out at the sun rising over the nearby hills. His last words were to Jean. 'You are wonderful,' he told her. Doyle was buried in his garden, just as he had asked, but when Windlesham was sold in 1955 his remains were moved to a quiet corner of All Saints churchyard in Minstead, near his summer home at Bignell Wood. The inscription on his marker reads, 'Steel True, Blade Straight'. It serves as a reminder of his determination not to abandon the struggle on behalf of the weak or oppressed, and never to give up in the face of adversity.

SOURCES AND CHAPTER NOTES

The following pages show at least the formal interviews, published works, or other archive material used in the preparation of the book. I should particularly acknowledge the help of Thomas Toughill, author of the best and surely definitive treatment of the Oscar Slater case (see bibliography), even if I may differ slightly from him in our ultimate conclusions.

Please note that I've sometimes referred to the subject of this book as 'Conan Doyle' and at other times simply as 'Doyle'. They are the same individual. He was born as 'Arthur Ignatius Conan Doyle', generally called himself 'Arthur Doyle' as a young man, and later adopted the compound surname from his great-uncle Michael Conan.

The unusually volatile recent exchange rate for the pound against the dollar has been a challenge, but I've tried to adjust both currencies throughout the text to show approximately what a sum of money in Doyle's time would be worth today.

Chapter 1

The question of Arthur Conan Doyle's real-life model for Sherlock Holmes has been addressed quite thoroughly over the years, not least by Doyle himself. 'It is most certainly to you that I owe Holmes,' he wrote to his old Edinburgh medical lecturer, Dr Joseph Bell:

> … and though in the stories I have the advantage of being able to place him in all sorts of dramatic positions, I do not think that his analytical work is in the least an exaggeration of some of the effects which I have seen you produce in the out-patient ward.

Bell, in turn, seems not to have actively discouraged his identification with Holmes, although he once modestly told a journalist, 'Dr Conan Doyle has, by his imaginative genius, made a great deal out of very little, [and] his warm remembrance of one of his old teachers has coloured the picture'. Perhaps it's fair to say that like almost every great fictional creation, Holmes was a composite of the real and the imagined. In the same spirit, Doyle drew heavily for the role of Professor James Moriarty on the German-born, Anglo-American criminal Adam Worth (1844–1902), who in 1876 spirited away Thomas Gainsborough's portrait of Georgiana Cavendish, Duchess of Devonshire, a painting he eventually returned twenty-five years later. 'The original of Moriarty was Worth, who stole the famous Gainsborough, [but] even that master criminal might have taken lessons from the Moriarty of Holmes and Watson, a figure of colossal resource and malevolence,' wrote Vincent Starrett in *The Private Life of Sherlock Holmes* (1933). Again, it was a case of Doyle basing his fictional type on a real figure, while drawing aspects of his character from other sources.

※　※　※

For further details of the Langham Hotel mystery, see Arthur Conan Doyle, *Memories and Adventures* (pp.130–32); and of the murder of Irene Kanthack, see Conan Doyle's *Our African Winter* (pp.182–84), as well as sources including Benjamin Bennett, *The Clues Condemn*, originally published in 1900 by Howard B.Timmins of Cape Town, but later revised and updated to include the events in Johannesburg of 24 November 1927.

Chapter 2

Conan Doyle's early life, and his experiences as a struggling provincial doctor and aspiring writer, have been thoroughly treated in a number of biographies. I should particularly mention John Dickson Carr's *The Life of Sir Arthur Conan Doyle*, Andrew Lycett's *The Man Who Created Sherlock Holmes*, and Daniel Stashower's *Teller of Tales: The Life of Arthur Conan Doyle*, all as cited in the bibliography. Regrettably, Doyle's home and surgery at Bush Villas in Southsea, the birthplace of Sherlock Holmes, no longer exists. Following extensive bombing of the area in the Second World War, Portsmouth City Council saw fit to finish the job and destroy many of the properties around Elm Grove. All that remains of Holmes today is a small plaque mentioning his origins nailed to the side of a red-brick block of flats. That notwithstanding, Michael Gunton and his supremely dedicated team at Portsmouth City Council very kindly put their Conan Doyle archive, largely the product of the Richard Lancelyn Green Bequest, at my disposal. I am grateful to them for their time and help.

※　※　※

For an account of Doyle's early occult experiences, see his *The Wanderings of a Spiritualist*, first published in 1921. I should also properly acknowledge Harry Houdini's 1924 book *A Magician among the Spirits*, a lively account of his own role in the post–Great War debate between the world's psychics and materialists, if not one that labours under any false modesty on its author's part. Doyle's 'The Adventure of the Resident Patient' was one of the stories collected in the cycle known as *The Memoirs of Sherlock Holmes*, and first appeared in *The Strand* magazine of August 1893.

※　※　※

Newspaper archives consulted included *Collier's Weekly*, *The Times*, the *Daily Express*, the *Daily Mirror*, the *Illustrated London News*, the *London Daily Illustrated Mirror*, and *The New York Times*. It's perhaps a reflection of our still imperfect knowledge of Conan Doyle that the name of his first wife is given as 'Louise' by some biographers, and as 'Louisa' by others. The second seems to me the more likely.

For archive material in this chapter I should also particularly thank the History Museum at the Castle of Appleton, Wisconsin; the US Library of Congress; the Magic Circle; and the staff of the Manuscripts Reading Room of the Cambridge University Library, where I spent rather longer in the course of a week than in my three years as a Cambridge undergraduate. I visited Conan Doyle's surviving homes at South Norwood, Hindhead and Crowborough.

Chapter 3

Arthur Conan Doyle's novels *The Refugees* and *A Duet with an Occasional Chorus* were first published in 1893 and 1899 respectively; I consulted the archives of the Cambridge University and British libraries, and the collection held by Portsmouth City Council, in seeking to better understand Conan Doyle's creative process, and his more recreational activities of the time.

✳ ✳ ✳

Doyle's letter to his editor friend W.T. Stead was dated 22 January 1893. Stead was to lose his life on the *Titanic*, only to apparently return in spirit form at intervals throughout the 1920s.

✳ ✳ ✳

Doyle's primary account of the sad case of Ella Castle of San Francisco and her excessive taste for souvenirs of her London visit appeared in the *Times* of 10 November 1896.

✳ ✳ ✳

Doyle's visit to the supposedly haunted house in Charmouth, Dorset, took place in June 1894, although he was to give a full account of it only in his 1930 book, *The Edge of the Unknown*. In his published version of events, Doyle adds the detail that the house in question had burned down shortly after his visit, and that the skeleton of a young boy was discovered buried

in the garden. It has proved difficult to corroborate that particular aspect of
the story.

For details of the events of May 1899 at Moat House Farm in Essex, see
Macdonald Hastings, *The Other Mr Churchill* (London: Four Square Books,
1966) and Carl Sifakis, *The Catalogue of Crime* (New York: New American
Library, 1979), as well as published accounts in the *Times*, *The Daily Telegraph*,
the *Illustrated London News* and the *Spectator*. For the story of the July
1907 removal of the so-called Irish Crown Jewels from their refuge in the
library of Dublin Castle, see Kenneth E.L. Deale, 'The Herald and the Safe',
included in *Memorable Irish Trials* (London: Constable, 1960), and 'The Great
Jewel Robbery (By Our Sherlock Holmes)', published in *The Leprechaun*,
August 1907, p.53.

※　※　※

Other periodicals consulted included the *American Weekly*, *Boston Herald*,
Chambers' Journal, *Light*, *Magic*, *New York Sun*, *The New York Times*, the *New
York World*, the *Saturday Evening Post*, *The Strand*, the *Spiritualist* and the
Sunday Express.

※　※　※

I visited the countryside around Great Wyrley, and should particularly like to
thank the staff of the Staffordshire Record Office.

Chapter 4

Several books have been published dealing (in some cases, exhaustively so)
with the strange events involving George Edalji and his alleged series of
cattle mutilations and other offences. Many readers may be familiar with the
loosely fictionalised treatment of the case in Julian Barnes' 2005 novel *Arthur
& George*. For a more drily factual account, see Gordon Weaver, *Conan Doyle
and the Parson's Son* (Cambridge: Vanguard Press, 2006) or Roger Oldfield,

Outrage: The Edalji Five and the Shadow of Sherlock Holmes (Cambridge: Pegasus Elliot Mackenzie Publishers, 2010). For more archival information, I consulted the papers and illustrations held on the case by the Staffordshire Record Office; the records of the *Indian Church Gazette*; the files of the *Cannock Advertiser*, the *Wolverhampton Express and Star*, the *Lichfield Mercury*, the *Birmingham Post* and *Pearson's Weekly*. The UK National Archives at Kew hold several papers on the case, among them Home Office File 989, which includes notes and correspondence to and from Honourable the Captain George Anson. Under ground rules of anonymity, I interviewed one of Anson's direct descendants who was familiar with family records of the case; his thoughts are included here only to give a degree of background context to the known facts. I should also acknowledge the insights provided by Home Office Files 986 and 988, UK National Archives, and of course by Arthur Conan Doyle's *The Case of George Edalji*, as cited in the bibliography.

✳ ✳ ✳

Innes Doyle's remark about 'Much talk of Edalji' appeared in his diary of 12 January 1907, and is quoted in Andrew Lycett, *The Man Who Created Sherlock Holmes*, p.321. There is also an account of the affair given in Conan Doyle's own *Memories and Adventures*, as cited in the bibliography. I also consulted Daniel Stashower's very fine *Teller of Tales: The Life of Arthur Conan Doyle* (2007), which rightly concludes:

> Conan Doyle believed the entire episode constituted an ugly blot on British justice. [However] recent investigations suggest that the final chapter of the Edalji case has yet to be written … Subsequent research indicates that Edalji may not have been entirely pure of heart.

Hopefully the account given here may go some small way to balancing the rival claims of those who portray George Edalji as an animal-ripping psychopath who hid behind a carefully maintained veneer of respectability, and others for whom he remains a potent symbol of the institutional racism of the British Police, and British society in general of his time.

Chapter 5

For specific details of the arrest, deposition and trial of George Edalji, see
Home Office File 986, UK National Archives; Statutory Declarations to
Home Office, 2 and 7 January 1904, Home Office No. 45/6, File 984;
Charlotte Edalji letter to Home Secretary, 8 January 1904, Home Office
No. 48, file 984; and Home Office File 989, which contains correspondence
and other notes to and from Captain Anson.

❊   ❊   ❊

The True Crime Files of Sir Arthur Conan Doyle edited by Stephen Hines, as
cited in the bibliography, gives examples of the sometimes forbiddingly
technical debate about the exact state of George Edalji's eyesight at the time
of the crimes of which he was convicted. Perhaps rashly, Doyle himself began
the exchange in the course of his two lengthy articles published in *The Daily
Telegraph* on 11 and 12 January 1907. Edalji in turn wrote in *The Telegraph* of
15 January 1907:

> I have several times been to optical experts and ophthalmic surgeons, with a
> view to getting glasses to suit me, but until Dr Kenneth Scott made a very long
> and careful scrutiny of my eyesight I have never got glasses of any use to me
> … but even these do not give me normal sight, as I find other people can see
> things without glasses at a far greater distance than I can with them. Another
> well-known ophthalmic surgeon declares my sight to be considerably less than
> one-tenth of the normal.

Further correspondence followed in *The Telegraph* of 16 and 17 January
1907, and at intervals both there and in several other papers, some of which
again condemned Edalji, and others of which began to agitate for an official
Home Office inquiry, as a result.

❊   ❊   ❊

Among other archive or published material, I read Herbert Gladstone's memo
of the case dated 6 June 1907, included in the Herbert Gladstone Papers,
British Library, File 46096; John Churton Collins, 'The Edalji Case', *National*

Review, March 1907; and George Edalji's 'My Own Story: The Narrative of Eighteen Years Persecution', *Pearson's Weekly*, 7 February–6 June 1907.

✳ ✳ ✳

Other periodicals consulted included the *Birmingham Midland Express*, *Birmingham Weekly Mail*, *Cannock Advertiser*, *Wolverhampton Express and Star*, *Birmingham Gazette*, *Lichfield Mercury* and the *Walsall Observer*.

✳ ✳ ✳

Arthur Conan Doyle's stories 'The Man With the Twisted Lip' and 'The Boscombe Valley Mystery' both appeared in 1891; his novel *The Valley of Fear* was published in instalments in *The Strand* between September 1914 and May 1915.

✳ ✳ ✳

An account of the Enoch Knowles case, under the headline 'Labourer Sent to Penal Servitude', appeared in *The Times* of 7 November 1934.

✳ ✳ ✳

I should again acknowledge the great help of both Liz Street and Rebecca Jackson, duty archivists at Staffordshire Record Office. Several other libraries and archives assisted with a variety of material on the Edalji case, including the Cambridge University Library, the Public Record Office of Northern Ireland, House of Lords Record Office and the John Murray Archive.

Chapter 6

For details on the case of Dr Hawley Harvey Crippen and his unfortunate wife Cora, see Douglas G. Browne, *Sir Travers Humphreys* (London: George G. Harrap & Co, 1960); John Dickson Carr, *The Life of Sir Arthur Conan Doyle* (London: John Murray, 1949); and Filson Young, 'Dr Crippen', in *Famous Trials* (Birmingham: The Legal Classics Library, 1985). I also consulted reports of the case published in *The Daily Telegraph*, the *London Globe*, the *Daily Chronicle*, the *Manchester Guardian* and the *Spectator*.

✳ ✳ ✳

For details of Conan Doyle's exposure to early twentieth-century criminal life in North America, see William John Burns, *The Masked War* (New York: George H. Doran, 1913); Harry Golden, *The Lynching of Leo Frank* (London: Cassell, 1966); Allan Pinkerton, *The Molly Maguires and the Detectives* (Mineola, New York: Dover Publications, reprinted 1973); and Conan Doyle's *Our American Adventure* and *Our Second American Adventure* (Boston: Little, Brown & Co, 1923 and 1924 respectively).

✳ ✳ ✳

For details of the Roger Casement case, see the Casement Papers archived in the National Library of Ireland, which include the trial notes of Casement's solicitor, George Duffy. Among many other biographies, I should mention H. Montgomery Hyde, *The Trial of Sir Roger Casement* (London: William Hodge & Co., 1960) and Brian Inglis, *Roger Casement* (London: Hodder and Stoughton, 1973). I also consulted accounts of Casement's trial and execution, and of Doyle's petition on his behalf, in the *Daily Express*, *The Daily Telegraph*, the *Manchester Guardian*, the *Pall Mall Gazette* and the *Spectator*.

✳ ✳ ✳

For details on Conan Doyle's latter-day belief in spiritualism, see his books *In Quest of Truth: Being a Correspondence between Sir Arthur Conan Doyle and Captain Hubert Stansbury* (1914); *The New Revelation* (1918); *The Vital Message* (1919); *The Wanderings of a Spiritualist* (1921); and, not least, *The Coming of the Fairies* (1922). I also consulted Massimo Polidoro's very fine book, *Final Séance: The Strange Friendship Between Houdini and Conan Doyle*, cited in the bibliography, as well as the archives of the *American Weekly*, the *Boston Herald*, the *Illustrated London News*, *Light*, *Magic*, the *New York World*, *Punch* and the *Saturday Evening Post*.

✳ ✳ ✳

Relatively little is known of Evan Powell, the colliery worker turned medium who apparently brought Arthur Conan Doyle's son Kingsley back to life at a séance held in Portsmouth on 7 September 1919. In later years he seems to have taken up mediumship in Paignton, Devon, where he frequently addressed clients in the voice of an American Indian spirit named Black Hawk. The *Scientific American* writer and psychic researcher Malcolm Bird later wrote that Powell, even when strapped to a chair, had been able 'to ring bells [and] have flowers fly through the air', describing this as 'the best séance that I had in England'. Conan Doyle continued to believe in Powell's ability to contact the dead, and the events that night in Portsmouth thus remain an important watershed in his life, if not the moment he abandoned his reputation as a sober-minded Scots doctor author and criminal investigator in the Sherlock Holmes mould.

※　※　※

Conan Doyle wrote to his mother on 9 May 1917, referring to his son Kingsley going to the front line, 'I do not fear death for the boy, for since I became a convinced Spiritualist death became rather an unnecessary thing, but I fear pain or mutilation very greatly. However, all things are ordained.'

Chapter 7

It is a pleasure to acknowledge the pioneering work done in the Oscar Slater case by the investigator and author Thomas Toughill, to whom I also owe a personal debt of thanks. Toughill's book *Oscar Slater: The 'Immortal' Case of Sir Arthur Conan Doyle*, cited in the bibliography, is the definitive treatment of its subject. No one who writes about Oscar Slater can fail to acknowledge this ground-breaking and peerless work. I might mention, too, that I was lucky enough to enjoy a sporadic but long-running correspondence with Toughill, who cheerfully answered my questions about Slater without ever making me feel a fool for having asked them.

※　※　※

William Roughead's *The Trial of Oscar Slater*, also cited in the bibliography, provides an invaluable transcript of the proceedings held in Edinburgh from 3–6 May 1909 before that formidable judicial figure Lord Guthrie. Conan Doyle was particularly struck by the 'intemperate' summing-up of the prosecution's case by the Lord Advocate, Alexander Ure. Ure drew the jury's attention to a number of what he called 'priceless inferences' which he drew from his 'forensic' study of the unfortunate Slater. Among these was the highly contentious view that:

> The [murder] was accomplished by a man who was on the hunt for jewels, not money – and who knew how to deal with jewels, how to make away with them when he got them. Jewels [he informed the jury] are difficult things for those who are not experts to handle if they do not come by them by honest means.

'Some of the Advocate's other remarks were equally surprising,' Doyle later remarked with some restraint, before adding of Lord Guthrie's instructions to the retiring jury, 'He commented with great severity upon Slater's general character, concluding with the words, "I suppose that you all think that the prisoner possibly is the murderer. You may very likely all think that he probably is the murderer"'.

✳ ✳ ✳

As well as Conan Doyle's own *The Case of Oscar Slater*, I consulted archives held at the Scottish Record Office (HH 16/109-112), and the Glasgow University Archives (GUA/FM/2B/5). I should particularly thank Barbara McLean of the Glasgow City Archives, and the staff of the Mitchell Library, Glasgow. Among periodicals consulted were the archives of the *Herald*, *The Scotsman*, the *Edinburgh Evening News*, the *Aberdeen Evening Express* and the *Scottish Daily Mail*. I'm also deeply grateful to Alex Holmes, who kindly visited the scene of the crime on my behalf.

✳ ✳ ✳

Conan Doyle's short stories 'The Boscombe Valley Mystery', 'The Adventure of the Blue Carbuncle' and 'The Priory School' were first published in 1891, 1892 and 1904 respectively.

✳ ✳ ✳

Doyle's assault on his teenaged son Adrian when the latter once rashly characterised a woman as 'ugly' is described in John Dickson Carr, *The Life of Sir Arthur Conan Doyle* (London: John Murray, 1949), p.279.

Chapter 8

For an account of Conan Doyle's psychic enquiries into the murder of Marion Gilchrist, see those of Doyle's papers in the archives of the Manuscripts Reading Room of the Cambridge University Library; the Reading Room of the British Library; and in the offices of Portsmouth City Council. The librarian at Longton Spiritualist Church kindly provided information on Doyle's sittings with the medium Annie Brittain. I also consulted the files of the *International Psychic Gazette*, *Light*, the *New Republic*, *Review of Reviews* and the *Proceedings of the ASPR*. I'm further grateful to the archivists at the Bodleian Library, Oxford; the New York Public Library; the Seattle Public Library; the FBI – Freedom of Information Division; the General Register Office; the Harry Ransom Center of the University of Texas at Austin; and the UK National Archives.

※　※　※

Thomas Toughill's observation, 'Slater was not a model prisoner ...' appears on p.182 of his book *Oscar Slater: The 'Immortal' Case of Sir Arthur Conan Doyle*, as previously cited. Toughill's remains by some distance the most thoroughly researched and consistently readable account of the Slater affair to be commercially published, and I warmly recommend it to any reader interested in learning more about the case.

※　※　※

Helen Lambie's article under the headline 'Why I Believe I Blundered over Slater' appeared in the *Empire News* of 27 October 1927. The rival *Daily News* published its interview with Mary Barrowman on 5 November 1927. Conan Doyle himself wrote to Stanley Baldwin on 13 November 1927, a letter reproduced in this book by courtesy of Glasgow City Archives.

On the same day, Doyle published an article in the *Empire News* in which he guardedly suggested that Marion Gilchrist's murder had possibly been less the product of an attempted jewel robbery gone wrong, and more some form of ghastly retribution for a past indiscretion, if true much the same sort of material Sherlock Holmes often worked with. 'Miss Gilchrist's behaviour suggests to me,' Doyle wrote, 'that there was some romance, some tragedy in this woman's life, dating perhaps far back, but having consequences now which were becoming manifest in her old age.'

* * *

The interview with Dr Francis Charteris appeared in the *Scottish Daily Mail* of 5 October 1961. Charteris' possible involvement in the murder would have made him only the latest in a long line of criminally minded doctors to have crossed Conan Doyle's path over the years, of whom Harvey Crippen was the most notorious.

* * *

G.M.A. McChlery's letter about Arthur Adams having thought Slater likely guilty of murder appeared in the *Scotland Herald* of 15 December 1993.

* * *

By a mild coincidence, the prison chaplain during much of Slater's time at Peterhead Jail was John Lamond, a friend and later biographer of Doyle. Lamond, too, remained convinced of Slater's guilt.

Chapter 9

I should again acknowledge the resources provided by the Manuscripts Reading Room of the Cambridge University Library, and the help of its curator Peter Meadows, and also those of the Rare Books Room at the New York Library. Every effort has been made to comply with the copyright provisions involved. The great majority of excerpts from letters exchanged between Arthur Conan Doyle and Harry Houdini are taken from Bernard Ernst and Hereward Carrington's *Houdini and Conan Doyle: The Story of a Strange Friendship* (New York: Albert & Charles Boni, 1932).

Michael Gunton and his colleagues at Portsmouth City Council were able to supply primary source information on Conan Doyle's dealings with several prominent mediums, among them 'Eva C.' and Kathleen Goligher.

Newspaper archives consulted included *Collier's Weekly*, *International Psychic Gazette*, *Light*, *Nation*, *New York Sun*, *Scientific American* and *The Times*. I also visited 20 Hanover Square.

Arthur Conan Doyle met Harry Houdini at Houdini's New York home on 10 May 1922. The primary source for the account of the magic demonstration that followed was Bernard Ernst and Hereward Carrington's *Houdini and Conan Doyle: The Story of a Strange Friendship*, as previously cited. Houdini's quote, 'before leaving with [Doyle], Mrs Houdini cued me', is excerpted from his book *A Magician among the Spirits*, cited in the bibliography.

Doyle gives an account of the Atlantic City séance of 18 June 1922 in his book *The Edge of the Unknown*, also as previously cited.

It's a curious aspect of their relationship that Houdini was then prepared to escort the Doyles to the ship for their return voyage to England, sending them off with a friendly wave and a subsequent telegram that read 'Bon voyage. May the Decree of Fate send you back here soon for another pleasant visit', while busily telling journalists, 'In the twenty-five years of my investigation, I have never seen or heard anything that could convince me that there is a possibility of communication with the loved ones who have gone beyond', the prelude to an all-out attack on the Doyles and their 'hoaxing tactics' at Atlantic City. Houdini's notarised statement, 'The Truth Regarding Spiritualistic Séance given by Lady Doyle' appeared in several New York Area papers on 19 December 1922. Not surprisingly, relations between the two men cooled as a result.

✳ ✳ ✳

For material on Mina Crandon, or 'Margery', see Houdini, *A Magician among the Spirits*; William Kalush and Larry Sloman, *The Secret Life of Houdini* (New York: Atria Books, 2006); Daniel Stashower, *Teller of Tales: The Life of Arthur Conan Doyle*; Arthur Conan Doyle, *The Edge of the Unknown*; and examples of Houdini's medium-baiting taken from *The Houdini Souvenir Program*, which was supplied by its copyright owners, Dick Brooks and Dorothy Dietrich of the Houdini Museum. Houdini's quote, 'Everything that took place was a deliberate and conscious fraud' appeared in the *New York Times* on 16 October 1924.

✳ ✳ ✳

I should again particularly acknowledge the help of the Manuscripts Reading Room of the British Library, and in particular Zoe Stansell. As well as the previously cited books, I consulted a variety of journals, magazines and newspapers, including the *American Weekly*, the *Boston Herald*, the *British Journal of Photography*, *Chambers' Journal*, the *Chronicle,* the *Morning Post*, the *Seattle Times* and *Variety*. I again drew on the resources of the Harry Ransom Center of the University of Texas at Austin, and of the US Library of Congress, which between them house most of Houdini's magic library, as well as his scrapbooks, photographs, innumerable newspaper cuttings, and journal and diary notes relating to Conan Doyle.

Chapter 10

For details of the Irene Williams case, see W. Lloyd Woodland (ed.), *The Trial of Thomas Henry Allaway (The Bournemouth Murder)* (London: Geoffrey Bles, 1929). For those of the Caroline Luard case, see H.L. Adam, 'The Summer House Mystery' in *Fifty Most Amazing Crimes of the Last Hundred Years* (London: Odhams Press, 1936), and Julian Symonds, *An Edwardian Tragedy* (London: Cresset Press, 1960).

✳ ✳ ✳

Arthur Conan Doyle's story 'The Problem of Thor Bridge', part of *The Casebook of Sherlock Holmes* cycle, was published in two parts in *The Strand* magazine in February–March 1922. It has since been alleged that Doyle lifted parts of his plot from a story called 'The Red Haired Pickpocket' by Frank Froest and George Dilnot, which appeared seven years earlier.

✳ ✳ ✳

For the Norman Thorne affair, see Leonard Gribble, *Famous Judges and their Trials* (London: John Long, 1957); Charles Higham, *The Adventures of Arthur Conan Doyle*, p.303; and Edgar Lustgarten, *Verdict in Dispute* (New York: Scribner's, 1950). An account of Conan Doyle's involvement in the case was published by an anonymous correspondent in the London *Morning Post* of 21 April 1925.

✳ ✳ ✳

For details of the Agatha Christie affair, see Jared Cade, *Agatha Christie and the Eleven Missing Days*, as cited in the bibliography; Horace Leaf, *Death Cannot Kill* (London: Max Parrish Publishing, 1959); and Patrick White, *Flaws in the Glass* (London: Jonathan Cape, 1981). There are also newspaper accounts of the case in, among others, the *Manchester Evening Chronicle*, 20 December 1926; *Lloyd's Sunday News*, 1 September 1929; and in retrospect, the *Sunday Times*, 18 January 1976. Conan Doyle published his own version of events under the headline 'Sir A. Conan Doyle and Christie Case: Psychometry and Detective Work' in the *Morning Post*, 20 December 1926.

✳ ✳ ✳

For further details of the Umtali Park murder of November 1928, see Arthur Conan Doyle, *Our African Winter* (London: John Murray, 1929), pp.175–82. Pages 228–29 of the same book contain Doyle's views on the case of Nicola Sacco and Bartolomeo Vanzetti.

✳ ✳ ✳

Other documentary material was kindly made available by the Cambridge University Library, the British Library, the Library of Congress, the Harry Ransom Center of the University of Texas at Austin, and Portsmouth City Council, as previously cited. I consulted journals, magazines and newspapers including the *American Weekly*, the *Boston Journal*, the *Evening Graphic*, the *Illustrated London News*, *Light*, *London Society*, the *New York Herald*, *Pearson's*, *Sphinx*, the *Star* (Johannesburg), the *Times*, *Two Worlds* and *Variety*.

✳ ✳ ✳

I'm particularly grateful to Matt Carpenter of the History Museum at the Castle of Appleton, Wisconsin, and to the staff of the UK Public Record Office and the New York Public Library for their help in obtaining diary notes, photographs or other archive material relating to Arthur Conan Doyle or the occult.

✳ ✳ ✳

Although all the above institutions and individuals helped in the preparation of this book, I should again stress that none of them had any editorial control over it. I am solely to blame for the contents.

BIBLIOGRAPHY

Baker, Michael, *The Doyle Diary* (London: Paddington Press, 1978)

Baring-Gould, William S., *Sherlock Holmes: A Biography of the World's First Consulting Detective* (London: Rupert Hart-Davis, 1962)

Barrie, J.M., *The Greenwood Hat* (London: Peter Davies, 1937)

Booth, Martin, *The Doctor, the Detective and Arthur Conan Doyle* (London: Hodder & Stoughton, 1997)

Brandon, Ruth, *The Spiritualists* (New York: Alfred A. Knopf, 1983)

Brown, Ivor, *Conan Doyle* (London: Hamish Hamilton, 1972)

Byrnes, Thomas, *1886 Professional Criminals of America* (New York: Chelsea House, 1969)

Cade, Jared, *Agatha Christie and the Eleven Missing Days* (London: Peter Owen, 1998)

Carr, John Dickson, *The Life of Sir Arthur Conan Doyle* (London: John Murray, 1949)

Conan Doyle, Adrian, *The True Conan Doyle* (London: John Murray, 1945)

Conan Doyle, Sir Arthur, *The Cases of Edalji and Slater* (Newcastle-upon-Tyne: Cambridge Scholars Publishing, 2009)

—*The Edge of the Unknown* (New York: G.P. Putnam's Sons, 1930)

—*Memories and Adventures* (Boston: Little, Brown & Company, 1924)

—*The True Crime Files of Sir Arthur Conan Doyle*, edited by Stephen Hines (New York: Berkley Publishing Group, 2001)

Cooke, Ivan (ed.), *Arthur Conan Doyle's Book of the Beyond* (Liss, Hampshire: White Eagle Publishing Trust, 1994)

Costello, Peter, *The Real World of Sherlock Holmes* (New York: Carroll & Graf, 1991)

Edwards, Owen Dudley, *The Quest for Sherlock Holmes* (Edinburgh: Mainstream, 1983)

Esterow, Milton, *The Art Stealers* (New York: Macmillan, 1973)

Gresham, William Lindsay, *Houdini: The Man Who Walked through Walls* (New York: Holt Rinehart Winston, 1959)

Guttmacher, Manfred S., *The Mind of the Murderer* (New York: Grove Press, 1962)

Harrison, Michael (ed.), *Beyond Baker Street* (New York: Bobbs-Merrill, 1976)

Higham, Charles, *The Adventures of Conan Doyle* (London: Hamish Hamilton, 1976)

Houdini, Harry, *A Magician Among the Spirits* (New York: Harper & Bros, 1924)

Jaffe, Jacqueline A., *Arthur Conan Doyle* (Boston: Twayne Publishers, 1987)

Jones, Kelvin I., *Conan Doyle and the Spirits* (Wellingborough: Aquarian Press, 1989)

Kellock, Harold, *Houdini: His Life Story* (New York: Harcourt, Brace, 1928)

Knowles, Leonard, *Court of Drama* (London: John Long, 1966)

Lachtman, Howard, *Sherlock Slept Here* (Santa Barbara: Capra Press, 1985)

Lamond, John, *Arthur Conan Doyle: A Memoir* (London: John Murray, 1931)

Lellenberg, Jon, Daniel Stashower and Charles Foley (eds), *Arthur Conan Doyle: A Life in Letters* (New York: HarperPress, 2007)

Lodge, Sir Oliver, *Raymond: Or Life and Death* (New York: George H. Doran, 1916)

Lycett, Andrew, *The Man Who Created Sherlock Holmes* (London: Weidenfeld & Nicolson, 2007)

Miller, Jonathan, *The Body in Question* (New York: Random House, 1978)

Nordon, Pierre, *Conan Doyle* (London: John Murray, 1966)

O'Donnell, Bernard, *The Old Bailey and Its Trials* (New York: Macmillan, 1951)

Park, William, *The Truth about Oscar Slater* (London: Psychic Press, 1927)

Pointer, Michael, *The Public Life of Sherlock Holmes* (London: David & Charles, 1975)

BIBLIOGRAPHY

Polidoro, Massimo, *Final Séance: The Strange Friendship between Houdini and Conan Doyle* (Amherst, New York: Prometheus Books, 2001)

Redmond, Donald A., *Sherlock Holmes: A Study in Sources* (Kingston, Ontario: McGill-Queen's University Press, 1982)

Roberts, S.C., *Holmes and Watson: A Miscellany* (Oxford: Oxford University Press, 1953)

Roughead, William, *The Trial of Oscar Slater* (Glasgow: William Hodge & Company, 1910)

Scott, Harold, *Scotland Yard* (New York: Random House, 1955)

Stashower, Daniel, *Teller of Tales: The Life of Arthur Conan Doyle* (New York: Henry Holt and Company, 1999)

Still, Charles E., *Styles in Crime* (New York: J.B. Lippincott Company, 1938)

Stone, Harry, *The Casebook of Sherlock Doyle* (Romford: Ian Henry Publications, 1991)

Tietze, Thomas R., *Margery* (New York: Harper & Row, 1973)

Toughill, Thomas, *Oscar Slater: The 'Immortal' Case of Sir Arthur Conan Doyle* (Edinburgh: Canongate Press, 1993)

Wagner, E.J., *The Science of Sherlock Holmes* (Hoboken, New Jersey: John Wiley & Sons, 2006)

Weaver, Gordon, *Conan Doyle and the Parson's Son: The George Edalji Case* (Cambridge: Vanguard Press, 2006)

Whibley, Charles, *A Book of Scoundrels* (New York: Macmillan, 1897)

INDEX